CAUGHT:
MONTREAL'S MODERN GIRLS AND THE LAW, 1869–1945

From the late nineteenth century to the Second World War, a 'young and modern' girl problem emerged in Montreal in the context of social and cultural turmoil. In *Caught*, Tamara Myers explores how the foundation and implementation of Quebec's juvenile justice system intersected with Montreal's modern girls. Using case files from the juvenile court and institutional records, this study aims to uncover the cultural practices that transformed modern girls into female delinquents.

From reform schools of the nineteenth century to the juvenile court era of the early twentieth, juvenile justice was a key disciplinary instrument used to maintain and uphold the subordination of adolescent girls. *Caught* exposes the attempts made by the juvenile justice system of the day to curb modern attitudes and behaviour; at the same time, it reveals the changing patterns of social and family interaction with regard to adolescent girls. Myers also uncovers the evolving social construction of these young culprits – *les jeunes filles modernes* with their penchant for *la vie legère* – by parents, church authorities, women's groups, social workers, the media, and juvenile justice agents. She illuminates the rich texture of these girls' public and private lives in the first half of the twentieth century, humanizing the stories of girls who were condemned for being too modern as they worked, played, and resisted the authority of parents, community, the church, and the law.

(Studies in Gender and History)

TAMARA MYERS is an assistant professor in the Department of History at the University of British Columbia.

STUDIES IN GENDER AND HISTORY

General Editors: Franca Iacovetta and Karen Dubinsky

CAUGHT

Montreal's Modern Girls and the Law, 1869–1945

Tamara Myers

UNIVERSITY OF TORONTO PRESS
Toronto Buffalo London

© University of Toronto Press Incorporated 2006
Toronto Buffalo London
Printed in Canada

ISBN-13 978-08020-9219-9 (cloth)
ISBN-10 0-8020-9219-5 (cloth)

ISBN-13 978-08020-9450-6 (paper)
ISBN-10 0-8020-9450-3 (paper)

Printed on acid-free paper

Library and Archives Canada Cataloguing in Publication

Myers, Tamara, 1964–
Caught : Montreal's modern girls and the law, 1869–1945 / Tamara Myers.

(Studies in gender and history)
Includes bibliographical references and index.

ISBN-10: 0-8020-9219-5 (bound)
ISBN-13: 978-08020-9219-9 (bound)
ISBN-10: 0-8020-9450-3 (pbk.)
ISBN-13: 978-08020-9450-6 (pbk.)

1. Female juvenile delinquents – Québec (Province) – Montréal – History – 19th
century.   2. Female juvenile delinquents – Québec (Province) – Montréal – History –
20th century.   3. Juvenile justice, Administration of – Québec (Province) – Montréal –
History – 19th century.   4. Juvenile Justice, Administration of – Québec (Province) –
Montréal – History – 20th century.   I. Title.   II. Series.

HV9110.M6M94 2006   364.36082'0971428   C2006-902202-X

University of Toronto Press acknowledges the financial assistance to its publishing
program of the Canada Council for the Arts and the Ontario Arts Council.

University of Toronto Press acknowledges the financial support for its publishing
activities of the Government of Canada through the Book Publishing Industry
Development Program (BPIDP).

This book has been published with the help of a grant from the Canadian Federation
for the Humanities and Social Sciences through the Aid to Scholarly Publications
Programme, using funds provided by the Social Sciences and Humanities Research
Council of Canada.

For my dad, Peter Myers, with love

Contents

Acknowledgments

This book began as a postdoctoral project in Montreal and was written largely in Winnipeg. Over the years and across the country many colleagues and friends have contributed to this project and have enriched my life along the way. To my many feminist friends with whom I share a commitment to critiquing the criminalization of women and girls, I thank you for your company and your inspiration, especially Andrée Lévesque, Mary Anne Poutanen, and Joan Sangster. Andrée, my doctoral dissertation supervisor, encouraged me to focus especially on girls and their relationship to the law. Joan and Mary Anne read various parts of the manuscript and offered their expertise and encouragement. Karen Dubinsky acted as a kind of postdoctoral sponsor, and I wish to acknowledge her early support for the project and the continuing encouragement she and Franca Iacovetta have provided as co-editors of the Gender and History series.

I spent many hours with the much-neglected juvenile court records under rather poor physical circumstances in various sites in Montreal. This filthy and awkward job was made bearable by fellow travellers. Criminologist Jean Trépanier and his team of researchers always demonstrated good humour and a wonderful generosity that I benefited from on many occasions. Jean's commitment to cooperative research and to thinking historically and transnationally about systems of juvenile justice are models in the field.

Staff at Library and Archives Canada in Ottawa, the Archives nationales du Québec in Quebec City, and the Canadian Jewish Congress National Archives in Montreal generously facilitated my research in those cities. I wish to acknowledge the Youth Horizons Foundation for granting me access to the Girls' Cottage School *fonds*; and the Honourable Michel Jasmin and the Honourable Ruth Veillet, who authorized my access to the Montreal Juvenile Delinquents' Court records. The research for this book was initially made possible by a Social Sciences and Humanities Research Council postdoctoral fellowship and then by subsequent standard research grants. I would also like to thank the University of Winnipeg for financial support. The University funded many research trips and enabled me to present this work at conferences in several countries. At the University of Toronto Press I wish to thank Len Husband for his hard work; also at UTP, Barbara Tessman and especially Pamela Erlichman deserve thanks for their fine editorial work. Two anonymous reviewers offered constructive suggestions and helped to make this a better book.

Members of the Montreal History Group contributed in many ways to this book. Students collected relevant newspaper articles while others offered commentary on the chapters. Lauren Cappell deserves special mention. This research collective not only helped to shape my thinking about the intersections of gender, class, and the law in Montreal's past, but also provided a space for critical historical inquiry. I would especially like to mention Brian Young, for his gentle criticisms and unflagging commitment to this project. Bettina Bradbury and Suzanne Morton offered very helpful suggestions about writing and encouraged me to maintain a close relationship to the MHG even as I became a Prairie person.

In Winnipeg I found a rich community of scholars and friends. At the University of Winnipeg James Hanley, Roy Loewen, and Serena Keshavjee and at the University of Manitoba Adele Perry, Jarvis Brownlie, and Sarah Elvins made me feel fortunate to be a historian in Winnipeg during this time.

Writing *Caught* demanded periods of intense solitude. For respecting that but also for drawing me away from the computer I must thank numerous friends near and far. Thanks to Sandra Clancy, Holly Dewar, Ken Dewar, Valerie Noftle, Mary Anne Poutanen, Megan Davies, Colin Coates, Keith Walden, and Maureen Malowany. Amy Richmond and Pauline Ripat offered many distractions usually involving great fiction, exceptional food, and copious amounts of wine. My partner Peter James created a loving home and a supportive work environment, making my task easier. His patience and humour in the face of the highs and lows of writing are cherished. For putting up with my half-presence, I thank my sister Friday Myers and her daughter Coco, who, at three and a half, is an astonishingly good teacher. I wish my late mother, Diana Myers, had been able to see this book, for she provided me with the stuff necessary to accomplish it. And finally it is to my dad, Peter Myers, that I dedicate this book. His respect and admiration for intellectual work and the written word is something I comprehended early in my life. Thanks.

CAUGHT:
MONTREAL'S MODERN GIRLS AND THE LAW, 1869–1945

Introduction

Girls and Juvenile Justice in Quebec

Les jeunes filles modernes were integral to the development of Quebec's juvenile justice system.[1] From 1869 to the Second World War the province's largest and most modern city, Montreal, played host to the rise of reform schools and a juvenile court and also an urgent social problem known as the young, modern girl. *Les jeunes filles modernes* became a feature of the industrializing landscape, as a public presence that revealed the apparent deficiencies in their material, spiritual, and moral lives. Modern girls appeared to manifest a homeless quality, belonging to a world beyond the *foyer* and the parish, where the bonds and bounds of traditional society had little consequence. Of course, the definition of what made adolescent girls modern changed over these decades: in the late nineteenth century, 'modern girls' implied streetwalkers; by the 1940s, they were independent adolescents participating in Montreal's 'wide open' night culture. Yet the problem they posed to their contemporaries shared commonalities: their close proximity to destitution and neglect; their eschewing of moral and cultural traditions; the apparent growing distance between them and parental, religious, and state authority; and their notorious relationship to Montreal streets. This 'problem' would attract the full weight of juvenile justice law and a continuum of institutions and agencies designed specifically for girls' rescue and rehabilitation.

Quebec juvenile justice advocates recognized that girls were not entirely responsible for their predicament. Indeed, profound structural changes in the lives of Montrealers shared the blame for the desperate condition of many homes, the brutal shifts in the economy that left parents unable to support their families, and the gendered labour market that seemed increasingly to have an unquenchable need for young girls and women but relegated them to the lowest and most vulnerable positions. As industrial Montreal emerged, the family and the domestic realm – the 'proper sphere' of girlhood – faced unprecedented challenges.[2] Were poor families and adolescent girls not victims of a modernizing city? Yet modern girls were also wilful in turning to the workplace and the street to earn a living rather than devoting themselves to the church and convent, and by the early twentieth century, spending their earnings on leisure rather than their families, sleeping late rather than attending mass, and eating, not their mothers' cooking, but food made in 'ethnic' restaurants. Sympathy for, and suspicion of, girls shaped the juvenile justice system.

Juvenile justice met the young modern girl in an era that embraced the malleable child and increasingly identified adolescents as reformable. Juvenile justice was born of the hopeful idea that rehabilitation was preferable to criminalization and incarceration. *Caught* explores the juvenile justice system's relationship to the modern girl. Like her, the juvenile justice system was not a static entity; rather, its laws, personnel, and character were historically contingent and had evolved over time. This book asks the questions, How did Montrealers come to identify certain behaviours or practices with delinquency? and What did the identity 'delinquent' – or indeed, *la jeune fille moderne* – mean for the thousands of Montreal girls who became inmates of reform schools or were brought before a juvenile court judge? In answering these questions I necessarily focus on the local history of juvenile justice because most of these systems involved municipally based courts and provincial legislation.

In 1869 Quebec, a two-year-old province in the new Dominion of Canada, embarked on a program of juvenile justice. Its history begins that year with legislation authorizing the creation of reform and industrial schools. Decades later, at the beginning of the twentieth century, such incarceration facilities assumed a more peripheral position in the juvenile justice system when the juvenile court and treatment through probationary schemes formed the core of the system. In 1912, the Quebec government established the Montreal Juvenile Delinquents' Court, which would operate as the province's only juvenile tribunal until 1940 when a second court was opened in Quebec City. In these critical decades Montreal became the locus of juvenile justice activity in the province. During the 1940s the provincial government made plans to transform Montreal's juvenile court into the Social Welfare and Youth

Court. Reform schools and the juvenile court were products of important legislative initiatives: the 1869 provincial act respecting reform schools, which established an alternative to prison for youths, and the federal 1908 Juvenile Delinquents Act (JDA), which set in motion the local establishment of juvenile courts. The JDA projected a national consensus that children, whether dependent or delinquent, were the responsibility of the state. As a vulnerable category of future citizens, they were to be spared adult punishments in favour of treatment that began in the child-friendly juvenile court and continued, if necessary, in youth facilities. Protection from inadequate parenting was guaranteed when the state expanded its role to 'super parent.'[3] These historical legislative and institutional initiatives have attracted academic interest in recent years, providing a backdrop to the little-examined history of juvenile justice and delinquency in the province.[4]

The province's involvement in juvenile justice led it to play a role in the national debates concerning the politics of childhood and youth and at the same time assert its cultural distinctiveness in administering to children. Notwithstanding that the 1908 JDA raised juvenile justice to the level of federal concern and a transnational project, child welfare remained a provincial responsibility and a jealously guarded right. Furthermore, while the Confederation era saw the forging of a national consciousness (which contributed to the production of a national JDA), in Quebec this politics was complicated by its colonial past. Since the British conquest of the French colony in the eighteenth century, the majority French-Canadian Catholics and the ruling British Protestants jostled for control over policies that affected the family and diverged over the meaning of nation.[5] In the expanding arenas of health, education, and welfare in the nineteenth century this divergence was physically manifested, with parallel hospitals, schools, and welfare institutions allowing for each to assert its cultural particularity. Yet the new juvenile justice institutions were not produced in duplicate, giving rise to a system imbued with the tensions and weight of duelling nations.

Local control did not lie solely with the provincial or municipal government. Juvenile justice in this period depended upon a dynamic voluntary sector whose membership shared a concern over modern adolescence. In Quebec this entailed a plethora of religious and lay organizations moving into the juvenile justice arena. Juvenile justice and its institutions then set the stage for local actors including legislators, justice officials, judges, probation officers, philanthropic and social service organizations, delinquents, and their families to give meaning to juvenile justice. That meaning was historically specific and shaped by political and economic concerns such as Quebec's 'national question,' immigration, industrialization, class relations, gender, and by majority and minority cultural communities vying for control over the definition of delinquency and the nature of treatment.

Although Montreal joined a number of North American cities in constructing its juvenile court, juvenile justice was articulated and pursued within a particular historical context – a city that was undergoing a significant political and cultural evolution. A port city of immense industrial and financial significance, Montreal was at once cosmopolitan, progressive, and modern, yet also home to conservatism, largely but not exclusively, promulgated by the Catholic Church. The juvenile court era overlapped with the rise of French-Canadian nationalism; therefore, questions concerning the survival of the French-Canadian 'race' echoed in the new institution. Religion and culture mattered to juvenile justice in Quebec because children and adolescents mattered to the future of the family, thus the 'race' and the nation. Juvenile justice became a site of religious, ethnic, and cultural struggle where peace was brokered through a confessional arrangement of cases and incarceration facilities. Yet the dichotomous understanding of Quebec society – franco/anglophone, Catholic/Protestant – is too simplistic for our purposes here because concerns over gender and adolescence cut across traditional linguistic and religious lines and lay bare the heterogeneity of each solitude.

Histories of legislation and institutions provide us with the historical framework of juvenile justice, yet they beg questions about process and practice. Juvenile justice – in the form of reform schools and juvenile courts – permitted the state to differentiate criminal cases according to age, but importantly it also opened the door to the policing of a broad range of minor acts of adolescent recalcitrance. What were the cultural practices that produced delinquents? Quebec juvenile justice was a means of targeting working-class children and youth; but child saving and juvenile justice were fundamentally gendered enterprises, both in the way he or she was singled out for protection and discipline and by the designation of who was best suited to process that child or adolescent.

In the 1910s the Montreal Juvenile Delinquents' Court brought in a comprehensive system of juvenile justice predicated on child-saving principles applicable to both boys and girls. But the system for processing delinquents saw girls and boys differently, mandating a critical role for adult women in juvenile court. In an era that celebrated public motherhood, female juvenile court workers assumed a legitimacy to supervise and regulate family life for delinquents of both sexes. The intimate nature of girls' delinquency hindered the possibility of male probation officers processing their cases. Investigation and treatment, then, fell to a congregation of surrogate mothers. By focusing on female delinquency this book addresses both the emergence of the female delinquent as an easily recognizable social problem and the development of female-specific treatment.

Ripe for Trouble: Modern Girls and Sex Delinquency

Girls embodied delinquency in a way boys could not. Adolescent girls' bodies were barometers of the future and made them, in the words of one probation officer, 'ripe for trouble.'[6] Their maturing sexuality and promise of maternity were read as harbingers of society's destiny. Parents and juvenile justice officials saw bodies that could not be constrained or contained, that left home for paid work, that swayed suggestively to modern music, and that were seemingly available for exploitation by men. In the nineteenth century, church-motivated female reformers and child rescuers identified female juvenile prostitutes as a social problem worth eradicating through reform school regimes. In the juvenile court era, as social change altered the work and lifestyles of adolescent girls and youth culture challenged the constraints of an older generation, sex delinquency was discovered in the streets, factories, dance halls, and moving-picture houses of the city. By the 1910s female delinquency was widely understood as a pattern of modern behaviour that included sexually suspicious, if not dangerous, nighttime behaviour and resistance to a model of passive femininity. *Les jeunes filles modernes* flouted gender norms that prescribed an invisibility for female adolescents. Juvenile justice promised to remove them from public view through a court experience where public witness was interdicted and by hiding them away in convent reform schools.

In early twentieth century Montreal we encounter a preoccupation with 'precocious sexuality.'[7] Parents brought complaints to the juvenile court about their daughters who spent nights away from home. The court responded by seeking scientific verification of girls' sexual experience through gynecological tests and demanding that probation officers record complete sexual histories. Boys did not face this physical and verbal intrusion. The court's conflation of girls' delinquency with sex delinquency has been upheld by scholars, who argue that 'bad girls' were problematic to twentieth-century society precisely because they were sexual.[8] Delinquent girls have even been celebrated: because of their sexual rebelliousness the first generations of delinquent girls have been labelled 'agents of sexual innovation and cultural change,' responsible for a sexual revolution.[9] We learn from the case of Montreal, however, that some girls appear to have sought out and embraced excitement and pleasure, but the gendered nature of juvenile justice extends beyond their sexuality. The juvenile court was a disciplinary instrument used to maintain and uphold the subordination of adolescent girls within a patriarchal family structure that was undergoing dramatic change. As Éric Pierre and David Niget argue for the case of early-twentieth-century French female delinquents, the delinquency designation was first of all the result of their economic status but further determined by the required submission to family and social order.[10]

In Montreal female delinquents who exhibited a penchant for *la vie légère*, or frivolous life, were called *jeunes filles modernes*. Modern girls were not a homogeneous group, though their stories generally substantiated and reverberated anxieties about gender, adolescence, and the autonomy of modern girls in urban life. Rather, like the category 'woman' before her, the modern girl proved to be complicated by her class position, her religion and ethnicity, and to a lesser extent, her ability to deflect the accusation of delinquency.[11] Modern girls' lifestyle changes collided historically with growing concern that the French-Canadian nation was in trouble; as nationalists fretted that the traditional family, the French language, and religious observance were on the wane, girls seemed at the root of the problem. French-Canadian nationalists concerned over the destiny of the family were not alone in constructing and naming a girl problem. Montreal's Jewish community perceived the female delinquent as a product of the strains of immigration and settlement and ultimately a threat to its reputation.

Female delinquency was also constructed, catalogued, and treated by professionals brought into the juvenile court. Medical doctors employed by Montreal's juvenile court focused primarily on the presence of hymens, pregnancy, and venereal disease, turning the court's attention to the delinquent body. Anglophones associated with the non-Catholic juvenile court committee looked to developments in sociology, psychology, and psychiatry to define and explain delinquency among girls. Consequently, anglophone delinquents were directed to the city's Mental Hygiene Institute, to be assessed by a new generation of experts who generated scripts about delinquent girls' biological mental deficiencies and broken homes. In pursuit of the etiology of female delinquency, experts of the human body, mind, and behaviour introduced social, environmental, genetic, and psychological factors to explain the crisis of wayward adolescence. Thus, it was through the anglophone element in the juvenile court that mental health experts initially forged a relationship with the juvenile court, engaging developments prominent in many Anglo-American jurisdictions. The female delinquent emerged as the product of new knowledges from the fields of medicine, psychology, and sociology.

Yet while medical and psychological experts, court authorities, nationalists, and community workers wrote and spoke volumes on the problem with girls, it was parents who often established the first narrative about the conduct of their delinquent daughters. Parental complaints reveal the complexity of girls' bad behaviour and of the family dynamics that led to a court appearance. These cannot be reduced easily to precocious sexuality and fears of unwed pregnancy. In bringing their daughters to the attention of the juvenile court, they defined what behaviour was sufficiently unacceptable to warrant declaring their daughters delinquent. A number of factors related to the family situation drove parents to call in the weight of the juvenile court to bear upon their girls.

Once in court, girls also participated in the discursive construction of delinquency in telling their stories to the litany of experts charged with investigating their cases. Often in the case of girls, it was their failure to assume and maintain their subordinate, dependent position in the family that got them into trouble. Some girls took the opportunity to respond to what they perceived to be an injustice in their lengthy interviews with female probation officers. Other girls denied allegations made against them; still others defended their behaviour. As American historian Anne Meis Knupfer claims, it is the 'collision, even collusion, of these stories' that is central to the history of gender and delinquency in the juvenile court.[12]

If the female delinquent was a social problem and the product of competing narratives, she was also an adolescent occupying a subordinate, but critical, place within the family. Using methods familiar to the social historian, I have pieced together adolescent girls' lives as they intersected with the juvenile court. This book covers the period in which adolescence takes its place as a distinct moment in the life cycle; in the words of one reform school worker, these girls were 'on the very threshold of life.'[13] Girls defined as delinquent in this era were not schoolgirls and they did not culturally identify with high school. By day they worked as domestics, factory hands, and waitresses, yet they were not on their own in the city like their older peers, who were known as 'women adrift.'[14] During their time off they indulged in what Montreal in these decades came to offer: a wide range of cafés, dance halls, moving-picture houses, and a lively street culture. Suspended between freedom and dependence – living under parents' roofs but working and exploring the commercial leisure attractions beyond the home – these girls participated in forging a new era, one that we know little about from the girls' perspective. Yet because they were caught transgressing parental authority and public expectations of them in an era that took great interest in adolescent behaviour, details of their lives and delinquencies remain available to us.

Delinquent Girls as Historical Subjects and Agents

Using court records to write a history of female adolescence and delinquency presents a variety of methodological challenges. Nonetheless, the paucity of research on girls in Montreal's history demands redress. Research for this book benefited from access to juvenile justice records containing private information about girls' lives.[15] I have used both official documents, including statistical summaries and annual reports of public institutions associated with the juvenile justice system, and more than one thousand juvenile court records concerning delinquent girls.[16] The dossiers of the Montreal Juvenile Delinquents' Court contain one or several of the following types of information: a deposition from the complainant; a standardized probation officers' form; court physicians' reports; correspondence from reform school personnel, the 'delinquent,' or members of her family; and a statement of case disposition. These records were not meant for public consumption (including by future historians) and both the Juvenile Delinquents Act and subsequent federal young offenders acts protect the adolescent in this regard. With this notion of privacy in mind, the probation officers probed the personal lives of adolescent girls, producing case records on each delinquent.

Case records potentially reveal more about their authors than their subjects; indeed, Karen Tice has used them to illuminate the development of case recording and the politics of professional writing, to better comprehend the professionalization of social work. In her work on family violence, Linda Gordon argued for the power of case files to elucidate the otherwise lost material experience of abuse survivors while not denying these sources were the product of the professionals who created them.[17] Other critics are more cautious about historians ability to generate 'experience' from case files: Annalee Golz, who examined family violence case files in Ontario, suggests exercising 'interpretive caution' in attempting to use such evidence to exact the experience of the historically silent, and examines the 'sociolegal' context in which their voices were recorded.[18] From this point we need to see the case file as constitutive of power relations. As Franca Iacovetta and Wendy Mitchinson remark: 'The "dossier" can be seen as the product of authorities exercising power over their citizens, or of a dialectic encounter between experts backed by state, medical, or religious power, and clients possessing far fewer resources.'[19]

In the contest between 'dominant' and 'subordinate' groups, one might lose sight of the important task of giving a history to the latter. Yet, as Karen Dubinsky argues, case file research holds great potential for uncovering 'private lives,' especially when wed with other sources.[20] Here I have used the case files generated on delinquent girls in conjunction with a variety of other sources to examine the practice of juvenile justice in Montreal as well as adolescent/delinquent girls' lives. Of critical importance to the histories of adolescence and delinquency are the seemingly mundane details about their daily lives.

Historical perspectives on the intersections of child saving, juvenile justice, and female delinquency have been generated from the disciplines of history, criminology, sociology, and women's studies. Studies of juvenile justice initially centred on class relations and the interventionist state, not gender. Juvenile justice historians cannot ignore the legacy of Anthony Platt's *The Child Savers*. His social control thesis argued that the state, represented by an emergent professional class, acted upon the working class through their children, using probation officers, surveillance, and coercion to transform the family into a bourgeois ideal. Like Platt, many scholars have conceded that the juvenile court did not adhere to the child-saving principles that the architects of the juvenile justice legislation advocated, and that the effect of the new courts – intended or not – was an oppressive regime aimed at the working class. A decade after the publication of *The Child Savers*, Jacques Donzelot similarly turned to the policing of families, promoting a conceptualization of the world of child protection work called 'the social.' In his work, juvenile courts, conjoining the domestic sphere of family and home and the public realm of law and politics, became a disciplinary force aimed at transformation of the working class. As part of a new intermediate space created by early social welfare programs, the juvenile court comprised bourgeois child-saving ideology, new specialists, and institutions and marked a massive intrusion into the private world of the working-class family.[21] In the name of child saving and protection of childhood, this new apparatus intimidated, policed, and disciplined families. Both Platt's and Donzelot's conceptualization of juvenile justice and the social have commanded a considerable response from feminist scholars and moral regulation studies.

Moral regulation studies, influenced by Michel Foucault, have specifically aimed at turning the focus beyond the disembodied state as the root of social control.[22] Moral regulation scholars explore the professional discourses, disciplinary technologies, and normalizing apparatuses that comprise the social. Central to moral regulation studies is the adherence to Foucault's insistence that power is diffuse and produces resistance. Linda Mahood, in her study on the policing of British families, argues for the inclusion of the 'disciplining of gender' and its integration with class, race, and sexuality.[23] At the same time, using a Foucauldian analysis of power and discipline, she promotes the social as a 'locus of resistance,' where the subjects of child-saving, working-class children, and their parents are more than passive objects of state power.[24]

Feminist historians have also rethought the social control paradigm. The acknowledgment that parental complicity was critical to the operation of juvenile courts forces us to reexamine social control arguments, which assert that the court was an instrument of the bourgeois state.[25] Feminist historians concerned with social welfare reform portray the relationship between programs or agencies and their clients as an interactive one in which clients are not rendered passive by the strong arm of the state. Linda Gordon, in her work on family violence, points to the immigrant and working-class families' use of state institutions to illustrate how power was more diffuse than social control theories permitted. Similarly, Mary E. Odem reconsiders Platt's argument in view of the fact that her work on the Los Angeles juvenile court demonstrates a 'triangulated network of struggles and negotiations among working-class parents, their teenage daughters, and court officials.'[26] Working-class families' ideas about their children's behaviour shaped how the court understood delinquency and punishment, notwithstanding the court's divergent views on the subjects. Certainly, struggles and negotiations occurred at all stages of the juvenile court process: between adolescents and parents, between parents and court officials, between probation officers and judges, and clearly between delinquents and probation officers and/or reform school administrations. At the same time, the regulation of adolescents was also a prerogative of more informal structures, such as voluntary agencies, with an unofficial relationship to the juvenile court.

To say that power was less hegemonic and more diffuse than social control theories had allowed does not suggest inattention to the hierarchy and nature of power and resistance. In this complex web of power relations, those clearly disadvantaged were the adolescents. Girls in early-twentieth-century Quebec were constructed as trouble because of their defiance of familial and social norms and rejection of their subservient (that is, feminine and youthful) position both at home and in the public world. For this they were verbally abused, beaten, raped, brought to court, placed under surveillance, and incarcerated. Yet, we can maintain Mahood's notion of the social as a 'locus of resistance' and examine how girls assumed agency, through both compliance and resistance. This resistance and agency was forged in the context of the maternal power and 'care' they were placed under in juvenile court and in reform school.[27] At times they invoked passive resistance and accommodation: other times they took advantage of the kinder, gentler regimes and walked away or erupted into uncharacteristic violent episodes. Not to be understated, too, is the fact that even when faced with paternalistic judges and threatened with incarceration, girls objected – verbally and physically – to their designation as delinquent.[28]

Female delinquency has attracted considerable attention in recent years from scholars outside Quebec. This work builds on a significant feminist literature on female criminality and punishment regimes.[29] As juvenile justice systems identified female youth as separate from the female criminals, historians pursued the delinquent adolescent girl.[30] American historians Mary E. Odem, Ruth Alexander, and Anne Meis Knupfer and Canadian historian Joan Sangster demonstrate the centrality of sexuality to the 'policing and protecting' of adolescent girls.[31] This contradictory imperative to simultaneously protect and punish has been a fundamental characteristic of the juvenile justice system from its origins in the late nineteenth century. Using a feminist and materialist framework (and, especially in the case of Knupfer, a poststructuralist approach) these historians show how female delinquents were products of historically specific, gendered, moral cultures and expert discourses. They reject the notion that these girls – although brought to court against their will and in many cases incarcerated – were victims, preferring to emphasize their agency and resistance.

Recent British and English-Canadian studies place the regulation of girls and juvenile justice regimes in the context of the development of the liberal welfare state. Tending to the question of citizenship rights and obligations with respect to policed girls in Britain, Pamela Cox examines their 'right to be rescued' but also how this right 'defined their freedoms in narrow and often highly illiberal terms.'[32] For girls, the persistent perception that because of their gender they needed protection led to an unshakeable restriction of their rights. Joan Sangster distinguishes between the models of citizenship juvenile justice promoted for boys and for girls: boys were entitled to/disciplined for social citizenship, whereas girls were targeted for moral citizenship and a future of 'restrained heterosexuality, domestic monogamy, and honest motherhood.'[33]

Quebec historiography has been very slow to recognize the regulation of girls and sexuality, outside Andrée Lévesque's work on interwar Montreal.[34] Studies on juvenile justice tend toward policies and institutions rather than gender regulation and girls. Sylvie Ménard's treatment of the Montreal boys' reformatory, for example, ably interrogates the Catholic order's administration but leaves aside critical questions of gender. Jean-Marie Fecteau's significant book on the regulation of poverty in Quebec pays scant attention to gender and the plight and experience of individuals affected by criminal justice regimes.[35] This book aims to address these silences by examining the implementation of a gendered juvenile justice system in a city and province where questions of 'race,' ethnicity, and class were ever-present.

This book examines three interrelated historical developments that help explain the construction and lives of 'delinquent' girls. The first is the rise and evolution of juvenile justice in Quebec, primarily under the Juvenile Delinquents Act; the second is the emergence of a (young and modern) girl problem in Montreal; and the third involves the experience of adolescent girls deemed juvenile delinquents before 1945. The example of Lorna H., whom we will meet in chapter 7, is instructive.[36] The Quebec juvenile justice system first interceded in Lorna's life in 1922 at age eleven to remove her from an 'undesirable' home situation. Although Quebec did not have a child protection act, the Montreal Juvenile Delinquents' Court was authorized to place abandoned or neglected children, which it did with the Society for the Protection of Women and Children. As Lorna blossomed into adolescence at fifteen, she increasingly ascribed to a young, modern female aesthetic that an older generation found problematic. In order to curb such behaviour and attitude, the juvenile court designated her as delinquent and sent her to the ethnically and religiously appropriate reform school, the Girls' Cottage Industrial School. She escaped from that institution, and survival on her own in Montreal speaks to the facility of adolescent girls to blend into an urban environment that, by the 1920s, offered them work, accommodation, and a thriving subculture. Once caught, Lorna was reincarcerated, this time at the other reform school for girls run by the Soeurs du Bon Pasteur, which had a reputation as being less pervious than the anglophone training school. My purpose in writing this book is to show the intersections of juvenile justice (in the form of institutions and rhetoric) and delinquent girls (as discursive subjects and adolescents).

Chapter Overview

This book proceeds chronologically and thematically in examining the Quebec juvenile justice system's intersection with girls' lives. In the first chapter, I chart the evolution of the structures of juvenile justice (federal and provincial legislation, and the birth of the Montreal Cour des jeunes délinquants/Juvenile Delinquents' Court) and the prevailing ideologies at play, specifically, child-saving in the Quebec context. Chapter 2 explores the origins and development of the girls' reform school set behind the convent walls at the Soeurs du Bon Pasteur provincial house. These nuns were chosen by the province not only for their capacity to offer 'tender and maternal treatment' to the nineteenth-century endangered girl but also for their observance of the Catholic faith and conservative social values. At the hands of the Soeurs du Bon Pasteur, a religious curative constituted the cornerstone of reform. This era in which juvenile justice was restricted to the incarceration phase of criminal justice would prevail until the 1910s and the juvenile court revolution.

How the female delinquent came to be a twentieth-century social problem is the subject of chapter 3. It examines how 'problem girls' were targeted for sexual regulation, a campaign that would be intensified by the new juvenile court. In the 1910s Montreal antivice reformers reported on girls' heterosocial adventures, broadcasting news of a frightening force in the city, the sex delinquent. Responding to the visible, youthful female presence in the city, especially at night, a host of female social reformers called for the state and charitable organizations to harness the girl problem. In the interwar period, francophone women's organizations focused on *les jeunes filles modernes*, girls whose defiance led them to reject a paradigm of femininity represented by their mothers. Young modern girls were cast as harbingers of the decline of the family, the cornerstone of French Canada. At the same time adolescence was undergoing significant revisions at the hands of experts whose discursive renderings of adolescent-girl conduct helped shape the juvenile court's comprehension and treatment of them.

Chapter 4 shifts the site of juvenile justice to the juvenile tribunal. Montreal's Juvenile Delinquents' Court opened in 1912, a triumph for progressive child-saving across Canada, and in Quebec for liberals like F.-X. Choquet, the first judge of the new court. It also marked a critical moment for women who were key to the promise of socialized justice. Although no woman ever presided over Montreal's juvenile court, 'maternal rule' was established in the early twentieth century by female probation officers. These 'mothers of all children' asserted their prerogative to investigate girls' lives, especially their homes and families. Maternal rule eventually gave way in the interwar period to a growing professionalism among female caseworkers. Maternal justice and professional social work methods were ultimately adapted to the cultural context, emphasizing the importance of ethnicity and religion to the Quebec juvenile justice system.

Chapter 5 asks the questions, Who were 'juvenile court' girls? and Who or what was responsible for their court appearance? Girls' conflict with parents and subsequently the law related to fundamental changes in the experience of adolescence in the opening decades of the twentieth century. Based on probation officers' reports, this chapter explores female adolescence and delinquency. Most of these working-class girls spent their days working and their nights with friends. Tensions with parents arose around domestic duties and paid work. At first glance what we discover is adolescent girls abrogating rules at home. Yet probation officers' reports also convey an adolescent culture forged by these girls where they laid claim to forbidden parts of the city and reconfigured city space on their own terms. Typically, the flaunting of sexuality and social autonomy got adolescent girls into trouble, yet as Joan Sangster has argued, 'while sexual regulation was undoubtedly a central impetus for the surveillance of adolescent females, the discursive construction of morally pure as opposed to bad girls cannot be disentangled from the material and social context framing and provoking girls' conflicts with the law.'[37] These girls were overwhelmingly working class and had been exposed to adversity in their early lives, including a combination of loss of one or both parents, acute poverty, domestic violence, and chronic alcohol abuse. In an ironic twist many 'delinquent' girls were brought to court by family members seeking to bolster their authority at home, only to find that probation officers judged the girls' home lives substandard and advocated surveillance not only of the adolescent but also of the family.

Chapter 6 examines female adolescent sexuality in the early twentieth century. In keeping with modern juvenile justice practice, girls' sexual histories were recorded by probation officers, as were the results of gynecological exams performed by medical personnel; these official documents were communicated to the judge, who rendered his decisions based on the information furnished therein. More than any other part of their experience with the court, the investigations into girls' sexual histories offered the adolescent girls the opportunity to construct their own narrative of their lives. Sexual histories therefore require a sensitivity to how girls made sense of their experience and how probation officers understood and constructed female juvenile delinquency. In seeking to understand the discursive rendering of girls' sexual precocity and girls' own hand in contributing to the construction of their sexuality, we should not forget the material experience of being brought to court, interviewed on such a private subject, and the intrusive gynecological examination. In this context girls' words are sought and given a place, a history.

While this book begins with the birth of juvenile justice in the reform school, it ends with girls carefully ensconced in another institution too, the training school. In the 1910s the Girls' Cottage Industrial School opened to bring to an end the incarceration of non-Catholic girls at the nuns' École de Réforme. The girls' training school, the first of its kind in Quebec, was fashioned as a thoroughly modern (secular) rehabilitation facility, in contrast to the convent reform school. Prevailing ideology regarding gender and sexuality, class and waywardness, were reflected in the programs, geography, and architecture of this new institution. 'Modern' girls resented modern retraining and chapter 7 examines their rebellions, concluding with two dramatic moments in the history of girls' incarceration in the province. The chapter ends with the violent riot at the nuns' reformatory school in 1945 and the massive escape of girls from the Girls' Cottage School in 1946.

This era of juvenile justice had particular ramifications for adolescent girls. Working-class girls spent these years working at low-paying jobs or helping with female labour at home. As youth, they were part of an emerging subculture that emphasized autonomy from the family and the pursuit of commercial leisure. As they were drawn away from traditional sources of surveillance and regulation at home and into the neighbourhood, they became an urban social problem – *les jeunes filles modernes.* Young, modern girls in Montreal sought out 'sites of perdition,'[38] eschewed 'a family spririt,' and created a generation gap. Juvenile justice opened the door to making private friction between parents and their daughters a public responsibility. As the first generation processed by the new system, girls were hauled into court for minor offences and placed on probation or in reform school, where they were to embrace a model of female adolescence prescribed by middle-class surrogate mothers, social science experts, and Catholic religious orders.

chapter 1

The Foundations and Framework of Juvenile Justice in Montreal

In the period from 1869 to 1945 girls in conflict with the law in Montreal were initiated into a legal process called juvenile justice. This system was one of several historical projects directed at the amelioration and regulation of children's lives. It comprised laws, institutions, personnel, and competing ideas about child welfare and youthful deviance, all of which were historically contingent and evolving. In these formative decades, Quebec introduced an abundance of legislation, constructed incarceration facilities, instituted a separate tribunal for youth in trouble in Montreal, and hired a coterie of personnel to focus on children's delinquency and dependency. Beginning with a rudimentary plan permitting children under the age of sixteen to be treated expeditiously by the criminal courts and placed in age-specific institutions, the juvenile justice system expanded to include a court featuring probation for those under the age of eighteen. For Montreal's delinquent girls, these were profound changes: a vagrant girl in the 1870s would likely have appeared in the city's Recorder's – the police court – and have been sent to the Soeurs du Bon Pasteur reform school; a girl similarly charged in the 1940s would have appeared before a 'children's judge,' been investigated by a female probation officer, and been physically and mentally assessed before being incarcerated or placed on probation.

This chapter examines the legal framework scaffolding and institutional innovations that created the status of 'delinquents' and where adolescents were judged and treated. These were not neutral processes: from the outset, juvenile justice reflected and prescribed normative gender, class, and ethnic values. In the early years of juvenile justice, the state was called upon to address the 'waifs and strays' problem, which largely concerned the visibility of 'undesirable' boys on city streets and to a lesser extent the growing juvenile prostitution population. Panic over the ubiquity of impoverished, idle, and seemingly parentless children led to the province's first gesture of juvenile justice, the laws concerning reform schools, which were intentionally created as sex-specific institutions to house destitute and morally wayward children. Responsibility for Montreal's long-standing reform and industrial schools fell to Catholic orders, giving this phase of juvenile justice a particularly private and confessional character, overseen by the city's Catholic elite. It was also largely shaped by gendered notions of salvation and rehabilitation.

The Quebec juvenile justice system would take a secular turn with the establishment of the Montreal Juvenile Delinquents' Court (MJDC) in 1912. This watershed in the local history of juvenile justice depended upon action of both the federal and provincial levels of government. In 1908 the federal Juvenile Delinquents Act (JDA) proposed a nationwide system of municipal juvenile courts but left it to each provincial government to actually create individual courts. The juvenile court therefore was a child of the JDA but also of provincial legislation that detailed the creation of specific municipal tribunals. With the JDA, provincial legislation, and the local juvenile court, the regulation of children broadened, and the state, rather than acting to rescue allegedly parentless children, began to target the working-class family. This new court embraced most of the latest thinking in North American juvenile justice reform, including prioritizing probation over reform school incarceration, decentring the child's offence, and, in rhetoric at least, blurring the lines between dependent and delinquent children. In this new process, gendered categories were quickly entrenched.

This chapter outlines the efforts of legislators and juvenile justice personnel to create a system intended for the protection and regulation of girls and boys, children and youth. It shows how juvenile justice in these years took its place in the political, social, and cultural environment specific to Montreal. Of chief importance was the ongoing negotiation between, and tensions among, Catholics and Protestants over care of children and youth. It also demonstrates the extent to which Quebec participated in the North American juvenile justice movement. The framework of juvenile justice in Montreal (beginning with reform schools and then a juvenile court system) is suggestive of the systems implemented in cities such as Chicago, Toronto, Los Angeles, and Winnipeg. On a superficial level the impact of these courts is similar: the juvenile court, with its broad definition of delinquency and its investigative officers wielding a middle-class morality, intruded on working-class families through the children. These court systems typically targeted female sexual delinquency and boys' property offences. Local politics and actors, however, provided the opportunity for these systems to diverge. For example, the Quebec government implemented compulsory schooling legislation only in 1943 and thus the Montreal juvenile court was not preoccupied with truancy the way it was in many other jurisdictions. Further, the deference of juvenile court authorities to psychiatric and psychological expertise seen in many progressive-era juvenile courts was less apparent in Montreal, especially prior to the 1940s. Lastly, the seemingly ubiquitous presence of female judges in juvenile courts in this era was not reflected in the Montreal situation, where patriarchal ideas about gender and the practice of law prohibited women from taking the bar and ascending the bench. Montreal took part fully in the North American juvenile justice movement, but what evolved in this city reflected specific social, cultural, political, and legal contexts that would in turn determine how delinquent girls experienced both regulation and justice.

Nineteenth-Century Child Saving in Quebec: Juvenile Justice Emerges

During the nineteenth century many Western countries embraced a spirit of reform directed at the improvement of children's lives called 'child saving.' This concern for child welfare was rooted in a belief that emergent urban, industrial societies had rendered children at once more vulnerable and vicious, requiring grand solutions beyond the parameters of home and family. Child saving produced a series of projects at the hands of charitable organizations, and eventually the state, that were aimed at the twin problems of the endangered and dangerous child. Most reformers extolled – initially, at least – the virtues of replacing the troubled family situation with an institutional environment designed specifically for that child.[1] This ethic of child rescue employed a contradictory combination of care/control and protection/punishment in an institutional setting.[2] The ambition of child-saving campaigns was to transform the landscape of hazardous childhood and deliver subsequent generations of obedient, industrious, and moral citizens. The city of Montreal was no exception to this reform spirit, although very specific local conditions framed the child protection movement and early juvenile justice projects.

Over the course of the nineteenth century, Montreal evolved from a small preindustrial centre into a significant industrial capitalist city with more than 216 000 habitants by 1891.[3] Tremendous growth and transformation of the urban environment and economy came at a considerable human cost, the face of which was the imperilled child. Abandoned and orphaned children were one dramatic side effect of the demographic tumult in the early-to-middle decades of the nineteenth century because the number of immigrants from the British Isles, especially impoverished Irish, and migrants from the Lower Canadian countryside grew and the city of Montreal was transformed. Private interests turned to the social problems of child destitution and dependence, recognizing orphans as a distressing consequence of the city's evolution. Like their counterparts in the northern United States and Britain, Montreal philanthropists and religious orders responded to the plight of 'innocent' children who lost their parents to famine, poverty, or desertion with 'institutionalized rescue work.'[4] In this city, social welfare institutions were carefully organized along confessional, or religious, lines: these included the Montreal Protestant Orphan Asylum (1822), the Asile des orphelins catholiques (1832), the Hospice Saint-Joseph (1841), and the St Patrick Orphan Asylum (1846). The early orphanages provided the basics of education, industrial training, and religious instruction, preparing the children of the poor for placement on farms or in urban homes, especially girls as domestic servants. Orphanages gained favour among nineteenth-century Montrealers as an alternative to the misery, ignorance, and poverty of working-class life and its proximity to temptation, sin, and vice. This trend in institution building would lay the groundwork for an explosion of institutions for problem children and the widespread practice of what historian Linda Mahood criticizes as 'using custody in a positive manner.'[5]

By mid-century, simplistic reckoning of the consequences of abandonment and poverty transformed an earlier problem of orphans into one of juvenile delinquency. Focus on the destitute child and family in the rapidly growing city resulted in the discovery of a different kind of gendered urban affliction that would require state intervention: street children. The juvenile justice system was designed originally as a response to working-class male delinquency, especially the 'waifs and strays' of urban life. In the nineteenth century, youthful male street culture became synonymous with juvenile delinquency.[6] A combination of the major features of industrial modernity – from urban poverty to cinemas to a decline in the power of the church – resulted in the growing presence of boys in public space. The modern city drew boys onto the streets as vendors, newsboys, delivery boys, vagrants, and thieves. Girls' presence on the street, especially at night, elicited concerns about juvenile prostitution and cross-class contamination featuring moral depravity and disease.[7]

This growing public presence of minors elicited action on several fronts broadly directed at the amelioration and regulation of children's lives. Gangs of idle, working-class boys in the streets of Montreal, for example, served as an impetus to establish schools under the Education Act of 1846; youthful prostitutes were increasingly contained in 'magdalen' asylums. The widespread visibility of youthful vagrants, prostitutes, and petty thieves evoked fear that childhood determined by crime on urban streets could only produce undesirable adults. According to observers, juvenile criminals were highly susceptible to nefarious behaviour. As British historian Heather Shore notes, by the 1830s, children played a fundamental role in the urban criminal 'underworld,' a geographic and social space that gained currency in the nineteenth century through fiction and contemporary accounts.[8] Methods of dealing with juvenile offenders were revealed to be limited: orphanages and asylums of nineteenth-century Montreal accepted 'deserving' children but left the criminal youth problem to the local jails. Concern that these institutions provided adult inmates with an opportunity to turn incarcerated children into permanent members of the criminal class motivated a shift toward differential treatment of youths in established prisons and jails.[9] The need for a new form of institution for delinquent juveniles was made all the more urgent by the perception that crime rates among children were on the rise.[10]

Nineteenth-century benevolent societies, city officials, and churches sought ways to protect children from the factory, the street, and importantly, the prison. Concerned citizens succeeded in pressuring the state to protect young people from the prison system and adult prisoners by placing juvenile offenders in new institutions. Symbolic of the rejection of the criminal justice system (as inappropriate for criminals considered young enough to be rehabilitated), youth reformatories effectively transformed young criminals into a new category – juvenile delinquents – and subjected them to a new regime of incarceration inspired by child welfare.[11] Sympathy for juvenile delinquents and the will to indefinite incarceration is aptly captured in the 1857 publication *Care of Our Destitute and Criminal Population:*

Poor little creatures, their lot is hard indeed. Treated as criminals before they can discern evil from good, and without any act of will of their own, locked up in a prison, surrounded by its demoralizing associations ... What

a load would be removed from the mind of the Judge in such circumstances, if it were in his power to send these little pests to an institution that
would at once protect society from their depredations, detach them from
their evil companions and from careless or vicious parents, that would keep
them under proper restraint and impart to them moral and industrial training, and so enable them to become useful members of society.[12]

Making children into 'useful members of society' was a gendered enter-
prise, beginning with the offences with which they were charged and further enforced by a sex-segregated rehabilitation regime.

Nineteenth-Century Legislative Innovations

Ambivalent attitudes toward juvenile criminality among child welfare
reformers (that it be treated severely and yet the individual be afforded
compassion) found its way into early juvenile justice legislation and institutions. By the 1840s, youthful offenders were singled out for their plas-
ticity and reformable nature; prison officials began promoting long
sentences to permit 'reeducation' of incarcerated youth.[13] In 1851 legislators for the Province of Canada resolved to promote special treatment
for juvenile delinquents, a mode of thinking that would come to domi-
nate juvenile justice practice in the latter part of the century. Included in
their resolutions was an identification of the needs of youthful first-time
offenders, creating a new category and opening the door to differential
treatment of inmates. While the common jails were deemed inappropriate to the mission of education, training, and discipline of children, the
reform school was proposed as a viable corrective to the common jail,
especially for young, first-time offenders. Eschewing the limited terms of
jail sentences, the proposals suggested keeping children locked up in
these new institutions for prolonged periods: 'it is essential to detain
children in institutions for as long as necessary to completely reform
them.'[14] These new reform schools, according to the resolutions, would
be funded by local taxes and the state.

   The 1850s represent a critical decade in the evolution of juvenile justice. The discourse of child protection in the legislature and in the popular press resulted in concrete action. Following the British example of
establishing industrial and reformatory schools, the Province of Canada
provided for the separate trials and punishment of youth[15] and in 1857
new reformatories signalled the trend toward a differentiated justice system for juveniles. Canada East established a *prison de réforme*, or reforma-

tory, to incarcerate those under twenty-one.[16] Unlike the reform schools of the late nineteenth century, but like the prison system, this institution was administered by the state, and a former prison inspector acted as warden.[17]

The reformatory, constructed in an old military barracks on Île aux Noix in the Richelieu River south of Montreal, was a short-lived experiment. From its inception it faced problems of mismanagement and was thwarted by its own objectives of mixing adolescents with older repeat offenders. And, despite its claim to be an institution of reform, it lacked a rehabilitation program, was home to severe discipline problems, and functioned ultimately as an adult facility – a common jail – that happened to hold young people.[18] The deficiency in rehabilitation regimes was further compounded by the fact that youth were admitted, irrespective of sex. Though few girls were incarcerated there, inspectors claimed its inattention to matters of gender inhibited true rehabilitation.[19] When an excuse to close the reformatory arose in the early 1860s, it was used to end this early experiment in juvenile incarceration: its proximity to the American border during the Civil War had made it untenable. With the reformatory closed in 1862, male inmates were transferred to St-Vincent-de-Paul and the girls to convents. Shortly after Confederation, another attempt was made to offer youthful offenders a different incarceration experience to that of jail and prison, where religious instruction and gender differences would become major organizing principles.

From 1869 to the creation of the Montreal Juvenile Delinquents' Court (MJDC) in 1912, reformatory and industrial schools constituted the foundation of the juvenile justice system. In 1867, the British North America Act placed the administration of prisons in the hands of the provinces, allowing local power dynamics to shape the system of youth prisons, quaintly renamed 'reformatory schools.'[20] Two years after Confederation, the province of Quebec embarked on a mission to institutionalize and reform wayward and dependent youth.

The 1869 Acts respecting Industrial and Reformatory Schools promised to transform the care and criminalization of children and adolescents in the province.[21] These acts resulted in a significant departure from the *prison de réforme*. Unlike that institution, which operated much like a jail for young people, the acts created 'schools' that were obliged to expand on the narrow imprisonment mandate of the 1857 experiment. The acts created a certification process for the establishment of industrial and reform schools, whereby the provincial government issued 'managers' the right to hold a specified number of children and make rules regarding discipline of inmates that were subject to the approval of the lieutenant governor in council. According to the legislation, the reform school was designated a 'reformatory prison' and was subject to the Act respecting Prisons for Young Offenders; the industrial school, on the other hand, was intended to offer children a chance for training in a variety of low-skilled jobs. Both types of institutions were required to 'educate, clothe, lodge, and feed' convicted youth and dependent children, respectively.

The distinction between the two types of facilities amounted to little more than the age of the children industrial schools held children under fourteen years, whereas reformatory schools received those under sixteen[22] despite the association of industrial schools with protection cases and reformatory schools with youthful offenders.[23] The act establishing industrial schools specified that children could be placed there if they were 'found wandering and not having any home or settled place of abode, or proper guardianship or visible means of subsistence,' as well as found destitute, orphaned, or having a parent in prison. The close connection between neglected children and delinquent behaviour, though, is clearly present in the act concerning industrial schools: the reasons for incarcerating a child in an industrial school also included being found in the 'company of thieves' or being uncontrollable, according to those in charge of him or her.

If the reform school system was an expression of new child-saving ideologies, in Quebec this was informed by the belief in Catholic redemptive strategies at the hands of priests and nuns. Thus, the development of reform schools illustrates the centrality of Catholic religious orders to nineteenth-century formation of the Quebec state and its intervention in the family. These 1869 acts, though not specifically defining 'managers' of reformatory and industrial schools as religious orders, mandated that children be placed in accordance with their religious beliefs. Not coincidentally, religion had been fundamental to the birth of the modern prison.[24] The purpose of the incarceration experience had become to isolate the prisoner, permitting time for reflection on criminal and immoral behaviour, and the opportunity to seek redemption from prison clergy. During the 1870s Montreal's two reform schools for girls and boys, respectively, were the work of religious orders. Emphasis on 'religious technologies of reform' opened the door for involvement of voluntary agencies, such as the Salvation Army, or religious orders, such as the Bon Pasteur nuns, in incarceration facilities.[25] Quebec child-saving policies enshrined a place for religious orders in the treatment of juvenile delinquency that would last a century.

This development was neither historical accident nor happenstance: the campaign for industrial and reformatory schools had sprung enthusiastically from ecclesiastical corners.[26] Under the 1869 laws, the state not only permitted but also fostered an organized, impressive presence of the Catholic Church and its institutions in the area of child rescue and reform, as we will see in chapter 2. For the remainder of the nineteenth century, Montreal reform schools were limited to those run by the Frères de la Charité de St-Vincent-de-Paul and the Soeurs du Bon Pasteur d'Angers. The confessional or religious orientation of institutions for delinquent and neglected children is but one example of the dramatic rise of the Catholic Church in Quebec society, especially in the realm of social services in the period 1850–70.[27]

The Catholic Church had actively pursued a larger role in the lives of Lower-Canadian Catholics in the wake of the Act of Union and its concomitant threat, assimilation. At the heart of this effort was Montreal's ultramontanist bishop of Montreal, Ignace Bourget (1837–76), who recruited religious personnel to parishes and dramatically expanded the presence of religious communities in the city. Bourget profoundly influenced Quebec society and its new institutions, including those run by the Soeurs du Bon Pasteur. Under him, the Catholic Church achieved a demonstrably larger role in the politics and social life of the province; the ultramontane vision of a Christian society faithful to Rome, where church and state were fused, began what Fernande Roy has called 'a veritable reconquest.'[28] During the latter half of the nineteenth century, the Catholic Church's place in the city and in the lives of most citizens was extended through a Catholic education system and the prominence of public religious observance and spectacle.[29] Bourget insisted on the supremacy of the church in all matters of religion and morality, thus claiming a right to safeguard the social order through its personnel and institutions.[30] This Catholic vision shaped new nineteenth-century juvenile justice institutions, making the reform schools an expression of the religious conviction that children should be isolated from the profane world, preferably in convents or monasteries where temptation did not drive them into sin.[31] The Catholic reform schools remained part of the Montreal juvenile justice system into the twentieth century, yet their status became peripheral with the passage of the JDA of 1908 and its provisions for juvenile courts.

By the early twentieth century, the Catholic hierarchy in Quebec increasingly turned its attention toward the socioeconomic problems brought about by urban and industrial growth, following the 1891 papal encyclical, Rerum Novarum. Building on a tradition located in early-

nineteenth-century institutions, Catholic social action now developed
rapidly, touching on a variety of problems facing children: public health,
punishing labour conditions, a need for expanding schooling initiatives,
and crime and delinquency. Throughout the twentieth century charitable organizations expanded to address the plight of troubled children
and adolescents and to absorb them into youth groups.

The latter part of the nineteenth century also saw the evolution of a
different thread of reform activism not as closely entangled with or motivated by the Catholic Church. Evangelical Protestants, social gospellers
and lay, or pan-denominational, social reformers simultaneously worked
at ridding 'their' city of vice and delinquency, child labour, juvenile prostitution, and the corruption of youth by adults. The founding in 1883 of
the Society for the Protection of Women and Children is likely the most
obvious development in this era. Eventually, Montreal's anglophone
Protestant community founded the city's Children's Aid Society (CAS)
in the first decade of the twentieth century. Its first president was, interestingly, a francophone, F.-X. Choquet. The selection of Choquet as president of the Montreal CAS demonstrates the permeability of the 'two
solitudes' in the early twentieth century. Choquet emerged from a tradition of nineteenth-century reform spearheaded by the political party,
the Parti rouge (eventually the Quebec Liberal Party), long-time opponents of the ultramontanists. Men such as Choquet worked within a
reformist, professional, francophone, and Catholic milieu but were also
able to transcend their own ethnic and linguistic community.[32] Working
in conjunction with educated elites of the Protestant and Jewish communities, and often with women, they sought legislative expression of their
social reform ideology. Their most important contribution to juvenile
justice would involve federal Parliament and a national children's bill.

The Federal Juvenile Delinquents Act and the Montreal Juvenile Court

Although child welfare constitutionally lay firmly within provincial jurisdiction, Canadian parliamentarians used their prerogative over criminal
law to initiate changes to the local practice of juvenile justice. The Canadian Criminal Code of 1892 recognized the young offender as a unique
category of criminal: it forbade convicting children under seven or those
under fourteen where the child had failed to comprehend that his or
her behaviour was wrong.[33] It also permitted courts to hold trials of juveniles separate from adult tribunals and without public witness. Two years
later, the Youthful Offenders Act reinforced these provisions in the

Criminal Code. This act stipulated that young offenders awaiting trial were to be held in custody apart from adult criminals. Significantly, the Act opened the door for new child-care agencies – such as local CASs – to play a role in processing juveniles, and it considered permissible as evidence a child's history and social context.[34] The legislation did not make special treatment of juvenile delinquents mandatory and most jurisdictions did not substantially alter the processing of young offenders.

For many Montrealers this legislative evolution did not go far enough, and thus began a campaign for a national children's bill, which would eventually be called the Juvenile Delinquents Act (JDA). The 1908 act was the product of intense lobbying and activism on the part of reformers known as the child savers, a new generation of social activists that was determined to systematize and professionalize the response to child welfare.[35] On the national scene the chief players were J.J. Kelso of Toronto and W.L. Scott of Ottawa, who founded CASs in these cities, modelling them on their American counterparts.[36] Yet, this was not simply an Ontario reform effort. Historians of the juvenile justice movement in Canada have tended to ignore Quebec's role in the process. Neil Sutherland's fine treatment of the JDA and the court system in English Canada excluded any discussion of Montreal;[37] yet, as the innovator of the federal bill, W.L. Scott knew well that convincing Quebec politicians and Montreal legal and religious elites was fundamental to the timely passage of the act.[38] In October 1907 Scott addressed Montrealers in a crowded public hall, arguing for a federal children's bill, a juvenile court, and a probation system. Both the francophone and anglophone newspapers greeted Scott and his ideas with enthusiasm, and as Dubois and Trépanier's quantitative and qualitative comparison of the Montreal and Toronto press coverage of the JDA campaign illustrates, Montrealers were anything but complacent over the issue.[39] Moreover, the largest petition in the country with more than 5000 signatures demanding the introduction into the House of an act concerning juvenile justice came from this city.[40] Support for a JDA appeared to unite cultural, religious, and linguistic communities. Along with the endorsement of the archbishop of Montreal, the JDA also gained approval from the chief detective of the Montreal police force, S.H. Carpenter; the governor of Montreal jails, C. A. Vallée; millionaires James Morgan and George Drummond; and Reverend J. Patterson-Smyth, rector of St. George's Anglican Church. Important women's organizations, such as the newly founded Féderation nationale Saint-Jean-Baptiste and the Montreal chapters of the Woman's Christian Temperance Union and Local Council of Women, constituted the juvenile court movement.[41] Prominent Montreal Liberals were also critical in guiding the bill through Parliament; of particular note was Senator Frédéric-Liguori Béique.[42]

When the federal government passed the JDA in 1908, it was hailed as a triumph for the child-saving movement and signified a pivotal moment for juvenile justice in Canada.[43] Child welfare reformers widely believed that the twentieth century would be marked by a humane and just system for young people. Following the passage of the act, the reform school era was replaced by one in which the juvenile court dominated juvenile justice. The separate court scheme formed the latter stage in a system that identified young offenders for special consideration, building on the establishment in the mid-nineteenth century of incarceration facilities for delinquent and neglected children under sixteen years.[44] In a particularly Canadian twist, the federal bill would not be hegemonic, but rather it included provisions for provincial control over the administration of juvenile courts. The juvenile justice systems constructed across the country mainly, if not exclusively, in urban areas were shaped not only by legislation but by provincial governments and the first generations of judges and probation officers.

Following the provisions in the JDA to establish a juvenile court, the Liberal government of Lomer Gouin moved to create a court in Montreal, aptly named the Montréal Cour des jeunes délinquants/Juvenile Delinquents' Court (MJDC).[45] This Montreal tribunal remained the province's only juvenile court until 1940. The MJDC, therefore, became the primary instrument of Quebec's juvenile justice system and a conduit for the province's child-saving aspirations.

In June 1910 provincial legislation permitting the city of Montreal to establish a juvenile court was passed.[46] The politicians' goal was to 'give juvenile delinquents an opportunity to redeem themselves without being classified as criminals.'[47] The legislators intended Montreals court to serve as a pilot project; if successful, subsequent juvenile courts would be constructed elsewhere in the province.[48] The attorney general of the province oversaw the court, vetting hiring, setting salaries, and at times interfering with the work of the court, as we will see in the firing of two female probation officers. This arrangement meant provincial politics permeated this local court, determining for much of the years from the 1910s to the 1940s that juvenile court judges were Liberal government appointments. As well, section 6 of the Act respecting Juvenile Delinquents, 1910 (1 Geo. V, chap. 26), which established the MJDC, stipulated that the juvenile court judge must be chosen from judges of the

Sessions, the police magistrates, or other city magistrates. This requirement, in an era when women were not yet called to the bar, effectively eliminated their chance to sit as juvenile court judges until the 1940s. This fact made Montreal's court an anomaly because many North American juvenile tribunals were headed by women. Most of the judges of the juvenile court between 1912 and 1945 were senior members of the bar, many with close ties to Liberal politics. The prominent judges included François-Xavier Choquet, who sat for a decade; he was followed by J.O. Lacroix, who was appointed in 1923 and who served until 1931; J.-Aldéric Robillard replaced Lacroix in 1932 and he was joined by Arthur Laramée in 1939; in 1941 the court's first Anglo-Protestant judge, J. Gordon Nicholson, was appointed by the provincial government of Adelard Godbout.

The MJDC officially opened in March 1912 on Champ de Mars Street in a converted house near City Hall.[49] This tribunal differed from other criminal courts – the Recorder's and the Sessions of the Peace – in several important ways. It used probation officers to investigate each case, held juveniles in a house of detention, and operated in conjunction with a citizens' committee. Juvenile justice would now reject key criminal justice principles of public trials and guilt determination: juvenile courts were held in camera to protect the delinquent from the wrath of the public, and the summary orientation of the trial meant the offence was trivial relative to the circumstances that led the youth astray.[50]

The name of Montreal's new court suggests that delinquency was its target, but the JDA and the provincial legislation gave the judge wide discretionary powers to process neglected children as well. Indeed, many fans of the juvenile court project claimed child protection was the main function of the new court.[51] Under sections 29 and 33 of the JDA, the MJDC could also prosecute adults for their contribution to delinquency among those under sixteen years of age.

Quebec juvenile justice in the juvenile court era became increasingly secular and liberal, reflecting remarkable political and social change in the province. The two traditionally powerful Montreal communities, represented by French Canadians and Anglo-Protestants, were easily represented within the new court, which had to accommodate a rapidly changing demography. Montreal grew swiftly with French-Canadian migration from rural areas of Quebec and with European and, to a lesser extent, Asian immigration.[52] That the court itself was not organized along confessional or denominational grounds is significant. Child welfare and other social services had long been the prerogative of the

Catholic Church, its religious communities, and various Protestant churches.[53] In the 1870s reform schools had been erected by religious orders that were financed in part by the provincial government. Although a child of the provincial state, the juvenile court reflected contemporary anxieties about nation, and therefore religion. In turn-of-the-century Quebec religion stood at the heart of the politics of 'race' and nation,[54] and this fact would resonate through all institutions, including the juvenile court. French-Canadian nationalists preferred that child welfare and other social services remain the prerogative of the Catholic Church. The 'race cry' was sounded over the threat that Catholic children were confined to the same juvenile court detention house as children of other religions.[55] The court's secular nature raised the ire of nationalists who saw the MJDC as too 'American' and not respectful enough of the role of the Catholic Church in child welfare.[56] This suspicion may have been fuelled by child welfare politics in Ontario, which, according to Nancy Christie, appeared to Catholics to be poised to 'gain ascendance for Protestant values in Canadian society.'[57] Negotiation, compromise, and accommodation produced a court system in Montreal that incorporated anxieties of Montreal's ethnic and religious communities: each child that passed through the court was carefully categorized according to its religious orientation, and investigation and treatment would be governed by this identity. The other identity that was critical in evaluation and treatment was gender. This categorization was not as incendiary as the 'race' question because it was considered obvious and indisputable to comprehend bad girl behaviour as distinct from boyish badness, and to treat them separately.

The Gendered Nature of Delinquency Law

Although the provincial government was responsible for personnel matters at the MJDC, the judges and probation officers followed federal juvenile justice law as well as provincial legislation concerning juvenile corrections. Under the 1908 JDA, delinquent boys and girls formed part of a new category of youth processed by the juvenile court system for behavioural difficulties, often at the behest of their parents and criminal activity brought to the court's attention by the police. The aim of the act was to create a category for differential or exceptional treatment under criminal law. A youthful lawbreaker was defined as between seven and sixteen years of age; after a 1921 amendment the age limit was raised to eighteen, although Quebec did not follow this trend until 1942. The young person was relieved of the 'criminal' or 'offender' designation and instead was labelled 'delinquent' and understood to be a 'misdirected or misguided child.'[58] A juvenile delinquent was described as 'any child who violates any provision of The Criminal Code ..., or of any Dominion or provincial statute, or of any by-law or ordinance of any municipality.'[59] This system inflated the kinds of behaviour that qualified as offences and caused adolescents in the early-twentieth century to be more policed than any previous generation for acts heretofore considered private.

The range of behaviour that could land an adolescent in juvenile court was amplified by a clause in the JDA defining the delinquent as one 'who is liable by reason of any other act to be committed to an industrial school or reformatory.'[60] Because industrial and reform schools fell under provincial jurisdiction, provinces could then further define what actions connoted delinquency. As provinces set about harmonizing their acts regarding the treatment of delinquent youth with the JDA, juvenile courts' jurisdiction over youth behaviour exponentially increased. Quebec Industrial and Reform Schools Acts of the nineteenth century had permitted criminal court judges discretionary powers to incarcerate adolescents for purposes of protection and punishment. Under these acts reform schools were filled with youthful offenders who had committed crimes or simply rejected parental discipline. Late in 1912 the Quebec legislature amended the 1869 provincial acts regarding reform and industrial schools to accommodate the new legal apparatus of the juvenile court. The amendment expanded on previous rights of guardians who could ask that their child be committed to an industrial school if they found themselves 'unable to control [their] child by reason of his bad or vicious habits.'[61] The amendment to this article outlined the following circumstances under which a father or mother, stepfather or stepmother, tutor or relative, could ask the judge to have the child committed to a juvenile reformatory: 'such child is deserting or abandoning, or that he has deserted or abandoned the home of the person who is in charge of him without permission or sufficient reason; or that he habitually disobeys the lawful and reasonable orders of his parents, or of the person in whose care or keeping he is; or that he is habitually idle; or that he is unmanageable or incorrigible; or that he habitually makes use of obscene or indecent language or that he is guilty of immoral conduct.'[62]

This amendment had very specific implications for the processing of delinquents. First, it would result in a dramatic rise in the number of children and adolescents coming to court.[63] Second, because neither the JDA nor the provincial acts defined 'unmanageability,' 'incorrigibility,' and 'reasonable orders,' it was incumbent upon juvenile court judges and probation officers, parents, guardians, neighbours, religious leaders, and even the press to identify what adolescent behaviour would be singled out for discipline. Third, the gender-specific – male – language of the amended act belies the fact that girls were found delinquent and that the meaning of misbehaviour was highly gendered, especially 'immoral conduct,' which was almost exclusively used to target female behaviour.[64] A 1924 amendment to the JDA further entrenched the sexual regulation of girls: the definition of juvenile delinquency was expanded to include those guilty of 'sexual immorality.'[65]

The gendered nature of delinquency meant boys were brought before the juvenile court judge for theft and damage to private property, whereas girls were targeted for immoral conduct. For example, in the MJDC's annual reports from the 1910s, clerk Owen Dawson vented his annoyance concerning the increasing number of delinqents – girls under sixteen coming to the court for 'leading immoral lives' and boys for burglary and shopbreaking.[66] In his 1926 study of the Shawbridge Boys' Farm and the Girls' Cottage Industrial School, McGill University professor J.W. Bridges observed that most boys were incarcerated for theft or stealing, whereas girls were sexual delinquents, though he admitted that it wasn't that the boys were not also sexually delinquent, 'but society sees fit to incarcerate boys for one offence, and girls for another.'[67]

The JDA and provincial acts concerning juvenile delinquency did not describe delinquency with any precision, opening the door to widespread interpretation of bad adolescent behaviour. Unlike adult crimes, juvenile delinquency was not codified, enabling court officials to reproduce prescribed bourgeois notions of adolescence, masculinity, femininity, and sexuality in producing delinquents. Even without precise descriptions of delinquency, people involved in the juvenile justice system had no difficulty in identifying and disciplining working-class girls and boys from the outset.

Conclusion

The introduction of juvenile justice to Montreal in the nineteenth century through provincially mandated reform schools and through the juvenile court in the early twentieth century systematically altered the relationship of the city's adolescents to law, the state, and their families.

Justice for youth was rooted in a belief that children could be saved – from poverty, illness, despair, crime, as well as from themselves and their parents. It emerged in a specific historical context that brought ethnic and religious tensions and negotiations to bear on child welfare and the treatment of troubled youth. It also provided a context in which local notions of gender, family, childhood, and adolescence could be played out on the young generation.

A politics of child protection produced the first reform schools in Quebec in the 1870s. That the province handed responsibility for these incarceration facilities to conservative Catholic orders reflected a particular political and social moment in nineteenth-century Quebec. Less an institution of state formation than a feature of the socially and politically ascending Catholic Church, the reform school reflected a distinct politics of child protection. By the early twentieth century, challenges to that conservative order came in the guise of the juvenile court movement. Spearheading the campaigns to de-institutionalize problem children was a liberal element within the province that was ultimately successful in 1912 with the establishment of the MJDC. In the juvenile court era, conservative critics observed the triumph of a dangerously Anglo-American model of juvenile justice. Beyond its progressive French-Canadian leadership, the juvenile court also saw the small but important anglophone minority manoeuvre to assert its philosophy of child protection, challenging what it saw as the Catholic stranglehold over the care of children and youth. In different ways, the Protestant and Jewish communities of Montreal took their place in this centre of juvenile justice, assuming control over 'their' children who were brought to court.

When Quebec authorized the establishment of reform schools, they were intended to be sex-specific institutions, confirming the notion that female delinquency differed from male and that treatment necessarily followed this distinction. The provincial government thus named a female religious order to run the first girls' reform school; boys were entrusted to a Catholic male order. Girls and boys came through the lower criminal court like adults but would experience incarceration in separate religious institutions: for girls this meant the female environment of the convent; for boys this meant a reformatory run by the Frères de la Charité. In the juvenile court era, male delinquency was more widespread than female, but delinquent girls constituted a weightier social problem. Gendered definitions of uncontrollable and incorrigibility permitted the differential policing of girls and boys. The category 'juvenile delinquent' had always been gendered; male and female delinquency were treated as distinct social problems though both came from the most impoverished and marginalized sectors of society. With the JDA and the early-twentieth-century juvenile court, delinquency continued to be constitutive of social relations structured by gender, class, and race.

Behind Convent Walls: Quebec Juvenile Justice in the Reform School Era, 1869–1912

Behind a stone wall surrounding the Bon Pasteur convent on Sherbrooke Street just east of downtown Montreal stood the province's first reform school for girls. Prior to the establishment of the city's juvenile court in 1912, girls judged delinquent, regardless of religious or linguistic background, experienced juvenile justice from behind these walls. How juvenile justice for girls began in a nineteenth-century Catholic convent reform school is the departure point for this chapter. It locates the Soeurs du Bon Pasteur reform school in the context of the nineteenth-century penal reform movement that promoted the creation and separation of specific age and gender categories of offenders. The Quebec government joined this international trend in 1869, when it authorized the establishment of separate reform schools for girls and boys, respectively. From their conception, these age-specific and sex-segregated institutions carefully insulated girls from the negative influence of older criminal women and bad boys their own age.

Reform schools were a manifestation of the broad trend away from punishment and toward treatment of social 'deviants' in the nineteenth century. The girls' reform school in particular was the product of three interconnected trends in nineteenth-century revisionist thinking: the transformation of attitudes toward the child in trouble; the rejection of the prison as appropriate for female convicts; and the emergence of the endangered girl as a social problem. Girls reform schools sprung up across North America and Europe in the latter part of the century, a reflection of the softening of attitudes toward both troublesome children and female criminals. These institutions filled the need to protect, through incarceration, young women who were increasingly known as juvenile girls. This chapter outlines these three discourses that promoted the idea that the child should be spared the grim experience of incarceration in jails and prisons, that an alternative female incarceration facility was necessary, and that adolescent girls and young women warranted protective custody.

In Quebec this development occurred at a time when religious orders were growing in number and in social and political prominence. Thus in 1869 the provincial government was prepared to delegate the reform school project to Catholic religious orders. Responsibility for the girls' reformatory school fell to the Soeurs du Bon Pasteur, a French order that had been recruited to the city twenty-five years earlier for their experience in regulating female deviance by confining women to institutions. The decision to entrust a Catholic religious order with the new facility was based on the assumption that girls in conflict with the law required spiritual redemption and proper socialization through maternal treatment in a sacred environment.

The historiography of Quebec's reform schools has privileged the politics of child saving that spawned the 1869 acts and industrial and reform schools.[1] Building upon the influential work of Jacques Donzelot, Renée Joyal argues that the philanthropic efforts to regulate children through new juvenile justice institutions in Quebec thoroughly reshaped the relationship between the private and the public spheres. The result was diminished paternal authority, and this paved the way for an invigorated interventionist state. Joyal points to these acts as the first dramatic intervention of the Quebec state into family life that would ultimately reshape the relationship between children and their parents.[2] Further, nineteenth-century juvenile justice and its physical manifestation, the reform school, comprised an emergent social arena connecting the state and the family, representing a new expression of power over the family and its members.[3] Certainly, the Quebec reform school legislation represented a new area of possible state intervention in the family: the control of delinquents and the care of neglected children. In the case of reform schools in Quebec the 'interventionist' state, though, was mediated by the religious orders that ran them. In contrast to the movement toward state control and management of prisons and reformatories elsewhere in Canada, in Montreal, the reformatory school for girls was administered by the Catholic sisters – a private venture – in exchange for a per capita subsidy from the provincial government.

While separate histories of the origins of the girls' and boys' reform schools have been written, they do not sufficiently interrogate the meaning of gendered juvenile justice in the late nineteenth century.[4] This chapter offers a corrective to the literature, demonstrating how juvenile justice policies and spaces were always gendered and that both delinquent girls and those in charge of them were gendered subjects. The girls' reform school was a product not only of child-saving rhetoric and policies but also of historically specific ideas about girls' proper and delinquent behaviour and the best way to transform the fallen girl into a future wife and mother. For girls in Montreal this meant internment in a convent run by chaste and pious nuns, programs predicated on saving their souls for the church and God, and lessons in accepting their station in life as working-class, French-Canadian women. In this way the Soeurs du Bon Pasteur played an important role in the expansion of conservative Catholic values among girls. This reform school indoctrinated the so-called weaker members of the flock and cloistered them from the temptations of a modernizing city and its 'foreign' influences. The reform school was one of many ultramontane projects that shaped late-nineteenth-century Quebec. This episode in juvenile justice history, where reform schools predominated, would peak in this period and, though not entirely dismissed, would eventually be supplanted by the juvenile court and new methods of treatment, including probation and training schools.

Through an examination of the politics and practice of the reform school project in the province of Quebec this chapter focuses on how and why sex-segregated, religiously based institutions emerged as the first stage of juvenile justice. Focusing on the Soeurs du Bon Pasteur, it examines the background, purpose, and regime of their reform school for girls.

The Rise of Gendered Incarceration

The reform school project originated in the penal reform movement that had sprung from eighteenth-century Enlightenment thought. Penal reform movements in Europe and North America produced a critique of inhumane physical punishment and deplorable jail conditions leading to the establishment of new incarceration facilities called penitentiaries.[5] In 1835, the Kingston Penitentiary, for example, embarked on a mission to rehabilitate the character of the prisoner through confinement.[6] Accompanying the conviction that inmates required treatment through manipulation of their environment was the new categorization of the deviant – especially with respect to age and sex. Categorization was facilitated first through separating certain groups (such as women or children) into wings of prisons, then into entirely new institutions, including reform schools.

In the 1840s at approximately the same moment that the urgent need to distinguish children from adults in prisons came to the fore, the horrors of housing women in local jails and prisons emerged in the prison reform movement. In most local jails men, women, and children had been lumped together; in an effort to stop the physical and sexual abuse of women in these jails as well as the moral and spiritual dissipation associated with incarceration, prison reformers at first advocated isolation of women into their own wings and then called for entirely separate institutions for women.[7] In the early nineteenth century Elizabeth Fry, a Quaker and English reformer, campaigned to reveal the injustices done to imprisoned women. Quakers were at the forefront of the prison-reform movement in general, arguing for a more humane and spiritual prison regime; Fry extended this to women, inspiring generations of female prison reformers in Britain and North America to launch prison-visiting schemes to expose the deleterious effects of incarceration on womanhood. By mid-century, a separate facility for female offenders, which came to be known as the women's reformatory, was promoted by voluntary middle-class female reformers in the United States and Britain who, following Fry's writings, denounced nineteenth-century incarceration methods as unsuitable for women. The women's reformatory movement and the child-saving movements coalesced to 'protect' female criminals and delinquents from adult jails and promote gender-appropriate institutions.[8] These institutions often became the business of middle-class female reformers who had lobbied the state for their establishment and were rewarded with employment in these new facilities.

The women's reformatory broke 'radically with custodialism':[9] everything from the program of rehabilitation to the architecture of the facility to its location was a rejection of the early-nineteenth-century penitentiary models and common jails. Its design fitted its purpose: conceived as 'extradomestic' female space, it was intended to evoke a maternal transformation in female prisoners who had clearly taken leave of their 'natural' state.[10] Rejecting the disciplinary regimes of anonymity and isolation that had come to predominate in penitentiaries, female prison reformers supported an individualized scheme for women inmates based on moral and religious teaching that emphasized women's maternal and domestic role in the larger society.[11] Facilities were constructed whose architecture, programs, and management suited women's 'gentle' and 'domestic' nature. In principle the architecture espoused by Jeremy Bentham and exhibited in the nineteenth-century penitentiary was rejected in favour of homier, cottage-style facilities. The equation of rural living with higher morality led the reformatory founders to build institutions in pastoral surroundings far from the menacing aspects of urban life from which most inmates came.[12]

Not only were female inmates to be physically separated from men and provided with gender-specific regimes, but they would also be supervised by exemplary female role models. Casting themselves as 'their sisters' keepers,' female prison reformers promoted themselves in the field of reformatory management through careful use of nineteenth-century maternal and separate spheres ideology. By laying claim to the womanly virtues of domesticity, piety, purity, and charity, they forged and legitimated a place for themselves in the public world of politics, organized religion, and social reform. American maternalist reform rhetoric ascribed to women a higher morality and a superior evangelical approach to social problems such as housing female convicts. With promises not short of redemption and salvation of fallen sisters, female prison reformers situated themselves as key players in the new female incarceration projects. Female custodians or matrons were selected for their alleged maternal force; as Kelly Hannah-Moffat argues, 'the expectation was that a mother's love and power could become a model for regulating, correcting, and normalizing deviant women.'[13]

The largely voluntary efforts of female prison reformers would eventually lead to the establishment of women's reformatories across the United States, Britain, and Canada. Toronto's Mercer Reformatory for Females, which opened in 1874, is the best-known Canadian example. Carolyn Strange and Kelly Hannah-Moffat have shown that the effect of maternalist politics in prison reform was to transform not only prison spaces for women but also the governance of female inmates.[14] American and British historians also agree that maternal reform meant programs featuring the training of women in moral lessons (to embrace chastity before marriage and fidelity within it) and homemaking.[15] Strange notes that the Mercer's aim was to inculcate the largely working-class inmate population with bourgeois notions of femininity.[16] Historians have also demonstrated the contradictory outcome of having sympathetic, nurturing, and domestic women in charge of female inmates: judges conceded to incarcerating women more often and for longer durations than men.[17]

The Soeurs du Bon Pasteur occupied an important role in this international trend toward gender-exclusive incarceration. The experience in the Montreal common jail had been far from conducive to reformation of either sex: by mid-century the 1837 edifice was overcrowded, the women's section was not sufficiently separate from the men's, and it lacked female staff to supervise the women inmates. As in other parts of North America and Europe, prison reformers in Montreal, including the inspectors of prisons and the clergy at the local jail, aimed to alleviate the horrendous experience of incarceration for women by handing them over to female religious orders.[18] During the late 1860s the inspectors of prisons, who had long been at the centre of debates over imprisonment in the nineteenth century, vigorously supported the role of the Catholic Church, especially in dealing with women and children in trouble, and began to argue for schools – not prisons – for youthful offenders.[19] Inspector W. Nelson claimed the key to reform for female inmates lay with the 'tender and maternal treatment' offered by nuns and that holding female inmates in asylums or charitable institutions run by nuns was 'easier and more economical' than state-run prisons.[20] When the 1869 Quebec Act respecting Reform Schools led to the establishment of Montreal's first institutions of juvenile justice run by religious orders it was determined that they would not simply be religious in orientation but that they would be fundamentally gendered spaces.

By the 1870s the Soeurs du Bon Pasteur housed several categories of 'deviant' women. The order began with the industrial and reformatory schools for girls and later that decade added the Montreal women's prison. The reformatory school for girls allowed the possibility for application of female-appropriate treatment in a Catholic context. While subscribing to the most basic principles of the women's reformatory – that female inmates required gender-specific treatment – the Soeurs embraced a system that was consistent with their religious custom and beliefs. If women's reformatories in the United States were part of a process of women's institution building in the late nineteenth century,[21] the girls reformatory school in Montreal was the Catholic equivalent, fitting into a large network of facilities run by female religious orders.

In 1869 the Soeurs were sought out by civic officials and the Montreal Catholic elite for their long experience in the field of rescuing fallen women in France and more recently in Montreal. In the 1870s they came to predominate in the area of criminal women and bad girls, constructing and managing the women's prison and the reform school for girls. This order of nuns differed from their contemporaries involved in the establishment of female state reformatories in Britain, the United States, and English Canada: they were not labelled reformers, nor would they likely have considered themselves such. They tended not to share in the middle-class, maternalist ideology behind the establishment of women's reformatories; rather, these nuns, selected for their piety and purity, were motivated by Catholic faith and a conservative social ideology. The nuns' ultimate purpose was to redeem the lost souls of wayward girls and fallen women; this could be best achieved through a cloistered religious environment.

The Soeurs du Bon Pasteur and the Endangered Girl

The selection of the Soeurs as managers of the women's prison and the girls' reform school was not coincidental. Established in the seventeenth century by Père Jean Eudes, an apostolic missionary and founder of a society of priests called Eudists, the Soeurs du Bon Pasteur focused on female sinners and their rehabilitation. In the eighteenth and nineteenth centuries these sisters embraced a 'fourth vow' beyond poverty, chastity, and obedience: to rescue fallen women, especially former prisoners and prostitutes.[22] Social service work with the penitent class of women was expanded in the early-nineteenth century under Mère Marie-de-Sainte-Euphrasie (Rose Virginie Pelletier), who added protection of girls to the order's mandate.[23] This mother superior had established an order at the *Institut de Notre-Dame-de-Charitè-du-Bon-Pasteur* in Angers, France in 1831. Ten years later the Bishop of Montreal, Ignace Bourget would visit her at this institution.[24] There, the nuns' activities relating to the rescue of 'fallen womanhood' would inspire him to recruit the order to Montreal.[25]

From the perspective of the Soeurs, the chance to branch into the western hemisphere was compelling. Under Mère Marie-de-Sainte-Euphrasie, more than one hundred Bon Pasteur monasteries had been founded.[26] The nuns wrote enthusiastically of Bourget's proposal: how could one refuse the chance to convert souls in '*La Nouvelle France*'?[27] Thus in 1844 four nuns from Angers left France to establish the Montreal chapter. As it is recollected in their fiftieth anniversary commemorative history, these nuns were instructed: 'Leave, go there [Montreal], far away by ocean, to open a new fold for the lost sheep of Israel.'[28] They would be joined in the latter half of the nineteenth century by many others from the same order who established institutions across Canada and the United States. The Sisters of the Good Shepherd of Angers first established themselves in Louisville, Kentucky, in 1842; by 1867 eleven 'convent-reformatories' had been founded in the United States.[29]

Their establishment in Montreal was eased by donations from the powerful Sulpician order and private sources, including Montreal businessman Olivier Berthelet and Madame D.-B. Viger. Viger donated land on Sherbrooke Street for their convent[30] and Berthelet contributed funds to construct it.[31] The convent was a large four-storey stone building with adjoining chapel. The large lot was walled along Sherbrooke Street and the side streets to cloister the community from the urban life that surrounded it.

Like other apostolic orders that were founded in Montreal in this period, the Soeurs du Bon Pasteur would carve a niche for themselves in community service, serving and regulating the popular classes from within the confines of the convent. Their particular work followed the wishes of Bourget, involving female criminals and delinquents, or what the sisters termed a 'runaway and rebellious flock.'[32] In practice their first attempts in the field involved a short-lived transition house for women recently released from prison.[33] Once in their Sherbrooke Street convent in 1847, they immediately accepted several categories of young girls and women: those under twelve years who were abandoned, orphaned, or mistreated, and older girls and women in trouble with the law. Following the 1869 acts, the provincial government granted them the responsibility of administering reformatory and industrial schools for girls; later that decade this order also assumed the management of Montreal's new women's jail on Fullum Street, the Asile Ste.-Darie.[34] By 1900 the sisters had acquired five institutions in Quebec.[35]

It was the sisters' ambition to reform fallen girls and protect the innocent from the sexual danger of the city, and they were not alone. These nuns formed part of a network of female orders concerned with fallen girls and women, which included the Soeurs de la Miséricorde, who had been sequestering, or in the parlance of the day 'rescuing,' fallen women since Rosalie Cadron-Jetté had founded a home for unwed pregnant women in the 1840s at the request of Bishop Bourget.[36] Evangelical Protestant reformers, working through their churches, were also struck by working-class girls' susceptibility to urban temptations as a result of the combination of living in the city without family (or just as bad, with neglectful parents), poor working conditions, and a lack of religious guidance.

In Montreal evangelical Protestants as well as the Catholic clergy had noted with dismay that as the city grew, so too did prostitution. Girls increasingly became the focus of concern about larger problems of commercial vice and the uncontrollable spread of venereal disease. Soon after its establishment in Montreal in 1884, the Woman's Christian Temperance Union (WCTU) turned its members' attention to the urban ills confronting young women. According to the WCTU, the increasingly public face of prostitution and the spread of brothels in the city apparently had a 'whirlpool' effect on young women, 'drawing to itself young lives.'[37] While chiefly an instrument of temperance, this group also saw itself as the arbiter or steward of the city's moral landscape. In the 1880s the Montreal WCTU added 'work for Social Purity' to their Evangelistic Department. Through its social purity department it also turned to the plight of young women in the industrializing city, establishing a variety of programs, including Travellers' Aid, Sheltering Home, and Reading Rooms. In its first decade in the city, the WCTU, convinced of an elaborate underworld scheme to trick women travelling alone to Montreal, posted placards in both English and French in railway stations outside of Montreal, warning unsuspecting women of the dangers that awaited them in the city. As 'respectable girls' from the countryside stepped from trains, the WCTU warned, they were allegedly met by individuals promising good jobs and housing but who in fact drove them into a 'life of sin.'[38]

Although the Soeurs du Bon Pasteur remained semicloistered and did not embark on public campaigns to round up public women and girls,[39] they awaited the arrival of girls who were deemed morals offenders by police, courts, and other authorities, such as parents and social reform agencies. On the street, those who noticed these girls belonged to an invigorated group of social and moral reformers who, inspired by evangelical Christianity, took to the streets to wage war on public drunkenness and prostitution. This benevolent work was largely gendered, with middle-class women laying claim to rescue work among young women and girls. The city's WCTU and Young Women's Christian Association, for example, focused largely on preventive measures to keep 'good girls good.'[40] Their emphasis on religious conversion, self-improvement, and the work ethic led them to construct boarding houses, employment bureaus, and recreation facilities. Unlike the Catholic nuns who focused on reforming girls from a vantage point inside incarceration facilities, evangelical Protestant laywomen engaged in public campaigns to rescue girls and women, and when necessary, directed them to institutions such as reform schools.

Andrée Lévesque has noted that with the rise of antivice reformers, attitudes toward the sex trade shifted dramatically over the course of the late nineteenth century from tolerance and regulation to eradication.[41]

The dramatic swing toward 'extinguishing the red-light district' of Montreal can be attributed in part to a desire to protect specifically young women from men and a mounting anxiety about women's presence on city streets. As prostitution became a social problem to be investigated, the more categories of fallenness emerged and mattered. In defining nineteenth-century social problems, reformers increasingly took note of the age and experience of the female vagrant. Christine Stansell locates this awakening in 1850s New York City when the sexual degradation of adolescent girls was identified and problematized. As she illustrates, this 'lively trade in juvenile prostitution' resulted from the eroticization of children, especially working-class girls, and gender and class iniquities of the mid-nineteenth century that made prostitution one of a few choices for poor girls.[42] The casual prostitution practised by these working-class girls was then framed as the precursor to a life of vice, disease, and unwed motherhood. In the nineteenth-century public discourse on fallen women, a cleavage emerged between the older career prostitute and the younger, more salvageable 'girl.' According to Linda Mahood, Scottish reformatories or Magdalen homes functioned to 'save' the latter category from collapsing into the former.[43] As new categories emerged, more women, especially younger and working-class, became 'potential clients' of reform institutions.[44]

Reform(able) Girls

Most girls caught in the emergent juvenile justice system were working class, impoverished, and likely seen as a visible urban nuisance. Girls who worked in the city's market stalls or on the streets selling whatever they could, along with those who were attracted to the excitement of street culture, were considered by respectable Montrealers to be abandoned, abused, and susceptible to the worst vices of industrializing cities – alcohol and prostitution. Far more than boys, girls appeared to be in moral jeopardy. Girls' poverty, abandonment, and youthful lack of will allegedly created an environment where they traded their virtue for material and emotional sustenance. According to reformers their public presence foreshadowed their moral destiny, which if left uncorrected amounted to life as fallen women.[45] The irredeemable consequences of a loss of virginity made rescue and reform critically important. Once fallen, of course, reformers condemned these girls to fill the ranks of the diseased and accused them of being a menace to the modern city. It was imperative therefore to rescue girls from this undesirable and dangerous path.

Very quickly the girls' reform school became a popular solution to the vagrant girl problem. In a 1875 *Montreal Witness* article, 'No Room in the Reformatory,' a reporter recounted the story of 'two females of bad character' who had embarked on a nighttime excursion on the snowy streets of Montreal in a stolen sleigh. One of the women, Hannah D., was but a girl of fourteen. In judging the case, the Recorder gave the older woman – a twenty-two-year-old – a ten-dollar fine or two months in jail; Hannah's youth and the lack of a responsible and present parent motivated the judge to send her to the Bon Pasteur reform school. The girls' reformatory, though, was full. In frustration, the judge sent her to prison for three months. As the newspaper noted, jail time would 'do little or nothing towards her reclamation from the fearful life she is leading.' The growing demand for space in which to incarcerate girls is directly related to the mounting perception of the need for exemplary women to rescue and reform the city's working 'girls' to keep them from a life of vice and away from the adult criminal justice system, where they would be turned into adult criminals; the nuns could effect change in their inmates.[46]

Late-nineteenth-century social critics and purity activists did not differentiate between women and girls who occupied the streets (especially after dark) and prostitutes, causing vagrancy to become one of the largest crime categories for female offenders at this time. Vagrant girls triggered the same response as prostitutes by virtue of their public activities, whether they were drinking, flirting, or loitering. A yardstick for morality, vagrancy arrests were constitutive of a discourse on social and sexual organization of public space. Too often, it seemed, the city's parks and streets provided young women with a freedom from parental authority and scrutiny. This is particularly true of female vagrancy cases, where girls found 'wandering' the streets or keeping morally questionable company went before the Montreal Recorder and were sent to reformatory school. The case of Jennie M. is instructive: fifteen-year-old Jennie was arrested for vagrancy in 1903. Since eleven years of age, she had worked outside her family home as a live-in domestic servant. Yet, prior to her arrest her disobedience was expressed in a failure to hold a regular job. Her father declared to the authorities that she had slept out nights and had been stopped by police in the streets accompanied by men. In the name of protection Jennie's social and alleged sexual behaviour (none had been proven) was punished. The Recorder sent her to the Soeurs du Bon Pasteur reform school for three years.[47]

The details of the case of Louisa S. reflect the general trend in policing female delinquency in the reform school era; her case and others

like it confirmed to contemporaries how socio-economic changes in
Montreal had imperilled young womanhood and legitimated the work of
the Soeurs du Bon Pasteur and the incarceration of adolescent girls. In
1907, thirteen-year-old Louisa was condemned to four years in the reformatory school for vagrancy. Louisa's mother, a widow, supported herself
and her daughter through laundry work, likely garnering a most meagre
wage. Lack of parental supervision and appropriate maternal care evi-
dently led Louisa to seek out young men and a youth-oriented street culture. Soon she was staying out overnight. In the context of familial
poverty, Louisa's mother expected her to find waged work, but she had
recently refused. With no work, the court was able to declare her a
vagrant and turned her over to the Soeurs for four years.[48]

A similar pattern is apparent in the case of Léda B., who was sentenced
to two years at the reformatory school for wandering the streets. In this
case, Léda had reportedly been a disciplined fourteen-year-old domestic
servant. According to her family, 'suddenly' she was spending nights out.
Arrested on Notre-Dame Street early one morning she was brought to
court where she was condemned as a 'coureuse de nuit,' literally a night
wanderer, an appellation akin to street walker.[49] Like older women
appearing in the lower criminal court before the Recorder, adolescent
girls arrested as vagrants were commonly suspected of prostitution,
although a vagrancy charge comprised a broad range of behaviour,
including a resistance to work and in the case of young women, real or
potential promiscuity. In the case of minors (those under sixteen), evidence gathered from aggrieved parents factored into the judge's decision. Cases such as Louisa's and Léda's were thought to illustrate how
running in the streets led to nightly desertion and then to juvenile prostitution. These two had been caught 'just in time' to prevent their moral
downfall; lengthy sentences with the nuns would 'protect' them from
imminent peril.

According to the Soeurs du Bon Pasteur, 'poor young girls' who came
before the courts fell prey to 'miserable persons' who paid girls' fines in
order to keep them in a constant state of dependence and sin.[50] While
confirming women's sexual passivity and casting working-class 'girls' as
victims of male sexual predators served to highlight the sexual threat to
young womanhood as never before, it also justified protection in the
name of incarceration. Girls who were on the streets were considered
orphans and authorities and parents alike seemed to favour reeducation
at the hand of the nuns. All of this thinking on the vulnerability of young
women would contribute to the forging of a clientele for the Soeurs du
Bon Pasteur's new École de Réforme.

Condemned to the Convent

From 1870 to 1915 the reform school was situated at the walled convent at the provincial house of the Bon Pasteur on Sherbrooke Street East in central Montreal. Despite the prevailing wisdom that pastoralness was fundamental to the female reformatory, such as those in Britain, the École de réforme was located in the urban centre; only in 1915 was the reformatory school moved to a more pastoral setting at Laval-des-Rapides.[51] In exchange for this work, the government eventually paid the religious order $5.50 per month for each child.[52] For boys, the Institut Saint-Antoine, a reform school, was created by the Frères de la Charité in 1873 on De Montigny Street in east-end Montreal; this Belgian order had also been recruited by Bourget in 1864.[53]

According to the act of 1869 the reform school was to receive girls under sixteen in conflict with the law: the École de Réforme took in girls for a period of 'not less than six months' for 'criminal offenses only.'[54] According to Véronique Strimelle, internment in the reformatory school lasted on average two years; many girls were incarcerated from two to four years,[55] spending much of their adolescence behind the convent walls. From its inception to 1915, the year it moved, approximately two thousand girls passed through the Bon Pasteur reformatory and industrial schools. In 1870 the reform school took in fifty-five girls; this number would drop in subsequent years and fluctuate between a handful and thirty girls per year.[56] Three-quarters of the girls were Canadian-born and francophone; another 20 per cent were anglophone, of English or Irish descent. Not until the twentieth century did the population diversify, reflecting recent immigration.[57] Delinquent girls incarcerated by the Soeurs du Bon Pasteur were typically thirteen to sixteen years of age, poor, and arrested for vagrancy.[58]

The very presence of a new institution called a school, not a jail, and run by a religious order inspired an increase in demand for rescuing – in fact, incarcerating – young women. In the reform school era, the range of girls' policed behaviour expanded, and sentences for minor infractions were lengthened as evangelical reformers fixed their attentions on the declining moral state of the city determined to deliver adolescent girls from certain moral catastrophe. While the reform school was intended only for girls who had broken the law, the industrial school act introduced the idea that bad behaviour at home could justify incarcerating adolescents. The reform school's sister institution, the industrial school, was mandated to take in 'protection' cases but also girls considered 'uncontrollable.'[59]

The case of fifteen-year-old Laura D. demonstrates how the mandates of the two institutions converged. In 1907, Laura, a working-class, franco-phone adolescent, was arrested for being disorderly and having no visible means of subsistence, also known as vagrancy. Like many vagrancy cases hers might be seen as simply the result of an urban police force attempting to clear the night streets of their unruly elements. However, in Laura's case, her mother – with whom she lived – had filed the complaint against her. She was indeed neither homeless nor without visible means; rather, in her mother's view, the heart of the problem was her 'intolerable' disobedience. Her mother claimed that Laura's refusal to work and evening social life were beyond her abilities to control. Before the Juvenile Delinquents' Court and the 1910 Quebec Act respecting Juvenile Delinquents opened the door to policing these behavioural problems, they were not sufficient to incarcerate adolescents in reform schools. In practice, however, adolescents such as Laura were labelled 'vagrant' and sent to reform school for bad behaviour as much as for law-breaking; in Laura's case, this was for three years.[60]

In the first decades of their management of the industrial and reformatory schools for girls, the nuns created their own system of differentiating between the populations of the two institutions: young girls who were deemed a bad influence were placed not in the industrial school but in the reformatory school.[61] By the 1890s the École de Réforme took in juvenile delinquents aged seven to sixteen who were sentenced by the courts, as well as industrial school girls whose actions were judged incorrigible. Incorrigibility was defined as resistance to authority and attempts to escape.[62] Quebec laws regulating the two facilities opened the door to the commonality of treatment for both categories, although the language describing girls' actions differed: a girl under fourteen found on the street was deemed to be 'wandering,' whereas a girl under sixteen was considered a 'vagrant.' This probably was a trend beyond the Montreal situation, as Michelle Cale suggests for the case of nineteenth-century British girls' reformatories and industrial schools; with overlapping administrations, the institutions shared common goals and methods.[63]

Although female reformatories of the nineteenth century were an obvious improvement over the mixed-sex jails that had preceded them, the history of girls' incarceration in reform schools is not one of straightforward progress. The gender-specific treatment of adolescent girls at the hands of nuns in private institutions did not necessarily benefit Montreal girls in conflict with the law. This outcome was common to most of the innovative female reformatories at the time, for, as Kelly

Hannah-Moffat has argued, female keepers of women's incarceration facilities did not eliminate, but rather, produced 'new relations of power/knowledge.'[64]

Within each institution and among them, the nuns operated a hierarchical system of categorizing girls and women. At the top of the hierarchy were the nuns, led by the mother superior. Beneath them were the novices (those in training), the *consacrées* (who had not yet taken their religious vows and who often lived among the penitents as good examples), and the *madeleines* and penitents (those who chose to live with the nuns after their sentences). A strict and inflexible rule at the convent dictated that the latter two were kept separate from the *protégées* and *préservées* (young girls considered protection cases), delinquent girls, and female prisoners reinforcing rank and hierarchy.[65]

In embarking on a mission to reform wayward girls, the Soeurs relied on a convent boarding school tradition that was predicated on isolation from the outside world and the cultivation of faith, honour, and virtue among the boarders.[66] The nuns undoubtedly received considerable support and direction from their ecclesiastic superior, Bourget's successor, Édouard-Charles Fabre. In the years preceding his ascension to bishop in 1876 Fabre had advised the nuns; like Bourget, he warned of the dire consequences of a mobile, industrial, liberal society and advocated the protection of Quebec's daughters by confining them to convents.[67] Invoking a Catholic parallel to the cult of domesticity ideal popularized by Protestant clergy and the bourgeoisie in nineteenth-century America, Fabre advocated isolation of girls to 'protect' their most valued characteristics: purity, modesty, humility, and piety.[68]

The nuns offered a moral cure for female delinquency featuring religious redemption. First and foremost the Soeurs du Bon Pasteur claimed to be saving souls through providing a cloistered environment removed from the temptations of urban society. Based upon the transcendent authority of the Catholic Church, the regime emphasized repentance and spiritual rebirth. To explain their work and role in Montreal, the nuns evoked vivid religious imagery centring on lost sheep, menacing wolves, and the shepherd saviour: 'The fold opened its doors wide to the lost sheep caught in the jaws of the ravaging wolf.'[69] Their concern was the protection of girls and women who by reasons of circumstance or through bad behaviour were at risk of being lost; their mission was to bring these girls and women back to the fold – reunite them with their faith and save their souls.[70] The fold, of course, was the church and the Catholic faith; the term 'lost,' while referring to the state of the women's souls, undoubtedly held sexual connotations for it often applied to vagrant women and girls, prostitutes, and rebellious females sent to them by families and civil authorities. The nuns themselves described their work: 'The uplifting of the fallen girl and woman ... will be the unique and essential function, the purpose of the order.'[71] Daily attention to religious learning in the form of prayer, Bible study, and catechism training was the cornerstone of rehabilitation at the École de Réforme.

Following the words of their founder, Mère Marie-de-Sainte-Euphrasie, the nuns upheld kindness and mercy as principles in their treatment of inmates.[72] Yet, in order to incite a conversion among their charges, the Soeurs embraced a model of incarceration not dissimilar to other nineteenth-century prisons. While at first glance the reform school may have resembled a Catholic boarding school, it also reflected nineteenth-century ideas about imprisonment. Although the nuns claimed that the inmates' day was divided into prayer, work, study, and recreation, manual labour occupied the largest part of it. The gendered nature of mandatory industrial work at the city's reform schools is evident in the type of work demanded of the inmates. The programs implemented by the two religious orders demonstrate the impact of sex-segregation in prisons. The Frères de la Charité emphasized industrial training suited to young men, including carpentry and furniture making, over rudimentary education.[73] Likewise the nuns did not emphasize formal education but rather domestic-oriented manual labour (in the commercial laundry) and domestic duties consistent with young women's low position in the social hierarchy of the city.

The Soeurs founded a commercial laundry in their reformatory school and the women's prison to meet both the financial demands of running such institutions and their desire to thwart idleness.[74] Nineteenth-century penal reformers had also targeted idleness as the root of criminality and the antithesis of their goal to develop productive disciplined citizens. The nuns promoted work as a 'moral virtue' and likely saw it as a 'vigilant keeper.'[75] At the same time, the laundry was the order's largest source of revenue.[76] The inspectors of prisons and reformatories observed that older girls worked in the laundry or in the sewing and mending workshops. All girls engaged in housework, which was organized according to the ability of the individual girl. In 1908 the nuns reported to the provincial inspectors that the work regime at the reformatory school was 'proper to their sex.'[77] The predominance of manual labour in the reformatory school fit with the Soeurs' determination to teach young working-class girls their station in life and probably followed Bourget's notion that each individual occupied an immutable position in the social hierarchy. Accordingly the nuns wrote that they attempted to instill in the inmates 'a justified pride to belong to part of the working class.'[78] The nuns likely hoped that the teaching of industriousness and one's station in life would contribute to the girls' successful reintegration into urban life after their sentences.

The nuns' aims in educating girls were basic. The nuns emphasized budgeting and household management; they promoted nutrition and denounced alcohol consumption in cooking classes; and they encouraged practical skills such as making, washing, and ironing clothing.[79] Illiterate inmates were given special classes; the rest spent limited time with nuns who had teaching diplomas. Education had a domestic arts emphasis consisting of daily sewing and cooking lessons that served to prepare girls to run a home.[80] Aside from work, prayer, and lessons in domestic arts the girls were given household chores to complete to keep the institution tidy and running smoothly. Finally, girls also engaged in some form of recreation. This might have involved singing hymns, and according to photographs, outdoor calisthenics. The nuns oriented their regime around 'honest' work, domestic duties, and Christian virtue to prepare a girl for her future – narrowly conceived as wife and mother.

Discipline and hierarchy were common features at the École de Réforme. Symbolic of the girls' submission to the nuns' authority was the daily donning of the black uniform and the close cropping of girls' hair.[81] Beyond religious retraining and manual labour, the reformatory school regime featured silence, surveillance, and isolation, all characteristic of nineteenth-century penitentiaries. The nuns modelled this feature of their regime on convent life where silent activity predominated. Silence was also embraced by the architects of the Auburn and Pennsylvania prison systems that emerged in the 1820s as a way to force the individual's reflection upon his or her deviant acts. The girls were also observed at all times. Perhaps the cruellest aspect of being a reform school girl in this era was the mandated isolation. Even though girls were housed in dormitories and worked together in the laundry, silence precluded easy relationships among the girls, and friendships were discouraged by the nuns to the point that girls seen to be forming intimate bonds were separated.[82] This emotional isolation forms what Foucault would call punishment of the soul, and it rendered a brutal punishment on adolescent girls.[83] This system was meant to evoke self-reflection, followed by confession, and then the long, nun-guided journey back to obedient girlhood. Intimate relationships, then, were acceptable only between penitent and nun.

More overt punishments were also meted out by the nuns who followed their founder's advice to avoid physical punishment and deprivation of food. Instead, a more 'effective' punishment involving humiliation was embraced.[84] The nuns called their disciplinary style 'mild and firm ... of a nature to greatly favor the fortunate changes [required of delinquents].'[85] According to Véronique Strimelle, punishment of this sort was used to confront five types of bad behaviour: resistence to authority, an absence of charity, inciting a revolt, immorality, and exhibiting a lack of piety.[86] Girls rebelled against the uniforms, humiliation, and religious indoctrination at the École de Réforme, sometimes with spectacular riots.[87]

Strimelle argues that the convent life experienced by the inmates of the École de Réforme was regimented and cramped and lacked the comfort and ample food girls probably craved. Yet, she suggests that the environment provided by the nuns was relatively better than the urban poverty from whence they came.[88] This analysis demands that we overlook the fundamental denial of liberty inherent in a reformatory school stay and see the nuns as welfare providers, not prison matrons. As Kelly Hannah-Moffat argues, schemes predicated on governance of women by women and maternal strategies gained widespread acclaim, yet produced contradictory results. As sisters of the good shepherd, their daily self-sacrificing work of tending to lost sheep suggests their role was benevolent: to watch over girls, provide them with shelter and food, and guide them back to God. Yet, this was a prison regime where girls were denied liberty and made to work. Many found themselves in this predicament because they had transgressed moral boundaries and the state saw fit to incarcerate them in poorly funded, private, Catholic institutions.

The Soeurs' reformatory school was virtually the only juvenile justice institution for delinquent girls in Montreal prior to the establishment of the juvenile court in 1912. Consistent with monastery-style facilities for children it reflected the design and religious aims of other Catholic institutions. In contrast to its contemporary – the women's reformatory – which featured individualized spaces for the inmates, the reform school held girls in large, anonymous dormitories. Girls were encouraged to break with their unsavoury pasts by embracing the religious-based rehabilitation program that had them dressing like nuns, observing silence and daily prayer, and learning the domestic skills required of working-class women. This reformatory school for girls operated as the only incarceration facility for adolescent girls until 1911, when the Girls' Cottage Industrial School was founded for all 'non-Catholic' cases. The Protestant training school would be designed to diverge from this reformatory school experiment of the nineteenth century.

An Era of Reevaluation

The Soeurs du Bon Pasteur maintained their reformatory school for girls during an era of radical transformation of Quebec society that would produce a dramatic shift in the practice of juvenile justice in the province. Even as Bishop Fabre persisted in recommending the cloistering of girls for their own protection in the latter part of the nineteenth century, ultramontanism was in fact on the decline. A child-saving reform ethic began to deny the wisdom of institutionalization and assert the preferability of a rehabilitated family life as a means of correcting delinquent girls.

Early in the first decade of the twentieth century, the promise of the girls' reformatory school began to falter. Complaints were lodged against the Soeurs for failing to prepare the girls for life in the city and for taking advantage of the girls' free labour. Eventually the meagre attention paid to education would similarly cast doubts on the wisdom of the reformatory school as convent model.[89] Undoubtedly this questioning of the Soeurs du Bon Pasteur's facilities was related to broader debates over child welfare evident in the rest of Canada that began to emphasize the problem of overinstitutionalization of children.[90] In the nineteenth century, the institution was considered a superior environment to the family home and, as Andrée Lévesque has shown, a girl's most prized possessions were ideally 'preserved within the walls of the convent.'[91] The Soeurs du Bon Pasteur's institutions evolved as well.

From 1870 to 1915 the reform school for girls was situated in a building at the provincial convent on Sherbrooke Street;[92] in 1915, the juvenile delinquents were transferred to another setting north of the city at Laval-des-Rapides, where the reform school joined the Catholic girls' industrial school, the Maison Ste-Domitille. The reform school occupied an old mill (a *moulin de crochet*) and was renamed the Maison de Lorette. For the forty years preceding the juvenile court's opening, the delinquent girl was cast in a leading role in the lost flocks of young womanhood, whose future was best secured by nuns; in the twentieth century problem girls were reconceived provoking a transformation of ideas about girls' culpability and how best to deal with them.

Conclusion

A combination of factors conspired to produce Montreal's first girls' reform school and locate it at a convent. The reform school was the physical manifestation of the idea that youth and females should be separated from adults and males, respectively. By the 1850s politicians sought to spare children the experience of the adult penal system, embracing the idea that as minors their characters were malleable and therefore salvageable. Through careful manipulation of the environment, they believed, juvenile offenders could be rehabilitated. In the latter half of the nineteenth century, penal reformers promoted sex segregation of inmates. Female inmates were especially singled out for new facilities that reflected and reinforced their alleged innate womanly qualities. Women's reformatories spread across North America in the 1870s. The development, expansion, and popularity of this new penal institution was directly related to the growing perception that urban industrial society threatened the chastity and innocence of young women. Indeed, the girls' reform school was designed as a solution to a very specific nineteenth-century social problem: the endangered girl. Female reformatories were born of the desire to regulate adolescent girls' sexuality through 'protective' custody. The women's reformatory model was predicated on domestic and maternal regimes but also religious instruction as a redemptive strategy. Quebec's 1869 laws establishing industrial and reform schools and the politicians' selection of the Bon Pasteur nuns to administer the girls' reformatory school led to the creation of an institution that would serve as a solution to nineteenth-century problems relating to children in general and female youth especially.

For four decades adolescent girls in trouble with the law experienced juvenile justice that was shaped by this religious order. The Soeurs conceived of the delinquent girl as part of a lost flock of young womanhood, who, through religious guidance, hard work and prayer could be redeemed. Outside the convent social reformers saw working-class girls on the streets perilously close to the century's worst vices of alcohol abuse and prostitution. And while the reform school was designed in law to receive only youthful lawbreakers, the system that created special categories of juveniles opened the door to incarcerating girls for reasons of moral turpitude and often for lengthy sentences. In Quebec, the reformatory school contributed to the expansion, not so much of the state, but of a particular Catholic vision of the future of French Canada. Only in the 1910s would the longstanding liberal opponents of ultramontanism influence juvenile justice in Quebec.

Les jeunes filles modernes: Reformers, French-Canadian Nationalists, and Experts on the Problem with Adolescent Girls

In 1910 a modern twist on an old seduction tale made headlines in the *Montreal Herald.* Certain city streets had become home to a new public nuisance, the male 'masher,' whose chief aim, according to the newspaper, was to hinder young women's ability to conduct their daily business of working and shopping. These men subscribed to a new youthful urban style that offended journalists and readers alike: smokers of 'cheap' cigarettes and sporting 'faddy' clothes and greased hair, they assumed a slouched position on busy street corners. An alarmist journalist attributed their body language not to a rebellious attitude but to venereal disease, elevating the masher threat from mere street nuisance to a menace to both young womanhood and the nation's future. According to the newspaper, these brazen, overtly sexual men, assumed to be pimps and procurers, 'fascinate and betray some unfortunate young girls and live a useless and parasital life on the proceeds of [their] shame.'[1] Yet, this public attack on the masher problem provoked one *Herald* reader to suggest that men were 'not always to blame,' for young women had drawn them out by 'parading' on city streets for the purpose of 'promiscuous flirtation.'[2]

This episode captures the shift in attitude toward young, urban women that would influence juvenile justice authorities and experts throughout the first half of the twentieth century. By then, an image emerged that challenged the idea that young lost women, especially vagrant girls, who had elicited compassion in the reform school era, were victims of male lecherousness. The masher story also reveals an ongoing uneasiness about young women's growing claim to urban space. Over the course of a day women and girls, as workers and consumers, might claim a legitimate place on streets without being associated with that despised public female character, the prostitute, but as the letter writer indicated, in traversing the space between home and work or store, some participated in creating a new urban phenomenon known as 'women's miles' – streets where they gathered in groups and flaunted their youthful female presence. These young women – often adolescent girls – participated in what Cynthia Comacchio suggests was an emergent 'youth culture expressed through leisure activity.'[3] By the 1910s 'modern girls' were seen 'unattended, promenading up and down' at the intersection of St Laurent Boulevard and St Catherine Street – in the heart of Montreal's red-light district.[4]

Changes in the work and leisure activities of young, working-class women and their expression of sexuality outside of marriage heralded a warning to parents, social leaders, and an assortment of new professionals, especially social workers. As adolescent culture challenged Victorian standards of conduct and propriety, the new social and sexual exploits of girls and young women galvanized social reformers who had organized to extinguish prostitution, that early-twentieth-century symbol of the subversion of the racial and sexual order. Revealed by social purity activists concerned with the presence of commercialized vice in the city, the sexual delinquency problem became a major preoccupation of female reformers and social workers during the 1910s and 1920s. In this era, melodramatic narratives of seduced innocents produced by an older generation of evangelical moral reformers were replaced with new qualitative data on the 'promiscuous young woman.'[5] Across North America female reformers and professionals alike called for direct state involvement to harness the girl problem through juvenile courts, reformatories, and public health measures. Whereas in the forty years preceding the founding of the juvenile court, reform school girls were lumped together with several categories of pitiable fallen women (including prostitutes and unmarried mothers) as part of the lost flock of womanhood, by the 1910s female juvenile delinquents emerged as a specific category of deviant, diagnosed and classified by modern social science. Although much literature on female delinquency at this time points out that the regulation of female delinquency was about anxieties concerning girls' new sexual appetites, a closer look at the construction of 'bad' girls and their experience in court reveals that they were also understood as symptomatic of a much larger problem.

In Quebec the conversation about delinquent girls extended beyond reformers and social workers. This modern problem provoked the Catholic clergy and French-Canadian nationalists because delinquency among girls was imbued with a host of related concerns: the wilful public face of female adolescence, the decline of virtuous womanhood, an 'open-door' immigration policy and the dilution of the French fact in Canada, the breakdown of the traditional family, and the general decline of religious devotion in the face of an urbanized and highly mobile society. Following the First World War, anxieties over the projected dire future of the French-Canadian family, which had particular implications for nationhood in Quebec, contributed to the construction of the 'bad' girl and fostered a need to control young women. In the interwar period, women's organizations belonging to the Fédération nationale Saint-Jean-Baptiste identified a new object for reform – '*les jeunes filles modernes*.' The Second World War and the homefront's delinquency panic exacerbated the modern girl problem.

This chapter introduces the female delinquent as an early-twentieth-century social problem and metaphor, and it examines how various actors – from Anglo-Protestant reformers to French-Canadian nationalists – understood Montreal's modern girl. In the 1910s, Montreal antivice reformers carefully scrutinized girls' heterosocial adventures, constructing and broadcasting a new frightening reality about their sexuality to the public. In the 1920s and 1930s modern girls became a target of nationalists who saw in their behaviour the seeds of decline for the family. In the 1940s girls' independent behaviour, coupled with mothers' wartime neglect of the home, fuelled concern directed at the modern adolescent girl. These discourses about delinquent girls generated outside the juvenile court informed the probation officers' investigations and reports on those girls. Informing probation officers' work was the documentation provided mainly by local women's groups about adolescent girls' modern lives and misbehaviour. At the same time, these decades were witness to the emergence of adolescence at the hands of experts – professional child-care and social workers, psychologists and psychiatrists whose discursive renderings of adolescent girl behaviour also contributed to the juvenile court's comprehension and treatment of them. New ideas about girls' experience during adolescence would shape their treatment in Montreal's juvenile justice system, although until the 1940s this psychological and psychiatric orientation in comprehending adolescent and delinquent girls was unevenly employed by juvenile court judges and probation officers.

Reformers and the Girl Problem in the 1910s

The Montreal Juvenile Delinquents' Court (MJDC) was born in an era of social reform where activists identified a variety of pressing urban problems from municipal corruption to public health to moral degeneration. Included as a target for improvement were 'problem girls.' Social reform campaigns and the search for 'sexual order in the city' set the conditions for the emergence of a female delinquency problem.[6] In Montreal, the social purity movement's target was residential prostitution in the city's infamous red-light district.[7] The vigorous campaigns to close brothels and end commercial prostitution carried with them a clarion call to save young womanhood; however, they had an unintended impact on adolescent girls. The reformers' 'scientific' investigations, use of legislation, and promotion of female police officers and social workers resulted in the construction and harassment of the female delinquent. Thus, in an atmosphere of heightened anxiety over vice and disease, sexual delinquency was discovered on the streets, in parks, moving-picture houses, and restaurants, and its definition broadened beyond prostitution to dating, joy riding, and dancing. Attempts to control it led to preventive and protective work with girls.

As the First World War raged in Europe, the debate over regulation and suppression of prostitution exploded in Montreal, turning a necessary evil into 'The Social Evil.' Certainly, the panic over prostitution and the white slave trade had given the citizens of Montreal cause to suppress the sex trade earlier, but the wartime atmosphere intensified beliefs about what prostitution represented. In the early 1910s Montreal clubwomen demanded that the 'international scourge', known as the white slave trade, be thoroughly cleansed from the city.[8] In February 1918 the *Public Health Journal* implored citizens to 'control the source of infection' – that is, prostitutes.[9] The escalation of the controversy was in part due to a panic over venereal disease and its potential to imperil the future of the nation; in fact, the 'epidemic' of syphilis and gonorrhea was seen as worse than the influenza scourge that hit Montreal in autumn 1918. Casting prostitution as the result of both an open-door immigration policy that welcomed white slavers and an economic system that left a class of poor women with little recourse but to sell their virtue, reformers launched an attack on the sex trade for its responsibility for the spread of disease and its threat to the racial and moral integrity of the nation. Reformers' alarm over prostitution can also be attributed to local conditions and the visibility of the sex trade in Montreal; not until after the Second World War and the 'grand sweep' of the 1950s was prostitution forced underground into a more clandestine form.[10]

Citizens' outrage over the seemingly lackadaisical approach of the police and municipal administration to commercialized vice coalesced in the founding of an antivice organization, the Committee of Sixteen.[11] These citizens saw a 'great city of churches and charities'[12] that had shamefully ignored the rampant growth of the red-light district, a 'spectacle of triumphant vice.' Modelled on similar committees based in New York City and Chicago, the purpose of the organization was to foster communication between societies and individuals concerned with prostitution and the spread of venereal disease. Its membership represented a variety of religious groups and leaders, many philanthropic organizations, and medical professionals. It was not to be exclusionary based on religion, language, or race, although a majority of its members came from the minority Protestant, anglophone population.[13] It claimed as its goals 'the reduction and final extermination of commercialized vice in the community.'[14]

Following a keen tradition of antivice reformers in New York City, Chicago, and Toronto, the committee launched a social survey of vice conditions in the fall of 1918. These moral surveys of the lives of working 'girls' had been motivated by a desire to end the nefarious global traffic in white women specifically, and local prostitution more generally. The committee's 'scientific study' of existing conditions of vice was intended to eradicate the 'ignorance and apathy' of Montrealers.[15] The report began with an exploration of the houses of prostitution in the red-light district: stationed outside five adjoining houses on Hôtel-de-Ville Avenue, the surveyors one night watched almost two hundred people, including American and British soldiers, come and go in the space of a couple of hours. They noted sober men entering only to emerge later drunk and cab drivers leaving brothels with cash payoffs in hand from managers.[16] Though their claim was to produce an 'unsensational' tract about vice in Montreal, the report relayed quite sensational items about interracial prostitution where: fifteen-year-old prostitutes (presumably white and Quebec-born) received Asian and black customers; widows prostituted their own daughters; an eleven-year-old boy contracted syphilis from a prostitute; and a young girl whose 'little mind was so filled with sexual matters that she was found to be abusing other children as well as herself.'[17] Three thousand copies of the committee's findings were disseminated, indicting civic administrators and police.[18] The impact of the committee's work was twofold: first, prostitutes working in the red-light district were subjected to an intense eradication campaign; second, the image of women as victims of male seducers began to wane as they were transformed into 'problem girls.'

An almost incidental result of the sexual purity campaign that focused on prostitution was the discovery of a new category of female deviant. In their first report of 1918, Montreal's Committee of Sixteen focused less on commercialized vice than on a seemingly more manageable problem: the sexual delinquent. The committee's report – Montreal's answer to Toronto's 1915 Social Survey – was a study of 124 'delinquent, wayward and immoral,' yet recoverable girls. Three-quarters of them were under the age of twenty-one. The great majority of those studied were not professional prostitutes and 'were not widely promiscuous.' Some were held responsible for their behaviour while others attracted some sympathy. Only a few fit the profile of the innocent who fell victim to pimps and procurers; most were the victims of moral neglect at home, illegitimacy, wretched living and working conditions, a lack of organized recreation, and 'mental deficiency.'[19] These conditions weakened girls' moral fibre making them vulnerable to white slavers, and ultimately ruined their futures.

Reformers were joined by female social workers in heightening the concern over the new social and sexual exploits of adolescent girls. During the First World War, problem girls became a subject of international concern. One of the most prominent new professional women of this era was Maude Miner, director of the Committee on Protective Work for Girls in the United States. Miner spearheaded a national campaign to prevent the moral downfall of teenage girls in the area of military training camp communities, and became an advocate for preventive and protective work in Montreal.[20] At the committee's first gathering in June 1918, Maude Miner gave her expert opinion on the conditions affecting 'young girls' in Montreal.[21] Her influence was direct: at the first meeting, this group, which was formed ostensibly in response to commercialized vice, decided that an agency for dealing with 'delinquent and wayward girls' was of immediate necessity.[22] Reverend Dr H. Symonds, rector of the Christ Church in Montreal and member of the Committee of Sixteen and the juvenile court committee, reproduced Miner's arguments about young women in a December 1918 publication. He wrote of young girls, influenced by the excitement of wartime, turning to army camps to fulfill their undisciplined desires.[23]

Although the Committee of Sixteen, Maude Miner, and Reverend Dr Symonds might appear to us to be weaving a tall tale to induce a moral panic, their scripts match the MJDC's probation officers' reports of delinquent girls in the same era. A familiar pattern emerged in the court: adolescent girls who held jobs during the day sought excitement after work at the cinema, the dance hall or the restaurant. One moment of weakness or vulnerability led to their loss of virginity and this then seemed to open the door to multiple sexual partners and even prostitution. For example, a fifteen-year-old French Canadian named Claudia A. appeared before the court in October 1918 for deserting her family home. Like many girls her age, she spent her days at factory work and her nights pursuing excitement. One night she met a soldier after going to the movies and she 'let herself' be seduced by him for $1. Six months after this fateful night, according to the probation officer, she was arrested at a brothel serving Chinese men.[24]

The Committee of Sixteen recognized that the lifestyles of adolescent working girls placed them in moral peril: members showed sympathy for the working girls of the city and their constant battle against the overwhelmingly negative influences of urban life.[25] With no chance of meeting potential romantic partners except on Dominion Square, St Catherine Street, or in dance halls and movies, girls were bound to develop unwise recreational habits. The solution, according to the committee, was chaperoned recreational activities organized by the city's churches and welfare societies. And when these young women fell through the cracks of these solutions, a surefire way to safeguard their moral health was an army of older, wiser women tracking them down under the auspices of the juvenile court (probation officers) or the police (female officers). Along the same lines, the committee called for supervision of young women released from the Girls' Cottage Industrial School and the École de Réforme, community and church protective leagues, and a system of temporary homes ('to help the rescued girl over the first critical period of starting "square again"').[26] These reformers would also argue for psychopathic clinics for the detection of feeble-mindedness, which we will see later also consumed professionals charged with explaining female delinquency.

The image of fallen womanhood as victims of male seducers began to wane in the early-twentieth century when it faced competition from the 'problem' girl. Social surveys of American and Canadian cities (New York City 1902, Chicago 1911, Toronto 1915, Montreal 1918) revealed a new image of the young working woman in the city – not the fallen woman but rather the recalcitrant adolescent. Surveys suggested that young, single, female employees of factories and shops by day were taking advantage of the new opportunities for commercialized leisure by night. They willingly met and engaged in sexual flirtation with strange men in dance halls, theatres, and restaurants.[27] Toronto's Social Survey rendered these girls 'occasional prostitutes' because they exchanged sexual favours for a night on the town. Similarly, in his antivice pamphlet, Montreal Reverend Evanston Hart made little distinction between women working in brothels and women who frequented moving-picture theatres and dance halls.[28] Girls were going wrong not because they had fallen prey to pimps, but because they were in search of a 'good time.'[29] In turn the girl problem captured the imagination of social reformers: Carolyn Strange has shown that 'women adrift' or single, wage-earning women in Toronto became the subjects of cautionary tales that 'link[ed] independence to danger, and pleasure to immorality ...' and girls specially were targeted with a new 'pleasure discipline' aimed at reforming their leisure habits.[30]

As the juvenile court period unfolded, female sexuality and delinquency became progressively bound as adolescent girls' social and sexual lives were subjected to new forms of surveillance and regulation. That the court would focus on adolescent girls' expressions of sexuality is no surprise. It opened in an era when the sexual delinquent developed into a major concern of the city's social reformers. Montreal's Committee of Sixteen documented adolescent girls' promiscuous social and sexual behaviour but lacked the means to discipline them. The juvenile court, though, would prove to be a more effective and consistent weapon for regulating girls' social and sexual behaviour.

Les Jeunes Filles Modernes: The Problem with Girls in Interwar Quebec

Witnesses to social change in the aftermath of the First World War decried the thoroughly 'modern' actions and attitudes of the nation's youth. As historian Cynthia Comacchio has shown for English Canada, modern adolescence meant 'youth problem' in the interwar period when an older generation observed with trepidation the youth culture's growing urban, commercial, and mixed sex appeal, likening it to another blow for the traditional family and subsequently the nation.[31] Quebeckers expressed a similar anxiety over youth culture which became all the more acute in the face of an apparent decline of the French-Canadian nation. The culmination of wartime dislocation, feminist struggles and successes, and dramatic socioeconomic change produced a highly gendered discourse concerning youth and the future of the nation at the centre of which were les jeunes filles modernes.

The interwar concern over modern young girls was in part Quebec's version of the girl problem. Concern over social habits and preoccupations of youth continued to mount as the First World War drew to a close.

A chorus of voices decried the condition of modern youth and its sub-sided sense of righteousness and morality. In May 1919 Abbé Gauthier, who worked with the Committee of Sixteen, addressed the Fédération nationale Saint-Jean-Baptiste (FNSJB) about the declining state of moral-ity in Montreal.[32] That year Montreal's Archbishop Bruchési issued a pas-toral letter on the same issue, and encouraged membership in the Ligue des Bonnes Moeurs.[33] The straying of modern girls from the decent mor-als carried with it more than individual failing – it forewarned of the disas-ter that awaited French Canada.

This mounting attention to Montreal's moral pulse derived from recent political setbacks and perceptions that French Canada was under attack. French-Canadian nationalists experienced the First World War as a sombre historic moment when the shortsightedness of Confederation revealed itself through the conscription of their sons into a British impe-rial war. The Canadian government's granting of the federal franchise to women in 1918 was also perceived as an external attack on French Cana-dians, disrespecting the traditional understanding of family hierarchy and power. In the wake of the First World War, the Abbé Lionel Groulx, gave voice to an emerging, defensive French-Canadian nationalism that at once invoked pride in French-Canadian heritage and institutions (lan-guage, religion, and family) and assailed the urban front of that society's decline. Preservation of French Canada began with the family, Groulx claimed in his classroom at the Université de Montréal and in the publi-cation, *L'Action française*. Bolstering the family took on special meaning in the context of news of the dramatic decline in the French-Canadian birth rate. A line was drawn between women's reticence to reproduce and modern girls' distraction by urban secular temptations such as mov-ies, jazz, and dancing. The independent lives of adolescent girls sig-nalled the worst assault on the future of the French-Canadian nation: Had they forgotten their place in the sacred mission of preserving and perpetuating the family?[34]

Where reformers in the 1910s had focused on adolescent prostitutes and young working women who compromised their virtue, the modern young woman in the interwar period drew attention to a much deeper problem of profound attitudinal change among adolescent girls at the war's end. The modern girl assumed urgency because she was both a prophecy and a manifestation of the moral and absolute decline of the French-Canadian family. The close relationship of family to nation in the interwar period made problem daughters all the more serious: as one school inspector claimed, 'The family [is] our true national fortress.'[35]

Juvenile justice athorities reflected this concern about individual girl's behaviour and its implications for the future of the nation; increasingly attention was diverted away from the girls' role in the family toward her responsibility for ensuring the survival of the nation.

After the First World War, the problem with *les jeunes filles modernes* captured the imagination of Christian feminists belonging to the umbrella reform organization Fédération nationale Saint-Jean-Baptiste. In the pages of *La Bonne Parole*, women carried the message of the Catholic Church against the instruments of modernity and their effects upon Quebec womanhood.[36] Federation women carried out Archbishop Bruchési's wish that pious female organizations engage in a crusade for modesty.[37] In *La Bonne Parole*, commentators noted that the crisis of loss, deprivation of material goods, and exigencies of wartime took a toll on the adolescent daughter, transforming her into a young, modern 'girl.' According to observers, the war effort coupled with familial demands on daughters to fill in for absent fathers and brothers, resulted in a higher percentage of adolescent girls leaving the *foyer* for paid work. Although working-class daughters had been engaged in paid work for decades prior to the war, the wartime atmosphere was blamed for weakening family bonds, resulting in the rise of independent-minded adolescent daughters.

Modern life was denounced for habituating girls into taking more 'personal initiative.' Accustomed to making purchases for the family, travelling alone on the tramway, hearing adult conversations on the street and at home, girls quickly amassed 'a small store of commercial, social, and indeed even political knowledge' that prepared them to act on their own.[38] The mention of girls' political knowledge reveals a central tenet of the critique of the modern girl phenomenon; it was also a cautionary note on feminist achievement (since the 1918 federal suffrage victory) and struggle in interwar Quebec for the provincial franchise. In the 1920s and 1930s Quebec feminists grappled with the backlash against suffrage demands. They felt it necessary to defend the sanctity of the family to the point where some rejected the goal of suffrage and instead looked to strengthening the wife's legal place within the family under the Civil Code. At the 1931 annual meeting of the FNSJB, the Ligue Catholique Féminine claimed the chief cause of moral decline among Quebec families to be the emancipation of women, which led them away from Christian duty and devotion.[39] The face of emancipation in this time period was the modern girl.

The attitude, comportment, and outlook of *les jeunes filles modernes* so distinguished them from their mothers' customs, habits, and behaviours that commentators called it a generation gap. Born of their wartime work experiences, an independent spirit was their most common feature. The author of a study of working 'girls' in Montreal complained that the experience of employment had given the adolescent girl confidence to assert 'she has the right to her complete freedom.'[40] In practice this translated into adolescent girls' knowledge of a complex world beyond the home and neighbourhood, a world to which their mothers had not had access. Where their mothers would have met with dishonour, girls went casually, from department stores to hotel ballrooms. Emancipated, liberated, and 'proud of their 14 or 16 years,' working girls 'flit around danger' on street corners, in parks, and at the cinema.[41]

If there was emancipation from tradition, it was expressed by eschewing their mothers' attitudes. Modern girls did not observe the rules of social class: 'Propriety has had its time,' according to them.[42] This translated into an absence of reserve and a revolution in language usage. Forbidden for previous generations, familiarity was all the rage for these girls. Independence from the old rules was also evident in their appearance. Commentators remarked that girls did not dress to please but to challenge prevailing ideas about decency; in modern girls' parlance they wanted '*épater*' or to shock the world around them. One commentator wrote: 'She puts on a cavalier air, smoking cigarettes and takes great pride in her dress.' In short, 'she has a good time.'[43]

Afternoon and evening movie-going were high on the list of amusements for the young modern girl. Its popularity among working adolescents galvanized the press, reformers, and civic authorities. In the first two decades of the twentieth century cinemas sprung up all over. As adolescents flocked to cheap moving-picture houses authorities tried to quell the stampede by implementing age restrictions and creating censorship boards to minimize the damage to good morals and decency.[44] In the 1910s provincial legislation forbade the entrance of minors to the cinema unless accompanied by a guardian, but the $50 fine functioned as little more than an added licensing fee.[45] The physical threat of this entertainment was driven home in 1927 when a fire at the Laurier Palace resulted in the deaths of seventy-eight children. Neither law nor threat to life and limb kept adolescents away from the movie houses. A study showed that there were sixty-four cinemas in the city in the early 1920s; with a price of admission ranging from 10 to 80 cents, they enjoyed an 'enormous' clientele.[46] The number of cinemas persisted: by the end of the Second World War more than seventy crowded the city's map.

In the interwar period members of the FNSJB, along with the Catholic clergy, juvenile court, and child welfare workers decried the impact of movies on youth, especially girls. Frequenting the cinema became one of the markers of delinquency: adolescents stole money to afford the price of admission and once there were inspired by big screen antics and actors. In a FNSJB study of how working girls spent their wages, it was noted that a good number of girls had a 'weakness' for the cinema, which was their principal leisure activity.[47] A survey reproduced in *La Bonne Parole* of 284 movies found 448 immoral, 6 antireligious, 93 antisocial, and 113 scenes of bad taste.[48] Free love, adultery, divorce, seduction, kidnapping, concubinage, murder, and suicide were typically featured in cinemas, one of the establishments juvenile court judge Lacroix called 'dens of perdition.'[49] Underlying the campaign against the cinema was the concern that Quebec youth were eagerly assimilating American culture. After the Laurier Palace fire, nationalist and Catholic forces demanded investigation not only into the physical site of the cinema but also into American movies.[50] American 'talkies,' like women's fashion and dance clubs were targeted by the Catholic Church in its campaign to preserve the morals of young people.[51] The FNSJB condemned the cinema and modern girls for wasting time and exposing themselves to an unhealthy environment that perverted their minds.[52]

The films brought new aesthetic standards to girlhood, including sex appeal emphasized with rouged lips, fashionable hairstyles, and the rejection of modest outfits.[53] Juvenile court judge Lacroix claimed the cinema provoked in young women 'the taste for indulgence and makeup.'[54] While this fascination with appearance – 'painting' and 'powdering' to excess – was a common feature of the female delinquent according to juvenile judge Ethel MacLachlan, in Montreal it was read as more than an adolescent problem.[55] Judge Lacroix confirmed the 'disastrous effect' of the cinema on girls in a story about five couples from 'good' families recited for a publication entitled *Parents chrétiens sauvez vos enfants du cinéma meurtrier*. The adolescents (all under the age of seventeen) went to the cinema one day; the excitement engendered by the movie so warped their moral compasses that instead of going home directly they stopped off at a park where they were later arrested for indecency.[56] Lacroix considered the love scenes in the movie too realistic and too passionate for those under sixteen, creating 'a deplorable mentality.' He advocated banning all children under 16 from attending the cinema.[57]

Modern girls' behaviour was certainly worrisome, yet it was what they weren't doing that caused the most concern. They were not preoccupied with marriage and a future subscribed by the four walls of the *foyer.* The lack of preparation of daughters for their role as mothers meant nothing less than their own deficiency when it came to modesty, morality, and dignity and a dubious future for the family.[58] Too many of them had failed to learn the essentials of homemaking from their mothers, being too busy working outside the home to bother with 'women's' chores. Working at the store or factory resulted in girls' loss of 'taste for domestic work.'[59] The result was, admitted one writer, that 'the family spirit ... is very weak among the majority of young girls in the city.'[60] Shirking domestic chores and lacking family-mindedness, modern French-Canadian girls threatened more than discord in their own homes.

Ultimately, the modern adolescent girl was seen to be delaying indefinitely the moment of creating a family. While the patriarch still held legal and economic power within the family, the woman was its moral centre, its foundation. If girls were not willingly embracing and preparing for their future, much more than individual lives were at stake. Family played a central role in the French-Canadian sense of nation. This was seen in historical and ethnic terms ('our race and our nation'):[61] 'The traditional French-Canadian family was accorded a preponderant role in history. It has left to the contemporary family admirable examples of what should be its strength and ideal. Examples of unshakeable faith, of heroic devotion, of tireless charity, of modest virtue and virtuous life: that is the legacy of ancestors.'[62] Yet in modern times, the troubled family threatened the entire social body and the nation.[63] The threat was clear: if the family was 'broken down, languishing, diminished, it will sow bad seeds that will poison the blood of the entire body, that will undermine the heart and head.'[64]

In this focus away from family toward herself, 'Christian simplicity' – a value treasured in a young French-Canadian daughter in the past – was replaced by a desire for '*luxe*,' or luxury and frivolity.[65] Modern girls in fact exhibited selfishness, refused the required self-abnegation, and lacked a 'parish spirit.' Some made their weekly appearance at mass but rarely engaged in any other program of the Church directed at adolescent girls. Their world did not stop at the boundaries of the parish. Add to this the problem with the modern home – it was no longer a sanctuary of religious devotion and observance – and the result was, according to one critic, 'the meal eaten, each family member pursues his own work, amusement, and pleasure.'[66] The dissipation of the individual girl was deemed responsible for endangering the family and nation.

Somewhere between prostitute and good Christian daughter lay *la jeune fille moderne,* a figure who emerged from the fires of the First World War and threatened the French-Canadian family and its sense of nationhood. Clerical nationalists in these decades, represented by Abbé Lionel Groulx, emphasized family, language, and religion. Individual adolescent girls were unimportant if they kept to the prescribed role within the family and remained protected within the *foyer,* until their wedding day when they fulfilled their sacred duty to bring forth the next generation. Modern girls, however, became an easy target for nationalists because of their visibility on city streets, at work, and in socializing outside the parameters of parish life. Worse still, their leisure and work habits exposed them to what Groulx and others would label 'foreign' – American and French movies, immigrants, and social spaces such as restaurants and dance clubs that were more multiethnic than the parish. The hardships faced by adolescent girls during wartime apparently resulted in a 'modern' lifestyle; because of its origins girls elicited some sympathy. Yet, like the girl problem of the 1910s when preventive work proved ineffective, protective work was mandated. Mothers and women's, girls', and youth associations were called upon to restore Christian family values to French-Canadian daughters; during the 1930s Catholic youth groups multiplied dramatically under the tutelage of the Catholic clergy.[67] More formal agents of authority like the juvenile court probation officers similarly followed the travails of the family, curbing girls' behaviour as necessary. The Second World War would pose an even greater challenge to traditionalists because mothers also 'deserted' the French-Canadian home.

'This Might Be Your Daughter!' The Second World War and the Delinquency Panic

The Second World War fuelled the flames of the problem of *les jeunes filles modernes.* Delinquency and youth made headlines in Quebec newspapers when the state recruited mothers out of, and fathers away from, the home. Montreal, a hub for recruited men, was also a centre of work, leisure, fashion, and entertainment. This combination meant Montreal's female adolescent population found jobs easily and was courted by the nightlife that thrived during the war. Two problems in particular focused attention on the female delinquent: freedom due to a generation of allegedly neglectful working mothers and the dramatic rise of venereal disease in Montreal during the war.

Wartime heightened girls' visibility. In Quebec the early 1940s was an important moment for youth because social policy brought adolescence and childhood into sharper focus. First, in 1942 the province expanded the age of the juvenile delinquent from under sixteen to under eighteen. Compulsory schooling was finally enacted in 1943, suggesting childhood now extended to fourteen. Further action by Montreal authorities during the war included a nocturnal curfew law for children under fourteen. These policy developments had the effect of concentrating adolescence between the ages of fourteen and seventeen; this cohort would attract considerable attention during the war, both for protection and control.

The fourteen to seventeen-year old girl saw opportunities during the Second World War that were not available to her older siblings during the Depression. Wartime adolescent girls moved easily beyond their own homes and domestic service. Whereas in the 1930s girls' work had been largely confined to domestic service, once the labour market rallied in the early 1940s, girls moved swiftly to factories, including munitions, and into restaurant and hotel work. Montreal continued to attract young women from rural Quebec who sought wages unavailable in their home towns. These developments alarmed onlookers. The Jeunesse Ouvrière Catholique (JOC), for example, called for protection of these young girls. The JOC was a youth group formed in the 1930s that was informally connected to the MJDC to help with Catholic cases.[68] At first the organization demanded that girls in the countryside stay home; then, its members argued that domestic service should change into a better occupation for girls with improved working conditions and training; and finally, the JOC decided that girls should delay moving into this work until they reached the age of sixteen. The JOC was one of many voices that raised the question of how to protect adolescent girls during the wartime crisis.[69] The buoyant wartime economy provided youth with relatively high wages but without moral overseers; girls seemed to lack discretion in spending both money and leisure time.

Initially the panic about delinquency was imported to the city. In 1941 British news reports identified and blamed a rising youth problem on the unsupervised wartime environment.[70] The press in Montreal first broached the topic as 'unrest' among the teenage population; unrest evolved into 'youth problem' and by 1944 it became a full-blown 'juvenile crime wave.'[71] Numbers fed the belief that youth were out of control. Countrywide statistics showed that the number of juvenile delinquents had grown from under 10,000 in 1939 to almost 14,000 in 1942, an increase of 45 percent.[72] By the end of the war *La Presse* declared: 'Youth crime has become the scourge of our time.'[73] Similarly in Montreal the number of adolescents before the courts grew from 2979 in 1940 to 3680 in 1942.[74]

The warnings that modern youth had gone bad continued to be gendered. In responding to the statistics confirming the rise of juvenile delinquency, the Canadian Welfare Council found that among boys the growth involved younger delinquents, aged seven to twelve. This shift was not replicated among the girls, whose involvement in delinquent action was not confined to any particular cohort.[75] Younger boys were accused of loitering and stealing while an older cohort of girls were responsible for 'uncontrollability' related to lapsed morals and the spread of venereal disease.

This delinquency panic was largely focused on 'latchkey kids,' those otherwise good children who had been abandoned by soldier fathers and working mothers. In this scenario, neglect apparently turned children into juvenile criminals. The Montreal Society for the Protection of Women and Children warned in 1942 that wartime caused a substantial increase in 'grievously neglected' children. Mothers were particularly singled out for failing to uphold their 'sacred duties' as they poured into factories leaving their children to fend for themselves. Quebec legislators, unions and Catholic hierarchy mounted a chorus of opposition to married women's work during the war. The clergy complained that work, even in the name of patriotism, was destructive of the French-Canadian family because it led women to temptation.[76] Explaining the apparent rise in juvenile delinquency in Montreal during the war, R.P. Valère Massicotte pointed to the absent mother who worked by day and sought to assuage the loneliness for her soldier-husband at night in the cinemas and similar diversions. This abdication of her role as 'keeper of the home and teacher' led Massicotte to denounce the employment of mothers with children younger than sixteen years of age.[77] The association of a delinquency crisis with the 'problem of the working mother' was well established by church leaders, community workers, juvenile court authorities, and the press. Whereas prior to the war mothers attempted to control modern girls, now they seemed to have joined them.

Popular culture and juvenile delinquency studies fanned the anxiety about how neglectful working mothers produced bad girls. A cautionary tale from the silver screen rivetted Montrealers in 1944. In March that year a Hollywood movie entitled *Where Are Your Children?* opened at the Snowdon Theatre in Montreal, coinciding with the city's Delinquency Prevention Week activities. Both the film and the well-advertised conference presented the problem of girls in wartime in overwrought style. In

La Presse ads for La Semaine de Sauvegarde de la Jeunesse délinquant began: 'The father is in Italy. The older brother is in the navy. The mother works all day in a war factory.' This situation inevitably produced delinquent teens, as the film pointed out. 'Problème social exposé à l'écran [Social Problem Exposed on the Screen]' confirmed one paper.[78] Others seduced viewers with sensational headlines: 'THIS MIGHT BE YOUR DAUGHTER!' (see figure 3.1).[79] The story followed the troubles of a seventeen year-old orphan girl who was sent to live with her brother and sister-in-law, two weary defence-plant workers. Put to housekeeping during the day, in the evenings the girl left her home to work at a lunch counter. Inevitably she met a boy who was also a product of a neglectful home. One night the two teenagers went off to a night club, thus beginning a chain of events that brought her to the attention of the juvenile justice system. A midnight joy ride developed into a tragic scene involving murder. The girl, although not directly responsible for the crime, was delivered into the hands of the juvenile court authorities. The movie's moral message was unmistakable: a girl's innocence was another war casualty. Wartime judges of Montreal's juvenile court, Robillard and Nicholson, confirmed that 'it's just what is going on in our courts everyday.'[80]

Delinquent girls in Montreal may have elicited some sympathy being the 'victims' of absent, immoral mothers, but they were also eyed suspiciously as the vectors of disease. Montreal had an ignoble reputation as a centre for prostitution and venereal disease, made worse during the war as statistics showed that rates for servicemen with VD were highest in Quebec.[81] Adolescent girls became the target of delinquency workers concerned about the effects of their modern lifestyles. It was no accident that the opening session of the Montreal's Delinquency Prevention Week (sponsored by the Junior League of Montreal, La Ligue de la Jeunesse Féminine, and the Jewish Junior Welfare League) began with the subject, 'Juvenile Delinquency and Venereal Disease.' The Ligue de la Jeunesse Féminine suggested that loose girls were responsible for the scourge.[82]

In the early 1940s the modern girl problem related to the adolescent girl's value as a worker and consumer, coupled with her orphanlike existence. Emancipated mothers had gained the provincial vote in 1940 and appeared to have eschewed their traditional place as the ever-present moral force in the home, leaving their daughters to follow suit. Commentators argued for a delay in sending girls out to work, prolonging childhood and the family's and school's ability to protect them.[83] Similarly, by expanding the age category of juvenile delinquent to under eighteen, the juvenile court authorities could monitor an older group of

Figure 3.1 From the *Montreal Gazette*, 11 March 1944, 6

girls in the name of protecting their virtue and preventing the spread of venereal disease. The juvenile court sprung into action, employing a juvenile morality squad to police adolescent hangouts and sending girls for VD testing.

Experts and the Modern Girl: Juvenile Justice and Theories about Female Delinquency

As girls' wayward behaviour was carefully documented by reformers, Christian feminists, French-Canadian nationalists, and popular culture, a variety of medical and social science researchers were positioning themselves as experts in a new field of study – the adolescent – to explain why girls became delinquent. Dramatic physical, sexual, and mental development associated with the transition from childhood to adulthood became the subject of medical and psychiatric discourses seeking to explain adolescent (mis)conduct.[84] In a similar vein to reformers, these experts of the human body, mind, and behaviour identified normative goals for adolescents based on their own class, gender, and racial biases. In their quest to define the normal child, they brought into sharp focus the problem or 'troublesome' child. There was virtually no moment in the twentieth century when the juvenile delinquent was not a subject of medical or social science research; indeed, the juvenile court became a veritable clearing house of diagnoses and prognoses on adolescence and delinquency. In their pursuit of the etiology of delinquency, experts introduced a myriad of factors – social, environmental, psychological, genetic, and physiological – that explained the crisis of wayward adolescents. While psychiatric and psychological determinism would prevail by mid-twentieth century, environmental explanations predominated in the first half.

Although coming late to the Montreal Juvenile Delinquents' Court (MJDC), most juvenile courts maintained a long and close relationship with psychiatrists and psychologists. Psychiatry had entered the criminal justice arena in the late nineteenth century over the issue of mental competence of the accused to stand trial and be held responsible for criminal actions. In contrast, psychiatry intervened in juvenile justice to provide evaluation of both intelligence and the emotional state of delinquents, not their capacity to comprehend the processes of law.[85] Largely preoccupied with the search for the cause of human conduct, psychiatrists and psychologists joined a tradition of building theoretical models to explain criminal and delinquent behaviour. In the late nineteenth century criminologists argued that an individual's morality was innate; thus criminals and delinquents lacked 'normal' moral structures, the result of hereditary defect. By the early twentieth century, criminal anthropologist Cesare Lombroso had popularized hereditarian causes of criminal behaviour thought to be manifested physically and mentally. Early psychological explanations of delinquency suggested a causal relationship between bad behaviour and an organic intellectual deficiency. Henry H. Goddard, author of *The Kallikak Family* (1912), and psychologist at the Training School for Backward and Feeble-minded Children in New Jersey, collapsed the delinquent and moron categories in his influential work on the causes of juvenile misconduct. This argument found favour with custodians of delinquents.[86] In Montreal, the Frères de la Charité, administrators of the Institut St-Antoine reform school for Catholic boys, supported a hereditarian model of delinquency well into the twentieth century, which, they explained, suggested why some of their charges were simply irredeemable.[87] Also convinced that delinquent girls were 'heirs of family defects,' the Soeurs du Bon Pasteur perceived delinquency to be an indication of a weak nature.[88]

In the 1910s as concern mounted over immoral and delinquent conduct, the heredity argument invigorated by the eugenics movement predominated in debates over causes of delinquency. This revitalized hereditarianism ostensibly focused on inherent mental capacity or intelligence, rather than innate morality/immorality. As psychiatry developed into a medical sub-specialty in the early-twentieth century, practitioners moved away from the study of the insane to the study of everyday behaviour, prescribing normality and abnormality. In attempting to make themselves relevant, these doctors were responsible for the successful dissemination of a psychiatric perspective because they spoke to contemporary angst about social change and human behaviour.[89] In their search for congenital defect through mental testing, psychiatrists found feeblemindedness among immigrant, poor, and delinquent populations. Psychiatry produced what Elizabeth Lunbeck has called 'geneologies of defectiveness,' tracing antisocial behaviour through generations as it served reform and eugenic purposes in targeting undesirables, from criminals to recent immigrants.[90] Fuelled by the results of widespread mental testing in the 1910s, the problem of the feebleminded grew as an explanation for social ills among the lay populations.[91] As several historians have noted the fear of a feebleminded population diluting the Canadian 'race' reflected a strong eugenic tendency among mental health reformers that was also disseminated by social reformers.[92]

Eugenic arguments that led to tampering with reproduction were not popular across Quebec, chiefly due to the powerful Catholic elite.[93] Eugenic ideas, though, were present in Montreal largely in anglophone reform circles. Beginning in the 1890s the National Council of Women of Canada had advocated investigating the rate of mental defectiveness in Canada. In subsequent decades in Montreal, the Local Council of Women (MLCW) presumed a link between delinquency and feeblemindedness and worked toward preventing delinquent girls from reproducing. They also advocated mandatory mental testing in schools, hospitals, reformatories, and jails, and brought in American experts to educate the public on the feebleminded. McGill University professor Carrie Derick, head of the MLCW's Committee on Mental Deficiency, was a strong proponent of mental testing in schools and the incarceration of the feebleminded in farm colonies.[94] At the 1915 child welfare exhibit, the MLCW organized, along with Derick's students, a presentation illustrating the 'Social Menace of Feeblemindedness.'[95] The point was to show the connection between feeblemindedness and social problems such as delinquency, unwed motherhood, and alcoholism. Their aim also included getting the province involved in treating those labelled mentally defective, a goal long frustrated until the LeJemmerais School was opened in the early 1930s. The MLCW proposed the segregation through custodial care of the feebleminded to prevent 'transmission of feeblemindedness' to the next generation.[96]

From the emerging professions of psychology, psychiatry, and social work came a host of intelligence (IQ) and personality tests that purportedly distinguished defective from normal. One of the most prominent tests in determining feeblemindedness was the Binet test, developed in France at the turn of the century and widely used in North America in the 1910s. Parisian psychologist Alfred Binet's 'quick test' was used to assess the mental age of school children. Results of the test encouraged classification of the subject according to mental age. Binet's test was widely used to determine evidence of feeblemindedness; the term referring to both a narrow category of 'morons' or those 'defectives with the most intelligence' but it was also used as a general description of 'defectives.'[97] Goddard is attributed with bringing the modified Binet test, now called the Binet-Simon intelligence scale to incarcerated populations.[98] Mental tests made feeblemindedness measurable, and scoring allowed professionals to slot delinquents into age groups: for example, Goddard assessed idiots at a mental age of two years or less, imbeciles at three to seven years, and morons at eight to twelve years.[99] Juvenile courts in Canada also resorted to IQ testing and used a typology of feeblemindedness and mental age to aid the judge in deciding dispositions.[100] The effect of the popularity of testing was the change in language describing delinquent girls: now they were not simply sexually precocious or immoral but were accorded a mental age that explained it. As a medical disorder, feeblemindedness was sharply gendered. In women, its major symptom was delinquency, which was indicated by sexually precocious behaviour and venereal disease.[101] Feeblemindedness was deemed to be a major cause of venereal disease that, by the 1910s, was considered an urgent national problem. Lucy M. Brooking of Toronto's Alexandra Industrial School for girls and the former boss of Nancy Stork, a superintendent at Montreal's Girls' Cottage Industrial School in the 1920s, published well-documented accounts of the slippery slope between mental deficiency and loose morality.[102] Linking feeblemindedness to sexual depravity in girls and women was used to justify incarcerating young women for their own good. Easy corruptibility of feebleminded girls made them 'a menace to society at large,' which led the directors to advocate the permanent incarceration of the feebleminded.[103] Feeblemindedness, then, indicated immoral sexual behaviour in women just as sexual immorality indicated feeblemindedness.

Feeblemindedness and hereditarian explanations of delinquency coexisted with environmentalism, especially at the hands of early-twentieth-century psychologists. Coincidental with the rise of juvenile justice in the late nineteenth century, the narrow definition of adolescence as a series of physiological changes expressed during puberty began to give way to psychobiology's pull. Largely influential in this shift was American psychologist G. Stanley Hall, a child study expert whose developmental approach was rooted in evolutionary biology.[104] In his 1904 study, *Adolescence: Its Psychology and Its Relation to Physiology, Anthropology, Sociology, Sex, Crime, Religion, and Education,* Hall established himself as the leading expert on the subject.[105] Hall described how the evolution of the child's body into an adult's precipitated a crisis for the adolescent. Unprepared for this 'normal' biological evolution, the adolescent experienced an emotional upheaval and was tormented by confusion. It was this precarious mental state that drove adolescent desire for adventure and freedom. To oversee the perils of adolescence and the successful psychological development toward adulthood, Hall called for adult supervision and guidance. He cautioned that failure to provide adolescents with proper direction and surveillance could result in a descent into delinquency. A Freudian, Hall admitted that sexual urges were a normal part of the maturation process, even for girls; however, if not thoroughly sub-limated, these feelings could easily lead girls into delinquent activity. Not unlike what reformers preferred for adolescent girls, Hall suggested that girls needed to channel their energies into dreams of motherhood.[106]

Hall's work on adolescence directly influenced Progressive-era sociologists concerned with the causes of female delinquency. Using social science methods of investigation, these researchers demonstrated the impact of society's failure to preserve adolescence as a prolonged dependent state. Pointing mainly to immigrant and working-class communities where crowded housing and substandard moral and physical hygiene were the considered the norm, and where adolescents left school early, entered the paid labour force, and spent evenings without adult supervision, sociologists catalogued the environmental problems associated with modern life. In an influential study of the Cook County juvenile court published as *The Delinquent Child and the Home* (1912) Chicago researchers Edith Abbott and Sophisba P. Breckinridge located the root of delinquency within the working-class and immigrant homes and neighbourhoods of that city.[107] The researchers conceded that the deficiencies of such family homes were largely the product of displacement and uprootedness experienced by newcomers to the city. Socioeconomic imperatives meant girls experienced crowded conditions, were forced to end adolescence early by going out to work, and were not properly warned away from the commercial pleasures of urban evenings.[108] Poverty and material deprivation coupled with the temptation of the theatre and other urban amusements were obvious environmental causes of maladjustment and delinquency.[109] The conditions of city life produced what Canadian female delinquency expert Lucy Brooking called 'the smart bad' girl who was responsible for the growth of 'promiscuous prostitution.'[110] While accepting that adolescent girls' desire for independence and adventure were part of the maturation process, the researchers determined that woeful neglect of these girls led to their downfall.

As early as 1915 William Healy, an American expert on delinquent behaviour, began to pull away from the inheritance model of causation. In 1909 Healy headed the new Juvenile Psychopathic Institute connected to the Chicago juvenile court. Within his first years of studying delinquency he questioned the pervasive attitude that crime was caused by mental deficiency and that delinquents were necessarily feeble-minded. In 1914 he renamed his clinic the Institute for Juvenile Research and began to promote the idea that monocausal arguments about delinquency were too simplistic.[111] In *The Individual Delinquent* (1915), Healy urged examination of a myriad of causative factors including but not limited to mental defectiveness, home conditions, education, and social milieu.[112] As Kathleen W. Jones points out, Healy's work marked a break with the hereditarianists in favour of environmentalism, although his position still called for the 'psychologizing' of delinquency.[113] His focus on the 'child's own story' and rejection of congenital delinquency echoed through delinquency studies in Montreal in the interwar period.[114]

Mental health experts disagreed over the cause of poor test scores as twentieth-century psychology moved toward environmentalism. The idea that humans are shaped by their external environment was hardly new but as Mona Gleason has argued, in order to legitimize psychological intervention, hereditarianism was exchanged for theories that located the cause of misconduct in the individual's environment.[115] At the same time the environmental origins of bad behaviour found appeal among agents of juvenile justice who held on to an optimistic notion that delinquency could be treated. Innate feeblemindedness was also challenged by educational retardation theories; social scientific explanations of waywardness pointed to the theory that the seeds of antisocial adolescent behaviour lay in the family home.

In the first decade of the MJDC's operations, the most popular argument about female delinquency pointed to environmentalism, blaming the social conditions of the modern city and neglectful parents for the problem of delinquency. Montreal probation officer Rose Henderson condemned 'the wolfish greed of modern industrialism' for rendering the schools, churches, and homes powerless to protect young people.[116] She railed against the predicament of the precocious wage earner, calling for the abolition of child labour and improvements to family wages and welfare that would obviate the need for youths' wages. Henderson argued that poverty was delinquency's 'most potent cause.'[117] An article in the *Canadian Nurse* published in the immediate years following the opening of the MJDC reported that 75 percent of the delinquents appearing before the court were children of men who made less than nine dollars per week. Still others were children of widows who left home to work in order to survive.[118] Rarely, however, was destitution in itself considered the cause of delinquency. Poverty compromised children's health, argued Toronto's Lucy Brooking: delinquent girls were almost always undernourished.[119]

Abandonment of good morals on the part of the adolescent coupled with an impoverished home situation opened the way for criticism of working-class parents. According to the nurse, the real cause lay in the family's intemperance and idleness.[120] Poverty also apparently drove parents to create undesirable surroundings for their families; some commentators asserted that delinquency was bred in crowded homes.[121] Overcrowding explained parents' lack of interest in individual children. Robert A. Wood and Albert J. Kennedy's *Young Working Girls* (1913) drew upon Hall's theories of 'mental excitation' in the female adolescent to explain immoral conduct, arguing that while modern society tempted working-class daughters out of their family homes and into lives scandalously close to prostitution, it was parental neglect that was to blame: 'Little effort is made to prepare the daughter for the opportunities and danger of her work life, and the girl has constantly to face situations unfamiliar to herself, and even to her mother, at a time when her judgement is unformed, and her emotions least controlled.'[122] Delinquent girls were understood as too inexperienced in life to resist temptation, stemming from years of parental neglect. Reverend Dr H. Symonds of Montreal's Christ Church concurred: female delinquents had 'no home training, no religious restraints, no foundations of careful and wise instruction and education.'[123] The Soeurs du Bon Pasteur believed that young women sent to the École de Réforme were victims of undesirable family situations, homes without faith, without morals.[124] Henderson saw delinquents as 'uneducated, undisciplined, and unprepared to earn a living or function in a democracy.'[125] Social welfare professionals agreed that the lack of training made the home less than 'the perfect institution for which we social workers strive and pray.'[126]

Irresponsible parents literally opened the door to temptation. Delinquency among girls was the result of the seduction of urban pleasures beyond the home. Observations that delicatessens and bowling alleys on the Main (St. Laurent Blvd.) drew adolescents and 'stimulate[d] gambling, late hours, and increased demand for spending money,' prompted the Federation of Jewish Philanthropies' Juvenile Aid Department to action. This 'after dark' behaviour was seen as exacerbating a rift between 'old school parents' and Canadian-born children.'[127] Like Abbott and Breckinridge, who argued that Chicago's delinquency problems stemmed from immigrant families' difficulties with adjustment to modern urban life,[128] Montreal social agencies similarly located delinquent troubles within the adolescents' environment.

During the 1920s and 1930s, the child guidance movement (and its psychologists and social workers) equated a mother's psychological 'maladjustment' with her delinquent offspring, causing one historian to claim that child guidance was 'synonymous' with mother blaming.[129]

Mothers' physical and emotional absence in the family allegedly produced psychologically troubled, immoral daughters. Experts like Sheldon and Eleanor Glueck and W.I. Thomas linked female delinquency to a lack of proper role socialization among girls, a prescribed duty of mothers. Mothers were blamed that girls failed to embrace passive femininity and identify with society's ultimate goal for them as wives and mothers. Attacks on the working mother and the emotionally neglectful mother did not stop during the Second World War, even while women claimed a patriotic right to paid labour.

Psychology's impact on work with adolescent girls is evident in Montreal's Big Sister Association (BSA), which in 1943 changed its name to the Girls' Counselling Centre. This social agency's determination to 'meet the needs of the adolescent girl' through casework led to its 'discovery' and identification of the 'broken homes, unhappy homes, cruelty and desertion' confronting modern girlhood.[130] It explicitly linked physical and mental health to a girl's potential.[131] Though the girl was given a leading role in this script of victimhood, BSA casework resulted in further regulation of her.

While environmental causes of delinquency indicted working-class families and the growth of commercial amusements for leading youth astray, professional mental health workers entered the juvenile court. Leading juvenile courts in the United States were early on appended with psychological assessment clinics; in Quebec this direct involvement of psychology was slower and uneven. Judges of the juvenile court applauded psychological and psychiatric contributions to juvenile justice although the province only approved of psychiatric evaluations for extreme cases. Not until the late 1930s did a child's mental assessment become a regularized feature of the court; until that time psychiatric examinations were restricted mostly to those who were institutionalized. Children deemed 'abnormal' by the judges' inexpert eye were sent to the detention home, where they were examined by a psychiatrist.[132] Psychomedical theories on juvenile delinquency did however come through the court in derivative fashion as psychiatric and psychological theories were popularized and as certain professionals were able to make their presence felt. These were largely individuals working in anglophone institutions, McGill University and the Mental Hygiene Committee.

Assessing Girls in Montreal

Trends in delinquency studies that alternately found causes relating to heredity and the child's environment were reflected among Montreal's elite institutions that dealt directly with the juvenile court. Anglophone reformers, psychologists, and physicians embraced feeblemindedness as a national cause in the 1910s. The relationship between delinquent populations and feeblemindedness was of particular interest to McGill University psychology professor Dr W.D. Tait and physician Gordon Mundie, who undertook to test inmates at several institutions in Quebec.[133] Dr Mundie visited the juvenile court and was so convinced that children appearing before the judge needed to be physically and mentally assessed that he attempted to create a position for himself at the court. He favoured 'special tests used in France and the United States' to determine the mental age of the child. He insisted that crime was produced by a 'lack of mentality,' meaning 'backwardness, feeblemindedness and high grades of imbecility.'[134] At that time the province was not willing to hire him, being satisfied with the casual services of Dr Villeneuve, medical superintendent of the Asile de la Longue-Pointe. Professor Tait took a different tack by studying delinquent subjects at private institutions including the Girls' Cottage Industrial School.[135] The school's directors appealed to Tait for evidence of feeblemindedness among their inmates.

The Girls' Cottage Industrial School (GCIS), recipient of all non-Catholic female cases from the MJDC, became a laboratory for psychological studies on delinquency in Montreal in this time period. It was one of the institutions that regularly engaged the Mental Hygiene Clinic and provided McGill University psychologists with research subjects. In the 1910s Tait had confirmed the GCIS board's worst fears – that all delinquent girls were feebleminded[136] – but the administration held onto the idea that girls could be classified according to mental age and given appropriate reeducation. Worries that feeblemindedness rendered their training and socialization goals unattainable were exacerbated by the fact that the provincial government had no programs or institutions specifically for this category of delinquent.[137] Witness a case in point where the GCIS invested time, money, and energy in one 'attractive' seventeen-year-old with a mental age of ten: within one year, the Committee of Sixteen found her to be 'living in the worst conditions pertaining to commercialized vice.'[138] By the 1920s the institution prided itself on developing a modern approach to delinquent girls who were of a 'very low grade of mentality.' Dr Gordon Mundie, now a member of the non-Catholic Juvenile Court Committee, was recruited to their medical advisory board and made frequent visits to the institution. Psychiatrist and professor of Mental Hygiene at McGill University W.T.B. Mitchell evaluated girls at the Mental Hygiene Clinic where he conducted research during the 1920s and 1930s.[139]

The Mental Hygiene Committee was founded as the Montreal wing of the Canadian National Committee on Mental Hygiene, which promoted the science of mental health and popularized psychology with the ultimate goal of diagnosing through intelligence testing and preventing mental disease. The committee operated a psychological and intelligence testing clinic where mental health professionals were trained; a decade later it became the Mental Hygiene Institute housed at McGill University. In the 1920s funding was sought through the national body and obtained from the Laura Spelman Rockefeller Memorial to establish two research departments in Toronto and Montreal. The Montreal research group was affiliated with the McGill University and directed by Professors J.W. Bridges and W.T.B. Mitchell.[140] The purpose of the funding of the Montreal research was to establish a mental hygiene clinic and tackle juvenile delinquency.[141] By the 1920s mental hygiene became an acknowledged component of public health with a confirmed aim to prevent delinquent behaviour. Those in charge of the Mental Hygiene Committee focused on education and training and consistently petitioned for proper psychiatric examination and treatment of juvenile court cases.[142] Mental hygiene clinics operated out of Royal Victoria and St Jean de Dieu hospitals.

The work of Professor Bridges on delinquency in 1920s Montreal demonstrates the shift away from hereditarianism; as he plainly wrote: 'It is possible that the most important etiological factor in the delinquency of these girls [at the GCIS] may be found in the home and its psychological environment rather than in any inborn mental or physical characteristics of the girls themselves.'[143] Bridges had been a research director for the Rockefeller-funded project on juvenile delinquency and in the mid-1920s studied the incarcerated delinquent populations at the non-Catholic, anglophone institutions that were fed by the MJDC. His approach and conclusions reflect broad changes in psychology and suggest he was inspired by Healy and his followers, who sought out not a single cause of delinquency but a range of social, environmental, psychological, emotional, and congenital factors that contributed to producing the delinquent girl.

In 1926 Bridges embarked on a study of thirty-three delinquent girls incarcerated at the GCIS. His aim was to consider the individual girls' backgrounds, temperaments, intelligence levels and emotional states. Employing a case study approach, he interviewed girls and the institutions' workers and ran a battery of mental tests. Like his peers, he was not so concerned with the delinquent act that had led to a court appearance and incarceration; he generalized that delinquent girls were sex delinquents (over half of this studied group were treated for venereal disease) and got on with the business of determining the roots of that delinquent behaviour. He began by describing the girls as a group: they were thirteen to twenty years old (average age, seventeen). In terms of 'racial stock' a majority were English, Irish, or Scottish, a minority were Jewish (3) and one was described as 'mulatto'; 20 were born in Canada, 8 in Great Britain or Ireland, 2 in the United States, and 3 'elsewhere'; two-thirds were from the city and one-third from the country; and parents worked at skilled, semiskilled or unskilled labour. Approximately half of the girls had been domestic servants, only 5 claimed to be students and the rest were likely 'idle.' These background factors seemed not to interest Bridges, unlike earlier Chicago studies that zeroed in on the working-class and immigrant neighbourhoods as creating the conditions for delinquency.

Moving on to temperament, Bridges used the observations of GCIS workers to compile generalities about this group of girls. Overall, Bridges conceded that the girls were 'fairly normal' in temperament, considering energy (some lazy and lethargic, others energetic and industrious), mood (variable to cheerful), social behaviour (sympathetic and generous), and anger (normal). Betraying psychology's tendency toward a gendered normativity he wrote of the girls' ego behaviour that most girls were 'submissive rather than assertive, bashful rather than brazen, and with a few marked exceptions followers rather than leaders.' In other words, for girls in the 1920s these were 'normal' because they fit with prescribed gender norms defined at this time by passive femininity.

The mental tests Bridges used assessed both IQ and emotional (in)stability. Girls scores on the National Intelligence Test and the Myers Mental Measure (a picture test) were low; given that their average age was seventeen, they tested like twelve-year-old children. About 15 percent were placed in the feebleminded category, 45 percent subnormal, and about 40 percent were considered average or a little above.[144] He attributed below-average IQ scores to scholastic retardation, arguing that many of the girls he tested had lacked any educational advantage. The role of education in preventing delinquency was increasingly embraced in sociology circles; Herman Ross's 1929 study of Montreal delinquency, for example, adopted this approach, arguing that the lack of compulsory education in Quebec led to high rates of delinquency.[145] For Bridges, though, IQ did not fully explain female delinquency.

Bridges also used two tests that measured emotional adjustment. Overall, Bridges concluded that delinquent girls were more unstable than ordinary adolescent girls, although even ordinary girls were more unstable than boys. Delinquent girls, he wrote, exhibited 'a premature manifestation of the instability of the average girl at later adolescence.'[146] One of the indications of such instability was their responses to questions pertaining to conflicts in the home, morbid depressions (feelings that nobody loved them) and fantasies (regarding adoption). When he compared the delinquent girls to a group of female University of Toronto undergraduates (which he acknowledged were older and socioeconomically more privileged) he found again that the delinquents were more troubled by insomnia, unhappiness, abnormal impulses, and conflicts at home, but college 'girls' had more difficulty in making friends, worried about 'little things,' and were more afraid of responsibility.[147]

In his conclusions Bridges acknowledged that this group of delinquent girls were not well educated, making some of them 'dull'; that they were more emotionally unstable and suffered some psychoneuroses; but that most consequential factor leading to their delinquency was the 'unfavourable home environment.' In fact, homes of delinquent girls were so socially and psychologically objectionable that he regarded girls' delinquency as 'merely a normal or expected response to an abnormal or socially undesirable environment.'[148] Like Chicago sociologists who focused on the 'disorganized' family,[149] Bridges seized upon the 'broken homes' theory of delinquency. A full 70 percent of GCIS girls came from homes in which death, separation, or desertion predominated. Normal mental development and social adjustment under these circumstances was virtually hopeless.

Bridges' 'broken homes' theory attributed the cause of adolescent downfall to a poor home environment in which a single parent had not provided proper discipline, supervision, and affection. Bridges invoked a model of bourgeois family life in which the father was the sole wage-earner and the mother held responsibility for educating and disciplining the children. This was echoed in the 1930s and 1940s when depression and war exacerbated already 'disorganized' home situations.[150] By the 1940s psychology had become so entrenched as an explanation for human behaviour and delinquency that parents were also now blamed for failing to comprehend their children's minds at this vulnerable transition to adulthood.[151] In 1946 La Bonne Parole sought out articles to explain the 'physical, intellectual, and moral crisis [of adolescence]: bodily disorder, a lack of mental stability, and inner confusion.'[152]

The steady progress toward a mental assessment of delinquents changed the language probation officers used to describe delinquent girls. In the late 1930s and 1940s probation officers' reports reflected upon girls' 'modern' personalities: vanity, nervousness, susceptibility to bad influences, lack of self-control, and instability became aspects of the delinquent girl personality. Using reports from the psychological clinic, a probation officer noted in 1942 that a particular girl was 'dull in general appearance,' exhibited 'no abnormal sexual tendencies,' but because of her low IQ and mental age of ten, was in danger.[153]

Conclusion

As the juvenile court era unfolded, rebellious adolescent girls attracted the unwanted attention of a host of new authorities who concerned themselves with the girls' changing social and sexual habits. Earlier, during the reform school era, working-class girls' flirtation with sexuality outside wedlock earned them the designation 'endangered'; now they were accused of being delinquent and modern. From antivice reformers, preventive and protective associations, women's organizations, French-Canadian nationalists, and increasingly social science and psychomedical experts came a campaign of resistance to the young, modern girl. From the pages of newspapers, vice reports, women's columns, religious and social work journals, and psychology manuals came a series of intersecting discourses on the 'girl problem,' quickly making the delinquent girl a familiar character on the urban landscape and in the popular vernacular of early-twentieth-century Canada.

In their quest to improve the overall moral hygiene of the city, social reformers created new definitions of delinquency. Setting out to clean up prostitution, a tenacious problem that had spilled over from the nineteenth century, Montreal's Committee of Sixteen targeted the city's redlight district in 1918. In doing so they embraced social science methods and the Social Survey, which uncovered the problem of wayward adolescent girls whose leisure habits too closely mimicked that of prostitutes. In documenting adolescent girls' pursuit of excitement, reformers helped to identify and define female delinquency.

In the interwar period French-Canadian reformers claimed another problem was on the rise, that of *les jeunes filles modernes*. They argued that the First World War had spawned a generation of adolescent girls who refused to be like their mothers, gave little thought to marriage and motherhood and who were altogether too interested in engaging in modern pursuits of work and entertainment beyond the *foyer*. These girls were problematic and delinquent not only because they risked their virtue but also because of the intense importance placed on the family in the survival of *la nation* and *la race canadienne-française.* The modern girl problem became even more visible during the Second World War as fathers signed up for military service and mothers 'abandoned' their families and homes. Mothers, it seemed, were bad wives and poor role models for their daughters during war: embracing their own youth, they found diversion from war and work in movies, dance halls, and in the company of other men. Wartime adolescent girls became the target for antidelinquency campaigns that sought to quell the VD 'epidemic' and return girls to their homes.

Where girls were deemed immoral and modern by reformers, parents, and clergy, they were also increasingly understood in psychological terms. As psychomedical experts brought testing to incarcerated delinquent girls, sexual delinquency became an expression of mental deficiency, or an indication of a corrupt environment. In the early decades of the twentieth century, adolescence and delinquency were subjects of expanding social science research. Equipped with new theories, mental health experts and social workers employed scientific measures to define normal and delinquent female adolescent behaviour. Expert theories on the cause of juvenile delinquency found a home at the MJDC because judges and probation officers saw themselves as child welfare experts and searched for causes of bad adolescent behaviour from other experts. This occurred initially only among the anglophone population where reformers, juvenile justice workers, and mental health professionals invoked the latest environmental and hereditary explanations of delinquency and implemented the new technologies of evaluation. Only in the 1940s did the MJDC embrace the idea that a psychiatric clinic played a central role in diagnosis and treatment of delinquents. Ultimately, juvenile justice sites – courts and reform schools – hosted a variety of competing knowledges all serving as tools of the probation officers and judges who decided the adolescent's fate. Yet as we will see in the next two chapters, the MJDC records demonstrate that as much as the court officials attempted to identify and categorize adolescent behaviour, on a daily level, the juvenile tribunal also became a contested site where parents' constructions of delinquent daughters at times collided with the expert knowledge and where girls themselves attempted to wrest a modicum of control from the web of juvenile justice.

'Maternal Rule': Gender, Religion, and Professionalization in the Juvenile Court Era

In February 1908, Montreal's *Daily Star* reproduced a *Punch* cartoon in which 'humanity,' personified by a woman armed with the Children's Bill, attempted to save a terror-stricken boy from a policeman and the local jail (figure 4.1).[1] The image of the imperilled child caught by the cruel realities of an unforgiving criminal justice system undoubtedly resonated with Montrealers who had recently joined the national campaign for a Canadian Juvenile Delinquents Act (JDA). The cartoon was a harbinger of sorts, for just months later the JDA achieved royal assent, ushering in a new phase of juvenile justice, characterized by the birth of the juvenile court. No longer limited to Catholic reform schools, juvenile justice in the juvenile court era took a secular turn, reflecting remarkable political and social change in the province. In Quebec it led to the establishment of the Montreal Juvenile Delinquents' Court (MJDC), which remained the province's only tribunal for youthful offenders until 1940. It could be said that by the second decade of the twentieth century, then, that the MJDC reflected *Punch*'s message: that a federal bill could save children from the adversarial criminal justice system and a cruel jail experience.

Beyond the importance of child saving, the inherent innocence of children, and the need for a separate juvenile justice system, the *Punch* cartoon was also making an obvious commentary on gender, advocating the importance of women to the promise of legal and welfare reform. The cartoonist deliberately cast 'humanity' as female, anticipating the auspicious presence of women in the field of socialized justice. Across North America, juvenile courts, like women's courts and family courts that would follow, became arenas of justice in which professional middle-class women prevailed as judges, probation officers, and social workers.[2]

PUNCH, OR THE LONDON CHARIVARI.—February 19, 1908.

SAVED FOR THE STATE.

Humanity. "GIVE THE CHILD TO ME."

Figure 4.1 In this *Punch* cartoon, humanity is depicted as a woman trying to save a young boy from the criminal justice system. (*Montreal Daily Star*, 29 February 1908, 9)

The fundamental female presence and elevated status of women in the juvenile court was widely thought to be a significant improvement over its predecessor, the Recorder's court. Yet, in Quebec, legal professionalism dictated that judges of this new court be restricted to magistrates with formal legal training: meaning men only.[3] Nonetheless, provisions were made specifically for the processing of girls by female probation officers who took on the responsibility of instructing the judge on the 'best treatment' for those found delinquent. Unlike various juvenile and family courts in Canada where women predominated, the Montreal court became a heterosocial arena made up of male judges whose function, they claimed, was to father, and female probation officers, who declared a maternal prerogative over adolescent girls and children.

The court's opening in 1912 intersected with a historical moment when maternalist politics animated women's reform efforts and the new female professions, and produced an explosion of female-controlled disciplinary measures directed at adolescent girls. Girls were subject to gender-specific treatment from judges and probation officers in juvenile court but also from a new collection of 'surrogate mothers' like policewomen and training school matrons. In practice maternal justice as juvenile justice permitted female reformers and new female professionals associated with juvenile court work to construct themselves as 'mothers of all children'[4] and in their work assume a moral legitimacy to supervise and regulate family life. This was generally embraced as a progressive measure because maternal power was (and is) so closely associated with an ethic of care, where mothers protect children and wield disciplinary force only in the child's best interest.[5]

Originally inspired by the spirit of child saving and maternalism, the first generation of female probation officers also participated in creating an emergent social work culture based on casework. These women were the first members of the juvenile court apparatus to meet with the alleged delinquent and complainant; on standardized forms their detailed reports gave a narrative structure to often messy lives and formed the basis on which the judge rendered his decision. Yet this is not a tidy story of the professionalization of social work, for women's work in the court was shaped also by community demands and expectations of them and of adolescent girls.

In the Montreal context the JDA's provisions for respecting the religion of the youthful offender was observed not only at the level of incarceration facilities but also at the level of casework. In the juvenile court, then, we find competing cultural prerogatives, especially among Catholics, Protestants, and Jews, regarding the welfare and the treatment of

children. Early-twentieth-century female probation officers were typically inspired by an ethic of 'doing good,' be it Christian charity or Jewish benevolence, and/or professional social service work. Rendering
maternalism and the emergence of female probation officers' professional identity as caseworkers more complex was the strict observation of
their religious affiliation.

   This chapter introduces the juvenile court and its early principal actors,
beginning with François-Xavier Choquet, the court's first 'fatherly' judge,
who avowedly parented the city's wayward, friendless, and dependent children in the new tribunal. Through the lens of maternalism, the chapter
highlights women's reform activism, the place of women in the MJDC,
and why it was possible to declare 'maternal rule' at work in this court. It
then examines the expansion of the court under Judges J.O. Lacroix, and
J.-A. Robillard. Since ethnicity and religion influenced child welfare and
juvenile justice ideals, the chapter concludes with an examination of the
work of two Jewish female probation officers and their attempts at serving
a community while subscribing to a new professional standard for caseworkers.

'Father' Choquet and the New Court: 'Not a Palace of Justice but a Home of Mercy'

'Since January 12th [1912], the child is treated as he should be, not as a
criminal to be punished, but as a delinquent to be reformed. He is not
tried, but he is questioned and advised by a fatherly judge, who is himself
assisted by a committee which is composed of responsible citizens, ladies
and gentlemen of the religion and nationality of the delinquent child.'[6]
The inaugural judge of Montreal's youth court was the distinguished sex-
agenarian lawyer, François-Xavier Choquet, a man known for his commitment to Liberal politics and child-saving reforms. Under him, the MJDC
embarked on a mission to deliver a new kind of justice where clemency
prevailed for those under sixteen. In his court, adolescents would be
spared the 'awfulness of justice,' offered his paternalistic advice, investigated by compassionate caseworkers, and most often sent home on probation. Choquet, who sat for ten years as Montreal's children's judge,
welcomed the expansion of the definition of delinquency and operation-
alized the major precepts of contemporary child saving, acknowledging
that criminal justice and private incarceration facilities had failed children under sixteen and in this new court, progressive action would be
taken. The generation of child welfare reformers like Choquet who

gained influence in the early twentieth century rejected institutional care in favour of the family environment to appease delinquency.

Born into a farming family in Varennes, Quebec, in 1851, Choquet spent his youth learning in prestigious institutions, including the Collège de l'Assomption and the Petit Séminaire de Montréal. He then pursued legal training in the office of well-known Rouge Louis Amable Jetté and at McGill College.[7] After being called to the Quebec bar in 1875, he spent the next twenty years practising at the law offices of prominent Quebec Liberals, including Jetté and future Senator F.L. Béique, Honoré Mercier, Cléophas Beausoleil, and Paul Martineau. In 1893 he was named Queen's Counsel and in 1898 was appointed judge of sessions of the peace, police magistrate, and licence commissioner.[8] In the first decade of the twentieth century Choquet also became a social reformer, advocating for child welfare and the federal JDA.[9] In this realm of activity, Choquet was joined by his wife, Marie Caroline Barry. The couple worked to establish the Children's Aid Society (CAS) of Montreal and Choquet became its first president.[10]

When Choquet was named the first judge of the MJDC there was overwhelming support for the government's decision. The press, with affection and deference, named him the Children's Judge and his recasting of a law court into a 'home of mercy' was lauded as a sign of progress.[11] Prominent women celebrated the government's decision. Mrs W.S. Maxwell of the CAS put it rather succinctly: 'My years of experience in Children's Aid work, leads me to believe that Judge Choquet is one of the *few men* who is eminently suited for this position.'[12] Even the visiting suffrage organizer Margaret Hodge declared, after having spent a day in his courtroom, that 'from a suffragist point of view' the court was 'splendidly conducted'; according to the newspapers, 'she did not think that even a woman judge could look after the children's interests better than Judge Choquet.'[13] Reverend Symonds observed that Choquet would be 'more than a judge ... He will be a father to the young delinquents [of Montreal].'[14] In his inaugural speech Choquet himself spoke of the court as 'a court ... of a good father, and not a criminal court.'[15] Choquet may have modelled himself on the famous Ben Lindsey of the Denver Juvenile Court who acted as 'father' to delinquents and based courtroom success on the promotion of character building in young men.[16] Both judges relied on the probation system to effect change in adolescent behaviour, and deferred to female probation officers to deal with female delinquents and their precocious sexuality.

Those who worked with Choquet similarly gushed over his leadership in the court: 'Only a man of great practical experience and one who understands human nature as does Judge Choquet could ever in a great complex cosmopolitan city like Montreal make the success which he has done of the Juvenile Court.'[17] The use of the term 'cosmopolitan' could very well speak to the fact that Choquet, while francophone and Catholic, had been educated at McGill University law school and moved easily within established anglophone and Protestant institutions, including the Montreal CAS.

For more than a decade Choquet served as judge of the MJDC, engaging child-saving ideas familiar to English Canada and Progressive Era reformers of the time.[18] At the occasion of the court's opening, Choquet declared the aims of the new court: 'Each juvenile delinquent will be treated not as a criminal but as a misguided child in need of assistance, encouragement and help.'[19] The Montreal court adopted a strong paternalistic character, functioning under the philosophy of *parens patriae*, where the state was responsible for acting in the best interest of the child. In the words of W.L. Scott, 'The State manifests itself not as an arbiter, but in its supreme function as the ultimate parent, the super-parent ... of those unable to protect themselves.'[20] Rejecting the atmosphere of the criminal courts and indeed notions of criminal justice was common to the first generation of juvenile courts. One Montreal probation officer called the juvenile court a 'child saving station ... where the letter of the law is in abeyance, and must take a second place to the greater law of conscience, love, science and justice.'[21]

Observers noted that the physical appearance of the MJDC distinguished this court from criminal courts. Its 'homelike' quality was immediately perceptible upon approaching the building: rather than a court of law, it was a converted house where one rang a bell to enter. The atmosphere, claimed a *Herald* reporter, was 'not of majesty but simplicity': 'In this quiet backwater of the rushing business stream is set the new juvenile court, marking Montreal's latest step forward in altruistic social development. No imposing Ionic pillars marks its entrance to convey their cold impression of the awfulness of justice, to the receptive juvenile mind. No stately officer of the Law's Majesty, uniformed and brass buttoned, lurks within its doors to pounce upon the youthful breaker of laws, and impress him with the enormity of his offence.'[22]

Inside the MJDC, a hallway led to the rooms that housed the judge, the probation officers, and the court clerk. The wallpapered rooms and carpeted floors further confirmed the homelike quality of this new court. What was missing was also important: 'There is no room ... [for] loafers or any of the riff raff which usually hangs around the corridors of the

Criminal courts.'[23] In introducing the juvenile court to the Montreal public, Choquet claimed: 'There will be nothing to suggest a criminal court ... no dock, no raised platform or bench, but the child will be brought into the room exactly as a father would bring his child into his parlor to talk with him and try to gain his confidence.'[24] Choquet held court in a relaxed atmosphere where justice promised to be 'more lenient.'[25]

Choquet clearly subscribed to modern techniques of child saving, especially probation.[26] In the fight to compel the province to establish a juvenile court in Montreal, Choquet vigorously supported the work of probation: 'What we need most ... are probation officers ... It is of supreme importance that a child's upbringing should be watched and recorded.'[27] Because Quebec did not have a child protection act, Choquet argued that it was crucial that the juvenile court be given sweeping powers in the realm of child welfare.[28]

The probation system and use of non-legal professionals distinguished the juvenile court from its predecessors.[29] Even Choquet, a formally trained judge, seemed not concerned with the lack of professional training among his probation officers. In his recommendations to the attorney-general he noted qualities such as voluntary work with the juvenile court committees and in the case of a male probation officer, the fact that he was 'father of a large family.'[30] This attitude can be explained by the way probationary work was conceptualized in the 1910s. As its antecedent was social reform work with the poor through visiting schemes, once introduced into the juvenile court it logically followed that benevolent work with children was sufficient preparation. This lack of professionalism is not to deny the importance of probation work to early-twentieth-century juvenile justice. The centrality of probation was captured in the words of W.L. Scott: 'Probation is the cogwheel in the whole mechanism of the court.'[31] The probation officer model was based on that developed by the CASs that predated the court; in fact, one of the legacies of the child protection movement was the juvenile court probation system.[32] In 1917 Vancouver's Helen Gregory MacGill launched a system of 'constructive' probation that she defined as a rigorous assessment of the cause of the delinquent action and close follow-up supervision of the family and juvenile.[33] Like MacGill and Scott, Montreal's Judge Choquet was convinced of the merits of probation for juvenile rehabilitation. This new generation of child-saving reformers promoted the family as the most important communicator of social and moral values; keeping the family together, therefore, with the supervision of a probation officer replaced the older idea of isolating and institutionalizing problem children.

In Choquet's court, probation work was divided according to the religion of the child: Catholic, Protestant, and eventually Jewish. In the early 1920s the Federation of Jewish Philanthropies (FJP) created a Juvenile Aid Department (JAD) and appointed a probation officer to work with the court. In 1930, though, there were still only two Catholic, one Protestant, and one Jewish probation officers to handle more than one thousand cases each year.[34] The juvenile court further observed ethnic and religious difference through the establishment of voluntary court committees (one for Catholics and the other for non-Catholics) to work with the judge on deciding the adolescent's future. The committees' purpose was often to avoid incarcerating young people by finding respectable homes and work for troubled adolescents.[35] Members of the committee could also work as volunteer probation officers.[36] The original committee split along religious lines and by the 1940s there were only two official committees of the MJDC, one Protestant and the other Jewish.

Another important innovation observed in the juvenile court era was a detention home, a temporary holding facility for children brought to court. Following a long-held assertion that arrested children should not spend any time in the proximity of adult criminals, this special facility was built to hold adolescents awaiting trial. Judge Choquet emphasized that there would be 'no waiting in police station cells for these young people.' Special facilities were built to hold adolescents awaiting trial: no arrested child would make contact with accused or convicted adults. The Detention House for Young Delinquents, a mixed-sex institution located upstairs from the juvenile court, served as a short-term jail for teaching youths discipline, morals and occasionally the rudiments of an academic education.[37] Education of inmates at the detention house consisted of twice-weekly sessions conducted by a volunteer teacher.[38] When the juvenile court moved in the early 1930s to 5030 St. Denis Street, detention home facilities were again built on-site, at the rear of the building.[39] Here there was room for approximately seventy young people, with dormitories, dining rooms, playgrounds, and a nurses' clinic. Boys and girls were both housed there, although in separate sections. Upon entry, 'suitable clothing' was provided as well as a visit with the court physician.[40] The detention home also included two chapels, one for Catholics, the other for Protestants. This facility was designed for minimal stays: the ideal maximum number of days being seven.[41]

Under Choquet's leadership the court appeared to live up to child-savers' designs: trials were summary and informal, separate facilities were used to prevent children from coming in contact with adult criminals, and constructive probation was implemented. As such it was referred to as a 'home of mercy,' and a 'child saving station.'[42] This it shared with juvenile courts in the United States and other parts of Canada. In certain ways the initial years of this court can be characterized by the euphoria of progress and change in the arena of child rescue and reform. Certainly the Montreal press lauded and respected Choquet's team at the MJDC in its effort to address problem families and rehabilitate challenging children. This juvenile court's mandate to process neglected and delinquent children was fulfilled by a relatively small staff with the court convening on a limited, part-time basis. The probation officers, such as Rose Henderson, Maria Clément, and her replacement in 1915, Marie Mignault, were selected for their child-friendly politics and received very little training. The first clerk of the court, Owen C. Dawson, also lacked legal experience but had worked in the CAS, had managed local boys' clubs and sat on the board of the Boys' Farm and Training School.[43] Choquet and his 'family' made sure the public saw their work through press coverage as benevolent, progressive, and successful.

Maternalism and Maternal Justice

Emerging in the late nineteenth century and gaining potency in the early twentieth, maternalism was an ideology that cultivated, promoted, and celebrated the virtues of motherhood.[44] These included several allegedly 'natural' tendencies of mothers toward their children – to care, nurture, feed, love – but also common-sense, charity, efficiency, and morality, which were positioned as complements to masculine characteristics. Female reformers invoked a maternalist discourse to explain why they should have access to political, economic, and social power; using 'public' motherhood, they argued for women's participation in the overhauling of corrupt and dangerous municipal regimes and the establishment of family- and child-centred social policy. In the welfare bureaucracies that emerged at the turn of the twentieth century, as Seth Koven and Sonya Michel remind us, female volunteers and professionals forged new relationships with the state, often relying on the power of the maternal symbol to justify their presence in this realm.[45] With the new juvenile court, the justice system became an important site for maternalist politics.

In keeping with the 'transformative' project that was the juvenile court, the patriarchal nature of other courtrooms was said to be tempered by women and 'maternal justice.'[46] This notion was embraced by contemporaries and is reflected in the work of juvenile court historians. The focus on women in juvenile courts has produced literature that verges on essentialism (women's work in the court being a function of their 'innate' character and maternal orientation) but also thoughtful explorations of the meaning of maternalism for these female professionals. In his now classic social control treatise on the child-saving movement, Anthony M. Platt described how civic-minded female philanthropists brought their 'housewifely' duties to the public realm and defined delinquency as a social problem befitting a therapeutic response.[47] His argument, though, pursues the women's class interests rather than their gender interest. In recent literature on American juvenile courts, historians have argued that the presence of women in these courts meant children were subject to a new kind of justice, one that was grounded in maternalism. Maternalists can be divided into two main groups: sentimental maternalists and progressive female reformers. Both groups worked for the establishment of juvenile courts in the United States: sentimental maternalists tended to be upper- or middle-class female volunteers who wanted to help dependent children and women; their progressive counterparts were often single, highly educated professionals who emphasized a social scientific approach to social problems and were considerably more sensitive to class and ethnic differences than the sentimental maternalists.[48]

Because those who advocated maternal justice tended to be female child welfare reformers, maternal justice rhetoric sounds much like that of the child savers who were responsible for late-nineteenth-century child protection acts and CASs. In their endorsement of a separate court for children and youth, therefore, maternal justice advocates overlapped with child savers. Common to both was a disdain for retributive justice, especially for children; a strong belief in social science, specifically the child study movement; a conviction that within a child's environment one could locate the cause of delinquency; and that the solution to delinquency was to be found in the family home, not in institutional care. In drawing our attention to the religious foundations and implications of child protection legislation (and the CASs) in Ontario, Nancy Christie argues that the shift toward the home as a social panacea for problem children is directly related to the rise of the 'maternal-centred family' and the 'moral dominance of mothers.' This shift, promoted by evangelical Protestant reformers such as J.J. Kelso, resulted in social reform programs such as child protection and juvenile courts, reflecting the heightened status of women in the family, Protestant churches, and politics.[49]

Maternal justice went further than child saving when educated professional women argued that innate differences between the sexes made women well positioned to not just influence but administer this new court of justice that dealt with the intimate details of family life. According to maternalists, the business of the court – private hearings, probation and follow-up work, and rigorous scrutiny of the delinquent's home life – required a woman's touch. W.L. Scott agreed: 'Women, intended by nature for motherhood, are better fitted for the work [of probation officer] than men.'[50] In reconceptualizing the juvenile court as a 'diagnostic and therapy centre' for troubled families, child welfare reformers were able to justify substituting surrogate mothers for legal professionals and therapeutic 'care' for legal procedure. The suspension of the rules of evidence and lack of representative counsel was rationalized because the goal of the tribunal was to treat, not to punish.

Claims of a kinder, gentler type of justice, have not convinced feminist historians who, in interrogating the nature of maternalist politics, have illuminated its coercive power over working-class and immigrant families. In her study of early-twentieth-century Los Angeles, Mary E. Odem has found that female-dominated justice had 'ambiguous consequences' for adolescent girls, because officials upheld a gendered notion of delinquency and in the name of protection, were severe in disciplining the overwhelmingly working-class, female sexual delinquents.[51] Kelly Hannah-Moffat argues in her work on women's prisons that 'maternal governing of women by women does not equalize relations of power in penal settings; instead, it naturalizes them.'[52] Amanda Glasbeek suggests that a language of familialism and gender solidarity in the Toronto Women's Court belied the fact that the court asserted the right of middle-class women as mothers to subordinate daughters of the working class.[53] In Vancouver, women across the political spectrum advocated a similar strategy to remedy the 'bad' family: 'tribunals with more comprehensive jurisdiction over domestic issues.'[54] In Quebec, the language of maternalism was similarly embraced by early female probation officers as women claimed a motherly prerogative over delinquent girls. Thus, the effect of maternal justice was to further extend the surveillance of mostly working-class or marginal families through juvenile, women's, or family courts.[55]

Maternalist Developments in Montreal

The Montreal juvenile court movement coincided with a heightened period of female reform in the city, and hundreds of women through their associations called for a new juvenile tribunal for the city as well as a range of legal measures aimed at policing adolescent girls. Advocating on behalf of the province's children animated both the Fédération nationale Saint-Jean-Baptiste (FNSJB) and the Montreal Local Council of Women (MLCW), which represented dozens of women's organizations. As early as the 1890s francophone and anglophone women's organizations had come together to solidify their social reform work with the aim of alleviating the worst conditions of industrial capitalism in Montreal. The MLCW first amassed the city's clubwomen[56] across linguistic and religious lines, to work on behalf of women, children, and the family.[57] Francophone women eventually felt constrained by the prevailing anglophone and Protestant character of the MLCW and in 1907 formed the FNSJB. Though Montreal clubwomen shared class privilege and their goals were generally consistent – to alleviate suffering and to bolster the family unit – the separation of the linguistic groups permitted the francophone women to openly embrace Catholicism in their reform activities.[58] The maternalism and Christian feminism espoused by the FNSJB provided its members with a basis for promoting child welfare reform on behalf of all children.[59] Advocating for a juvenile court and policewomen to patrol neighbourhoods was just one part of the FNSJB's work in its early years: in an attempt to preserve the home and strengthen motherhood (both physically and morally) its members established les Gouttes de lait,[60] and other maternal assistance programs, a children's hospital, and campaigns directed at protecting and policing minors.[61] Implicit in their demands for a juvenile court and benevolent activities on behalf of mothers and children was an understanding that families that produced delinquent and dependent children required moral surveillance. The FNSJB's cofounder, Marie Gérin-Lajoie, publicly admonished mothers who quietly worried about their children but who did not act in the public realm to improve their lives: 'You will complain that your son dissipates his health and fortune in the neighbourhood bar, you will be overcome with sorrow at the sight of your daughter whose virtue is gradually being eroded by immoral theatre ... and still you do not attempt to remedy these evils.'[62]

Although women were denied the basic rights of citizenship, namely, to vote and run for political office, female lobbyists played a critical role behind the scenes promoting and guiding the legislation through Ottawa and Quebec City. Specifically, members of the MLCW generated public support for the JDA, bringing W.L. Scott to Montreal in the autumn of 1907 and organizing a CAS.[63] Beyond the MLCW's general support for the JDA and juvenile courts, anglophone women in the Montreal CAS worked closely with Scott to ensure the successful passage of the act in 1908. The MLCW lobbied hard for a women's reformatory and passed resolutions in 1910 advocating that legal guardians replace parents who shirked their responsibilities regarding their children.[64] Caroline Béique, one of the founders of the FNSJB in 1907 and the wife of Liberal senator F.-L. Béique who was instrumental in securing the successful passage of the JDA in Ottawa, worked alongside other clubwomen in Montreal to see that Premier Lomer Gouin passed the requisite legislation establishing a juvenile court in 1910. She claimed in her memoirs that as head of the FNSJB she was invited to join a group of women lobbyists; for three years they met at her home each week to plan their campaign.[65]

The 1910 provincial legislation gave Montreal clubwomen hope and opportunity. While it would take two years before the juvenile court was ready to begin its work, women prepared for full involvement. Many women, including Madame Béique, became volunteers in the court's first citizens' committees, which oversaw the disposition and treatment of delinquent youth.

Anglophone and Protestant maternalists also took the opportunity of the court's opening to establish a long-awaited alternative to the Soeurs du Bon Pasteur's École de Réforme. Since 1870 girls in conflict with the law, and more often with parents, had been sent to this reform school; forty-one years after the nuns began incarcerating girls, a new institution for girls opened. The Girls' Cottage Industrial School (GCIS), an anglophone and largely Protestant institution derived from a tradition of reform influenced by a combination of juvenile and maternal justice ideals, not to mention Protestant fear of, and prejudice against, Catholic institutions. In 1911 the GCIS was founded by Montreal philanthropists Beatrice and Mary Hickson in response to the lack of facilities for non-Catholic and English-speaking delinquent girls they imagined would be produced by the juvenile court. The GCIS began as a home in Outremont that supported a handful of girls and a matron. Within the first year, the school moved to a larger house in St. Lambert on the south shore of Montreal. Two more moves were necessary before it settled in the Eastern Townships, sixty miles from Montreal, where it stayed from 1922 to 1946.[66] Many of the volunteers on the board were also prominent members of other organizations such as the MLCW and the antivice organization, the Committee of Sixteen. The administrators worked closely with the new court's female probation officers. For those cases that warranted not probation but institutionalization the court could now send non-Catholic cases to an institution other than the nuns' reformatory.

The other major accomplishment of women's organized efforts that directly impacted on delinquent girls was the placing of women on the Montreal police force.[67] In the 1910s the pressure to hire women onto Montreal's police force came from two main sources: Montreal club-women and the New York Bureau of Municipal Research. The former supported the installation of women on the force because of the nature of women's police work and its goal – 'the purification of morals.'[68] Women's organizations maintained an important role of supervising the work of the policewomen. A study conducted by the New York bureau revealed problems inherent to Montreal's civic administration, including the police service, and advocated a new Committee on Public Safety and the hiring of at least three women officers.[69]

In the summer of 1918 the chief of police hired two francophone and two anglophone women. Perhaps because of incomplete recordkeeping or the policewomen's seeming unimportance, the only records of these women's experience on the force that remain are those of Elizabeth Wand. Wand was a bilingual, trained nurse and social worker who had worked in New York City and Montreal and had a long history of volunteer work, including with the Parks and Playground Association of Montreal.[70] As a policewoman she regularly attended the juvenile court and the city's industrial and reform schools. Although she did not have the power to arrest or serve warrants, Wand relied on coercion and moral suasion to discipline adolescent girls. Policewomen's work lay fallow between the two World Wars, but in the postwar era women joined the Montreal police services as members of the Juvenile Morality Squad.

The Montreal woman's movement directly influenced the establishment of the new MJDC, a new training school for non-Catholic girls, and a female police force. Armed with maternalist convictions, more Montreal women became directly involved in the juvenile justice system and in regulating adolescent girls.

'Maternal Rule': Female Probation Officers in Juvenile Court

Relative to other areas of the legal profession juvenile courts permitted professional women easy access. The institutions themselves were often the end result of successful political lobbying on the part of maternalists and first-wave feminists[71] who promoted the value of children – as future citizens – and women's key role in guiding them as mothers-at-large.[72]

Contemporaries celebrated the confirmation of women's knowledge and power over children in the public realm. Because the new court system was imagined as a not-too-distant cousin of the nascent welfare system rather than the criminal justice system, women 'figured there without impropriety.'[73]

As maternalism gained political power its influence began to bear fruit. In the decades following the JDA of 1908, female judges and probation officers were appointed to many juvenile and family courts in Canada. Perhaps the most famous female magistrate was Helen Gregory MacGill of Vancouver, who has been attributed with bringing child saving to Vancouver in 1917.[74] Ethel MacLachlan, who presided over the Juvenile Court of Regina, was very vocal in the campaign for a JDA and joined Charlotte Whitton's Canadian Council on Child Welfare in the 1920s. These reform victories, though, did not herald female accomplishment in the male-dominated criminal justice system as much as they signalled the political acceptance of women's domain over children and family life in the public realm.[75]

But to what degree did women and maternal justice ideals prevail in the largely francophone and Catholic culture of Montreal and under the paternalistic Choquet? Given the context of early-twentieth-century Quebec, should we presume that women would play a large role in the new court? In this era the Catholic Church still maintained governance over the delivery of maternal aid and child welfare. For example, the Soeurs du Bon Pasteur had already predominated in the field of girls and women in trouble with the law. As well, Catholic laywomen had justified their presence in the world beyond the *foyer* in terms of safeguarding the French-Canadian family; as Denyse Baillargeon argues, the women in l'Assistance maternelle de Montréal defined their work as a 'social, patriotic, and religious endeavour.'[76] Women, then, had moved into the area of child welfare when it was organized around religious differences and privately run. With this new state institution women would find themselves marginalized to a degree by the fact that no woman was ever named judge.[77]

In spite of the growing consciousness that women could and perhaps should administer juvenile justice, they were conspicuously absent from the top post at the MJDC. In Quebec, women were excluded from the bar until 1941, and therefore technically there were no female judges available.[78] However, according to the JDA, the judge of the juvenile court was to be a 'justice,' and justices were not required to be lawyers. Yet, even in jurisdictions where women were nominated to the juvenile or family courts, there existed considerable opposition from 'legal professionalism' advocates who opposed the appointment of justices deficient in legal training.[79] At the same time, as the local press suggested, Choquet and his successors were legal professionals but also 'fatherly,' confirming the privileged place of men in Quebec families and society. According to the 1910 Quebec legislation concerning the establishment of Montreal's juvenile court, judges were to be chosen by the Conseil des ministres from among the judges of the sessions of the peace. In Montreal the dominant political and legal culture meant all juvenile court judges from 1912 to 1949 (when the juvenile court was replaced by a social welfare and youth court) were male members of the Quebec bar.

Notwithstanding the fact that a woman *never* presided over the Montreal juvenile court, Rose Henderson, one of the MJDC's first probation officers, was still able to declare the juvenile court to mark the 'extension of maternal rule into the larger life of the community.'[80] When Henderson proclaimed the maternal nature of the court, she was writing, not about Choquet's gender, but rather of the predominant ethic at work in this new court and about probation officers gaining access to family homes. For Henderson, what distinguished this new court was its fundamental rejection of the juvenile court as a criminal court: 'The cold letter of law has but little place in solving the problems of mothers and children,' she wrote in 1916. This parenting role of the judge fit well with Henderson's notion of juvenile justice. Her maternal justice ideals and the *parens patriae* philosophy held by Choquet had much in common: to view the delinquent not as a youthful offender but as a child in need of protection.[81] Like the women of Hull House who played a major role in the early Chicago juvenile court, Henderson believed that the court's mission was 'formation, not reformation.'[82] Henderson described the new tribunal as being a protector rather than a destroyer of human life. Using thinly veiled gendered language she declared the ideals of the juvenile court: 'to protect the child, educate the community as to causes of crime, and degeneracy, and render justice – not more tyrannical, but more merciful, a more intelligent instrument for the defence and protection of the unfortunate victim, rather than a tool of retribution and destruction.'[83]

Although the court was hierarchical, with male judges firmly ensconced at the top, women did figure prominently in the court's first years, owing in part to the prominence of Rose Henderson who wrote and lectured about the court and was willing to engage the press on issues of child welfare and delinquency. As one observer noted in 1914: 'I am glad to see the woman probation officers have so much power.'[84] The court relied heavily on probation officers to investigate home life to evaluate the root of the delinquent behaviour; who better than women had the expertise to evaluate the city's homes and children's lives?

The court opened with a modest three probation officers, two women and one man. The two women, considered 'child-loving,' were recommended because of their years of experience working with both the Montreal CAS and Choquet.[85] Rose Henderson processed all non-Catholic cases and Maria Clément dealt mainly with Catholic girls.[86] Clément was replaced in 1915 by Marie Mignault, who worked in the court for fifteen years.[87] The boys were processed by male probation officers.

Maria Clément first became involved in probation work in 1907 with the nascent Montreal CAS. Although she had no university training, she spent time late in 1907 with the Ottawa branch of the CAS and was coached in the methods of probation by none other than W.L. Scott.[88] Scott himself felt she compensated for a lack of experience by being blessed with the 'right disposition,' common sense, and optimism.[89] At that time the Montreal CAS president was Choquet who would eventually have Clément installed in the new court in 1912. After her brief training in Ottawa, Clément worked at the request of police magistrates, investigating family situations of juveniles brought to court.[90] As the probation officer responsible for Catholic girls brought to the court, she likely saw her role as parallel to women's benevolent activities that similarly focused on children. In these organizations the importance of assisting and maintaining the integrity of the French-Canadian family was predicated on Christian charity principles and on the primacy of religious devotion.

Rose Henderson is better known to students of Canadian history for her work as a pacifist and labour activist than for her work with the juvenile court in Montreal.[91] Born in Ireland, she spent years in Boston before coming to Montreal with her husband, an accountant with MacDonald Tobacco. After his death she pursued social service work and obtained a job at Choquet's court. She made Montreal her home in the first two decades of the twentieth century, during which time she worked for women's suffrage and a variety of social welfare causes such as mothers' pensions.[92] Although assumed to be Protestant, she was a practising Bahà'í,[93] and although her background and appearance were conservative middle class, she was far more radical in political outlook and action. Through the 1910s she became increasingly interested in social justice issues, especially the plight of the working class and pacifism.[94] In 1919,

Henderson was one of the prominent women who came out in support of the One Big Union and the Winnipeg General Strike.[95] Her pacifism[96] and radical leftist politics sparked outrage in the aftermath of the First World War. In 1919 the Sons of the Empire sent a strongly worded resolution to Premier Gouin demanding her resignation: 'In view of her pronounced and oft-repeated Bolshevistic utterances,' they argued, she should be 'replaced by the widow or mother of some soldier who fell in action during the War of 1914–1918.'[97] The state's determination to punish those associated with the Winnipeg General Strike and Henderson's visible and vocal association with labour radicalism may have led to an early end to her career at the MJDC. Henderson was one of many whose property in Montreal was seized in the aftermath of the General Strike. In mid-1919 the deputy attorney-general of Quebec, Charles Lanctot, took 'interest' in documents she held at home and at the juvenile court.[98] She did not refute the charges against her but decided to make a 'confession of [her] principles,' eloquently defending her socialist position and denying that she advocated anything other than 'constitutional methods' of political and social evolution.[99] Following raids on her home and office, Henderson was suspended and three months later she resigned her post.[100] In the 1920s she moved to Ontario and eventually stood for election as a Co-operative Commonwealth Federation candidate.[101]

Although Henderson was well educated and considered herself a professional, new credentials took second place to the maternal characteristics that best describe her qualifications for the job of probation officer: 'The Probation Officers must have the mother-heart to win the children's hearts and obtain their little secrets.'[102] In fact, she told the *Montreal Daily Herald*, 'No one should go into child work without study and love for children.'[103] (In adult courts, no one advocated that officials love adults or criminals!) The president of the Trades and Labour Council, upon visiting the court in 1916, similarly remarked upon the 'motherly concerns' of Henderson, which he found an appropriate complement to Choquet's 'fatherly interest.'[104] Maria Clément similarly expressed this child-saving view of probationary work: 'The Probation officer is a friend of the child and of his parents ... the purpose of the Juvenile Court is not to punish the child but to cure him.'[105] The belief that love for children was natural in women was used to argue that women were well suited for probation. The maternal justification for women's presence in the new court system was similarly employed by 'club mothers' and female professionals attempting to establish themselves in American juvenile courts.[106] By promoting probation work as the expansion of mothers' work, educated professional women strategically constructed themselves as indispensable for the success of progressive juvenile justice.

While Choquet maintained ultimate authority in adjudicating cases, the outcome of the trial was based on the input of these new court officials, such as Maria Clément and Rose Henderson – caseworkers known as probation officers or *agents de surveillance* or *d'enqueteur* – whose job it was to investigate the family, work, and school lives of all adolescents appearing in court. This work was intense and onerous, involving multiple interviews and much form-filling. It is likely that these women spent much of their time seeking answers to the questionnaires and writing up delinquents' dossiers.

The first job at the court for probation officers was to interview the adolescent girl along with the complainant, often the girl's parent. In rendering the story, probation officers generated scripts on girls; yet probation officers' work was at least in part influenced by the priorities set out by the forms they were required to fill in. The court opened and operated in an era where recordkeeping and standardization of procedures and forms were the hallmark of efficiency and progress, and a legacy of the scientific charity movement of the late-nineteenth century.[107] Montreal probation officers followed a legal tradition of recording information on children in conflict with the law that predated the court's opening by two decades. In an 1892 Act to Amend the Law respecting Reformatory Schools, the Quebec government required that a judge or clerk at a trial of a child record the evidence of each witness against the child and submit them along with a baptismal certificate, a copy of the complaint and the following personal information regarding the child: age; address; names of parents; place of birth; whether or not the child had always lived with parents and if not with whom and where; the 'habits and antecedents of the child'; and the precise details and circumstances and nature of the offence.[108]

The MJDC had a legal responsibility as a court of record to produce and maintain case files on each delinquent, the exact shape of those reports were the result of prolonged national debates. W. L. Scott saw the standardized form and its contents as vital to ensuring consistency, thoroughness, and professionalism across Canada.[109] The earliest forms asked name, address, age, place of birth, religion, parents' names and occupations, charge, character of girl and parents, girl's employment history, and comments on the physical and moral hygiene of the girl's

CANADA,
Province de Québec,
District de Montréal.
CITÉ DE MONTRÉAL.

ICOO-I-12

Cour des Jeunes Délinquants.

La Dénonciation et Plainte de

de   de   dans le
District de Montréal, pris sous serment ce
jour de   dans l'année de Notre-Seigneur
mil neuf cent   par le soussigné, Monsieur
Juge de la Cour des Jeunes Délinquants, agissant dans et pour la Cité de Montréal,
lequel   déclare :

Je demeure au No.   de la rue

Assermenté et reconnu dévant moi à Montréal
les jour, mois et an plus haut mentionné

_____
Juge de la cour des jeunes delinquants

Greffier de la Cour
des jeunes Delinquants

Figure 4.2 Complaint form, Montreal Juvenile Delinquents' Court, n.d.

COUR DES JEUNES DELINQUANTS

Rapport de l'officier de surveillance à la demande
de la Cité de Montréal.

-o-o-o-o-o-

Nom de l'enfant.................................Âge...........

Domicile...

Lieu de naissance..

A Montréal depuis.....................Religion.................

Date de la sentence...................Terme....................

-o-o-o-o-o-o-o

Nom du père....................................Âge...........

Domicile...

Au Canada depuis..................A Montréal depuis............

Lieu de naissance..

Occupation........................Salaire.....................

A-t-il des biens?..

Nom de fille de la mère.........................Âge...........

Domicile...

Lieu de naissance..

Au Canada depuis..................A Montréal depuis...........

Occupation........................Salaire.....................

A-t-elle des biens?..

Nombre,âge et occupation des enfants?..........................

....

vv...

....

Remarques: Les parents semblent-ils être en état de payer?

-...

Autres remarques...

....

....

Date........................

vv........................

(Signature)

Figure 4.3 Early probation officer's report form.

COUR DES JEUNES DELINQUANTS

No. ....

Rapports de l'Officier Enquêteur

Montréal, ... 19

Nom de l'enfant ....Age ....
Adresse ....Nation .... Religion ....
Date et lieu de naissance... du baptême ....
Occupation .... Instruction ....
Délit .... Précédents ....
Punitions ....
Cigarettes ....Drogues ....Cinémas ....Liquers ....Danse ......Pool ....
Nom du père .... Nation................. Religion ....
Adresse ....
Occupation .... Salaire $ ....
Séjour au Canada ....à Montréal ....
Nom de la mère .... Nation.................... Religion..............
Adresse ....
Occupation .... Salaire $ ....
Séjour au Canada .... à Montréal...........................
Nombre d'enfants dans la famille ....Garçons................. Filles ....
Nombre de pièces ....Loyer mensuel $ ....
Nombre de pensionnaires .... Chambres louées....................
Tenue de la maison .... Etat sanitaire ....

ENQUETE ET RAPPORT SUR LES SUJETS SUIVANTS:

a)   Dans quel milieu vit l'enfant ?

b)   Quelles sont ses dispositions sous le rapport de la propriété d'autrui ?

c)   Quelle est sa conduite à l'égard de ses parents, de ses maîtres, de ses patrons ?

d)   Quels sont ses compagnons et ses rapports avec eux ?

e)   Quels sont ses défauts dominants ?

f)   Comment emploie-t-il ses loisirs ?

g)   Où et comment joue-t-il ?

h)   Quels sont ses goûts et aptitudes ?

Figure 4.4   Probation officer's report, c. 1930s/1940s.

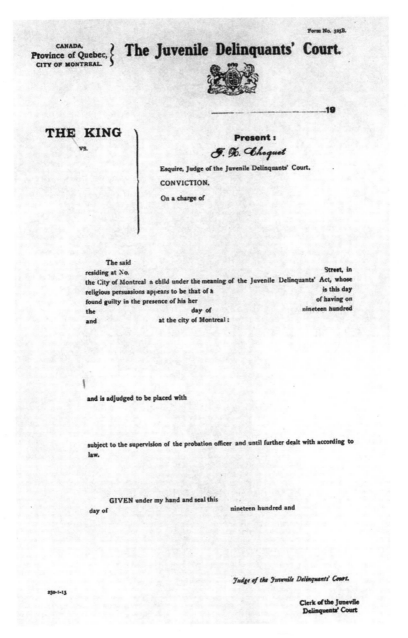

Figure 4.5 Conviction form, Montreal Juvenile Delinquents' Court, c. 1912–22.

Figure 4.6 Crest of the Montreal Juvenile Delinquents' Court.

home. As well, the form provided for comments on behavioural indices, such as whether she smoked or attended the cinema. Later that decade officers' reports asked about rent, boarders, girls' prior arrests and education history. In the interwar period the forms expanded to include questions about the girls' habits, use of leisure time, temperament and personality, and emotional and physical environment. Probation officers contributed the centrepiece of knowledge on each case through their reports, embarking on a process of translating what they heard from their 'cases,' parents and other interested parties into 'textual realities.'[110] They did so by laying out the relevant factors contributing to the adolescent's difficulties, often referring specifically to the girl's family/work/ social situation; it was incumbent upon the probation officer as the expert to then recommend a solution. As Karen Tice explains in her history of case reporting and social workers, 'Record-keeping is a formalized way of knowledge and recounting that potentially subdues and transforms individual biography into professionally translated and abridged versions.'[111] The probation officers' forms appear to conform to the goals of early-twentieth-century juvenile justice for they are concerned primarily with the delinquents' cultural and moral environments.[112]

Mother Blame

For all the public discourse concerning the court's maternal devotion to the city's children, the practice of maternalism and *parens patriae* was not always kind to early-twentieth-century working-class families. Under Quebec law and custom, minor children were the property of the male patriarch (usually their father). In this hierarchical arrangement, wives and mothers were to provide sustenance, moral, and religious guidance to children but were, according to the Quebec Civil Code, not given the right to correct or discipline children.[113] Male culpability was related to a father's overbearing disciplinary style or failure to provide sufficiently for his family (and anything that hindered his ability to do so, such as alcoholism or laziness). Social commentators and the juvenile court officers saw mothers' duty firmly in the home; while not trespassing on a father's disciplinary rights, they were to create conditions – often by setting an example – where children would learn a high moral standard. At the hands of child-care experts, mothers have been held responsible also for the character, emotional life, and behaviour of their children, especially daughters. These issues would creep into the language of Anglo-Protestant and Jewish women's organizations and juvenile court officers. In francophone Catholic circles, emphasis was placed on religious observance and modesty. At the juvenile court, Montreal mothers were cast as wilfully incompetent or simply ignorant in their role of supervising and training adolescent girls. They were meant to be on the lookout for daughters' hasty turn toward modern life.

Maternalists in the juvenile court set up the dichotomy of good mother/bad mother, leading to vigorous mother blaming in the juvenile court. Although the stated purpose of probation was to investigate youth in trouble, not surprisingly, probation officers took the opportunity to measure working-class families against the bourgeois ideal, especially concerning child raising. In juvenile court, mothers were judged responsible when their children got into trouble; the roots of the girls' delinquencies were often traceable to their mothers' character and behaviour. Only those whose characters were beyond reproach and whose homes exhibited exemplary moral and physical hygiene were spared blame. Mothers, according to juvenile justice authorities, were too lenient or too strict; if they worked, they were neglectful; if their homes were untidy or deemed unhygienic they were unfit. Being a 'good mother' meant being entirely *not* responsible for a daughter's delinquency *and* reporting the girl to the court. However, a catch-22 situation was at play here: the status of having an uncontrollable daughter led the court to search for how the mother had elicited such behaviour in her offspring.

Because the solution for delinquent behaviour among youth often was better mothering, working class mothers were criticized for working outside the home and found to be unsympathetic by probation officers. As Margaret Little has pointed out, those involved in the juvenile court movement, including Rose Henderson, often connected the rise of delinquency with working mothers.[114] As explained by one of her colleagues, Henderson was 'forced' to think about mothers' pensions because of her work, finding that 'children of good mothers are going bad because their mother is obliged to go out to work to support the family, and the children are left uncared for.'[115]

Like many progressive maternalists in the United States associated with the Children's Bureau (1912), Rose Henderson articulated an appreciation of the class bias inherent in the court. 'Enough facts daily occur to prove to us what money and position can do with the law,' she wrote in 1916, 'while the poor pay the full penalty every time.'[116] In attempting to educate the public about the roots of delinquent behaviour, Henderson offered a basic analysis: 'The children of the poor are brought to court for stealing, and the children of the rich and middle classes, commit the same sins and are not brought to court. Children steal for only two things, food or amusement, although girls beginning to grow up will steal for a bit of finery or clothing. If they had all the candy they wanted they wouldn't steal it. They need the carbon in the systems, and they need amusement, so they steal for car-rides and moving picture shows. The middle class and the rich parents can give their children candy and take them to the theatre.'[117]

A few years later Henderson similarly argued that the causes of delinquency were comparable to those that caused disease and insanity, including hunger, worry and unemployment.[118] She was a strong advocate of the state providing urban spaces for children to enjoy themselves and to keep busy, such as playgrounds and skating rinks: 'Every mother knows that the greatest punishment a child can have is to make it sit quiet.'[119] Yet she took the position that poverty and weak, ill-prepared mothers produced juvenile delinquents: 'The child born of a domestic or industrial drudge, chained to the baby-cradle, cook stove, or machine, linked to poverty, knowing nothing of the arts and sciences, or of child rearing, uneducated, unprepared for life, can only produce after her kind; and it is usually her kind who fill the brothels, insane asylums, jails, reformatories, and penitentiaries.'[120]

Unthreatening, naughty children who stole did not predominate among Henderson's female cases, however. Most of the adolescent girls Henderson interviewed were sexually active teenagers, not children who could not sit still. In the 1910s girls' flagrant sexuality became a much talked about social ill and the juvenile court joined many other institutions that sought to discourage it. Faced with the *jeunes filles modernes*, and their seemingly negligent families, Henderson, like her Catholic colleagues, upheld a model of bourgeois propriety and scientific child rearing as a panacea for troubled youth. A bourgeois model meant conformity to heterosexual marriage and the sexual division of labour where mother stayed home to raise the children. Importantly, girls' delinquent acts were placed in the context of their prescribed role as future mothers. Although Henderson did employ the language of sentimental maternalism in suggesting that mother love was an appropriate credential for her work in court, during her years in Montreal at the juvenile court she can be described as what Molly Ladd-Taylor called a 'progressive maternalist.'[121] Henderson invoked a maternalist rhetoric that at once demanded the state take more responsibility for maternal and child welfare and denounced working mothers. Her position was undoubtedly based on contemporary economic and political systems, but her work in the court permitted access only to band-aid solutions within individual families, not a revolution.

A critique of the economic system still led her to blame mothers for neglecting their role at home. During times that accentuated family dislocation, such as the First World War, the court made frequent reference to working mothers and their failure to raise their children properly. In her 1916 report on eight-year-old Enid W.'s disobedience, Henderson remarked that the girl 'has a step mother who insists on going out to work and leaving the child.' While Enid's father brought her bad behaviour to the court's attention, Henderson took sympathy on the child, who appeared to be neglected at home. The probation officer focused her criticism on the working stepmother, not the child's father: 'The mother should stay home and look after this child; if not she must find some other home or else [Enid] will soon learn the evils ways of the street.'[122] In this case Enid was taken away from the family for one week and then sent home on probation.

If women who went out to work were bad mothers, so too were those who were neglectful or abusive and those who were a poor role model for daughters. Dorilla T. was arrested for vagrancy and loitering in the summer of 1912. When her home life was investigated, Maria Clément found that both her stepfather and her mother drank: Madame T. had just finished two months in jail for drunkenness and disturbing the peace. The probation officer spoke of 'irregularities' in the home, evidence probably derived from the girl herself, who claimed she would prefer to be placed with a good family as a domestic. The probation officer summed up the case for the judge: the daughter is 'kind hearted, seems devout and a hard worker' but the mother was 'without principle.'[123]

In this case the girl's recognition that she was overwhelmed by bad influences at home spared her committal in a reform institution; in a case earlier that summer, an adolescent was not so lucky. In June 1912 the Montreal police brought Clementine F. to the MJDC for committing an indecent act in public. Maria Clément admitted in her report that the fifteen year old did not seem truly delinquent but rather had been influenced by older friends and her mother, who 'lived a life of debauchery and drunkenness.' This not-so-bad girl was committed to the reform school.[124] A minor offence and a bad mother in this instance led to a three-year term for this adolescent.

A recurring theme in the court records is that delinquency on the part of adolescents was due to the leniency of mothers or their inability to properly manage children so that institutionalization was required. Too often, according to juvenile court judge Choquet and the probation officers, mothers failed to be strongminded and were therefore guilty of benign neglect. One mother before Judge Choquet told him that she loved her errant son. 'Ah, that's the trouble,' Choquet replied, 'You love them too well. You are too soft.'[125] In January 1914 Henderson investigated the case of Emily E., a fourteen year old accused of vagrancy, a prostitution-related offense. Henderson thought the girl 'a moral degenerate,' having been found in a brothel frequented by Asian and Italian men. The girl's home and parents made the grade in terms of character and hygiene; however, Mrs E. was not absolved of responsibility for the girl. A mother 'not sufficiently strong willed' to manage her daughter was inadequate – the girl was sent to reform school for four years.[126]

In another case involving juvenile prostitution, the judge similarly sent a girl to reform school for several years. In this case it also appears that the parents lost control of the girl, the result being she wound up in a brothel. The parents pleaded for clemency for their daughter and promised greater scrutiny of her actions. Within a year the daughter was back in court, arrested again for being found in a brothel. The judge admitted the girl was 'inclined to immorality' but that her mother's leniency was also to blame: 'Unfortunately she has a very lenient Mother, who can never believe that her daughter has fallen.'[127]

Far worse than benign neglect was a mother's incompetency. Fanny F.'s mother probably did not expect to become the target of the court's wrath when she brought her daughter before the court for stealing. Fifteen-year-old Fanny had never been arrested before, but Henderson found that she had been truant and judged her character to be 'not good.' Her parents on the other hand had 'good characters' but Fanny's mother was 'incompetent.' As a result, Henderson claimed, the girl was being raised in a 'poor dirty badly managed home' leaving her with 'little opportunity to be anything but bad.' Henderson blamed the mother, who was 'always being tied to a baby,' for forcing the family to be 'huddled together like animals' and neglecting the older children, who were left to fend for themselves. Fanny was sent to the reform school for two weeks, undoubtedly to teach her a lesson and then home under the watchful eye of the probation officer.[128] Henderson was not typically critical of working-class families for being poor; rather, she was critical of mismanagement – of homes and fertility.

Even when probation officers could not substantiate claims of bad mothering, there were cases where girls were still punished. Ruth J. was brought to juvenile court by her adoptive mother for stealing one dollar from her. This girl had never been arrested before but was having some trouble in school and her mother alleged that Ruth was passing notes to boys and exhibited signs of 'immorality.' In rebuttal the girl told Rose Henderson that her mother treated her cruelly. Henderson could not get anyone to substantiate the mother's harshness but felt that the child needed to be taken away from the family. The probation officer wrote to the judge that the 'child is not naturally bad but needs to be with some one who will be firm and kind with her.' She was sent for several months to the Bon Pasteur reform school for girls.[129]

While mothers might be shamed in court for their role in creating a substandard home environment, it was the daughters who were incarcerated as a result. And, because girls who came to court were often accused of engaging in adult activity (sex), they were regularly deemed bad candidates for rehabilitation under probationary schemes; the women probation officers recommended they be sent to reform school. Thus, notwithstanding the rhetoric that suggested the family was the appropriate institution to educate, socialize, and rehabilitate children, often the maternalists in the court advocated an alternative to a mother's 'natural' love. Henderson's faith in the progressive nature of the training school is revealed in her 1915 column in *Woman's Century*, where she lauded its potential to produce economically independent young women.[130]

Ostensibly the purpose of probation was to avoid incarcerating young people, yet as many have argued, it permitted the state access to homes where court workers diagnosed 'problems' and attempted to implement normalizing measures.[131] Choquet claimed that in the 2000 cases he saw in 1913, only 6.5 per cent were placed in reform schools; the rest remained with their families under the 'potent' influence of parents and probation officers.[132] In the first year of the MJDC's operation, girls who came before Choquet – having been assessed by Maria Clément and Rose Henderson – were incarcerated at a much higher rate than Choquet claimed. In 1912 an astounding 45 per cent of girls who came to court were incarcerated. This is much higher than the statistics for the rest of the decade: as Jean Trépanier has found, from 1915 to 1919, only 13.6 per cent of minors who came to court were incarcerated.[133]

The gender imbalance witnessed here is likely due to the persistence of the desire to 'protect' wayward young women – from families and themselves. Often Henderson noted that the benefits of probation would be lost on the girls that she interviewed, either because of their bad behaviour or that of their mothers. 'There is nothing to be done for this girl but put her in some institution,' Henderson advised Choquet on more than one occasion.[134] Similarly Clément wrote, 'Surveillance at home would not be sufficient.'[135]

In the Montreal juvenile court, 'maternal rule' then, was an assertion that women had the expertise to investigate the home life of juvenile offenders. When the court opened in 1912 the probation officers and judge approached the accused (delinquent) not as an individual, but rather as part of a social system that had failed. As a result, a delinquent could be punished (or rehabilitated) on the basis of her own bad behaviour or simply on the poor household environment and her mother's character. By the end of the first decade, the court's approach shifted somewhat toward a more intense focus on the girl's actions. This reflects trends outside the court where social workers and policewomen were increasingly seeing delinquent girls as wilful rather than as products or victims of home environments.[136]

As progressive maternalists, probation officers were highly critical of working mothers and took easily to mother blaming. While mothers were subjected to self-righteous tongue lashings, it was the 'delinquent' daughters who were incarcerated at times for poor home environments. The gender solidarity one might have expected due to the maternalist politics at work was as elusive in juvenile court as it was in the contemporaneous campaigns for suffrage and mother's allowance.[137]

Both Clément and Henderson, once face-to-face with delinquent daughters and their mothers, chose to rely on other women at work in this gendered juvenile justice system: nuns who ran the École de Réforme (Soeurs du Bon Pasteur) and the laywomen who ran the Girls' Cottage Industrial School. Both reformers had confidence in these distinctive incarceration facilities for girls: Clément with the Soeurs du Bon Pasteur whose convent-reform school focused on religious instruction, domestic work, minimal education, and learning one's station in life; and Henderson with the Girls' Cottage School superintendents who ran a model female reformatory to prepare girls for bourgeois married life. Unlike their Catholic and Protestant counterparts' desire to institutionalize delinquent girls, probation officers in the 1920s and 1930s would take a different tack.

The Expansion of the Court and the Professionalization of Juvenile Justice Work

In the interwar era, the growing and awesome demands of delivering juvenile justice to the city resulted in the dissipation of the euphoria endemic to the Choquet period. From 1919 to 1939, the inadequacy of the original facilities and the poor training of the juvenile court workers met with the constant criticism of an imperfect system. Eventually the municipal and provincial governments approved and funded a new court building and new actors applied innovative ideas to juvenile justice practice in this turbulent era.

Replacing Choquet in 1923 was J.O. Lacroix, a Université Laval – educated lawyer, judge of sessions, and former Recorder for Ville St. Pierre. For eight years, Lacroix ran the juvenile court. Likely selected by the

Taschereau government for his Liberal politics, he was less visible than his predecessor or successor J.A. Robillard. During Lacroix's time the court continued to expand but persisted on a part-time basis. In these years complaints were heard about the inadequacies of the facilities and Lacroix complained publicly about the need for a rejuvenated court.[138]

During the 1920s Lacroix saw an increasing number of delinquents but like Choquet had little staff. He never had more than a handful of probation officers, so relied on a less than effective system of probation: each month about two hundred children reported to the court with letters from teachers or parents attesting to their good behaviour. By the mid-1920s the juvenile court and the detention house were bursting at the seams.[139] One observer of the court in 1930 noted that it wasn't just the building that was tired, but the judge himself. Lacroix, 'an elderly French-Canadian ... [with] no special training in child psychology,' appeared to McGill graduate student Herman Ross as part of the problem plaguing the court.[140] Ross also noted what had frustrated Lacroix: too few probation officers and the lack of medical and psychological examinations at the court, which set it apart from other juvenile courts of this era. Lacroix's ideas for change included a domestic relations court, raising the age of delinquency to eighteen (which had been permitted by federal law since 1921), and a new building.[141] When Lacroix fell ill in late 1931, he was temporarily replaced by L.P. Lacaisse.

The MJDC evolved from its settlement house–like existence when it was relocated to a new building in 1932. Eschewing the 'home-like' atmosphere of the Champ de Mars Street location, the new court occupied an imposing three-storey civic building north on St. Denis Street. Accompanying the physical move was the hiring of a judge whose reputation and personality approximated Choquet's. In 1932, J. Aldéric Robillard, a sixty-two-year-old lawyer, began a new era at the court in which the juvenile court operated on a full-time basis.[142] Although the Robillard era overlapped with a major economic depression and his court faced opposition from the Union nationale government in the latter half of the 1930s, the court implemented important changes and continued to expand.

Robillard enjoyed tremendous popularity with the Montreal press. Referred to as the 'father of Montreal's family of children,' Robillard courted the press, inviting reporters to witness his good works in the juvenile court, which he suggested was less a tribunal than a 'family forum.'[143] Upheld as a kind and compassionate judge, he managed approximately forty to fifty cases per day and continued the limited parole system used by Lacroix: every Saturday dozens of children came to court with letters in hand attesting to their good behaviour. Similarly, the Juvenile Aid Department of the Federation of Jewish Philanthropies, which placed a probation officer in the court made a point of noting Robillard's cooperation and generosity with their worker.[144]

During the Robillard years an important shift was made toward medical and mental health assessment of children brought to court. Like his predecessors, Robillard supported the ideas of thoroughly investigating each delinquent, including psychological assessments. Although still not routine for all children coming before the court, those placed in the detention home were increasingly tended to by a physician, and those appearing to the judge or probation officers to have significant mental health problems or simply odd behaviour were sent for psychiatric evaluations. While the provincial government was slow in providing the requisite funding for a juvenile court clinic, private interests involved in the mental hygiene movement made their way into juvenile justice. The main impetus for the testing of juvenile offenders came from psychologists and psychiatrists at McGill University and those involved in the city's mental hygiene movement, especially the Mental Hygiene Institute.

From the 1910s to the 1940s medical doctors were used by the court to assess delinquency cases. While mostly concerned with the presence of hymens, pregnancy, and venereal disease, Doctors Amiot and Lebel gave shorthand commentary on girls' mental state, often stating that it 'appeared normal.' Juvenile court judges such as Lacroix advocated full physical and mental examinations of delinquents; however, because there was no psychiatrist attached to the MJDC, he used the committee's clinic when possible and consulted with other psychiatric experts.[145]

Meanwhile, the juvenile court sent Catholic girls they thought were 'abnormal' to psychiatrists at the province's hospitals for the insane or the new La Jemmerais School for the Feebleminded at Mastai, Quebec. These psychiatrists were called upon to determine if cases warranted institutionalization in such asylums. In the 1930s and 1940s, for example, Dr Daniel Plouffe of the Bordeaux Prison Hospital for the Insane examined girls for the court. He often found girls slightly behind in terms of intellectual development but not sufficient enough to intern them. He did note, though, that many girls from a moral standpoint expressed 'perverted tendencies' and could use some education and training at the reform school.[146]

By the latter 1930s the Depression resulted in increasing numbers of youth appearing in court. The numbers eventually merited the appointment of more staff, including another juvenile court judge in 1939, Arthur Laramée, who came with experience in the Saint Vincent de Paul Society.[147] Two years later the reformist Liberal government of Adélard Godbout appointed to the court J. Gordon Nicholson, a forty-three-year-old McGill University graduate, lawyer and army veteran. He became the court's first anglophone judge.[148] Not only did the staff at the court expand, the Second World War saw numbers of juvenile delinquents soar. This trend was exacerbated by the Quebec government's decision in November 1942 to raise the age of the juvenile delinquent to under the age of eighteen. In the 1940s the juvenile court used a psychiatrist, Dr J.E.A. Marcotte, at the city's Department of Health to examine delinquents for mental age and IQ. His reports came to play a large role in both Catholic and non-Catholic cases.[149] In 1945, the province established a Child Aid Clinic attached to the juvenile court which included an expert in psychology or psychiatry.[150]

Female Jewish Juvenile Aid Workers in the MJDC

During the interwar period, the professionalization of casework at the juvenile court developed. This era also overlapped with the integration of Jewish probation officers at the MJDC. Women's work at the juvenile court was initially divided between Catholic and non-Catholic (largely meaning Anglo-Protestant) cases, yet prominent members of the Jewish community organized early in the court's history to have influence over Jewish juvenile delinquents. In the same way it negotiated with school boards for special consideration, the Jewish community was able, by 1921, to place a Jewish probation officer at the court. This act was part of Jewish Montrealers' long struggle for inclusion and civil rights in a society defined as the heart of French Canada. In the interwar period preservation of its language, Catholic faith, and rural heritage left Jews on the periphery of citizenship. A growing population, Jewish Montreal demanded political and economic inclusion and expected rights to social service endeavours, parallel to those launched by the Catholic and Protestant communities.

In the interwar years two women predominated in juvenile justice work. Dorothy Sigler and Esther Levitt acted as probation officers at the juvenile court while embracing a model of caseworker that went far beyond the juvenile tribunal, frequently engaging the network of Jewish social service agencies to avoid sending children to court. The careers of Sigler and Levitt are good examples of how important the community was to the disposition of delinquency cases as well as how the female probation officer's identity evolved generally in the 1920s and 1930s. Through the 1920s the Juvenile Aid Department of the Federation of Jewish Philanthropies worked to bring attention to the problems of Jews living in the 'congested' area bordered by Sherbrooke, Mount Royal, St Urbain, and St Denis Streets. This department lasted until 1938 when its function was subsumed under the rubric of the Federation's Child Welfare Bureau, and delinquency became a secondary issue to the plight of orphans and foster care.

From early in the court's history, Jewish Montrealers were represented through membership on the non-Catholic court committee which oversaw probation and advised caseworkers. The non-Catholic probation officer, Rose Henderson, played a role in inciting the community to get involved.[151] In the 1910s prominent Jewish Montrealers Lyon Cohen and Max Goldstein played a distant role in the disposition of Jewish cases that Rose Henderson vetted.[152] These 'West End' Jews probably had little in common with the downtown immigrant children who came before the court. Montreal's Jewish community was undergoing an enormous transition at the time: since the 1880s Montreal had been a recipient of the Ashkenazic diaspora in which Jews fled persecution and poverty in Russia, Austria-Hungary, and Romania. This 'Great Yiddish Migration' resulted in a Jewish population increase in Montreal, from 811 in 1881 to more than 45,000 in 1921.[153] The Yiddish-speaking Jews of this era settled along St Laurent Boulevard, whereas the financially well-off older Jewish community that included Cohen and Goldstein, moved from downtown to the west end. The former became the objects of Jewish social service initiatives largely under the auspices of the Baron de Hirsch Institute.[154] From the 1890s onward the institute established medical clinics, schools, and brought together social agencies primarily to meet the needs of recent immigrants.

Delinquency among Jewish adolescents developed into one of the chief targets of the new Federation of Jewish Philanthropies (FJP) of Montreal. It was part of what middle-class and elite Jews saw as the Yiddish slum problem. Recent immigrants brought from *shtetl* in Europe a strong sense of nation based on common language, education, religious observance and dietary practices. In the 'slums' of Montreal, this largely poor community of peddlers, garment workers, and small shopkeepers stood out relative to the wealthy Westmount Jews who were battling for integration into the anglophone community by downplaying cultural differences. Declaring the slums of Montreal worse than the ghetto life from whence they came, one commentator in the *Canadian Jewish Chronicle* wrote: 'The danger lies not in our best homes nor in those of our middle class, but in the poor hovels that constitute our slums lurks a danger that we Jewish people cannot afford to shut our eyes to … in that disreputable district lives a large percentage of our Jewish boys and girls.'[155] The established Jewish community saw the trying conditions of immigration and settlement, of downtown vice, crime, illness, and slums as its problem. It was through the FJP that this older community sought to relieve the distress of the Jewish immigrant and impose its ideal for the future. In 1918 the FJP incorporated; it would fund, coordinate, and expand Jewish social service in the city. Following its founding, a new goal emerged: to rescue and rehabilitate Jewish youths.

In the late 1910s, the FJPs' Committee on Correctional Work reported an alarming trend in Jewish teens being sent to the Boys' Farm and Training School and the Girls' Cottage Industrial School. Importantly, there was a perception that the influx of immigrants in the previous two decades had given rise to a delinquency problem. Judge Choquet argued that 'many' juvenile delinquents were of 'foreign extraction … whose parents have but lately arrived in the country, and who know nothing of the laws and language of the new land.' While many newcomers to Montreal were Catholic and Protestant, Choquet pointed out that many delinquents were of a 'different religion,' in all likelihood, meaning Jewish.[156] The problem with these immigrant parents, he wrote, was that they 'are obsessed with the idea of making money; consequently the duties of citizenship are almost ignored.' He railed against immigrant parents for hanging on to their 'distinctive and separate' ways, impeding their children's assimilation.[157] Choquet was not alone in his perspective: Max Goldstein also pointed to the 'problem' of 'foreign' Jews responsible for ghettos, who failed to assimilate and who tarnished the reputation of all Jews.[158] While the overwhelming majority of children appearing before the judge were French Canadians, perception that delinquency was a foreign problem resonated both inside and outside the Jewish community. What seemed to be true was that Jewish adolescents were overrepresented in the juvenile court. In an attempt to generate support for its cause, the Jewish Big Brothers suggested that Jewish delinquents accounted for one-third of all cases before the juvenile court.[159] According to the MJDC's Annual Report of 1921, Jewish delinquents made up 10 per cent of all cases but only approximately 6 per cent of the city's population.[160] Herman Ross, a McGill sociology student, found that in 1929, 'Hebrews' made up 7.19 per cent of juvenile court cases but only 4.8 per cent of the city's population.[161] Juvenile delinquency was reconceived as a Jewish problem, as this rhetorical question posed by the FJP suggests: 'We ask you Jew to Jew – Are we to allow our Jewish boys and girls to go the path of waywardness and delinquency?'[162]

As a remedy to a mounting youth problem, the FJP turned to casework and by 1921 had established a Juvenile Aid Department (JAD) and hired a worker.[163] The department quickly focused on the origin and character of Jewish delinquency. The volunteers and workers assumed this social problem was rooted in the 'ghetto' that had developed along St Lawrence Boulevard. 'The Main' brought temptation to the adolescents of the plateau; homes ruined by the conditions of immigration and settlement in crowded tenements had created a Jewish delinquency problem. The worker identified the Jewish delinquent as 'the underpriviledged [sic] child, the child of the back alley, the crowded and unattractive home, the low moving picture, poolroom, and redlight district.'[164] Commercial amusements, such as bowling alleys, dance halls, and the delicatessen stores on the Main, appeared to attract adolescents, inspiring them to keep late hours, gamble, and they drove the need for greater spending money. According to the chair of the JAD, this behaviour sparked tension between 'old school parents and Canadian born children.'[165] The sorry lack of recreational facilities and the crowded neighbourhood laid the groundwork for adolescents to be misled and caused a rising number of them to be caught in the juvenile court.[166]

When the JAD began, it opened an office in the Herzl Dispensary at 632 St Urbain Street on Montreal's Plateau neighbourhood. The dispensary brought aid, practical help, and bourgeois moral guidance to the working-class immigrant community. Beyond probation work with the Jewish cases in the MJDC, the worker also dealt with referrals from the Council of Jewish Women, the Family Welfare Department, the Baron de Hirsch Institute, schools, and parents. Each adolescent was thoroughly examined physically and mentally as necessary at the Royal Victoria Hospital psychiatric clinic, the Herzl gynecological clinic, the Mental Hygiene Committee; all eyes and ears were checked for weakness and disease. In the first year the worker spent 42 days in court, made 204 visits to homes and 14 to clinics, conducted 93 interviews, and visited the Girls' Cottage Industrial School 7 times.[167]

Under the JAD Jewish juvenile aid work expanded dramatically to a general interest in the 'health, welfare and morals of Jewish girls and boys.'[168] Pre-delinquent, troublesome, and unadjusted children would preoccupy the JAD's workers and administration who sought preventive measures to stave off delinquency.[169] One of the solutions proposed in 1925 to remedy the problems of unemployment (idle youth) and the lack of healthy recreation (creating the conditions for delinquency), was a new settlement house. By the mid-1920s the Jewish population had moved northward along St Laurent Boulevard toward Mount Royal and stretched from St Urbain in the west to St Denis in the east. A settlement house in this newly established Jewish area became a central project of the JAD. In her proposal for a new settlement house on Mount Royal Plateau, JAD chair Millie Berliner argued that preventive work was central to juvenile aid, and that the cause of much delinquency could be thwarted with this new organization. The settlement house would function as a 'rendez-vous' for adolescents and become an educational centre where 'old school parents' could be helped to understand the world of their Canadian-born children.[170] A Jewish settlement house called Neighborhood House opened within two years at 3958 Laval Street and became a constituent member of the FJP in 1928. Settlement workers opened a library, organized a mother's club, and held classes including the Red Cross, Brownies, Girl Guides, and Boy Scouts. By 1936 it was said to offer 'counter attractions to the empty glamour of commercial amusements and street corner excitement.'[171] It also performed an important assimilationist function for the Jewish community, where English language classes were held and it became an 'interpreter for children of modern times, and parents of old world thoughts and ideas.'[172] Neighborhood House worked to establish recreational centres to keep children occupied outside school hours, and for 'health instruction, and general development of and respect for good citizenship.'[173] For predelinquents, the JAD called for solving the problems of unemployment and a lack of recreational facilities in the immigrant neighbourhoods.

When Dorothy Sigler became a probation officer at the MJDC in 1921, a new era of social service work had begun. The first wave of female probation officers was gone and their maternalism had been eclipsed by a new professionalism spearheaded by social workers. Where Rose Henderson and Maria Clément professed their mother-love for children in the MJDC, Sigler and her successor Esther Levitt found little resistance when making their way into juvenile justice and therefore dropped the essentialist female justification. The earlier female probation officers were hired because they were women; in social service work they represented the halfway point between the lady volunteer of the nineteenth-century settlement houses and the professional social workers that emerged in the 1920s.

There is no evidence that Sigler and Levitt embraced the language of maternalism or traded on their gender identity in their work with the JAD. Rather, they are good examples of the shift toward professional, objective, and dispassionate social work. As modern social workers they saw themselves as caseworkers – mediators among families, the state, and social service agencies. They were professionals who used the most modern techniques of investigation, evaluation, and diagnosis. Yet, as Walkowitz argues for the case of New York City where the FJP became the centre of Jewish social service work, this is a good example of the 'limitations of the secularization' of social work.[174]

Certainly Sigler and Levitt were not hired solely for their professionalism; they were hired explicitly because of their religion. Levitt's facility in Yiddish was particularly noted. Quebec's deputy attorney-general authorized the hiring in February 1921 of Dorothy Sigler (at this time Feigleson), as probation officer for the MJDC, responsible for Jewish cases.[175] Her salary was six hundred dollars per annum, equivalent to the other female probation officers' wages.[176] By the time she took a leave of absence in 1927, from which she would not return, her wages had doubled and the FJP, along with the Council of Jewish Women, augmented her salary by fifty dollars per month. During the 1930s she served on boards and committees of the JAD and Neighborhood House. Esther Levitt was Sigler's permanent replacement. In 1928 Levitt left the Family Welfare Department at the FJP to take up casework with juveniles at the JAD. For a decade Levitt was publicly congratulated by the FJP for her faithful and devoted service, efficient and zealous attention to her duties, and efforts to keep abreast of the progress made in the field of social work.[177]

The creation of preventive agencies like Neighborhood House helped to divert some of Sigler and Levitt's casework. Ultimately, settlement houses represented an older model of social service where they functioned as the work site of the volunteer charity worker. In the interwar period, the female 'worker' as she was called, took to the streets following a family casework model. As professionals, Sigler and Levitt energetically collected information on delinquents and their families, assessed home and school lives, examined the neighbourhood and job sites. As Walkowitz has illustrated, this generation of caseworker, as social workers called themselves in this era, employed a sociological form of casework, creating narratives of families and playing mediator.[178] Not restricted to examining the delinquent alone, the caseworker investigated family finances, examined marital, school, and psychological problems, and assessed all personalities involved. For each problem encountered, the worker directed the family to the appropriate agencies, often another agency at the FJP, to obtain legal aid or loans, employment, housing, medical attention, and psychological and psychiatric help. They sent troublesome teens for mental and physical tests, helped incarcerate them in reform schools or set them up with Jewish Big Brothers and Sisters, found jobs and even opened an after-school program to help combat disaffection at school. Except for several Protestant agencies, like the reform schools, this was kept within the Jewish community.

Sigler and Levitt embraced what Karen Tice calls the fundamental tenet of casework: recordkeeping. Case writing lent a scientific and professional guise to their work. Of course, the MJDC was a court of record and probation officers were required to submit specific information and observations on standardized forms; yet, the purpose of the Jewish caseworkers in keeping records was not strictly for the judge and the legal process. The objective of their case recording was to carefully document the travails of the most troubled part of the Jewish community so that the problems could be catalogued, remedies found, and ultimately the community rid of such impediments to proper citzenship. They were not simply interested in juvenile delinquency, rather in expunging from the Jewish community the conditions that created delinquency among its youth. Generally only half their caseloads were generated through the juvenile court, the rest came from recommendations to the JAD. Therefore, their case conferences most often occurred outside the court, within the Jewish philanthropic milieu.

As 'workers,' Sigler and Levitt rigorously sought to distinguish themselves from the feminine volunteer tradition and the narrow, unsystematic casework of their predecessors at court. Their work was not sentimental – they were not mothers of all children- it was empirical and depended on professional distance and expertise: as Tice notes, 'documentation of causality and conditioning factors became the hallmarks of scientifically sophisticated social workers.'[179] In the early 1930s the director of the (American) Training School for Jewish Social Work argued that the job of social worker required 'objectivity, a search for basic causes, avoidance of undue and hasty generalizations, a passion for verification, and belief in control and improved technique.'[180]

As early supporters of the mental hygiene movement in Montreal, these social workers also adopted borrowed terminology from psychiatry and psychology. Where the juvenile court was slow to move beyond basic binary assessments of juvenile delinquents (sane/insane), the anglophone community (both Protestant and Jewish) rushed into more complex mental examinations to explain and ultimately resolve wayward behaviour. These probation officers were closely connected with the Mental Hygiene Institute.

Both Sigler and Levitt integrated the language of typologies into their reports. Although not explicit about what a 'degenerate type' or 'ignorant type' was, these were important markers. They relied on the experts to be much more specific; for example, Sigler noted in one case: Dr Mundie (of the Mental Hygiene Committee) found Fannie C. to have achieved a mental age of nine and a half according to the Binet-Simon test and an IQ of 72. Her psychiatric examination revealed a diagnosis of 'borderline mental deficiency.'[181]

The Jewish probation officers' reports provide us with insight into their approach, language employed, and the battery of professionals and tests relied on in each case. In the winter of 1924–25, Rachel C, a fifteen-year-old daughter of Russian Jews, was brought into court twice by her parents for desertion.[182] Dorothy Sigler's investigation showed that Rachel absented herself from home to be with her boyfriend, Alphonse F. who worked for the Rex Moving Picture Theatre. She had been with Alphonse for three days when she was apprehended. At the occasion of her first appearance in court, she was discovered – by medical examination – to be a virgin and was therefore sent home with a warning to stay away from her boyfriend. (Rachel's case resembles others: daughters of working-class, immigrant parents fell for young men of a different religion and when parental discipline threatened to interfere with the relationship, they deserted their family home and ended up in juvenile court.) This couple paid little heed to the warning and planned to get married (he had promised to convert to Judaism). Perhaps self-conscious of her role in creating a narrative, Sigler made extra space on her form for 'the girl's story.' While this section is not verbatim, and in fact is interrupted with admonishments from Sigler in third person ('the worker attempted to go over the seriousness of the situation with her and point out its dangers, but Rachel's reaction was very childish'), she was demonstrating an important new facet in social work technique.

In 1928 Esther Levitt left the Family Welfare Department at the FJP to take up casework with juveniles at the JAD. Levitt's job as Jewish probation officer began on 1 April 1928 and for a decade this single, articulate, professional woman dealt with youth on the streets. More than other workers at the court, she appeared to have professional credentials, attending the American National Conference of Social Workers annual meetings and lecturing at McGill University's Department of Social Service on the JDA and its application. She also attended special classes at the Mental Hygiene Institute to keep up to date with the latest in child rearing.[183] In the name of efficiency, she sported around Montreal in the 1930s in her Ford Coupe visiting schools, children in reform schools, attending juvenile court sessions, and visiting families at home.[184]

Levitt transformed many juvenile delinquency cases from the Main into family casework, finding employment, foster care, relief, and fully supporting the shift toward mental health clinic involvement in dealing with families.[185] In 1938 Levitt's job at the juvenile court was abruptly terminated by the provincial government. Because only the Jewish probation officer was fired the situation deserves some attention. In the interwar period, especially the 1930s, some anglophone and francophone Québécois acted on what they perceived to be a Jewish threat. This crisis was related to the growing presence of Jews, who were threatening because they were not Christian, and often not English- nor French-speakers. Many were part of a thriving working-class community on Plateau Mont Royal and many espoused radical labour politics. There were also Canadian-born Jews who had to some extent integrated into Montreal society and were now attending universities and becoming professionals.[186] As Pierre Anctil has found, the proportion of Jewish students grew to 25 per cent in 1924–5 at McGill University, traditionally a preserve of the city's Protestant elite. In response, covert measures were taken by the university administration to reduce the numbers of Jewish students.[187] This reaction to the competition posed by Jews was replicated in francophone institutions: interns at Montreal hospitals threatened to strike over the hiring of a Jewish intern at Hôpital Notre-Dame, and on campus at the Université de Montréal public condemnation of the Jewish presence was heard.[188] Outside the institutions, in the 1930s, the *Achat chez nous* program was directed against Jewish merchants and *Le Devoir* ran editorials on the 'Jewish problem.' It was in this context of heightened anti-Semitism that Levitt was fired by the Quebec government of Maurice Duplessis.

In June 1938, the attorney-general's office made what an FJP member called a 'regrettable move' and fired Esther Levitt.[189] For years the provincial Liberals were able to pass out juvenile court posts as patronage. When Maurice Duplessis's Union nationale came into power, this was felt eventually among juvenile court personnel in the mid- to late 1930s. Levitt was not the only juvenile court worker to be targeted, but her firing was the most blatant. Her abrupt termination was explained in a memo authored by Edouard Asselin, the deputy attorney-general, who argued that her twelve-hundred-dollar salary was not put to good use because she held two other positions, at the Herzl Dispensary and the Baron de Hirsch Institute.

It was true that the probation officer worked at the offices of the JAD at the Herzl Dispensary and collaborated with the Baron de Hirsch Institute, especially its Family Welfare Department. It is also true that the FJP rewarded her financially for this work, topping up her salary by approximately thirty-five dollars per month. Third, and perhaps more damaging, was the complaint that her attendance at the juvenile court was sporadic: she appeared in juvenile court mornings only and gave 'all sorts of pretexts for not coming in the afternoon.'[190] It is highly unlikely that Asselin nor anyone from his department requested attendance records from the courts under their jurisdiction; MJDC annual reports certainly did not specify this information. Therefore someone from the juvenile court must have played informant. Asselin admitted that court clerk and deputy judge Paul Monty 'often tells me' that she is 'absolutely useless.'[191] He also noted that she was from the electoral district of St. George, likely meaning that the government owed no patronage to this ward. Further, perhaps most mysteriously damning, was the fact that her loyalty was under suspicion.[192]

The Non-Catholic Juvenile Court Committee had not been notified of this action and protested, as did W.R. Bulloch, member of the Legislative Assembly for Westmount-Montreal, yet to no avail.[193] In response to these protests, the deputy attorney-general avoided the personal attacks and rather focused on how few Jewish cases came before the juvenile court – so few as to not warrant a Jewish probation officer.[194] In attempting to tease out what prompted the government to fire Levitt, several possible scenarios come to mind: first, the financial argument – the province was attempting to save money. Yet the firing of Levitt saved the province only twelve hundred dollars. Second, the numbers argument: did the diminutive size of the Jewish population in Montreal and the small percentage of Jewish juvenile delinquents mean that a Jewish probation officer was not warranted? The numbers of Jewish children before the court had not changed enough for this to be substantiated. Third, was it anti-Semitism that led to her being singled out and fired? Certainly the Quebec of Maurice Duplessis was no stranger to this kind of prejudice, and she may have been fired for being Jewish and serving the Jewish community on the province's purse. Walkowitz, who looked at Jewish social workers in New York City, noted that the context of the Red Scare of the interwar period meant that even middle-class social workers were tainted with suspicion, targeted as being 'seditious socialist' social workers.[195] This would not be the first time that the MJDC fired a female probation officer for radical politics: in 1919 Rose Henderson was investigated by the Mounties as part of a national round-up of alleged insurgents following the Winnipeg General Strike. Henderson was also fired by the attorney-general. Unlike Henderson, Levitt was not a vocal opponent of the class system and did not advocate radical social change.

It may be that anti-Semitism was at play in a less overt way: Levitt, in her attempts to keep Jewish children out of the court (perhaps because she felt the justice system was anti-Semitic and lacked separate incarceration facilities for Jewish delinquents) might have unwittingly done herself out of a job. From Levitt's monthly and annual reports it is clear that she worked to keep young people out of court and her caseload involved many delinquents who she handled by herself.[196] According to her reports her caseload had increased, not diminished. On behalf of the Non-Catholic Court Committee and the Montreal Children's Aid Society, Frank M. Horner wrote Asselin, admitting that Levitt had worked out cases with families and schools, thus avoiding the juvenile court and iron-ically 'saving the Government a good deal of money.'[197] By increasing her non-court caseload and by taking afternoons to complete this work, she opened herself up to criticism from certain juvenile court judges and the administrators of the system who were not concerned with child welfare alternatives. In the wake of her firing, the JAD was amalgamated into a Child Welfare Committee (which would become the Child Welfare Department and the Jewish Child Welfare Bureau) under the Family Welfare Department. This committee took over Levitt's pay and she continued for several years with probationary work unofficially.[198]

What began as a progressive experiment of integrating three strains of juvenile aid work (Catholic, Protestant, and Jewish) in the juvenile court broke down in the 1930s over legitimacy and rights, with the Jewish community temporarily losing out. Jewish juvenile aid work then continued on the periphery of the system. Levitt's firing can also be read as a product of uneasiness over the ascendence of professional women in the justice system. When Sigler and Levitt gave up their claims as mothers of all children, they challenged the narrow venue available for women in that system. The MJDC never hosted a female judge and so female probation officers were meant to work symbiotically with the male head of the court. Levitt, with all the accoutrements of professionalism, including a car, attendance at important international conferences, and assumptions about the most modern way of dealing with delinquents likely challenged judges who preferred an older model of female subordinate. Because the JAD's annual reports throughout the 1930s commended highly the cooperation of Judge Robillard with their worker, it was likely Paul Monty, clerk and deputy judge who was especially hostile to her. Esther Levitt continued to work for the FJP in the Child Welfare Bureau until early 1945 when she quit, blaming the incompetence and lack of goodwill demonstrated by the male executive of the board. '[A]s a professional woman,' Levitt wrote, her conscience forbade her from accepting community money for compromised work.[199]

Conclusion

In 1912 the opening of the MJDC signalled the beginning of the second phase of juvenile justice in Quebec. Choquet and his team of child savers embarked on a mission to spare delinquent children the 'awfulness' of the criminal justice system. In this 'home of mercy' the court workers claimed to embrace an ethic of care over retribution. Significant changes were realized in the court: youth awaiting trial were held in the detention home, not the common jail; probation officers investigated the private lives of the delinquent; most youths were sent home under the watchful eye of the probation officer. As well, unlike other areas of legal practice, women were able to secure a fundamental role in this new juvenile justice system.

In the first decade of the twentieth century Montrealers fostered the notion that public child saving was women's prerogative. Clubwomen endorsed a children's bill – later to be called the Juvenile Delinquents Act – and a new Children's Aid Society was formed. Progressive female reformers united across linguistic and religious divides to promote a new court for the city, and in acceding to the right of the fatherly François-Xavier Choquet to establish this new child-saving station, celebrated the female presence in the court. Rose Henderson and Maria Clément vetted female cases for Choquet, carefully separating Catholics from non-Catholics. They professed that mother-love and maternal knowledge guided their work; cases from the court demonstrated this often turned into mother blaming rather than an opportunity for gender solidarity. Their understanding of the 'problem' of delinquent girls and the influence of standardization through forms meant girls were treated similarly. Both women overwhelmingly approved the gendered system of incarceration and the need to remove girls from families in favour of surrogate mothering at the hands of the Soeurs du Bon Pasteur and the lay Protestant administration at the Girls' Cottage Industrial School. In the interwar period the court expanded and shifted toward a more professional model of juvenile justice. Female Jewish probation officers in the 1920s and 1930s rejected the earlier pattern of maternal investigation and chose instead to direct their cases away from the court and the incarceration facilities. Dorothy Sigler and Esther Levitt did not use the language of mother-love; rather, their work exemplifies how women's work at the court shifted toward professionalization beginning in the 1920s. It also demonstrates how cultural communities embraced antidelinquency work as part of their assertion of citizenship. Unlike the reform school where juvenile justice was part of the nation-building exercise for the established Catholic hierarchy, the MJDC, as centre of Quebec's juvenile justice system in the early-twentieth century, reflected and accommodated the city's three main ethnic and religious groups.

chapter 5

A Girl's Place: Family, the City, and Juvenile Court

For most juvenile court girls, adolescence was marked by the end of schooling and a series of low-paying jobs, resulting in an increase in independence from family and neighbourhood. The Montreal economy readily and indiscriminately absorbed the cheap labour of the young and female of Montreal-born and immigrant, francophone and anglophone, and Catholic, Protestant, and Jewish communities. Work sites, such as the city's tobacco and textile factories, facilitated a public meeting and mixing of young people from across ethnic, religious, and linguistic lines, unlike the parochial and often gendered school system. With their wages, these girls could be found in dance halls, moving-picture theatres, restaurants, and even brothels, stealing themselves away from traditional sources of surveillance. As we saw in chapter 3, adult anxieties over social and political change contributed to the definition of the modern girl and in critical ways helped to script how an adolescent girl might go bad.

This chapter focuses on the experience of female adolescence in the first half of the twentieth century to demonstrate how economic, cultural, and social contexts configured specific bad behaviour. The experience of adolescence and the breakdown of parental authority over adolescents were constitutive of broad urban transformations. Traditional family ties that normally bound adolescent girls to a specific place in the household strained under the impact of rapid change in adolescent girls' lives. Parents and guardians reacted with a range of emotions to daughters' growing demands for autonomy and turned to the juvenile court to bolster their waning authority. This explains why few of Montreal's delinquent girls were charged with contraventions of the Criminal Code; rather, they committed 'offenses against their parents' – swearing, breaking curfew, disobedience, and running away. In their depositions to the juvenile court, parents described daughters who refused to play their traditional, subordinate, feminine roles within the family. This rejection of their place in the family was often central to girls' cases in the court.

Suspended between freedom and dependence, delinquent girls were brought to court for attempting to renegotiate the terms of adolescence and their role in the family. Because Quebec did not have compulsory education until 1943, girls' cases rarely revolved around truancy and, unlike the delinquent girls of the post–Second World War era, these girls' teenage years were not shaped by high school but by familial duty to younger siblings and aging parents, by poorly remunerated waged work, and by new gathering places. Girls who earned their own wages participated in the lively downtown nighttime culture that included cafés, movies, joy riding, and milling about street corners. Unlike previous generations these girls gathered in groups seeking out new hangouts and acquaintances. This lifestyle, what one probation officer called 'the frivolous life,'[1] was a rejection of familial tradition and discipline and girls' low status in the family hierarchy. A number of facts about these thirteen to sixteen-year-old girls are striking: they were indisputably on the move in the city, reconfiguring city space on their own terms; they were savvy in the face of arduous situations at home and on the street; they shared in bearing the brunt of economic hardships and 'broken families'; and few of them were free of adult worries and situations.

Regardless of the particular activity that landed them in juvenile court, as a group, female delinquents were identified as agents of immorality and, given the combination of their age, gender, and unwillingness to surrender to filial discipline, they became a force to contend with. Their independence – personified by the working girl and cultural consumer – was read in sexual terms. As we will see in the next chapter, girls' sexuality came to predominate in many cases; yet, as experts in adolescent behaviour, juvenile court authorities endeavoured to identify the underlying conditions that contributed to the making of the female delinquent. Probation officers' investigations led them into the homes and lives of adolescent girls and revealed the particular constellation of factors that produced female delinquency.

This chapter begins with an examination of girls' delinquencies as presented in official statistics and in the dossiers from the juvenile court. It then shifts the focus back to the family home where adolescent girls' disagreements with parents about their wages, curfews, choice of romantic partners and friends, and their desire to frequent the cinema, dance halls, and restaurants precipitated court intervention. An important emphasis here is the rebellious actions girls resorted to when in conflict with family members, especially talking back, swearing, and establishing an allegiance to peer groups over the family. Often they employed the ultimate weapon of defence against familial obligations and court reprimand: running away. A host of push-and-pull factors are explored to explain why Montreal girls so often chose to reject their identity of daughter and their place within the family. Ultimately, the juvenile court records are filled with cases of girls who were disciplined for contesting their place in the family as daughters and workers, and on the streets of Montreal as consumers of commercial leisure.

Girls' Offences

Under the Juvenile Delinquents Act (JDA) and the provincial acts concerning juvenile delinquency, each year from the 1910s to the1940s, the Montreal Juvenile Delinquents' Court (MJDC) processed between 1000 and 4000 young people for infractions of the Criminal Code and/or delinquency offences and as protection cases (see table 5.1). Girls represented a solid minority of these cases, comprising annually between 10 and 20 per cent of cases. In the first decade, the number of girls appearing in court ranged from over 100 to more than 300 annually. Through the interwar period and the Second World War, the number of girls appearing before the court swung from a low of 127 (1923) to a high of 533 (1941). While the court processed both delinquency and dependency cases, the numbers of girls brought to court for delinquency dramatically overshadowed the protection cases of 'neglect' and 'abandonment,' and at times the two were treated interchangeably.

The majority of girls appearing in juvenile court were Catholic and born in Canada.[2] Roman Catholics accounted for between 85 and 90 per cent of delinquent girls; Protestants for approximately 10 per cent; Jews for less than 10 per cent; and Greek and Russian Orthodox for approximately 1 per cent.[3] In 1918, 76 per cent of girls were French Canadian, Catholic, and born in the province of Quebec. Canadian-born Protestants represented 6 per cent, Irish Catholics 2 per cent, and Canadian-born Jews 1 per cent. Seven percent were Catholics of British origin. Recent immigrants from outside Britain accounted for another 7 per cent: Italian Catholics, 3 per cent; Russian and Austrian Jews, 2 per cent; Belgian, Russian, Portugese and Lithuanian Catholics, 2 per cent. Delinquents in general were born in Canada, although many had 'foreign-

Table 5.1 Juvenile Court appearances by sex, Montreal Juvenile Delinquents'
Court, 1914–1945

Year	Girls	Boys	Total	Girls as % of total
1914	124	945	1069	11.5
1915	131	877	1008	13
1916	144	861	1005	14.3
1917	205	1043	1248	16.4
1918	263	1193	1456	18.1
1919	329	1397	1726	19.1
1920	294	1398	1692	17.4
1921	232	1265	1497	15.5
1922	156	1033	1189	13.1
1923	127	1299	1426	8.9
1924	254	1474	1728	14.5
1925	240	1516	1756	13.7
1926	155	1204	1359	11.4
1927	243	1368	1611	15.1
1928	176	1191	1367	12.9
1929	171	1170	1341	12.8
1930	153	1318	1471	10.4
1931	209	1473	1682	12.4
1932	241	1672	1913	12.6
1933	300	1853	2153	13.9
1934	472	1976	2448	19.3
1935	417	2105	2522	16.5
1936	286	1965	2251	12.7
1937	419	2321	2740	15.3
1938	388	2175	2563	15.1
1939	464	2408	2521	14.5
1940	484	2387	2871	17
1941	533	2647	3180	16.8
1942	480	2964	3444	14
1943	423	2210	2633	16
1944	323	1674	1997	16
1945	342	1560	1903	18

Sources: For 1914: Labour Gazette (March 1915), 1057. For 1915–21, 1925,
1934–5, 1937 annual reports of the Montreal Juvenile Delinquents' Court
(ANQ-Q, Attorney-General's Correspondence files or as reported in the
press). For 1922–4, 1926–33, 1936, 1938–45, Canada, Dominion Bureau of
Statistics, Juvenile Delinquents (for years ending 30 September).

Table 5.2 Religious and ethnic background of girls whose
cases came before the Montreal Juvenile Delinquents' Court,
1924

Religion	
Roman Catholic	84.6
Protestant	11.5
Jewish	2.6
Unknown	1.3
Nationality/Ethnic Origins of Girls' Families	
French Canadian	68.5
Canadian	10.0
English	3.4
Scottish	2.6
Irish	2.6
Italian	2.2
Polish	2.2
Russian	0.8
American	0.8
French	0.4
Roumanian	0.4
Lithuanian	0.4
unknown	5.6

Source: MJDC, dossiers, 1924

born' parents. In 1924, reports of girls' religion, nationality, and/or ethnicity suggest that the majority before the court were French-Canadian Catholics (see table 5.2).

Even with the strong showing of Quebec daughters in the court a strong a correlation between delinquent conduct and immigrant areas of Montreal was assumed. In Herman Ross's study of the juvenile court's work in 1929, he carefully plotted a 'delinquency crescent' on a map of Montreal, highlighting the neighbourhoods whence the delinquents came. His crescent began in Point St Charles (a traditional English, Scottish, and Irish immigrant area), and continued through St Henri before it arced north toward the Plateau Mont Royal (home of Jewish and Italian immigrants) and Rosemont. Strictly speaking, none of these areas were exclusive to first-generation Montrealers, but what they do share is low-income housing, factories and shops, and a transient population. Wealthier francophone and anglophone districts like Outremont and Westmount were conspicuously absent.

Table 5.3 Girls' offences, Montreal Juvenile Delinquents' Court, 1912, 1918, 1924

Charge per year	1912 no. (%)	1918 no. (%)	1924 no. (%)
Theft	15 (21)	31 (17)	24 (11)
Vagrancy	48 (69)	43 (24)	18 (8)
Incorrigibility	–	46 (25.5)	34 (15)
Desertion	–	43 (24)	109 (48)
Immorality	–	3 (1.5)	29 (13)
Other*	7 (10)	14 (8)	13 (6)
Total	70 (100)	180 (100)	227 (101**)

*Other charges include: 1912: selling newspapers without a licence (2); indecent act (1); disturbing the peace (1); forgery (1); begging (1); assault (1). 1918: indecent act (7); assault (2); disturbing the peace (3); loitering (1); housebreaking (1). 1924: found in a disorderly house (2); neglected and delinquent (2); pregnant (1); indecent conduct (2); false alarm (1); assault (1); trespassing (1); throwing stones (1); disobedience (1); not indicated (1).
**Percentages rounded to nearest .5 or rounded up.
Source: Female delinquency cases heard before the Montreal Juvenile Delinquents' Court, 1912, 1918, 1924. ANQ-M, Fonds Cour des jeunes délinquants de Montréal, dossiers for each year.

Beyond sex, social class united the juvenile court girls. Dossiers from the court reveal that families with delinquent children were not only working class but experienced acute economic uncertainty and poverty. Although one could argue that the court was class-conscious – delinquents were rarely from middle-class or elite families – class was not recorded in a systematic way. From the dossiers they left, probation officers tell us about the impoverishment of families due to death, illness, or the absence of a parent. Class is also evident in the high priority given to wages an adolescent daughter could contribute to the family and the low priority given to educating daughters: working-class girls who came to court generally had little schooling, although most could read and write. Illiteracy did predominate in as much as 24 per cent of female cases (1919), but typically the proportion was less than one-fifth of all delinquents.

Girls' charges collapsed around a limited number of offences, as demonstrated by an examination of all-female delinquency cases that came before the Montreal juvenile court in 1912, 1918, and 1924 (see table 5.3). In 1912, girls were overwhelmingly charged with vagrancy (48 of 70 girls, or 69 per cent). The typical juvenile offences of incorrigibility and desertion do not appear to have been used in the juvenile court's inaugural year. By 1918 incorrigibility and desertion competed with vagrancy for the top offence among girls; each accounting for approximately one-quarter of girls' delinquent offences. Vagrancy continued to decline in importance in 1924, sliding to 8 per cent of girls' cases. Much more prominent in 1924 was desertion, accounting for 109 of 227 cases, or 48 per cent. Incorrigibility as a girl's primary offence also diminished in 1924 – to 15 per cent – while immorality cases began to rise, to 13 per cent or 29 cases. Indecent conduct comprised a small but statistically important portion of girls' offences over these decades. Throughout the period 1912 to 1945, theft was a constant offence on the list of delinquencies committed by girls, as they were brought in for stealing from parents, department stores, employers, and strangers.

Incorrigibility as an offence or description of delinquent girl behaviour held tenaciously during these decades. This catch-all label was used by court clerks, probation officers and judges to sum up a variety of circumstances and actions. Approximately one-quarter of female delinquents were charged with the status offence 'incorrigibility' toward the end of the 1910s. During the 1920s the incorrigibility declined, likely subsumed under another offence. Many of the girls' cases indicated multiple or hyphenated offences that included incorrigibility, although it was not the stated primary offence. In the Depression years, the incidence of incorrigibility among girls rose to more than two-thirds of girls' cases; during the Second World War, it comprised approximately 60 per cent of female delinquency cases. Official statistics from 1930, 1935, 1940, and 1945 indicate incorrigibility remained the most common reason for a girl's appearance in juvenile court; vagrancy remained under 10 per cent, and desertion also fell from nearly one-quarter to less than 10 per cent over these years (see table 5.4).

Incorrigibility complaints largely came from parents or guardians who witnessed adolescent daughters breaking rules at home. Family members offered comprehensive summaries of daughters' subversions of family rules and expectations. Incorrigibility comprised a litany of minor complaints: the delinquent daughter didn't listen, lied, swore – Christ! *Maudite chienne* (bitch)! – and was rude and disrespectful. Alone, these grievances were rarely the central cause of the parental complaint; they were frequently accompanied by a failure on the girls' part to keep her job, or proper hours, or to come home at all, as we will see.

Incorrigible girls were often 'deserting' daughters. Girls who deserted their family homes quickly became a major preoccupation of the Mont-

Table 5.4 Offences committed by Quebec girls by year, 1930–1945

Offences	1930 no. (%)	1935 no. (%)	1940 no. (%)	1945 no. (%)
Minor offences				
Incorrigibility	57 (50)	125 (70.6)	290 (63.6)	216 (59)
Desertion	26 (23)	9 (5.1)	14 (3.1)	52 (6.3)
Vagrancy	7 (6)	15 (8.5)	14 (3.1)	23 (6.3)
Indecent conduct	13 (11)	13 (7.3)	82 (18)	50 (13.6)
Disturbing/peace	2 (1.8)	8 (4.5)	43 (9.4)	1 (0.3)
Begging	2 (1.8)	7 (4)		
Breach of municipal by laws	2 (1.8)		3 (0.7)	13 (3.5)
Infraction of school act				10 (2.7)
Drunkenness				1 (0.3)
Disorderly conduct			8 (1.8)	1 (0.3)
Trespassing			1 (0.2)	
Disobedience			1 (0.2)	
Loitering	4 (3.5)			
Indecent language	1 (0.9)			
Unsatisfactory on probation				1 (0.3)
Minor offences, total	114	177	456	368
Major offences				
Aggravated assault		4 (5.4)		1 (2.9)
Common assault	6 (15)	3 (4.1)	3 (6.1)	4 (11.8)
Theft	30 (75)	62 (83.8)	31 (63.3)	15 (44.1)
Breaking and entering	1 (2.5)	3 (4.1)		
Theft (other)	1 (2.5)	1 (1.4)		2 (5.9)
Damage to property		1 (1.4)	5 (10.2)	5 (14.7)
Immorality	2 (5)		8 (16.3)	1 (2.9)
Burglary				3 (8.8)
False pretenses				1 (2.9)
Forgery				1 (2.9)
Escape custody				2 (4.1)
Abduction				1 (2.9)
Major offences, total	40	74	49	34

Source: Dominion Bureau of Statistics, *Juvenile Delinquents*. Annual statistics for years ending September 30.

real juvenile court. By 1918, 25 per cent of female delinquents came before the court for desertion. By 1924 more than half of female court cases centred on formal complaints of desertion. Montreal Police Department arrest statistics confirm the centrality of desertion in police work with girls: in the 1920s between one-third and one-half of girls or

Table 5.5 Girls' offences, Montreal Juvenile Delinquents' Court, 1930s and 1940s

Charge per year	1930s no. (%)	1940s no. (%)
Incorrigibility	117 (49)	89 (45)
Desertion	26 (11)	22 (11)
Theft	26 (11)	10 (5)
Loitering at night	13 (5.5)	7 (4)
Disturbing the peace	19 (8)	7 (4)
Immorality	6 (2.5)	40 (20)
Assault	9 (4)	2 (1)
Vagrancy	5 (2)	2 (1)
Other*	18 (7.5)	17 (9)
Total	239 (100.5)	196 (100)

*Other charges include: 1930s: found in a disorderly house (3); neglect (2); not indicated (3); city by-law infraction (1); damage to property (2); drunkenness (1); begging without a license (3); false alarm (1); playing ball on the street (1); and attempted suicide (1). 1940s: neglect (4); protection (6); damage to property (5); attempted arson (1); forgery (1).
Source: Female delinquency cases heard before the Montreal Juvenile Delinquents' Court, based on a two-month sample in each of the following years: 1930, 1932, 1934, 1936, 1938, 1940, 1942, 1944. ANQ-M, Fonds, Cour des jeunes délinquants de Montréal, dossiers.

'*fillettes*' arrested had '*désert[é] ses parents*' (deserted the homes of their parents).[4] Considered a far more serious offence when committed by a girl than a boy, female desertion was policed vigorously. For example, in the peak year for girls' desertions, 1924, 102 girls were arrested for deserting compared to 61 boys. However, the overall ratio of girls to boys arrested that year was 192 to 834.[5] From a sample of girls' cases covering the 1930s and 1940s the number of desertion offences seen by the police and in the juvenile court declined, although the issue of a girl's absence from home was dealt with regularly through the elastic offence of incorrigibility (see table 5.5). In fact, throughout the entire period, girls' incorrigibility involved some form of desertion.

An examination of the description of the offences over time shows some interchangeability between incorrigibility, desertion, and even vagrancy. The flexible definition of juvenile offences was ensured by the JDA's imprecision and based on interpretation by local personnel. The records from the MJDC do not indicate who assigned the offence to each girl's case. Likely it was the probation officer assigned to the case or the court clerk who filled out the 'Information and Complaint' form. Vagrancy, unlike incorrigibility and desertion, predated the juvenile justice system and had a specific definition in the Canadian Criminal Code. Traditionally an anti-'tramp' law, vagrancy was used against women mainly to target prostitution, those who lived 'without visible means of subsistence,' and who disrupted public order, especially at night. 'Vagrant' girls who came before the juvenile court had 'refused to work and kept late hours and bad company,' 'slept away from home,' or were 'living on the streets,' found 'wandering by night' or 'in a house of prostitution.'[6] Others were accused of running away, fooling around with boys on park benches at night, and even being found on board a ship in the company of sailors.[7] A vagrancy charge was also used against teenage girls whose parents ran, or were implicated in, disreputable establishments. The juvenile court could have made these cases ones of child endangerment but chose instead to make them delinquents: in 1918, for example, Blanche was arrested for vagrancy when her mother was apprehended in a disorderly house; another two sisters were charged with the same offence that year when their father was arrested for selling liquor without a licence and keeping a disorderly house. In 1924 a girl was charged with both being abandoned and vagrancy because her mother kept a house of prostitution.[8]

At times, girls' behaviour defied easy categorization. In 1924 one girl was charged with 'vagrancy-theft-desertion' and eventually spent three years in the Soeurs du Bon Pasteur reform school. The police officer who arrested and brought her to the juvenile court did so on suspicion she had committed theft. The probation officer's further investigation found that she had had sexual relations with a 'black man' who had paid her ten dollars and from whom she had stolen a bag. Her family stated to the probation officer that she had regularly deserted her home, leading to the additional desertion charge. Further it was noted by the probation officer that she held no job and 'didn't do much.'[9] The vagrancy charge could indicate suspicion that she was a prostitute, that she was idle, or both.

While it is true that some girls were arraigned for prostitution-related offences, for example 16 (or 12 per cent of female cases) in 1915,[10] only a minority of girls' cases were designated major offences, including those involving prostitution, as table 5.4 indicates. The vast majority of girls who came to juvenile court were not prostitutes but many were suspected of sexual promiscuity. Parents were able to discipline sexually delinquent daughters by calling them 'incorrigible' or accusing them of desertion. Thus, generally it was not their numbers that made female delinquency an urgent problem but rather the nature of their offences caused their presence in the juvenile justice system to be of great concern. Like social reformers, parents and court officials recorded evidence of adolescent girls' sexual delinquencies. Parents brought daughters to court with complaints of their incorrigibility and unmanageability and many revealed their adolescents' irrepressible sexuality. The range of behaviour parents included in their descriptions of sexual delinquency included dating (or choosing an inappropriate boyfriend), sleeping out overnight, and even claims or fears of prostitution. Repeatedly throughout the first decade of the court, the clerk's annual reports pointed to the alarming growth in delinquent girls who were 'leading immoral lives.'[11]

Processing Female 'Delinquents'

There were several paths to juvenile court. Continuing a tradition from prior to the juvenile court's opening, the municipal police force acted as the front line in criminal justice enforcement and agents of a rudimentary welfare system.[12] A perennial function of the Montreal force was to deal with 'lost' children, in fact, more than two thousand such cases per annum in the early 1930s. The police also arrested girls for public order offences (indecency, drunkenness, vagrancy, theft), offences under the JDA (desertion, incorrigibility), and breaches of municipal regulations (soliciting without a licence, curfew).[13] Working with the MJDC, the police brought young people to the detention house and the juvenile court, swearing out complaints against juvenile thieves, vagrants, and those who had deserted their homes.

Several officers specifically handled requests from the juvenile court and dealt with minors who were arrested. More boys than girls were subject to police intervention, although a substantial minority of girls' cases were always brought to the court's attention by the police. In 1912 police signed the complaint in 30 per cent of girls' cases, likely related to the high rate of vagrancy charges that year. Over the course of the 1910s and 1920s this began to decline proportionally, to 23 per cent in 1918 and 19.5 per cent in 1924. From a sample of cases in the 1930s and 1940s police initiated less than 20 per cent of girls' cases. Complaints lodged by parents to the court about runaways, however, were followed up by the police, suggesting a more complex involvement of the police than these statistics demonstrate. The Montreal police service assigned several officers to deal with juveniles and the MJDC. These officers reported work with lost and abandoned children, runaways, vagrants, and thieves. Girls arrested by Montreal constables had committed infractions against public order, usually being found on the streets or in public places at night. The annual reports of the Montreal police indicated a broad definition of 'child,' an age category that was left flexible and unspecific.

Police work with children and adolescents intensified in the late 1930s with the introduction of the Juvenile Morality Squad. An increasingly important part of police work, this squad began as an assemblage of a few officers and grew to over thirty in 1946. The main aims of these officers were to bring adolescents to juvenile court for morals offences and to investigate juvenile hangouts, such as restaurants and movie theaters. During the 1940s the police brought in to court or local police stations thousands of children who had broken the municipal by-laws on curfew.[14]

Private citizens could also bring forth complaints to the juvenile court. Parents and relatives of the girl in question were the most numerous of these. The strong association of female delinquency with incorrigibility and desertion correlates to the role of parents in bringing their daughters to juvenile court. As I have argued elsewhere, parents volunteered their children for correction at the juvenile court.[15] Familial complaints accounted for a substantial proportion of female cases that came before the court. In 1912, 59 per cent of cases were the result of complaints lodged by the girls' relatives or guardians (see table 5.6). In 1918, 58 per cent of the 180 cases of female delinquency were introduced by complainants related to the offender. This high rate of parental complaint was specific to girls: according to a 10 per cent sample of boys brought to court in 1918, 28 per cent were there because of relatives and guardians.[16] In 1924, 68 per cent of complaints against girls were lodged by relatives or guardians, the majority of those by mothers and fathers (55 per cent of the total).[17] From a sample of cases from the 1930s, relative-initiated complaints diminished somewhat while remaining at a solid 40 per cent.[18] During the early 1940s a sample demonstrates that familial complaints accounted for 43 per cent of cases[19] (see table 5.7).

Common female juvenile offences, incorrigibility and desertion, were based in domestic relationships beyond the usual policed public domain and therefore contingent on family members or guardians to bring them

Table 5.6 Persons responsible for bringing complaints against girls, Montreal Juvenile Delinquents' Court, 1912, 1918, 1924

Person	1912 no. (%)	1918 no. (%)	1924 no. (%)
Relative or guardian	41 (59)	105 (58)	155 (68)
Police	21 (30)	41 (23)	44 (19.5)
Third party	4 (6)	31 (17)	18 (8)
Not indicated	4 (6)	3 (2)	10 (4.5)
Total	70 (101)	180 (100)	227 (100)

Source: Female delinquency cases heard before the Montreal Juvenile Delinquents' Court, 1912, 1918, 1924. ANQ-M, Fonds, Cour des jeunes délinquants de Montréal, dossiers for each year.

Table 5.7 Persons responsible for girls' appearance at the Montreal Juvenile Delinquents' Court, 1930s and 1940s

Person	1930s* no. (%)	1940s** no. (%)
Relative or guardian	95 (40)	85 (43)
Police	42 (17.5)	29 (15)
Third Party	66 (28)	35 (18)
Probation Officer	18 (7.5)	46 (23.5)
Not Indicated	15 (6)	1 (0.5)
Other*	3 (1.5)	–
Total	227 (100.5)	196 (100)

*Other includes truancy officer for the Catholic School Board.
Source: Female delinquency cases heard before the Montreal Juvenile Delinquents' Court, based on a two-month sample for each of 1930, 1932, 1934, 1936, 1938, 1940, 1942, 1944, ANQ-M, Fonds, Cour des jeunes délinquants de Montréal, dossiers for each year.

to the court's attention. In cases where girls were flouting convention and rejecting curfews, if they were caught on the streets at night they might be arrested for deserting their homes, but usually it was parents who filed complaints against their daughters. Parents therefore assumed a policing role for the courts, initiating a process in which they would also stand as key witnesses and offer recommendations as to appropriate punishment.

Other adults swore complaints against adolescents, including parents or guardians of children who were perceived to be victimized by the accused. Organizations that held 'pre-delinquent' girls, such as the nonsectarian Protestant Summerhill House or the Soeurs du Bon Pasteur's Maison Ste. Domitille brought forth girls who deserted, were acting out, or uncontrollable. Complaints of agencies such as the Society for the Protection of Women and Children grew in the interwar period. Beyond agencies that dealt with problem families and girls, another group can be identified as instrumental in bringing complaints against girls: security guards. Security guards at department stores where girls shoplifted were responsible for commencing the legal process against them.

Once a girl was brought to court a probation officer was assigned to her case. Probation officers' standardized forms required the worker to generate information on the girl, from the general to the specific. Noted from the earliest of forms were her parents, their nationality and occupations, and the moral and physical conditions of her home. These forms became increasingly more detailed over time and more oriented toward the character and personality of the girl and her family. If the information to be collected took time, the girl would be remanded to the detention house or the Soeurs du Bon Pasteur reform school. From the juvenile court's early days, the overwhelming majority of girls were sent to see a doctor to verify the state of their hymens. This involved a session with a physician either at the Soeurs du Bon Pasteur convent or at the detention house. Brief remarks from the doctor were integrated into the girl's case file. For the court appearance, the girl was brought before the judge with the probation officer and the relevant witnesses and her guardian. The judge then discussed the case and rendered his decision.

The 1938 case of Anne-Marie B. demonstrates the process of juvenile justice experienced by girls under the JDA and through the MJDC. On 16 June 1938 Anne-Marie's father filled out a 'Information and Complaint' form at the juvenile court, stating that for about six months this fourteen year old was 'incorrigible, uncontrollable, habitually disobeying all [his] legitimate and reasonable orders, running in the streets during the day and part of the night, refusing to go to school, and deserting his home without cause or reason.'[20] That same day Madame P. Aubertin, a Catholic probation officer, took extensive notes on her and her family, mostly notably about her absent mother whose address was unknown. Aubertin's report details where the family had lived over the course of Anne-Marie's life, the family history of poverty and welfare, and perhaps most importantly, both her and the father's side of the story. In front of Judge Robillard Anne-Marie pleaded guilty; her court date was fixed for 27 June and she was sent to the detention house attached to the juvenile court. The case was delayed one week for reasons not specified and she remained in detention until 4 July. On that day she was declared a juvenile delinquent and made a ward of the court until she turned twenty-one years of age. She was given a suspended sentence under the following conditions: listen and respect her father; go to school; stay at home in the evenings and never go out during the day without her father's permission and specifically stay away from restaurants; and report to probation officer Mrs Aubertin every Monday.

Within one week the court issued a new citation at the request of her father who claimed she was in violation of the conditions of her suspended sentence for having deserted his home. The same day the new citation was ordered she was sent to detention where the court doctor performed a medical exam. The doctor's report comprised two main categories – general exam and local exam – and 'remarks.' Under general exam, the doctor gave checkmarks for 'mental' and 'physical'; under the more detailed local exam, the doctor checked off eyes, nose, ears, mouth, throat, and endocrine glands as well as most of the large body systems. In his general remarks he noted that she was 'deflowered.' The next day, Judge Robillard sentenced her to three years at the Soeurs du Bon Pasteur's reform school, the Maison de Lorette, but gave her one last chance: internment would begin only on the day she again failed to uphold the conditions of her suspended sentence.

On 16 September a new citation was ordered by probation officer Aubertin for desertion. Again she was sent to the court doctor who noted her last menstrual cycle, that she was 'deflowered,' though he found no sign of leucorrhea nor, according to the Neisser test, of gonorrhea. He also remarked that Anne-Marie admitted to having sexual intercourse once, several months earlier. That same day, in front of Judge Paul Monty, she pleaded guilty. On 26 September she was again before Judge Robillard who made good on his threat to incarcerate her for three years.

One and a half years later Anne-Marie was brought to court by the head administrator of the Maison de Lorette for staging a riot at the girls' reform school. Robillard held an investigation into the episode on 18 April 1940 with the implicated girls present. Anne-Marie's father's presence was also requested. According to the nun deposed, Anne-Marie led seven girls in a violent attempt at escape. The police were called in to reestablish order and the girls were brought back to juvenile court. In a written report, the mother superior of the Maison de Lorette expressed a desire to avoid taking any of these girls back to this institution. The judge then had to decide what to do with Anne-Marie and her accomplices. Robillard decided to send her to another convent operated by the Soeurs du Bon Pasteur. Apparently the riot girls' goal had been a transfer to the women's jail (a Bon Pasteur institution), where sentences were two years less a day, but Robillard might have thought it unadvisable to send girls to mix with a criminal adult population. He chose instead Maison Ste-Hélène, for the duration of two years.

Shortly after her new sentence of two years was announced, Anne-Marie was transferred to the detention house and appeared before Judge Robillard at the request of her paternal aunt. On 6 May 1940, Anne-Marie, her aunt, and two sisters appeared before the judge with an ambition to allow her to return home to her family. Robillard was convinced by the sisters' strong affection for Anne-Marie and her promises of exemplary behaviour, and sent her home under conditions similar to those he set out in 1938, with the added corollary not to see any girls whom she met at Maison de Lorette. This arrangement lasted the summer. In September 1940 her aunt brought yet another complaint against her for disobedience. In the weeks that followed, the probation officer located her mother, and on 8 October 1940 Anne-Marie boarded a train for Ontario to begin a new life with her mother. Her juvenile justice record ends there, at the age of seventeen.

Anne-Marie's case demonstrates juvenile justice was both lenient and coercive, that it depended on family members' determination to use the court to correct and discipline girls, and that it could be a multiyear experience. It also demonstrates that girls' cases could be complex, involving a variety of behaviour that was considered contrary to normative femininity. The medical investigations of Anne-Marie focused on her body, not her stage of mental development, which was typical in this Montreal court well into the 1940s. And, while Judge Robillard favoured probation and the family home as the site of rehabilitation, he was still willing to use long sentences at reform school to effect treatment. When an adult female presented herself as able to care for Anne-Marie, as in the case of her aunt and eventually her mother, the court agreed to avoid further incarceration.

Delinquent Days

Girls were brought to court by their parents and guardians because of tensions concerning their domestic duties or working lives beyond the home. In 1926 fifteen-year-old Juliette H. was brought to court by her mother for incorrigibility.[21] As in other cases involving female delinquency, when she was asked about her loss of virginity, she told the story of how, when she was twelve, her brother had seduced her. On the basis of these facts alone the court would see her as a sex delinquent, yet the case had little to do with her sexual experience. Parents' motivations were complex and cannot be reduced to the need to control precocious sexuality, as the case of Juliette suggests. Juliette's difficult behaviour was brought to the court's attention in the wake of her father's death. His death left the family of eight children in desperate circumstances: the responsibility of supporting the family fell to the oldest son, while three younger boys were sent to institutions. The girls, including Juliette, were kept at home because of their age and value as domestic workers. According to her mother, Juliette had already become an exasperating adolescent prior to her father's death, never listening, refusing to help at home or keep a steady job. When she did work she changed jobs frequently. Now that her father was dead, leaving a pregnant widow, Juliette's cooperation at home and her potential earnings took on even greater importance. Juliette's mother wanted the court to help reassert her authority in the home over this adolescent who was prone to acts of violence and directing such epithets as '*maudite chienne*' at her mother. Mostly she wanted Juliette to bring home her earnings and help her sisters with household chores. Juliette's case points to the importance of identifying the constellation of events and behaviours that resulted in the construction of her as a juvenile delinquent.

Parents engaged the court at critical transitions in a girl's life, such as the end of schooling. Where truancy appears to have been a major preoccupation of juvenile courts elsewhere in Canada,[22] it was not a central concern of Montreal parents or the juvenile tribunal. Probation officers often commented on the poor education of female delinquents but accepted the role of adolescent daughters in the working-class family economy. Conflict over that responsibility prompted family members to engage the court to correct a daughter's behaviour. When moments of familial stress – death, desertion, remarriage, acute poverty – coincided with a daughter reaching the age of twelve or thirteen, it meant the end of schooling and the beginning of more responsibility in the family. Although by the early-twentieth century the trend was toward girls staying in school longer, when exigent circumstances arose families pulled their daughters out of school.[23] This pattern is reflected in cases from the juvenile court. Limited schooling and a dependence on girls' labour in the home reflected the subordinate, yet critical, place of girls in Quebec's working-class families and appears to have transcended boundaries of ethnicity and religion. In 1930, the fourteen-year-old daughter of Russian Jewish parents, Goldie L., was brought to juvenile court for shoplifting. She had been very successful in school until her father's desertion forced her to seek paid work. In response to losing the family's breadwinner, Goldie's mother appealed to the Federation of Jewish Philanthropies for help and sent her daughter to work. According to her story, which her mother corroborated, the transition to paid work at Imperial Tobacco was at the root of her delinquent behaviour.[24] Now that her daughter had left school, Mrs L. lost control of her to an influential peer group. Similarly, Noella R., a French-Canadian teen, was permitted to leave school at thirteen after her mother died and her father remarried. She found work in service and gave the two-dollar weekly salary to her stepmother.[25] She was brought to court by her stepmother for disobedience just months after the death of her father. School leaving was also common following the death of a mother when it was deemed necessary for the adolescent daughter to take care of family members and the housework. It was not unusual for a probation officer's report to reveal that, for example, a fifteen or sixteen year old had been in charge of the home since she left school at thirteen following her mother's death.[26]

From the records of the MJDC, it appears that the parental prerogative of setting household tasks caused considerable friction, and disputes over duties could lead to court intervention. Typically, girls owed respect and obedience to their fathers and were obliged to aid their mothers in the home. In immigrant and Canadian working-class families teenage daughters were expected to make meals, clean house, care for dependent siblings and parents, and contribute to the family economy.[27] As Bettina Bradbury has contended for the latter part of the nineteenth century, decisions about family members' work represented 'a complex and often unconscious balance between basic need, existing ideology and practice regarding gender roles, the structure of the economy, and the particular economic conjuncture.'[28] Bradbury notes the tradition of older girls replacing or helping mothers at home-work such as sewing and supervision of young siblings and care of elderly or infirm family members. In mid- to late-nineteenth-century Montreal, adolescent daughters only worked outside the home if they were the oldest child in the family with no or very young brothers, or in the case of destitute families where all children were sent to work at about age fourteen.[29] In return for being part of this family order they received 'the necessities of life': food, shelter, clothing, and protection.

From the perspective of the court record, we see that the equilibrium of this paternalistic, patriarchal system sometimes broke down during adolescence. This was particularly true in cases where adolescent girls' role in the family suddenly changed as in the case of death or illness of their mothers. Eldest daughters frequently assumed the responsibilities of raising younger siblings and maintaining the household in the absence of mothers. Fleurette C., a seventeen-year-old French Canadian, appeared in court in the autumn of 1923 and was placed with the Soeurs du Bon Pasteur as a voluntary case. She was sent home in December to look after her siblings when her mother fell ill. For a month she coped with the demands of eight siblings, a working father, and an incapacitated mother, being 'good with the children and capable of doing the sewing and cooking.' She eventually ran away from these responsibilities, preferring to be paid for this work in a brothel rather than remain at home.[30]

Adolescent girls' identity became increasingly contradictory in the early twentieth century. They were meant to be domestic, subordinate, and dependent, yet the labour market and family financial needs led to a departure from this prescribed ideal, sparking intergenerational tension at home. Like Fleurette C.'s parents, many working-class families depended on daughters to maintain their roles within the confines of the family home, while others needed the wages they could contribute. The vast majority of juvenile court girls had at least some first-hand experience of wage earning. Montreal's labour market increasingly attracted adolescent girls; families knew it as did adolescent girls.

The issue of paid labour was key to female delinquency cases. Disagreements arose at home around where a girl worked, how she disposed of her wages, and oftentimes her failure to keep working. In fact many cases brought to court that appear to us as sex delinquency cases often contained an element of tension around employment. Because adolescents in Montreal were commonly expected to work for wages, those who rebuffed parental demands over this issue found little mercy in the court. Along with parents, probation officers defined well-behaved girls as those who worked consistently and brought home their wages. Both daughters and sons played a vital role in the working-class family economy, especially as they entered adolescence, and the juvenile court often disciplined those young people who reneged on their obligations. And while juvenile court officer Rose Henderson spoke out vehemently against child factory labour, calling it a 'social and race hindrance,' she did not suggest that fourteen and fifteen-year-old girls be spared factory work.[31]

Because girls' days were likely shaped by waged work, the MJDC carefully examined their work history, providing us with insight into the work experiences and patterns of adolescent girls. The most common waged job held by adolescent girls and the one deemed appropriate for their age, gender, and alleged need for supervision was domestic service. Being placed in a private home or going *en service* marked an adolescent girl's initiation into the labour market. Traditionally the largest employer of women, domestic service was mostly taken up by those in the most precarious economic situations: recent immigrants, young women from the Quebec countryside, and working-class adolescent girls when a family's economic circumstances demanded it. By the second decade of the twentieth century domestic service was rapidly declining as the most important female employer. In 1891 domestic service occupied 41 per cent of the female workforce in Canada, but by 1911 only 15 per cent of the Montreal's women workers were domestic servants. Yet it remained an important opportunity for girls entering the labour market.[32]

Domestic service jobs varied greatly, were readily available, and generally paid very little. In the 1910s delinquent girls who had been domestic servants claimed they earned between four dollars and twelve dollars per month or roughly one to three dollars per week.[33] The pay for adolescent domestics improved during the 1920s (between two and a half and six dollars per week) but this was reversed during the 1930s. Thirteen or fourteen-year-old girls typically earned about two dollars weekly during the Depression. Paltry wages did not mean the work was not arduous: probation officer Marie Mignault noted that for two dollars a week, one fourteen-year-old had a baby to care for and considerable housework including laundry and washing and waxing floors.[34]

Parents and court officials considered domestic service an effective way to maintain surveillance of working daughters. For example, in the summer of 1918, Elsie M., a fourteen-year-old Protestant girl from a working-class district of Montreal, became entangled in the web of the juvenile justice system having deserted her place of employment. Over the course of the investigation it was revealed that Elsie's mother, the wife of a man serving overseas, thought placing her as a domestic servant with a Westmount family would keep her off the streets.[35] While she was proved wrong in this case, many parents and probation officers sought out private home environments for adolescent girls where they could become domestic servants under the watchful eye of an employer. In this case, Elsie's mother then opted for placing her daughter at her own expense in reform school.

For the same reasons that women left domestic service – lack of privacy, poor wages, constant surveillance, and long hours – adolescent girls did too, only to return when there was little other choice. Shortages of domestic servants were noted early in the First World War; the Fédération nationale Saint-Jean-Baptiste's (FNSJB) employment bureau, l'Assistance par le Travail, found in February 1915 girls looking for work preferred a period of unemployment to domestic positions.[36] A year later a similar mention was made that 'young girls have given up good [domestic service] places, attracted by the pay offered in factories.'[37] During the Depression years, girls who came to court generally were out of work or were domestic servants. Expanded opportunities for work during the Second World War meant fewer girls claimed to have experience as domestics; generally they spent more time in factory, sales, and increasingly office work.

Since the latter part of the nineteenth century, the Montreal economy had depended on and benefited from the cheap, unskilled labour of adolescent girls. Factory work pulled adolescent girls away from domestic service into a gendered labour market, providing them with more freedom, better wages, and opportunity to develop workplace relationships with peers. During periods of labour shortage or buoyant economic times, girls' job possibilities expanded yet these opportunities evaporated at the first sign of slowdown, forcing girls out of work or back to domestic service.

The growing numbers of girls and young women working outside the home prompted investigations into their experience. Reports to the 1913 Royal Commission on Industrial Training and Technical Education found that the garment, textile, and tobacco sectors absorbed large numbers of female workers and that minimum wage in most factories was two dollars per week.[38] The Montreal Child Welfare Exhibition held in October 1912 provided a sample of 260 working girls that revealed the following: 57 per cent (149) began working before their sixteenth birthdays; 64 per cent (165) left school before they were sixteenth; half began work to help support their families, while the rest worked to support themselves; 10 to 10.5 hour days was typical for textile industry jobs, 8 to 9 hour days for clothing factories.[39]

A trend of increased opportunity for young girls and women in the industrial sector developed in the 1910s, exacerbated by four years of war. Within the first month of war in late summer 1914, a 'temporary boom' was noted in industries that depended on women's work, especially textile, boot and shoe, tobacco, and clothing factories.[40] The demand for female labour in general persisted throughout the war though seasonal variations in employment were also evident. The *Labour Gazette* noted the increased demand for waitresses and laundresses.[41]

During the 1910s many juvenile court girls had worked at multiple jobs by the time they were fourteen, moving between domestic service and factory work, and earning between four and five dollars weekly. This meagre wage would not support a girl who lived without family: in the fall of 1914 the WCTU acknowledged the inadequacy of these wages by proposing a girls' home for 'young girls' earning five dollars per week or less.[42] The FNSJB acknowledged the low wages and precarious position of adolescent female workers by opening dormitories for those girls who could not afford their rent.[43] The Royal Commission on Industrial Training in 1913 suggested that boarding outside the family could not be done in Montreal for less than three or four dollars per week.[44]

In a positive labour environment girls tended to change jobs regularly, perhaps reflecting their precocious working age or an attempt to exercise some control in a market where low-paying unskilled jobs were not difficult to obtain. The 1918 case of Aline D., a fifteen-year-old French-Canadian girl, illustrates the adolescent girl's work pattern. After leaving school at eleven, she worked in a private home for a weekly wage of $1.50. This was followed by factory work: first, in a cotton factory where she made $9.25 every fifteen days, to another unspecified factory where she worked for two months making $4.50 weekly, then to a biscuit factory where she lasted only one week.[45] Another girl, Liliane R., left school at thirteen and went directly into factory work at a cotton manufactory where she made $5 weekly for one year; she left that job to take up a position at the Sweet Caporal Cigarette factory where she earned $4.50.[46] She had quit this job two weeks prior to her mother taking her to court for incorrigibility.

Age and the job market sometimes conspired to make adolescent girls unemployable. During the 1930s for example girls found their opportunities severely circumscribed, especially those who had little education or training. In 1939, Montreal's Big Sister Association (BSA), which took referrals from the juvenile court, reported that girls who 'left school at 12-13-14 years of age ... [were] wandering aimlessly about, dodging in and out of employment bureaux' and were in danger of never finding work.[47] For this youngest of the adolescent cohort, the BSA attempted to redirect them back to school. In their protective work with girls, operating an employment bureau meant dealing with the tendency among employable girls to 'drift' from domestic service (that the BSA had recommended) to factory and store jobs. The girls' wandering was not the only problem they confronted: 'petty stealing, late hours, [and] wearing employers' clothes' generated additional work for the BSA.[48]

While girls' motivations for leaving jobs are not clear what is evident is that this behaviour aggravated parents and the court. The court saw the failure to remain in one job as evidence of recalcitrance, and mental hygienists pathologized this behaviour labelling the girls 'occupational wanderers.'[49] The pattern of the fifteen-year-old adolescent girl having several jobs and bouts of unemployment causing conflict in the home persisted to the 1940s. In the 1940s girls found jobs for seven to thirteen dollars per week at cigar, cigarette, shoe, cookie, and cheese factories. Unlike their older siblings who had limited options during the 1930s Depression, these girls enjoyed a widening of employment options accompanied by better pay. Adolescent girls continued to be an important labour force during the war, especially in the service sector, often stepping into jobs vacated by women and boys. Restaurants, hotels, and department stores eagerly searched for girls to employ during the war. Dorothy L. claimed that in 1943 and 1944 she earned ten dollars a week plus food in her many restaurant jobs.[50] Office girls who rarely came before the juvenile court earlier now appeared claiming wages of fifteen dollars per week. Sixteen and seventeen-year-old girls were now also working in restaurants at ten dollars weekly plus tips and food.[51]

Throughout the Depression but even during the Second World War girls' wages were rarely sufficient for them to live independent of family. The wages were often considered (by employers and families) to be part of the family economy, not as girls' sole source of support. Even the two dollars many domestic servants earned each week was counted on, especially during the Depression when many families lived on municipal aid (Secours Direct). Probation officers' reports from this brutal decade indicate that some children weren't in school because they were inadequately dressed.[52] The balancing act conducted by families was subjected to a probation officer's scrutiny. In the case of Noella R., the teenager worked at a demanding domestic position during the Depression for two dollars per week, handed over her entire salary to her stepmother. The probation officer put a stop to this situation: not only was Noella removed from this job (because it was too much for a fourteen year old) but she was placed as a live-in domestic servant and was authorized by the court to keep her five-dollars monthly salary to care for herself.[53]

The meagre amounts of money girls could earn kept them dependent on families but their status as wage-earners permitted them some independence. Therefore it is not surprising to find that tension in the family revolved around girls leaving home for work. As women's historians have demonstrated, the decisions taken around which family members worked for wages depended on factors relating to the family life cycle as well as to negotiation and conflict; this intergenerational conflict was particularly heightened among immigrant families because of parents' anxiety over the teenagers' independence, especially once they had access to paid employment.[54] Yetta H., a Russian Jew, told her probation officer that she desired the 'freedom and independence' one obtained through earning a living. Her desertion was justified, she believed, because her parents prevented her from working. On running away, this sixteen year old secured a job first in a candy factory (which she lost because she worked too slowly), and then in a hotel washing dishes for five dollars per week plus her board.[55] It was in the hotel that she was arrested for deserting her family. The probation officer focused on Yetta's desertion as the problem, ignoring her parents' concerns about a young woman working outside the home: 'There is no reason why she should not be allowed to earn her own living provided she lives with her parents and obeys them.'[56]

Similarly, an Italian family that had come to Montreal just months before the outbreak of the First World War also resisted their daughter's aspirations to work outside the home. Sixteen-year-old Leontine deserted in 1918, she claimed, because she wanted to work in downtown Montreal and her father's house was simply too far. Like Yetta, she easily found employment and was soon caught.[57] In this case, the probation officer pointed to Leontine's respectable parents and sided with her mother who wanted her at home, not at the factory.

From the court's perspective, working-class families appeared to have prioritized daughters' work discipline and relinquishment of wages. This is highlighted in a 1924 case where fifteen-year-old Dorothy E. deserted. In her words, she failed to return home when she was unable to secure a job. Brought to court by her parents, Dorothy was eventually sent home on probation. She would return within six months, though, in an attempt to escape a hostile family environment. Her mother begged the court to place her in reform school to protect her from her father whose quick temper flared over his daughter's continuing failure to find work. For a combination of her own wilfulness (illustrated by her desertion) and a need to safeguard her, the court incarcerated Dorothy for two years.[58] Work discipline then was traded for incarceration.

Girls appearing in the MJDC before 1945 generally spent their days working at home or for wages. As Montreal's economy demanded more cheap, female labour, adolescent girls left domestic service and turned to the city's cigarette, food, and clothing factories. Eventually working-class adolescent girls would also find work in restaurants, shops, and offices. Working daughters must have been a relief to, and a curse for, the working-class family; intergenerational tension regarding home duties, wages, place of work, and rejection of work discipline transformed these young workers into juvenile court girls. The daytime trend toward waged work would directly affect girls' perception of what was possible at the end of the day, in their spare time.

Nighttime Delinquencies

When Herman Ross declared in his 1929 study of the MJDC that 'delinquency is largely a leisure time problem,' he might have understated the case.[59] A youth-oriented leisure industry had exploded in Montreal in the wake of the First World War. Even on the coldest nights, Montreal in the first half of the twentieth century hopped with venues sporting the latest in music and dance trends and vast numbers of moving-picture houses and restaurants. Adolescents pursuing American movies and jazz, French cinema and fashion, shed old-fashioned rules about modesty and propriety and forged a new urban youth culture. Comprising more than 50 per cent of Quebec's population, young people (under twenty-five) constituted a demographic and cultural force.[60] For adolescent girls, leisure or spare time was fairly restricted, limited to hours after the completion of work and chores in the latter part of the evenings and weekends, thus delinquency was also largely a nighttime problem. It's no wonder then, that parents and juvenile court girls provided volumes of detail about how adolescents spent their spare time away from family, the church, and the neighbourhood.

Although factory work did not provide sufficient wages to permit adolescents to live on their own, it did enable them to indulge in nightly activities at the growing commercial establishments that filled the city's downtown core. Trouble arose as parents tried to restrict girls from availing themselves of such attractions. The daughter who worked full time and contributed to the family economy often expected, in exchange, freedom for leisure pursuits and control over some of her wages to purchase life's necessities and even luxuries. Girls' presumption of some freedom associated with their new status as wage-earners punctuated juvenile court records. In the words of one probation officer: 'Now they are working, they feel they can do as they want.'[61] At the same time, girls' understanding of the city expanded dramatically as they travelled through both familiar and strange neighbourhoods to work, claiming larger parts of the city than their parents and the juvenile justice authorities thought appropriate.

The most common leisure pastime was attending the movies. Interestingly, this appears to have irked the court more than parents, who might well have indulged as well. Within six months of the court's opening 'frequents moving pictures' appeared on the probation officers' official form. It was a rare delinquent girl who did *not* admit to spending time at the cinema. From chapter 3 we know that the cinema was very popular with Montrealers and that dire consequences were predicted for girls who were lost to the prevailing Hollywood messages of romance, scandal, and new aesthetic standards, such as rouged lips and sex appeal. Girls skipped school to attend matinees, or went after work and on the weekends. And notwithstanding entrance restrictions on age and adult accompaniment, in the 1917 annual report for the juvenile court, clerk Owen Dawson claimed: 'Practically every child before the court admitted that there was little difficulty in entering the Picture halls unaccompanied.'[62]

While delinquent daughters who frequented the movies may have developed rich fantasy lives, girls who joined the dance craze were more worrisome. Dance hall girls often broke curfews as they took part in Montreal's thriving nightlife. Cafés, cabarets, and dance halls stayed open until dawn, with adolescent girls keeping pace.[63] All-night gyrations on the dance floor suggested girls were truly out of control. At one of the popular night spots in the 1910s and 1920s, St Catherine Street's Jardin de Danse, girls did the latest versions of the fox-trot and the waltz with young men.[64] 'She passionately loves to dance,' wrote one probation officer in 1912 of a girl later found in a brothel.[65] According to her mother, Irène C. left home one night in February 1918 to go dancing and did not return for three days.[66] Before engaging the court to rein in daughters, parents tried to wrest them from these hot spots. One mother stated her actress daughter had 'gone bad since she began frequenting the Palais de Danse.' Her pleas to the owners to refuse her daughter entry were met with laughter.[67] Another mother, in search of her daughter who had run away, found her on St Laurent en route to a dance hall.[68] Parents and probation officers found confirmation of their suspicions about dance hall culture from the girls themselves: one pregnant teen admitted in the mid-1920s that the police should put the Jardin de Danse under surveillance because alcohol flowed freely and young people appeared to be under the influence of drugs.[69]

The close association with loss of sexual control lay at the heart of the anxiety about the dance craze. Not only did the dance hall provide an unchaperoned free mixing of the sexes, but as American historian Anne Meis Knupfer writes, the new dances – 'contortions' of the waltz and two-step – were 'sexually suggestive and subversi[ve] of middle class refinement.'[70] Girls used melodramatic tropes to deflect their own sexual adventures at the dance hall: Marguerite C. claimed she was seduced at the exit of a salle de danse; Gertrude R. also claimed to have been seduced following a night of dancing.[71] As girls danced into the early-morning hours, they often could not, or would not go home. In cases from the 1920s, 1930s, and 1940s, girls as young as thirteen pursued Montreal night life and failed to return home.[72]

Music joints permitted the mixing of the sexes but they also abandoned traditional ethnic and religious organization of Montreal institutions and neighbourhoods. When parents spoke of 'bad' friends, it concerned adolescents often not from their neighbourhoods, parishes, churches, or synagogues. Young people, be they English or French Canadian, Catholic, Protestant, or Jewish, immigrants from Poland, Italy, or Britain, moved together on the dance floor rewriting the social boundaries that constructed their daily lives.

As dangerous as dance hall life appeared to families and court officials, the proliferation of restaurant culture further outlined girls' vulnerability and weakness. Girls increasingly worked in restaurants and frequented them in their spare time. Restaurants were places to meet friends but also befriend strangers. Irène J., for example, went suitcase in hand to a restaurant in the late summer of 1918 where she met a girl keen to find a place to rent and together they found a room.[73] In 1942, a fifteen-year-old pregnant girl infected with venereal disease was said to have worked in a restaurant 'where she learned to be bad.'[74] Parents and court workers found restaurants objectionable because they were often run by 'foreign' men. Greek and Chinese restaurants hired young working-class girls to work in these new hangouts for young people. Again girls' own tales of restaurant life helped to construct the restaurant as dangerous: several girls claimed that restauranteurs had attempted to seduce them.[75] One girl openly told of her experience at a Greek restaurant, claiming nothing untoward had occurred; the probation officer wrote in her report that she suspected this girl had been seduced by the Greek restauranteur.[76] In 1924 a Jewish girl, Freda S., was found working in a restaurant owned by a 'coloured' man, serving African Canadians.[77] In court, crossing such racial and ethnic boundaries became evidence of delinquency and was met with firm punishment, often incarceration.

By the 1940s frequenting restaurants became part of a larger package of bad adolescent girl behaviour. Girls now admitted overwhelmingly to smoking and drinking alcohol.[78] Two sisters brought to court in the winter of 1944 both worked at restaurants, admitted to regularly attending the cinema (the fourteen-year-old sister two or three times per week) and the older sister extended Saturday night dances to 6 a.m. Sunday.[79] Violette F., a fifteen-year-old French-Canadian adolescent confessed to going to restaurants and smoking and drinking wine three or four times a week with boys and girls her age.[80]

The need to control daughters' pursuit of dances and restaurants in their spare time was related to the concern over the potential for seduction and heterosexual adventure, but parents were also troubled by the larger issue of girls' demonstrated lack of responsibility in the home and the family. Girls exchanged family for peer-group socializing, especially with girlfriends. Parents complained that girls spent multiple evenings out with 'bad' friends, ate in restaurants rather than at the family table, prompted by the company and encouragement of girlfriends.

A constituent part of this female youth culture was the decline of 'modesty' and the emergence of a new beauty aesthetic. Mothers and daughters fought over adolescent girls' pursuit of glamour and their flagrant vanity; on report forms, probation officers specifically addressed the question of a girl's vanity beginning in the 1930s. Daughters' rejection of modest dress and pursuit of makeup and fashionable hairstyles signified their independence and pointed to their subscription to the 'cult of the body.'[81] For example, one girl ran away at the threat that her mother was going to cut her 'beautiful locks' of hair. Her mother complained to the court that the girl 'liked to have a good time' and was afraid that her vanity might lead her into temptation. Cutting her hair would have solved the problem of her vanity, literally cutting off the girl's visible, corporal sign of autonomy.[82] Similarly Lucy G. told her probation officer that she wanted glamour and excitement, and preferred to wear slinky black clothing rather than the simple clothes her mother bought for her.[83]

Girls got ideas about glamorous or luxurious lifestyles from American and French movies, and local women's magazines like *La Revue Moderne*. They sought out accroutrements for their lifestyle at the department stores in central Montreal or in the 5 and Dime cent stores common to most neighbourhoods. In large American cities social reformers warned that the department store whipped young women into a state of consuming desire where they would stop at nothing to satisfy their yearnings for glamour.[84] In Montreal, working class-girls frequented Dupuis Frères, Eaton's, Woolworth's, and Simpsons, poring over cosmetics, lingerie, and fashion accessories. When girls could not afford what they desired, they stole it. Girls shoplifted articles that would enhance their feminine appeal and match their nighttime adventures: silk bloomers and garters from Morgan's department store; powder and perfume from 5 and Dimes; jewellery, compacts and lipstick from Woolworth's; powder and silk dresses from Eaton's.[85] One girl stole a 'bright' scarf from a department store in 1926 which was said to represent 'a shortcut to the glamour which her undisciplined and unsatisfied youth demanded and which her lack of funds prohibited.'[86]

Conflict inevitably arose about adolescent girls' use of spare time and their participation in the city's new youth culture. The generations that arrived at adolescence from the 1910s through the 1940s sought nighttime adventure at cafés, restaurants and movies; they expressed an aesthetic style that conformed more to that of movie stars than their mothers; and they laid claim to urban space beyond their own neighbourhoods in the company of friends and strangers. Parents attempted to rein in this behaviour, especially as girls' sexuality appeared to be propelling this nighttime adventure.

Dating Delinquents

Parents clashed with daughters about the rules of courtship. For their part, parents expected to maintain surveillance over courting youth, especially daughters, to ensure that appropriate mates were chosen and a girl's virtue remained intact. Their daughters increasingly found ways to wrest control over dating away from their guardians. Working-class girls in Montreal gained increasing freedom to associate with boys and young men when they began working at around age fourteen. This led to group dating – afternoon or evening outings among several adolescent workmates or neighbours – which might include walks, movies, dances, picnics in summer, and ice skating in winter.[87] Group outings could and often did lead to the pairing off of young people. Yet, as Denyse Baillargeon tells us in her study of Montreal families during the Depression, parents considered evening dating a step toward marriage and therefore tended to give permission for such socializing only when girls reached the marrying age of sixteen or eighteen.[88] As leisure pursuits drew adolescents away from the neighbourhood, girls' independence regarding dating appeared to increase giving parents reason to call on the juvenile court when they suspected their daughters were in danger of sinning and ruining their reputations.

When parents complained about daughters who broke curfews and stayed out all night, they implicitly or explicitly were accusing them of sexual promiscuity. To the court, parents fretted that their daughters were too young to be dating and challenged their choice of beaux. For example, parental disapproval of her boyfriend incited Germaine C. to desert even after warnings from the juvenile court. In January 1924, fourteen-year-old Germaine was brought to court for skipping school and being rude to her parents. In the probation officer's investigation it was revealed that she had let her eighteen-year-old boyfriend Henri 'touch her under her dress.' The court made her promise never to see him again and to listen to her parents who threatened to commit her to the Soeurs du Bon Pasteur reformatory for girls. Three months later she snuck out of her parents' house through a window because she 'could no longer live without Henri.' Together they rented a cheap room as Monsieur et Madame D. in Montreal's red-light district. There she was 'seduced.' For two weeks they lived as a married couple. Henri was arrested and Germaine was brought back to court where the doctor confirmed that she was 'deflowered.' Eventually she was sent back home to her parents. Tormented by her incarceration in the Bon Pasteur awaiting her trial, Germaine threatened to kill herself and pleaded for the chance to be with Henri.[89] Ignoring her threats, the court ruled the romantic relationship precocious and worked to constrain it by pressuring the family to impede any communication between Germaine and Henri.

In these cases the evidence of sexual activity obscures other concerns of parents, such as the ethnicity or religion of their daughters' dates. In this period it was not uncommon for adolescent girls to visit dance halls in the city's prominent red-light district. Gladys G., for example, refused to stop going to dances with her boyfriend every week and come in before midnight. More critical to her case than her nighttime pursuit of adventure was the family conflict over Gladys's boyfriend. Her father, she claimed, refused to accept him because of his religion. This English, Anglican family objected to Gladys, fifteen, dating a francophone, Catholic man of twenty. When she refused to stop going to dances with him every week and obey her curfew, her father apparently threatened to kill her. Probation officer Frances Hains took the young couple's side in this family conflict. Although they had been 'immoral,' the boyfriend had promised to marry girl. When asked by the judge if she was 'a good girl,' he replied, 'Yes, for me.' The probation officer recommended that she not be sent home but rather to work and remain under the supervision of the court until marriage.[90] The father clearly perceived his right to use the juvenile court as a means of punishing his daughter's precocious sexuality and refusal to observe his wishes which in this case involved not only late-night activity and dating but religious and ethnic transgression in choice of love interest. Gladys convinced the court that due to her violent home life and her 'immoral' state, marriage was preferable to incarceration or being sent home.

Ethnic tensions were also featured in the 1928 desertion case of Nina O., a thirteen-year-old Montreal-born daughter of Italian immigrants. Nina confessed to both having been seduced by her seventeen-year-old boyfriend, Alfred, and to loving him dearly. To the probation officer she explained how she had tried to act properly but her parents refused to receive her French-Canadian boyfriend. Her father protested the youths' romantic involvement, physically punishing his daughter for dating Alfred. In protest she left home one day and the adolescent lovers spent one week in a room in the red-light district. Acting on the father's complaint of Nina's desertion, the probation officer explored the family acrimony over Nina's choice of boyfriend and her sexually precocious behaviour. Although Nina's father expressed unambiguous suspicion of French Canadians (whom he believed beat their wives) his daughter's damaged reputation and loss of virginity led him to overlook his original objections to Alfred and concede to a prompt Catholic wedding.[91]

Race further complicated these cases. Generally the racism of parents and probation officers was illustrated in their determination to keep white adolescent girls away from men of Asian and African descent. In the early-twentieth century, the Montreal Chinese were associated with narcotics and gambling and therefore any association with Chinese men tainted a girl as delinquent. In cases that resemble those 'romance' stories above, when race was a factor, the outcome was not generous to the girls. Aurore M., an actress who was seduced by a soldier during the First World War, was charged with desertion in September 1918. During the war, she had dutifully worked in a munitions factory, but she and her younger sister were much more interested in the local theatre and turned their attention to acting. Aurore eventually landed a job with a touring company and went on the road. At this time she met an African-American man from Massachusetts whom she alleged was responsible for her pregnancy. Although he proved to be single and Catholic, her parents refused to allow them to marry and filed a complaint against her for desertion.[92] At this time in Quebec history, being pregnant on a wedding day was not uncommon;[93] however, interracial marriage in this case was forbidden. The court concurred, determined to keep her away from her lover, Aurore was placed on probation, likely to end up at the Hôpital Miséricorde where she would be encouraged to give up her baby to the orphanage.[94]

Girls who came to court for incorrigibility and desertion had sometimes committed dating delinquencies. In the same way that girls found leisure activities beyond their neighbourhoods, so went dating. Parents called in the juvenile court to discipline daughters who appeared to be compromising their virtue; yet it was not the sexual nature of dating alone that bothered parents. Girls who came of age in Montreal in the first decades of the twentieth century dated outside of their ethnic and religious groups. This appears to have particularly upset parents and the court to a lesser extent. Neither parties approved of interracial dating and acted swiftly to prevent adolescent girls from pursuing such liaisons.

Running Away

As we saw earlier, in the middle of an April night, 1924, Germaine C. slipped out of her family home through an open window. Across Montreal she travelled to meet her boyfriend at 188 St Laurent Boulevard where they rented a room as 'husband and wife.'[95] Not two months earlier, Alice M. also deserted her home to escape the physical abuse of her father. While on the run she and a girlfriend similarly rented a room at 188 St Laurent Boulevard.[96] Both girls were caught, taken into the MJDC and punished.

The juxtaposition of the two cases suggests that a range of issues caused girls to desert their family homes; it also hints at the potentially central role played by certain areas of the city – not to mention the reputation of certain streets such as St Laurent Boulevard – in girls' desertions. In the juvenile court, girls' misbehaviour was largely interpreted in sexual terms, but it was not sexual behaviour alone that concerned the court and parents: desertion of the family home was almost as critical to determine if a girl would end up in court as the suggestion of promiscuity. Desertion meant far more than a threat to female chastity for it signified daughters' abdication of their subordinate, yet integral, role within the family hierarchy. In leaving home and neighbourhood, girls successfully eluded familial control and circumvented community surveillance.

In early-twentieth-century Montreal, delinquent girls often ran away. In deserting their homes girls achieved autonomy to pursue their own pleasure. Yet it would be a mistake to reduce this behaviour to sexual adventure. One could use probation officers' reports to chart these travels as a 'journey of sex,'[97] however, this would obscure other facets of girls' desertions. Their flights from home were about much more than having sex; desertion was an important means of resistance. As we saw earlier, some girls ran away to avoid arduous household responsibilities or paid employment; others were seeking urban adventure and excitement at the city's dance halls, restaurants, skating rinks, and moving-picture theatres against the prohibitions of their parents.

Generally, parents turned to the juvenile court only when a pattern of deserting had been established. In attempting to make sense of the high percentage of female desertion cases in the Montreal juvenile tribunal, it is important to place them on a continuum of behaviour that attracted the court's attention. The typical early-twentieth-century delinquent daughter was described as being '*sorteuse*' (from the verb *sortir*, to go out) or having '*découché*' (slept out over night). Desertions, then, could consist of habitual nights out over a period of time as well as behaviour we now identify as running away.

Runaways' efforts to escape the home were often eventually thwarted by parents and the juvenile justice authorities, but the urban environment of Montreal at that time promised temporary refuge and anonymity. Parts of the city core were deemed dangerous to adolescents; yet, runaway girls managed to negotiate Montreal's streets thanks mainly to support networks of female (and to a lesser extent male) friends, the ready availability of paid work, and the proliferation of cheap rental accommodation.

The reasons girls deserted are as numerous as the girls themselves, and as Carolyn Strange has articulated, historians cannot definitively ascertain why girls ran away.[98] According to probation officers, what led girls down this path of 'debauchery' was a combination of the girls' weakness for the modern city and a lack of rigour in parenting. As hundreds of girls revealed their passion for dance halls, bowling alleys, the cinema, restaurants, and 'the streets,' one might conclude that the probation officers had it right. During the Great Depression running away appeared to offer escape from 'family strife' as well as an opportunity to pursue urban adventure. The press noted in 1935 that after the stockmarket crash Montreal became 'a veritable port of missing girls' as girls from the countryside flooded into the city. In response to this runaway crisis, attempts were made to apprehend fourteen- and fifteen-year-old travelling girls at railway stations.[99] These girls, in turn, would be brought before the juvenile court judge.

In terms of derelict parenting, while it was true that the court assumed negligence produced these undisciplined adolescents, it was the girls who were brought to court. In their defence, girls provided diverse reasons for their absence. Girls' explanations were frequently tales of resistance: at times eloquently, and in detail, they revealed what they perceived to be unfair treatment at home. Girls often justified their behaviour in terms of a once mutually advantageous familial relationship gone awry. They admitted to running away because: their leisure activities strained family life; they wanted to work on their own terms; they had chosen inappropriate boyfriends and were prevented from dating; or family members had physically and sexually abused them. As Joan Sangster has shown for Ontario teens who ran away at mid-century, many working-class girls found there was very little reason to stay.[100]

Many desertion cases gave emphasis to stories of domestic physical violence. Mothers and fathers, and sometimes brothers and sisters, punched and kicked their daughters and sisters, threw them on the floor, threatened to shoot them and banished them from their homes. It is unlikely that at this time parents would conceptualize corporal punishment meted out to invoke discipline as abuse, notwithstanding the North American child protection movement.[101] Discipline was a common excuse for violence; indeed, it was often seen as justifiable by juvenile justice authorities as much as parents.

In Montreal some parents claimed that they were correcting their children for refusing to obey, especially daughters who refused to come home before midnight or who stayed out all night. Linda Gordon has attempted to explain the abuse of children in working-class Boston as discipline – a result of the limited ability of parents to protect their children from the dangerous city streets.[102] When fourteen-year-old Ida D. deserted she claimed that she had been hit repeatedly by her parents who justified the violence as a response to their daughter's habit of spending nights on the streets. The probation officer emphasized in her report that Ida liked the streets and boys too much for her own good and investigated her sexual experience; the escalation of physical violence in the home, which Ida claimed prompted her desertion, became secondary to her indiscretions.[103]

Some girls admitted that tensions over their nighttime sorties provoked violence that led, in turn, to desertion. In 1924 Adrienne C. deserted her family home to join her boyfriend. When asked to explain her actions, she cited the brutality of her father: rather than being motivated by lust as her parents would have it, she was attempting to escape a beating. Her parents claimed the violence was justified to break her habit of staying out until midnight. Despite family insistence on severe corporal punishment, she argued that the father's actions were indefensible and that it was she who had been wronged.[104]

Fifteen-year-old Lilian D. was brought to court because her behaviour had been 'bad' in the past year; according to her mother, she attended the cinema and did not come home at night. Lilian retorted that her mother had frequently beaten her with daily cuffs to the head, kicks and punches. Because Lilian was culpable of sexual transgressions she did not garner the protection of the court. Though her mother's bad reputation led the court to reject its favoured program of probation, it determined instead to send Lilian to reform school for a minimum of two years for 'protection.'[105]

In 1928 Ida B., an Italian immigrant, deserted because she had broken the gramophone and was afraid of being beaten by her brother who frequently hit her. The father constantly scolded the girl. The probation officer wrote that the mother backed up her daughter's story, saying the father was 'like a devil' and that 'life at her father's was hell.'[106] In this case the girl was examined and found to be a virgin. That, along with the lack of evidence that Ida had attended the cinema or smoked cigarettes, and the fact that she had sought out her sister and her godmother during her desertion brought her the sympathy of the court.[107] In another case, ten-year-old Marie-Jeanne had deserted because her father beat her. She, like Ida, found an older married woman to care for her. Because she was also a virgin, she was pitied and placed in an industrial school.[108]

A variety of factors pulled adolescent girls from their homes. Certainly the reputation of Montreal's red-light district undoubtedly played a role in runaways' decisions to leave their families. Social boundaries in the city were supposed to function to restrict prostitution to certain areas like the red-light district and keep young women away and their virtue intact; yet, for girls this district held an irresistible attraction. Through delinquent girls' confessions to probation officers, the MJDC probed the city's notorious downtown core. Carefully, these court workers noted the names of dance clubs, restaurants, and location of boarding houses and hotels that opened their doors to adolescent girls. An association with certain streets and addresses in and around the red-light district worked to taint these adolescent girls with the brush of the ultimate condemned female, the prostitute, and her counterpart, the factory ('good time') girl. As Boyer points out, 'determinations of virtue' were based on dress, demeanour, and place.[109] Of course, the juvenile court would eventually seek out the state of a girl's hymen to make that determination; until then, her presence in this disreputable area meant her identity slid easily toward delinquent. This was even more true for girls who came from this area. However, this does not tell us what the girls were doing – if they were prostitutes, sex delinquents, or urban adventurers. In fact, experiences of runaways have been little explored except by sociologists and criminologists working since the 1970s on the problem of homeless youth.[110]

Girls did not heed the warnings of the social reformers regarding the risks of the red-light district. Rather, with their own sense of Montreal's moral geography, they chose to go there when they ran away. Deserting daughters found jobs and temporary lodgings, and spent evenings with lovers and friends at dance halls, moving-picture houses and even in brothels. This is not to suggest that these adolescents were or became prostitutes; rather, they found this area provided them with adventure and anonymity that most neighbourhoods did not. Where reformers saw brothels, disease, and depravity, girls who came of age during and after the First World War, saw a compelling world defined by youth and defiance of authority, be it parental, church, or state.

Girls came to the red-light district from working-class districts of Point St Charles,[111] St. Henri,[112] and Rosemont,[113] and streets in the francophone east end.[114] For other girls the trip to the clubs, restaurants, and hotels was a matter of blocks, not miles. In 1924, Marie-Rose C., for example, lived with her mother on St Elizabeth Street, one block north of St Catherine and the red-light district. Madame C. herself ran a boarding house and rented rooms to unmarried couples. When Marie-Rose deserted she went south and east into the red-light district, first to St Denis Street then to La Gauchetière Street where she went *en chambre* – to a rented room – with her boyfriend.[115]

In response to the rising number of single wage-earners, tourists, and migrant workers in the city, rental accommodation boomed in the early-twentieth century. Establishments offering rooms to rent ranged from brothels to boarding houses, from the makeshift to the respectable, a point not lost on women reformers hoping to control the moral environment of the city.[116] By the 1910s the single-woman-boarding phenomenon was noted and problematized. In its annual report of 1916–17, the Young Women's Christian Association remarked that 'never before in the history of Montreal have their been so many girls employed in banking institutions, stores, offices and factories, and never before in the history of the Association has it been so difficult to secure satisfactory accommodation for these girls.'[117] The First World War exacerbated the need for accommodation for women workers, leading the Montreal Local Council of Women (MLCW) to remark on the uncontrolled spread of boarding houses.[118] Katherine Chipman of the MLCW's Reformatory Committee claimed in 1918 that the licensing and supervision of all boarding houses and apartment houses 'would be of great advantage and assistance in a much needed vice crusade.'[119]

In response to the growing population of independent wage-earners in Montreal, religious orders and women's organizations tried to keep pace with demand, opening subsidized lodgings based on the linguistic and religious divide: French-Catholic women stayed at Le Foyer (located on Champ de Mars and Mansfield), and others on St Hubert, St Denis, and Viger Streets in central Montreal; Irish-Catholic women stayed at Killarney House on La Gauchetière Street; and Protestant women used the YWCA's dormitories on Dorchester Street, a rooming house on Ste Famille and a boarding house on Mackay Street.[120] This inexpensive accommodation could be had at a price. The Catholic Foyers, which housed roughly fifty women each, for example, cost just ten dollars per month in the 1910s but offered little privacy. Women living there did so under constant supervision. The YWCA boarding homes likewise offered women a place to live – as many as 2500 in 1916–17 – but they were expected to live up to the spiritual and moral ideals of the Y. The Royal Commission on Industrial Training and Technical Education reported in 1913 that boarding outside the family could not be done in Montreal for less than three or four dollars per week.[121] Commenting on the high cost of living Montreal presented to the working girl, American Maimie Pinzer declared the city too expensive for a stenographer to live decently.[122]

Other constituents also acknowledged increasing demand for rooms-to-let. Families, single women with children, and brothel keepers also rented rooms by the day and week. A long tradition of doubling up of families and taking in male workers expanded to accommodate the working woman.

The proliferation of cheap rooms rented by the day caught the attention of many girls wanting to slip anonymously into the city. These rooms proved to be an effective short-term solution for runaways: inexpensive enough to be attractive yet too costly to become a permanent residence. During the First World War a room on St Justin Street in the red-light district cost two and a half dollars per week, about half an adolescent girl's salary. Irène J., a fox-trotting delinquent mentioned earlier, solved her financial difficulties by doubling up with another girl at a boarding house on St Justin. In the 1920s a room could be had for a weekly rate of four dollars still a considerable portion of a girl's seven dollars salary.[123] Rates for rooms did not change substantially, for by 1944, Jeannette L. was still able to rent a room with her girlfriend for four dollars a week.[124]

Most girls found rooms at establishments that did not question their age, their company or their activities. To the consternation of the probation officer investigating the case of Marie-Rose C., the boarding housekeeper did not object when this adolescent received her boyfriend in the room during her two-week stay.[125] This was not always the case, however, as Irène J. found out; not all keepers permitted female tenants to have men in their rooms.[126]

Independence for adolescent girls did not mean negotiating Montreal by night on their own: networks of girlfriends encouraged and sustained their desertions. Many deserting daughters slept at the homes of relatives or friends when they could. Girls relayed stories of meeting girlfriends, venturing to dance halls or cinemas, and together finding a place to spend the night. For instance, Alice M. spent one week at a girlfriend's home, and then with another friend she went 'en chambre' on St Laurent Blvd.[127] Similarly, Mary R. met her friend Sadie F. and together they spent the night at another girl's home.[128] Married girlfriends, often themselves still teenagers, offered runaways a place to stay.[129]

In hearing girls' tales, probation officers frequently concluded that relationships between girls were at the root of delinquent acts. Primarily, these relationships interfered with parents' ability to discipline daughters and even replaced familial bonds. Critical of girls' friendships, probation officers rejected the notion of mutual relationships among teenage girls, insisting instead on a hierarchical model of leaders and followers. A common refrain of probation officer Rose Henderson was that girlfriends were not 'desirable companion[s].'[130] Girls like Sadie F., mentioned earlier, who had already come before the court, were automatically blamed for leading Mary R. down the wrong path.[131]

Older girls were singled out as particularly bad influences. Rita R., one of the few girls before the court to have made it to business college, deserted according to the probation officer, because of the influence of 'sophisticated' girls she had met at school.[132] Dorothy Sigler, the probation officer responsible for Jewish cases, reported that Rita had developed a habit of 'absenting herself' from her family and blamed her susceptibility to 'moving picture romance' for giving her the courage to desert. Rita claimed that her father's harsh discipline (a humiliating slap on the face when he found she disobeyed him and attended a party) was the cause. She took $25 from her bank account and $100 in Victory Bonds and went *en chambre* with a girlfriend. The following day Rita met up with girlfriends, including Marjorie, a parcel girl at Holt Renfrew, who was known to the court for her multiple desertions from convents and a suicide attempt. Marjorie took Rita to a party where she was later arrested for desertion, drinking beer, and smoking cigarettes. Because of her history and her 'sophistication' Marjorie was deemed the bad influence and given an indeterminate sentence.[133] Rita, on the other hand, was saved by her virginity and the probation officer's suspicion that her father was excessively physical with her: Sigler recommended she be sent home on probation.

Probation officers were frequently suspicious of girlfriends because of the seeming ease with which they lied to protect one another; mothers similarly found that girlfriends were known to cover for their daughters.[134] Distrust of girlfriends speaks directly to the fear that the traditional family had lost its power to control adolescent girls. Gordon writes 'weakened family and community networks meant that adolescents relied on peer approval and companionship, and often came to disdain their parents, while parents could not trust these peers to protect children and orient them toward secure futures.'[135] Rather than see girlfriends as safer company than the wily men so often described in the press, probation officers worked to separate girlfriends in the long term. Though silent on the subject of same-sex involvement, the court's antagonism toward girls' relationships could be read as fear of or desire to prevent lesbian relationships.

Girls engaged in several modes of sexual exchange, from prostitution to bartering for shelter and food. Undoubtedly some girls entered the city's thriving sex trade. The story Eva L. told of her desertion confirmed the worst fears of probation officers. She claimed to have been coaxed into deserting by her friend Rita S. After work one Saturday they met at a house of prostitution on La Gauchetière where Eva made between three and four dollars. From there two men took them to St Elizabeth Street where they lived for two weeks in a room paid for by the men. Then they went back to another brothel on La Gauchetière where Eva paid one and a half dollars a week for a room and earned fifty cents profit on each 'trick.' At this last place Rita's mother caught up with the girls and had them arrested.[136]

Scholars now recognize the close connection between physical and sexual abuse at home and prostitution.[137] Having few economic options in the first half of this century, it is not at all surprising to find girls escaping dysfunctional family situations only to find themselves victimized by men on the streets. Irène M.'s drunken father habitually hit his four daughters and their mother. In the middle of winter 1924 he threw all of them out of the house onto the street. Irène chose not to return and wound up at '*mauvaises maisons*' (a euphemism for brothels), where she stayed for four weeks. She came home on her own recognizance but departed again. Eventually she was arrested for being found in a disorderly house.[138] She had been supporting herself through prostitution.

Cases of runaway girls entering prostitution are extreme examples; more common were the cases of girls going to rooms with young men they knew and exchanging sex for the price of the room. This sexual bartering system – called occasional prostitution by the worried middle class – appears to have been characteristic of adolescent sexuality, where girls learned early to turn male sexual interest into some form of material benefit.[139] Fourteen-year-old Simonne T. left home on Christmas Day 1931 with her brother and simply did not return home until she was found several weeks later walking on Boulevard St Laurent after dark. Having left her brother, she sought out her twenty-one-year-old boyfriend in the heart of the red-light district. He rented a room for them at 74 St Catherine Street East. Although they had dated for months before the desertion, according to Simonne it was when they went *en chambre* that he seduced her.[140]

Mary Odem has suggested that California runaways in this time period traded on their sexuality in their struggle to survive on their own[141] and recent research has found that many runaway girls become involved in prostitution or an exchange of sexual activity for food, shelter, or money in order to survive.[142] An example of this is the case of girlfriends Anny V. and Annie B. who left home late in 1933 and lived together for seven weeks in a cellar on St Laurent Boulevard near St Catherine. These girls struck a sex-for-money-and-food arrangement with a sixty-year-old man.[143] Exchanging sex for shelter or food speaks to the material reality of life for these girls who could not earn enough to be independent of their families.

Adolescent female desertion was threatening because of the perceived danger the city presented to unchaperoned young women; it was also threatening because of the independence and self-sufficiency exhibited by girls in the face of their alleged peril. In some cases the girls' desertions reveal their keen ability to survive away from their families. Others illustrate the social and economic disadvantage of being adolescent and female. Considering the tremendous risk involved, it is perhaps surprising that so many girls chose to run away. It is for this reason that it is important to examine why they left.

Conclusion

Girls' conflict with parents and subsequently the law relates to fundamental changes in the experience of adolescence in the opening decades of the twentieth century. In the juvenile court, parents accused daughters of incorrigible behaviour and probation officers recorded the basic patterns of female adolescence. For working-class youth in Montreal formal education ended with the start of puberty; by thirteen or fourteen years of age girls had entered a new phase of the life cycle marked by waged work and greater responsibility in household production, aiding, if not replacing, their mothers. Tensions at home arose when girls refused to follow parental demands and expectations regarding work, both inside and beyond the home. Education and work histories reveal that most juvenile court girls played an important role in both the family and the city's economy at this time. Girls were often initiated into the labour market through domestic service, where the work, surveillance, and low remuneration were thought to mimic a girl's place within the home. By the 1910s, opportunity for unskilled factory work drew girls away from domestic service and into the cigarette, food, and textile industries. The 1920s saw service-sector expansion that widened the variety of jobs available to girls: adolescents found work in restaurants, hotels, and department stores. Cases from the long Depression of the 1930s reflect the reality that girls were likely the first fired from better-paying service and factory jobs and forced to seek out domestic-service jobs. Many of the girls who came to court during the Depression were unemployed and, unlike their older sisters, had never found consistent wage work. The Second World War once again opened the doors for girls in factories and service-oriented jobs.

Girls' worlds expanded rapidly when a youth-oriented leisure market developed and girls chose to direct their wages and energy into adventure rather than the family economy. Adolescent girls also occupied an important place in the amusement industry, being chief consumers of movies, dance trends, and beauty aids. Unlike previous generations these girls were on the move in the city, often in pairs or groups meeting strangers and indulging in the latest movie or dance. This behaviour produced conflict at home as girls broke curfew, deserted, spent their wages on themselves, and rewrote the rules of dating. Parents attempted to counter the strong pull of adolescent girls toward this life of work and leisure beyond the home, especially with the help of the juvenile court. In turn, girls expressed further resistance, confirming their own design of what would be their place in twentieth-century Montreal. The growing independence of young women, the weakening of traditional structures of authority, and the changing nature of the Montreal landscape that seemed to facilitate girls' wayward adventures created an imperative for the court to punish them.

'Did You Bleed?' The Juvenile Court, Girls' Bodies, and the Sexualization of Female Delinquency

The roots of early-twentieth-century girls' transgressions lay in the assertions of their autonomy and nothing symbolized the inherent danger of their independence than girls' 'immorality.' Quebec moral authorities denounced *les jeunes filles modernes* for their role in the ubiquity of 'lust, sexual pleasure and immodesty' in Montreal. Antivice reformers and the medical establishment focused on venereal disease and prostitution rates, while the Catholic clergy determined that young unmarried women should be ignorant of their own sexuality and all but the most deviant were free of sexual desire.[1] To arrest the trend in unmarried sexual relations and the loss of female virtue, the church responded with (largely ineffectual) prohibitions on the unchaperoned leisure activities of young people. All actors engaged in the struggle against girls' rejection of the twin virtues of chastity and modesty pointed to the inevitability of a ruined reputation leading to ostracization and failure to fulfil their true destinies as wives and mothers. While prostitution, venereal disease, and familial shame spoke to the concrete dangers of adolescent female sexuality, it was unwed pregnancy that most alarmed parents, the church, and lay reformers. This was not a new or small problem. Montreal housed an establishment for single mothers dating back to the mid-nineteenth century. In the juvenile court era, the Hôpital de la Miséricorde was a formidable institution for pregnant Catholic girls and young women who found themselves pregnant outside wedlock; Bethany House, a parallel home for unwed pregnant and English-speaking girls contributed to 'solving' this problem. Unwed pregnancy, a telltale sign of girls' immodesty and sin, delivered girls to a specific set of carceral experiences. The juvenile court facilitated the pregnant girls' journey between reform school and the Miséricorde or Bethany House.

The Montreal Juvenile Delinquents' (MJDC) Court did not limit its focus to the pregnant girl whose body exposed her modern, bad behaviour. Rather, its officers were riveted to the exploration of adolescent girls' attitudes toward, and experiences of, sex. Girls' sexuality suggested the independence of working-class girls; sexuality, as Christine Stansell notes, 'was both a consequence of social autonomy and its metaphor.'[2] Even if girls' sexual activity did not result in pregnancy, disease, or a life of commercial vice, their habits and lifestyle represented the alarming growth of young women's freedom. The irreversible loss of virginity therefore became a sign of girls' immorality but also of their autonomy. Thus when parents complained of the freedom and independence that girls indulged in, the court embarked on an inquest into the sexual expression of this behaviour. But parental complaints were not simple, unmitigated complaints of girls' precocious sexual adventures. In fact, as discussed in chapter 5, sexuality played a significant role in girls' cases yet it was not the lone culprit responsible for their appearance in court. Parents used the juvenile court to interrupt girls on a path that might have led to pregnancy or dishonour; even then it appears that parents did not act precipitously. While the parents' complaints cannot be reduced to girls' sexual escapades, the court kaleidoscoped girls' behaviour, focusing investigations largely on sexual affairs and in effect constructing a secular confessional where the girls were told to bare all.

When the juvenile court was established in 1912, therefore, one of its major preoccupations was the 'precocious sexuality'[3] of adolescent girls: parents told court officials they suspected their daughters had been immoral on nights spent away from home; court-ordered gynecological exams determined if the girls had lost their virginity; probation officers recorded sexual histories; and judges asked girls to reveal the names of their male seducers. The result was that an incorrigibility or desertion charge evolved into a quest to prevent, restrain, and punish premarital sex.

This chapter explores the court's interrogation of adolescent girls' sexual histories. From the early years of the court through the 1940s, female probation officers insisted that alleged female delinquents divulge the details of their sexual pasts beginning with the 'first seduction.' To complement or challenge the sexual history, the court ordered gynecological examinations for all girls who came before the judge, effectively turning the suggestion of sexual culpability into irrefutable medical 'truth.' While girls' sexual expression – or just the hint of it – resulted in their relationship with the juvenile court, the construction of adolescent girls as *jeunes filles modernes* and sex delinquents by probation officers and other court officials shaped girls' experience of the juvenile justice system. That is, rather than erase girls' sexualized identities the process of court appearance and evaluation ultimately fuelled the construction of girls as sexual and problematic.

Juvenile court records tell us plenty about judicial attitudes towards adolescent courtship and sexuality. While it is fairly easy to identify the anxiety that greeted girls' sexual precociousness, it is much more difficult to grasp how girls understood and experienced sex and the process of disclosing intimate details to the court. This chapter is an attempt to explore the girls' stories of sexual encounters and get beyond the court's and parents' moralizing and their discursive renderings of adolescent sexuality. The nature of the case file, which was generated and mediated by female probation officers, male physicians, and judges, makes it difficult to exact 'experience.' More than any other part of female delinquents' experience with the court, the investigations into their sexual histories offered them the opportunity to tell their stories and construct their own narratives.[4]

Girls' admissions regarding their sexual experience did not conform to a single script of victimization or wanton sexual adventure, which undoubtedly troubled the court. Many girls were brought to court for being sex delinquents and 'problem girls' – dancing, dating, and breaking curfew with their peers – but when court officers inquired into their *first* sexual experience, it allowed girls to subvert attention away from their most recent delinquency and talk of childhood incest, rape, and seduction. Others took the opportunity to try to redefine their sexual liaisons with boyfriends as respectable, not delinquent. The court heard that for girls sex was about violence, passion, defiance and, at times, economic vulnerability. The purpose of these stories was to elicit compassion, to escape punishment, and even to seek revenge on those who had violated them. Likely this was the first time an authority figure had ever asked these girls to tell their stories. Only by the 1940s, did girls' attitudes towards the regulation of their sexual lives appear to change: while most still did not want parents to know the details, sixteen and seventeen-year-old girls readily claimed their sexuality with frankness and an audacious lack of humility.

The juvenile court's role in regulating adolescent girls – unlike that of the church or family – involved an attempt to ascertain why girls became sexually deviant, which helps explain why lengthy case histories were taken. The probation officers endeavoured to establish how vulnerable girls became teenage sex delinquents and generated a wealth of evidence that pointed to girls' material circumstances and weak status in the family. The poverty of many girls was acknowledged by the court, and its workers knew well what girls learned early: that economic imperatives accentuated the fact that their bodies were commodities to be exchanged for material benefit. It is no wonder that probation officers asked frequently if girls accepted money for their sexual indiscretions. Girls' subordinate position in the patriarchal family also left them open to regulation of courting behaviour and sexual abuse.

In struggling to deal with the overwhelming ordinariness of sexual expression among girls the court might have arrived at a sophisticated analysis of girls' sexual 'deviance' that acknowledged the class and gender structures that worked against girls in childhood and adolescence. But it did not. Rather, juvenile court officials reduced individual sexual acts to evidence of delinquency and upheld the authority and power bestowed on parents in the family hierarchy in which girls occupied the lowest rank. Parents brought their daughters to court to reinstate familial control and to reassert their prerogative over female members of the family. This state institution then meted out punishment to girls who broke religious and social rules about chastity.

Girls' Sexuality, the Juvenile Delinquents Act, and the Court

Although sexual delinquency predominated in the cases of adolescent girls brought to juvenile court, nothing in the 1908 Juvenile Delinquents Act (JDA) would have suggested that girls' precocious sexuality was its target. It might be safe to presume that because most turn-of-the-century female lawbreakers were charged with offences related to prostitution that juvenile justice activists hoped to use the JDA and juvenile courts to punish and protect juvenile prostitutes. Certainly contemporaneous American juvenile court acts included 'frequenting a house of ill-repute' in descriptions of juvenile delinquency.[5] The calling of young sex-trade workers delinquents rather than prostitutes or criminals exemplifies the primary goals of the juvenile justice system of rescuing adolescents from careers of crime and rehabilitating them into good citizens. And yet, the juvenile court gained jurisdiction over regulating female adolescent sexuality far beyond the parameters of juvenile prostitution. Facilitated by 1912 amendments made to Quebec legislation identifying desertion and immoral conduct as delinquent behaviour, parents and police were empowered to bring before the courts delinquent daughters who exhibited a precocious sexuality. Criminal Code offences, such as vagrancy, and delinquent actions, such as desertion and immoral conduct, were used by families and state authorities to restrain sexual activity of adolescent daughters.

With the juvenile court apparatus firmly entrenched in 1912, girls' sexuality was targeted in unprecedented fashion. Adolescent prostitutes and vagrants who worked in the city's sex trade now fell within the juvenile justice system, but so too did girls who dared to be on the streets after curfew and who had established habits of spending wages frequenting dance halls, moving-picture houses and restaurants. In fact, with this new mechanism to control female sexuality, adolescent girls were caught in a web of surveillance that extended from the family home to the streets to the juvenile court.

Twelve years after the establishment of the court, the JDA caught up with the MJDC's practice. A 1924 amendment to the JDA added to the definition of juvenile delinquent anyone 'who is guilty of sexual immorality or any other form of vice.' There was no equivalent statement in the Criminal Code governing Canadians over the age of sixteen.[6] The stated aim of the amendment was to gain jurisdiction over young women who were considered 'semi-prostitutes' or 'occasional prostitutes' although in practice it would be used to police working-class female sexuality.[7] The 1924 amendment was a juridical response to recent upheavals over female sex delinquency in English Canada. According to Toronto juvenile court judge H.S. Mott, boys and men could be convicted for having carnal knowledge of a female minor under the seduction legislation in the Criminal Code but a gap in the Criminal Code meant 'there was nothing to charge her with.'[8] The 1924 amendment filled this gap, although it is clear from its female delinquents' files, that the juvenile court in Montreal had already assumed its right to target young women and girls in this way.

In using the law to regulate female sexuality, the Montreal juvenile court also contributed to the medicalization of the 'problem' of girls' precocious sexuality. Medical doctors played an important role in this process from the earliest days of the court. Because girls embodied delinquency, medical expertise was used by the court as a way to read the delinquent's body for sexual activity. This role persisted throughout the period under study and expanded to cover regular venereal disease testing during the Second World War. In facing the judges of the juvenile court, allegedly bad girls had to confront laws that defined their actions as delinquent and medical evidence that told a story about their bodies that they would have to explain.

'Qui t'a débauchée?' Constructing Innocence, Demanding Justice

Throughout the first half of the twentieth century, female probation officers at the MJDC spent much of their time writing adolescent girls' sexual histories. In interrogating the girls' sexual histories, they put a name, place, and date to the 'first seduction,' which often occurred years prior to a girls' court appearance. The focus on virginity allowed the court to create a crude topology of female delinquency ranging from innocent and redeemable to debauched and depraved. Because of its deep religious and social meaning and the weight of its irreversibility, the loss of virginity was taken very seriously; while a girl's 'ruined' body could never recover physically, with carefully constructed rehabilitation schemes a girl might be redeemed morally.

The court ordered gynecological examinations for girls as part of the background investigation into female cases. Regardless of religion or ethnicity, girls were taken to the Soeurs du Bon Pasteur convent on Sherbrooke Street for gynecological exams performed by a male doctor.[9] A verdict of 'clean and virginal' would undoubtedly lead to an easier time with the judge, but most of the girls were in fact branded 'deflowered.' Under such circumstances, the girls were up against the 'scientific' proof of their sexual delinquency (incomplete hymens) in court. This focus on the relationship between sexuality and delinquency was entirely gendered as delinquent boys were spared the sexual interrogation and invasive physical examination.

Girls who came before the court for offences not remotely related to sexual activity were also sent to the physician for examination. The hymen assessment provided the court with a narrative beyond the facts of the delinquent action. In 1938 two sisters aged thirteen and fourteen appeared in court for disturbing the peace following a neighbour's complaint (which did not involve anything sexual). Both were found to have intact hymens and the issue of their sexuality was dropped.[10] An egregious use of the physical exam can also be found in the case of a sixteen-year-old girl brought to court as an 'abandoned' child. Juliette F., an orphaned domestic servant, was brought or came to court several times in 1934 because her placements were untenable. The court took responsibility for this protection case, attempting to find appropriate settings for this domestic worker. The probation officer contacted individuals and organizations to find a more satisfactory placement. Within a little over one year, Juliette was subjected to three physical exams to determine the state of her hymen. Repeated verdicts of 'intact' sent a signal to the court that this was, in fact, a 'good' girl, deserving of protection.[11]

An example of a 1932 case involving theft demonstrates how the court turned entirely away from the criminal act toward a girl's sexual history. Marie Rose B., a fifteen year old, was accused of stealing two watches, a pair of glasses, and some cash. Probation officer Lecompte carefully pieced together the story behind the theft, and Dr Amiot performed a gynecological examination. Although Marie Rose denied her role in the theft, she could not deny the physician's findings that she was 'deflowered' and infected with venereal disease. When Judge Robillard interviewed Marie Rose, he exhibited little interest in the stolen property and her denial of the charge. Rather, Robillard wanted to know the frequency with which she had sexual relations and the extent of her knowledge concerning the venereal disease.[12]

Having obtained the medical proof of a girl's sexual activity, female probation officers and juvenile court judges sought out the origins and nature of her first time: *'Qui t'a débauchée?'* they asked. Like the unmarried mothers in Regina Kunzel's study who were asked 'how did you become pregnant?' delinquent girls faced with the question *'Qui t'a débauchée?'* were able to 'appropriate, subvert, and resist the dominant discourse' about their sexuality.[13] The passive construction of the question – crudely translated, 'Who debauched you?'- depicted girls as objects acted upon by men and opened the door for them to avoid responsibility for their loss of virginity. Girls told probation officers that they had been seduced by strangers, family members, and adult men known to them through their families. By 1919 the age of consent laws made it criminal for men to have sex with adolescent girls between fourteen and sixteen years of age, suggesting that they were criminally responsible for such actions, not the girls. However, all too often, the court simultaneously condemned 'predatory' male behaviour and blamed girls for exhibiting a precocious sexuality. As one probation officer wrote, '[she] has admitted her immorality and her medical certificate shows that she has been tampered with.'[14]

Stories about their first seduction follow patterns that therefore illuminate adolescent girls' own sense of vulnerability but also agency where they confessed to youthful sexual discovery and redefined moral codes of conduct. What girls said undoubtedly shocked the court as narratives of seduction, rape, domestic sexual abuse, and adolescent romance flooded the juvenile tribunal. In admitting sexual experience, girls defiantly claimed it did not make them delinquents, at times proffering love as a justification for their actions or demanding retribution for the seduction and rape of their bodies. As well, girls changed their stories; for example Madeleine P. offered several versions of her sexual history, which involved denial (until the physician labelled her '*débauchée*'), a boyfriend, several unnamed men, and a forty-year-old man who promised her money.[15]

A few girls denied the veracity of the physician's claim that a ruptured hymen necessarily indicated sexual activity. In court, girls countered that bicycle accidents, Tampax, or even the gynecological exam explained why their medical exams betrayed them.[16] A thirteen-year-old girl who was also asked to explain a damning doctor's report remained resolute when asked, '*Qui t'a débauchée?*' she replied, 'No one.'[17] Girls sometimes looked to the female probation officer for an ally against the male doctor: one seventeen-year-old 'incorrigible' told her probation officer, 'I never acted badly with the boys I go out with' and that she only touched her 'private parts' in washing herself after menstruation. She claimed that the physician then threatened her into confessing to masturbation; she did, 'so that he would leave me alone.'[18] But to the probation officer, she claimed, she delivered the truth. Rebuttals and denials were isolated, however, for eventually almost all girls offered their tales of adolescent sexual adventure, seduction, rape, and domestic sexual abuse.

Only during the 1940s did girls question the basis for the focus on their sexuality. The roots of this change lie with changing sexual mores but also expansion of the age category (to eighteen) over which the juvenile court had jurisdiction. Girls – young women, really – sixteen and seventeen years of age discussed their sex lives with such audacity that probation officers felt compelled to comment. Seventeen-year-old Dorothy L. appeared 'very frank,' wrote a probation officer in 1944: 'She speaks of her immoral conduct as if it were something very natural.'[19] As well, girls more frequently admitted to masturbation and telling mothers about their sexual experiences.[20] In a case from 1943, Jeannine D. brazenly smiled at her probation officer, Simone Lefebvre, when interrogated about her 'immoral conduct.' This seventeen-year-old admitted to having as many as twelve to fifteen sexual relationships. When asked if she worried about getting pregnant, she said no, that the men used condoms or withdrew before they discharged. Nothing sexually abnormal, she reassured Lefebvre. The probation officer communicated to the judge that the 'girl' simply did not comprehend the gravity of her immorality.[21]

Sexual Adventure and Romance

Parents' inability to control their daughters' activities and choice of male company was often the cause of a girls' juvenile court appearance. While it might have been expedient to deny sexual activity or responsibility for it, girls sometimes did claim their sexuality and defend it.[22] Young men, girls' boyfriends, therefore entered the record as the perpetrators of the 'first seduction.' Many girls labelled sex delinquents were involved with boyfriends and admitted to harbouring fantasies about marriage. Even expressions of appropriate feminine goals did not deter the court from punishing the girl for her loss of virginity. Even so, many girls were defiant in asserting their understanding of romance and courtship in the face of parental and court disapproval. For their part, the probation officers were most interested in whether the girls had been coerced or paid to commit 'immoral' acts and in dousing the fires of budding romance.

The urgency of teen romance comes through clearly in girls' explanations of their desertions. In Chapter 5 we saw how frustrated romance led to defiance in the form of running away with boyfriends. Girls' determination to have these romantic attachments acknowledged in the face of parental opposition extended to a defence of their sexual involvement. In these cases girls admitted to sexual relations (as did some of the boyfriends interviewed) and quickly excused their actions with an assertion that they had made up their minds to marry. Julie M., an eighteen year old, was charged with desertion when she left home for a live-in domestic-service job. Her parents preferred that she remain at home, contribute to the housework, and abandon her habit of staying out late at night and sleeping in mornings. Critical to the case was conflict over Julie's refusal to help her parents sell papers at their street kiosk. She complained about selling newspapers on the streets where passers-by verbally abused her. Further she felt she needed to make her own money to buy the clothing her parents refused to provide. She defended her sexual and romantic relationship with her boyfriend, claiming that they intended to marry. Her parents vehemently opposed this union, claiming she was too young and her boyfriend not capable of supporting a family. According to Julie, proof of the wisdom of this ambition included his stable job at one of the city's newspapers and her positive influence upon her boyfriend. Since they began dating, he attended church regularly, including confession every fifteen days.[23] Unapologetically, this young woman invoked her own sense of sexual morality. Despite her solid defence, the court chose to reinstate her parents' authority over her.

A precocious marriage lay behind a desertion charge for fifteen-year-old Isabelle in 1924. A recent immigrant to Montreal from Scotland, she worked in a candy shop for a time before marrying an American of Greek background and moving with him to a rooming house. Isabelle's parents appealed to the juvenile court, claiming she had been married under the false pretense that she was twenty-one years old. To avoid interference from the court, the couple moved to the United States where the court authorities attempted to track them down; the couple must have moved quickly, though, because the case was eventually withdrawn with no suggestion in the court documents that the girl was ever found.[24]

In 1944, Denise C. described to her probation officer a year-long affair that had included sexual relations beginning five months into the courtship. The probation officer labelled what she described an immoral life, full of clubs, cafés, and dance halls. Denise admitted the couple often spent nights out, going to hotels and clubs, and drinking alcohol. She also admitted to having sex in her mother's otherwise empty house, and cavalierly admitted to oral sex with her boyfriend. To the doctor who examined her for the presence of hymen and tested her for venereal disease, she minimized her sexual transgression by admitting to having sexual intercourse only once, perhaps an assertion that this fact permitted her to claim respectability. The conditions of her suspended sentence were that she give up this romantic attachment and her 'immoral life.'[25]

The threat of another episode in juvenile court sometimes was enough to keep girls away from their paramours, but not always. Juliette, for example, persisted in dating Renald even though her mother forbade it. So she lied, sneaked around, and was generally able to maintain her romance with Renald until she pushed her mother too far: one night in January 1930 she didn't come home at all. Her mother refused to believe that she was out with girlfriends and brought her to court to teach her a lesson. To the probation officer, Juliette's mother accused Renald of being a drinker and demanded that the court put a stop to their romantic attachment. The doctor's report verified that she had been 'deflowered.' She was sent home with a suspended sentence under the condition that she abandon all relations with Renald. This would prove intolerable for Juliette and she was soon brought to court for violating the terms of her suspended sentence.[26] Girls such as Juliette likely told the probation officer about their boyfriends and romantic lives to appeal to their sense of fairness, believing that their parents were indefensibly harsh and intolerant of their social lives. Girls who insisted that they intended to marry the boyfriends who were implicated in their damning medical exams invoked their own rules about respectable sexuality. They differentiated themselves from girls who had had a succession of relationships and sexual encounters and who were perceived to be generally sexually available, rather than only selectively so.

Seduction

Girls might have been brought to court for breaking rules related to courting but when asked who first seduced them, some girls blamed an *inconnu*, a stranger. It was to the advantage of daughters to use well-worn tales of seduction and danger to convince both parents and the juvenile court that they had been objects of prey. Characteristic of such narratives of sexual danger was the portrayal of women and adolescent girls as passive victims.[27] The late-nineteenth-century panic over missing and fallen young women gave rise to federal laws and local protective agencies intended to safeguard female chastity, but ultimately it contributed to the regulation of the social lives of young, single women.[28] Historians have argued that laws and courts were used in the late-nineteenth and twentieth century – mainly through the criminalization of seduction – to protect female sexuality;[29] yet as Karen Dubinsky has argued, a legal sleight-of-hand meant that protection 'slid easily into surveillance.'[30] The regulation of female sexuality was given high priority in new laws and courts as well as by social agencies.[31]

Since the late-nineteenth century widespread fears about Montreal's thriving sex trade and its links to an international web of prostitution led to assumptions about a seemingly ubiquitous threat to young women's virtue. Tales of seduction and the white slave trade were rampant in the press in Montreal at the turn of the century and continued through the interwar period.[32] A year after the 1886 Charlton Act had passed in the House of Commons criminalizing seduction, the Montreal Woman's Christian Temperance Union, committed to protecting women who travelled alone to Montreal, posted placards in English and French in railway stations to warn unsuspecting women of the dangers awaiting them.[33] In 1912 the *Montreal Witness* offered a story on City Alderman Blumenthal's rescue of an eighteen-year-old woman who had been forced into an 'evil life' in Montreal's underworld after having been seduced.[34] Stories of girls being victimized for purposes of commercial prostitution proliferated, and as late as the 1930s the Fédération nationale St-Jean-Baptiste, warned parents against letting their daughters take certain jobs lest they be pawns in the white slave trade.[35]

In the 1910s the juvenile court began hearing from girls who claimed to have unwittingly and sometimes unwillingly placed themselves in danger. Seduction stories were often set far from girls' homes and communities and increasingly employed that emblem of modernity, the automobile. The car became a prime location for seduction because it combined a sense of adventure, freedom, privacy, and risk. Girls were likely warned against accepting car rides, which made them all the more appealing to adolescents and good material for seduction tales. When sixteen-year-old Regina C. was brought into court in 1924 for deserting her home, for example, it heard that one summer night a year earlier she had been seduced following a stranger's invitation to a car ride.[36]

As Beth Bailey notes, courting couples experienced the automobile generally as a positive social transformation, turning dating into an American pastime.[37] The other side of the story, as the Lynds' study of 'Middletown' in the United States reveals, suggested that the automobile introduced new levels of 'sexual peril' for women, being 'houses of prostitution on wheels.'[38] Parents and court officials were undoubtedly aware of this evolution in courting and emphasized the vulnerable position of young women once settled in the passenger seat. From the early years of the juvenile court the problem of men luring young women into cars had been identified as 'a not uncommon way of victimizing ... children.'[39] Some working-class adolescent girls eagerly accepted rides in cars yet in doing so sacrificed control of the situation to the driver.[40] One Montreal girl claimed she accepted a ride with a young man with whom she worked and 'this is when it happened.'[41] In response to the question regarding her first seduction, Marcelle T. claimed that at twelve she had met a boy in the street who offered a ride in his automobile. It was a slippery slope from accepting a ride to a night in a hotel in Montreal North where she was 'deflowered.'[42]

In these cases involving car rides, girls' stories functioned to highlight their susceptibility to the promise of adventure and men's wiles and demands, and they promoted their innocence. Such a tale perhaps helped Lucienne M. by distracting the court from the details of her life in a disorderly house where she worked as a prostitute. Her first time, she alleged, involved being taken by force in an automobile.[43] Another means of minimizing their own sex delinquency was to claim to have been unconscious. Béatrice M. insisted that she had been hypnotized and seduced while in St Jérôme, Quebec, visiting a friend in the circus.[44]

In the girls' stories of their first seduction, unnamed men formed an elaborate cast of characters: likely boyfriends who girls refused to name; those who the girl did not know or care to remember; or the more pernicious person who lured the unsuspecting girl to her 'fall.' In the typology of sexual villains, as Dubinsky and Givertz note, none provoked more anxiety than the stranger.[45] The stranger diverted attention from men, including boyfriends, the girls wished to protect. Though nameless, the stranger was at times a familiar character on the Montreal landscape. According to antivice reformers Montreal, a port city, had a chronic problem of transient men, especially soldiers and sailors.[46] During the wars, girls frequently pointed to the menace of the predatory soldier. During the First World War adolescent actress Aurore M. claimed to have been seduced by a soldier.[47] Another adolescent girl confessed to have dated a soldier and going to the moving-picture houses; but then one afternoon he attacked and seduced her.[48] In June 1942 two adolescent girls accompanied a group of young men on a joy ride. They were gone for most of the night and Thérèse E. claimed she was afraid to return home because her father had warned her that breaking curfew would be met with reform school. Off to St Laurent Boulevard the girls went where they encountered a number of soldiers, one of whom took her to a room and 'debauched' her.[49] The court, while recognizing that the morals of soldiers were less than ideal, focused its attention on the campaigns to control 'khaki-mad' girls rather than the servicemen.[50]

Although the court may have believed the girls' stories of their first seduction, their unrepentant behaviour – involving desertions and further sexual experience – meant they were a danger to themselves and society. Juvenile court officials expressed fear that adolescent girls who were easily enticed into sexual relations with men would just as easily wind up in the city's thriving sex trade, like the case of Lucienne M. earlier in this chapter. These girls were described as easily led or influenced by both men and older girls, as moral degenerates, and sometimes as feebleminded. While seduction tales and the vulnerability of young women still struck a chord with reformers, parents, and juvenile court workers, by the end of the First World War, the culpable sex delinquent had transcended the victim prostitute as the city's problem female. The tales of seduction then encouraged the court to incarcerate these girls in the name of protection and redemption.

Force and Coercion

For adolescent girls brought to court, rape and sexual coercion were all too common experiences. In explaining their stories girls rarely used the word 'rape' or 'sexual molestation' but it was not unusual for a girl to claim that 'he forced me.' This explanation for their lack of virginity shares many similarities to the seduction defence: it pointed to their innocence and for some garnered the sympathy of the court. These cases depart from seduction cases in that the men involved were named and often they were older men who had some association with the family or neighbourhood. Like the incest cases discussed later, the details of these cases often surprised family members and required the girl have an impeccable reputation to be believed.

Cases of rape underscore the danger present in a girl's domestic environment. Opportunity for rape occurred where a boarder had been left alone with daughters. In 1924 Yvonne B.'s stepmother brought her to court for being pregnant. The court sent Yvonne to the maternity hospital but not before it heard the details of her sexual history. When asked to reveal who had seduced her, she accused a thirty-four-year-old boarder of raping her three times in her parents' absence. Although she did not come to court on her own to demand redress – it was her stepmother who had brought her to court to punish her for being pregnant – once there, she denied any culpability. In order to be taken seriously, though, two facts had to be established: that Yvonne resisted her attacker and that he had a dubious reputation. Yvonne explained her earlier silence on the issue as a response to his threats and maintained that she struggled against him but was unable to escape. The bad character of the boarder – a man with four children placed in a variety of institutions around the city, with irregular work habits, and who was often under the influence of alcohol – meant in this case he was arrested and sent to Bordeaux jail. She, in turn, was sent to the maternity hospital.[51]

The court maintained a sceptical attitude toward girls' stories of rape and coercion. 'Incorrigible' fifteen-year-old Fernande was, according to the probation officer, like most working girls: she liked her freedom. Madame D. had brought her daughter to court in June 1944, frustrated over late nights spent in the company of an unnamed young man. Fernande deflected attention away from this suitor when she was asked to explain why her medical exam had revealed she was no longer a virgin. To the probation officer and the court physician, she claimed that at age ten her mother had forced her to share a bed with a boarder, whom she named for the court. Her mother denied this allegation, insisting that her daughter was vengeful and lying. The probation officer was similarly suspicious about the verity of the girl's tale, although it shed enough doubt on the moral condition of the home that the court was inspired to place her at the Soeurs du Bon Pasteur provincial house for two years.[52]

Thirteen-year-old Rose A. confessed to all her mother's complaints about her behaviour in the juvenile court. The catalogue of typical adolescent misbehaviour – missing school, leaving home without permission, refusing to help around the house, not listening to her parents, and coming home late – had little overtly to do with sex. But when the probation officer inquired into her sexual history she revealed that the widowed father of her neighbourhood friends had seduced her 'by force.' When Judge Lacroix asked for details, she explained how this man had taken off her culottes and raped her. In his interrogation of Rose, the judge was clearly attempting to determine if she was truly raped: Did you scream? Did you bleed? Was this the first time? Have you been with others?[53] The court interviewed the man in question but it appears that the court was undecided about who to believe. In order to monitor Rose she was made a ward of the court until age twenty-one; the records are silent as to whether the man was pursued by the law.

In another case, an uncontrollable adolescent girl with bad friends shared the blame for being coerced into sexual relations. In 1938, Fleurette G., a thirteen year old, was hired to clean floors for fifty cents by a man known to her. According to her, he touched her and wanted to have sexual relations with her. She refused to have sexual intercourse and oral sex with him but claimed he forced her to let him touch her while masturbating, for which he gave her money. The doctor claimed that the hymen was 'nearly intact.' The probation officer found her honest and her story believable but still she was made a ward of the court until twenty-one and given a suspended sentence under condition that she obey her father and never go out in the evening and only during the day with permission.[54]

According to the evidence they provided to the juvenile court, then, girls also entered into sexual relations for monetary gain. As we saw in chapter 5 girls' economic vulnerability could leave them open to sexually coercive situations. Sexual exchanges of this sort happened close to the girls' homes and in areas where probation officers would have suspected such deeds to occur, like the red-light district. Although the court was quick to believe that unscrupulous and depraved men preyed on adolescent girls, probation officers were also likely to assume that girls' bodies and minds were contaminated as a result, which justified incarceration or strict surveillance.

In 1936 a pair of sisters and their girlfriend were stopped for begging without a licence. As they told the court, the sisters, aged twelve and furteen, had been asked by their mother to raise money because their father had failed to provide proper support. The interrogation of these girls followed their daily exploits as they begged for coins in their neighbourhood. When asked about boys, they admitted to various sexual episodes in parks and alleyways. The girls' desperate need for money became part of this scenario, as they engaged in masturbation for between five and fifty cents. One of the girls admitted doing it three or four times a week during the summer. The court judged these girls delinquent and they were given a suspended sentence under the conditions that they go to school and refrain from begging and bad behaviour with boys.[55] In the case of girls accepting money for sex, it is difficult to discern the level of coercion and of agency involved. What is clear is that probation officers seriously considered what girls exchanged for meagre amounts of money and aimed to prevent the pattern from continuing. The girls' purpose in telling the caseworker of such incidents is ambiguous: perhaps they hoped it pointed to the dismal state of their impoverished lives or they may have hoped to avert accusations of precocious sexual desire.

In certain cases a pattern of taking money in exchange for sex led to incarceration, regardless of the economic or social vulnerability of the girls implicated. One night in 1936 two fifteen-year-old French-Canadian girls were arrested on the streets. They were found that night wandering because they did not have the money for admission to a club. Their story to the probation officer involved several incidents of exchanging sex for money or for services, such as a car ride. One of the pair admitted to going to Chinatown where they were paid ten to fifteen cents for manual masturbation sessions.[56] No doubt the location of this sexual exchange confirmed racist assumptions about the licentiousness of Chinese men, but it was the girls who were considered wilful and punished. The girls' behaviour was met with a harsh sentence of three years in reform school.

Sixteen-year-old May, a Chinese-Canadian girl who was brought to court by her father for desertion, told the court she had been coerced into sexual relations for much-needed money. This arrangement had been struck when her father's friend realized that she was poorly paid and in desperate straights. At first the man, also Chinese, agreed to give her money as a gift but after several months he began to demand sex. She admitted to having given in to this man under the threat that he would tell her father. Although sexual relations occurred only once, she found herself pregnant. Fearful of her father finding out she agreed to leave the city with this man and take a job at a hotel north of the city. Her father appealed to the court to bring her back. Her story of coercion appeared believable to her family and the court, although one might imagine that she, like many other juvenile court girls, would not enjoy the support of the court. The probation officer noted that a childhood spent in Montreal's Chinatown was necessarily deficient in proper role models and moral guidance. May, though, seemed an otherwise obedient daughter and good student. Nonetheless, she was placed in the detention house for weeks, where it was determined that she was pregnant. This was followed by internment at a maternity home for eight months. The Chinese man was fined $100.[57]

Probation officers likely did not expect that the sexual histories would reveal rape or the coercion of sex for money. Girls who were considered of a tender age or whose reputations were beyond reproach were able to find a sympathetic ear at the court. Others whose involvement in sexual acts appeared to be ambiguous were punished for it. These cases of rape or potentially coercive sex underscore girls' sexual vulnerability and also suggest the juvenile court was ineffective in protecting it.

Domestic Sexual Abuse

A common revelation in the adolescent girls' confessions to probation officers was that the 'perpetrator' of their first seduction was an older male relative or 'social father' (most often boyfriends of mothers).[58] Domestic sexual abuse was not specific to one decade or era: it persisted throughout the time period under study. According to their stories, these girls experienced abuse in their pre- or early-adolescent years, or the abuse began following the death of the mother. The sexual abuse stopped once the girls were able to get away from home through employment or running away. In Linda Gordon's study of domestic sexual abuse she determines that the victims conformed to one of two scripts: in the first, mothers were often absent, leaving a feminine void to be filled by the isolated incest victim; in the second, the sex delinquent 'acted out,' using her sexuality outside the home, sometimes in exchange for money or reward that would then lead to her appearance in juvenile court.[59] To the Montreal juvenile court came many who fit the latter category of incest survivors – those who acted out against their families, who often deserted the family situation, and who revealed this family secret when brought to court. In this court, girls' allegations of domestic sexual abuse faded relative to evidence of their own promiscuity and recalcitrance. Men, therefore, were not often pursued in the court system.[60] This must have frustrated girls whose juvenile court appearance was the closest they came to telling their stories and demanding justice.

Incest in this period was covered by the Canadian Criminal Code and subject to severe punishment. Under the code, it was illegal for fathers and mothers to have sexual relations with their children, or for sex to occur between sisters and brothers, and grandparents and grandchildren. Along with male members of the family, daughters were subject to punishment unless they argued successfully that they were taken by force. A conservative Roman Catholic family tradition also served to reinforce patriarchal relations within the family.[61] In her study of incest cases in Quebec from 1858 to 1938, Marie-Aimée Cliche has argued that the authority of Quebec fathers to physically discipline children 'for their own good' opened the door to further abuse.[62] Familial imperatives that daughters obey patriarchs appear to have further isolated victims. As Cliche's study has shown, incest cases made a rare appearance in the province's criminal courts. Along with Cliche, Karen Dubinsky and Joan Sangster have shown in their studies of incest in early-twentieth-century Ontario that the 'paucity' of criminal charges for incest can be historically related to a combination of victims' guilt, familial pressure on the victim to recant, and girls' choice to escape the abusive situation rather than to confront it in a law court.[63]

Incestuous relations, as revealed in juvenile court cases, emphasize the power of male relatives over girls. In the 1970s feminists mounted a compelling argument that rape (and by extension, incest) was about power, not sex;[64] however, over the last two decades the scholarship has reacted to correct this 'desexualization' of rape and recognize that incest is indeed about the appropriation of women's bodies and our culture's acceptance of male sexuality as dominant.[65] In her study of rape and heterosexual conflict in turn-of-the-century Ontario, Karen Dubinsky wrote: 'An analysis that diminishes the sexual component of rape cannot help us illuminate the crucial role sexual violence plays in heightening women's sense of shame and in making the pursuit of sexual pleasure such a minefield for women.'[66] Girls employed a variety of methods in resisting sexual violence, including running away from home and subsequently using their bodies to support themselves. In the context of the juvenile tribunal the centrality of adolescent female sexual behaviour meant suspicion fell on those who accused family members of sexual abuse.

The early-twentieth-century juvenile court was created to discipline children but also to protect them, and it was ostensibly a move toward recognition of children's rights.[67] In this way we would expect to find this a compassionate and receptive forum for girls' allegations of abuse; however, it is in these cases where the ambivalence about protecting and punishing female sexuality is most conspicuous. Under articles 29 and 33 of the 1908 JDA the juvenile court judge had the authority to condemn adults for leading minors into delinquency. Because court officials did not see the causal relationship between incest and subsequent delinquent behaviour, these articles were not typically used in this way. As Elizabeth Pleck has argued, for the case of family violence in general, what prevented reform against its occurrence were traditions upholding family privacy, parents' rights, and the primacy of family integrity.[68] Joan Sangster suggests that while officials blamed incest on the poverty and immorality of parents, they were blind to the material reality of patriarchal relations within families and to sexual abuse as 'an instrument of masculine power and control.'[69] Critics of the early juvenile court fault the institution for violating the rights of working-class families to privacy; however, in these cases upholding 'family' rights meant individual girls' rights were obscured.[70] The Montreal court sometimes extricated girls from the danger of their home and at other times left them with the family to maintain its integrity.

Characteristic of many female delinquency cases involving incest was the fact that the abuse occurred years prior to the court appearance. In these cases, where the abuser no longer posed an immediate danger to the girl, the fact of incest was largely ignored in the proceedings. In the case of Marguerite G., a thirteen year old brought to court in 1938 for a variety of delinquent acts, the probation officer learned that her maternal grandfather had raped her six years earlier. Her father had brought her to court for refusing to attend school, running in the streets at night, and using insulting language. The probation officer's investigation into her sexual history unleashed a long record of domestic sexual abuse. The court found that she had of her own volition entered into sexual relations at age twelve but this was years after she had been raped by her grandfather. A male cousin also raped her. When her parents separated she lived with her mother and her lover, who, according to Marguerite, also made sexual advances toward her. Because her father's home did not appear to pose any danger to her, she was returned to him. In order to discipline her the court recommended to the father to send her to a boarding school.[71] The court in this case did not burden itself to prosecute the male abusers in her family, rather it focused on correcting her current delinquent behaviour.

In other cases the victim was punished, as was the case of Laura B., a French-Canadian adolescent from a small-town. Laura's case is rare among other cases of incest: in 1922 her father had been found guilty of mistreating and raping her and condemned to fifteen years in prison.[72] This came about because when she was eleven years old a local priest had complained to the provincial police that Laura was being mistreated by her father. The judge prohibited the child from living with her 'unfit' mother, who, according to rumour kept a house of prostitution. Therefore, shortly after the arrest of her father, Laura was sent to an aunt in Montreal and when that arrangement fell through, the attorney-general authorized placing her at another home also in Montreal. By the summer of 1922 her guardian declared Laura to be uncontrollable and she was placed at the Catholic reform school for girls, the Maison de Lorette. After two years in the reform school, the juvenile court judge authorized her commitment to the reform school and continued her status as ward of the court until age twenty-one.

Other sexually abused girls were found delinquent by the court and sent to reform school for a combination of punishment and protection. This occurred when the court was unable to prove incest or was reluctant to believe the girl's story, assuming it was yet another 'pardon tale.' The story of a thirteen year old, Violet M., is a case in point. In the summer of 1928 Violet's mother had brought a complaint against her for desertion, immorality, and being generally hard to manage. Violet confessed to the 'immorality' but blamed her father for her downfall. She rescinded this charge later stating that a boy, whose name she could not remember was responsible. In this case the home situation was judged by the probation officer to be physically and morally dreadful: both parents were alcoholics, Violet's father had been jailed at Bordeaux for non-support and abusive conduct toward his wife, and Violet's older sister had accused their father of incest. The probation officer, E. Fales-Jones, avoided addressing the issue of incest in the family, as Violet's story had apparently become muddled. She wrote: 'Careful investigation shows that this girl is untruthful, immoral, and very difficult to control, that she needs constant supervision, and careful retraining.' Judge Lacroix sentenced her to the Girls' Cottage Industrial School (GCIS) until her eighteenth birthday. Subsequent to her court appearance, the Society for the Protection of Women and Children intervened on her behalf and Monsieur M. was charged under Article 29 for abusive behaviour toward his daughters. The juvenile court agreed that Violet be made a ward of the society until age twenty-one. Four years after her initial appearance in court Violet's case was reexamined, prompted by demands of her father to have her released. In a letter from Dorothea Heney of the GCIS to the juvenile court judge, she summarized that Violet had been threatened by her father in 1928 to withdraw her accusation of incest. Her sister had not recanted and Monsieur M. was found guilty. The official GCIS line suggested that Violet's four-year sentence was about protection. At the time of her sentencing, however, the four years was clearly about punishment and retraining.[73]

Common to the home lives of female juvenile delinquents were violence, instability, alcohol abuse, and exposure to adult sexual activity. Nowhere was this more explicit than in cases involving father-daughter incest. The Montreal police picked up eleven-year-old Juliette L. of Ville Emard (a Montreal suburb) for vagrancy early in 1924. The history of this girl that was presented in probation officer Marie Mignault's report reveals the classic elements of this kind of abuse: an absent mother and an isolated girl dependent on her father. During the First World War Juliette's parents were imprisoned (unfortunately the records do not indicate for what offence) and she and her four siblings were placed with their grandfather. Because Juliette's mother died at war's end, once Monsieur L. was released from prison, he took charge of the children. Apparently he remarried but by 1923 that marriage had ended. At that time her father, now having only Juliette, moved into his brother's house. They shared a room and its sole bed. Juliette claims she was awoken one night with her father on top of her. Aware on some level of Juliette's predicament, her aunt offered the girl another bed elsewhere in the house, but Monsieur L. refused the change the sleeping arrangements. From her uncle's house they rented a room, again with one bed and stayed there one month. One day her father hit her and she 'deserted,' taking refuge at a former neighbour's. While the police charged Juliette with vagrancy, the juvenile court probation officer defined Juliette as 'a neglected and abandoned child' and recommended her placement at the Maison Ste-Domitille industrial school for girls run by the Soeurs du Bon Pasteur until age fourteen.[74]

In some cases involving father-daughter incest, the father was responsible for bringing charges against the girls for sex delinquencies.[75] In the following case the father, a widower, described his actions as 'loving' his two daughters whom he regularly sexually abused. The father had the girls charged with desertion because they came and went as they pleased and he had evidence that they were involved sexually with boys. An investigation into their situation resulted in a long list of the girls' lovers. However, what was also revealed in the juvenile court was that from the ages of ten and twelve these girls had been sexually and physically abused. At eighteen and sixteen years of age, respectively, Germaine and Gabrielle L. attempted to resist this pattern of domestic sexual abuse and interfered with their father's power over them; they were turned over to the juvenile court by him, charged with desertion and theft.

In this case, the mother died in 1914 and the girls were brought up in convents. In 1920 their father resumed custody of his daughters and moved into the grandmother's house. When Germaine was twelve he 'taught' her how to 'give him pleasure' and for five years this continued. She spent entire nights with him once they lived in the same house. He told her that 'she had to serve him as a wife'[76] and that she was not to talk about it. Germaine's situation exhibited the classic traits of what Linda Gordon labels as domestic incest: the father was committed to and dependent on the eldest daughter as a manager of his household and as sexual partner.[77] At 18, Germaine had never worked outside the home and claimed to be afraid of her father. She was severely punished by her father the one time she attempted to leave his house seeking out a sympathetic aunt. Upon her return he beat her. He also beat his younger daughter, who was sexually abused from the age of ten or eleven. Both sisters were sexually abused by the father but responded to it differently: Germaine, the older daughter, almost always obliged him and was rewarded with clothes and money; Gabrielle, on the other hand, resisted her father and was denied the necessities of life. Gabrielle managed to escape for short periods, taking up work outside the home.

By the autumn of 1924 the power dynamic in the household was breaking down and the father had lost control of his daughters. It was then that he sought the help of the juvenile court to discipline them. The evidence of sexual abuse led the probation officer to criticize the father's behaviour, but the evidence of sex delinquency caused her to recommend that the younger sister be placed in the reform school with the nuns of the Bon Pasteur for rehabilitation. The juvenile court doctor found Germaine to be pregnant by her father and she was probably sent away to have the baby.[78] Because the girls were acting out as sex delinquents, they were not constructed as victims of a sexual predator – their desertion was not understood as a response to an abusive home life, and they were denied the protection and sympathy of the court.[79] The records are unclear as to whether the father was ever prosecuted.

The pattern of domestic sexual abuse in the preceding case had continued for five years and, ironically, once it began to breakdown the father turned to the law to reestablish and bolster what he saw as his right to his daughters' subservience and obedience. Feminist scholars interpret incest as a brutal form of the socializing process of femininity to which most girls are exposed. In this case incest functioned to reinforce male supremacy, docile femininity, and the primacy of family life.[80]

In cases where mothers were not absent, father–daughter incest inevitably problematized relationships between the mothers and their daughters. In cases where the mother was present, what explains their failure to protect their daughters? This question raises issues of the relative power between husbands and wives, wife battering, and in the other extreme, complicity in the abuse. Alice G.'s mother brought her to the juvenile court for desertion in early December 1918. The oldest of five children, Alice was sent out to work at a glove factory, bringing home five and a half dollars weekly. Alice's parents did not get along, especially when her father drank: earlier that autumn he had locked his wife out of the family home. During her mother's absence, Alice's father raped her. According to the probation officer, Alice was defiant against her father, having him arrested. From jail he wrote and asked that she rescind her allegation. After three months in jail he was released on bail, and again he insisted she take back her story, threatening her to the point that she had to make a quick escape through a window. Meanwhile the mother had returned and had her daughter arrested for deserting. In cases involving incest, girls often felt that they had nothing to lose by leaving home.[81] The charges against Alice were dismissed once the father was found guilty. The mother's actions in this case can be explained in a number of ways. First she, like many women, may have been dependent on her husband and wanted to keep her husband out of jail by making the daughter look like the troublemaker. She may have also been jealous and angry at the daughter, blaming her for family discord. On the more positive side, Alice's mother may have wanted the court to place her out of reach of her husband who had not yet been found guilty.[82] In this case the daughter seems to lack the paralyzing shame that often accompanied incest and prevented girls from escaping abusive situations.

Girls were also abused by their older brothers. The way girls experienced incest with older brothers is difficult to establish; the structure and meaning of sibling incest suggests it might have been less brutal than father–daughter incest although it undoubtedly was coercive as older brothers wielded more social and familial power than their sisters. In two 1918 cases girls were brought to court for immoral conduct and both claimed they had been seduced by their older brothers. Both were typical wartime, recalcitrant, adolescent girls, attending the cinema, refusing to hold down jobs for any length of time, and having sexual relations (mutual masturbation and intercourse) with boys. In the case of Aline D. her brother seduced her at twelve; this boy was not pursued, however, because he was a soldier in the prestigious French-Canadian 22nd Regiment. Adrienne D. was seduced by her older brother at age thirteen. Both girls had been brought to court by their fathers as sex delinquents and were incarcerated in the reform school as voluntary cases.[83] Once the girls had acted out, separating themselves from abusive situations and becoming involved with other men, the court officials interpreted the problem as the girls' precocious sexuality, not domestic sexual abuse.

There is no evidence that the brothers in the preceding cases were pursued in court for having sexual relations with their sisters and indeed it was rare for a boy to be brought in on such a charge.[84] In this case, a fifteen-year-old boy committed incest with his seven-year-old sister. In 1916, the father of Wilfrid C. exposed this family secret after becoming increasingly frustrated with his son's behaviour: Wilfrid refused to go to school, hung out in the streets, and came in late. An absent mother – she had died a year earlier- and the two older brothers living away from the family provided the opportunity for Wilfrid to abuse his younger sister, Simonne. Wilfrid worked in a cigar factory and was occasionally responsible for his little sister. In his deposition the father wrote: 'On or about the first day of July 1916, Wilfrid C. my son age 15 years did cohabit and have sexual intercourse with his sister Simonne age 7 years against the law in such case made and provided Criminal Code 146 Sect 204.' Little Simonne was sent to a doctor for physical confirmation and the doctor wrote: 'There is ample evidence of coitus having occurred ... The hymen has been partially ruptured and there is recent injury.' Wilfrid admitted committing incest with his sister about twenty-five times. He was sentenced to three years at the École de Réforme for boys. In this case the father was clearly repulsed and angered by his son's sin.[85] While clearly illegal and repugnant, sibling incest was simply not a traditional concern of this court. Why this case came to court and others did not can be explained perhaps by the large difference in age between the boy of fifteen and the girl of seven. Also, the little sister was unquestionably constructed as a victim in this case: a daughter – the youngest child and only girl in the family – had lost her mother and was considered too young to be a sexual delinquent. The father may have been motivated by mounting frustration about the boy's general behaviour, and the evidence of incest pushed him to involve the court, despite the ignominious nature of the delinquency.

Girls who made allegations of incest in the juvenile court were often required to do so in front of their abusers. Rita B. was brought in to court in 1924 for having deserted her family; during her desertion she rented a flat and was having an affair with a married man. When asked to reveal the name of the man who had first seduced her, she declared to the judge that her stepfather had raped her several years prior to her juvenile court appearance. The judge then asked for a clarification: 'Your stepfather who is here?' 'Yes,' she replied. The judge then turned to her stepfather and asked what he had to say in reply to his stepdaughter's testimony. He stated her claims were false. 'Even if your wife would say it's true?' the judge queried. One could almost hear his contemptuous reply, 'Yes; is she able to provide witnesses?'[86] Her stepfather knew well that the lack of witnesses and a family's reluctance to break the silence around domestic sexual abuse sheltered him from legal prosecution.

Girls sometimes transformed their stories from the time the probation officer privately recorded events to the trial where family members would be in attendance. The distressing nature of this legal affair may have forced some girls to reconsider their allegations of incest or confess they had fabricated them. When her mother had her arrested for desertion, Agnès D. retorted that at home, her father had wanted to seduce her. Facing the threat of having to answer to her family before the judge, Agnès asked to be pardoned for maligning her father.[87]

The declared *modis operandi* of the juvenile court was to get to the root of delinquent behaviour and put adolescents back on the right track toward honourable lives of thrift, work, and obedience to parents. There is little evidence that female probation officers (who one might think would be empathetic to incest allegations) or juvenile court judges used incest claims as a way of understanding adolescent girls' delinquency. Social scientists at this time had constructed incestuous activity as a social problem; however, it was not employed as an analytical tool to explain girls' (bad) behaviour. McGill University psychology professor J.W. Bridges proposed a broken homes theory of delinquency to explain delinquency in Montreal in the 1920s. In his study of incarcerated anglophone girls he identified a history of sexual abuse. Typical, he wrote, was the girl 'at seven years of age [who] was led into sexual relations with her foster father.'[88] In the case histories of one of the Montreal girls reform schools, the caseworkers wrote of a father who 'had always shown an unusual interest in his daughter ... and she has accused him of incest but [as] this is difficult to prove in court no action was taken against [him].[89] Linda Gordon found that sociologists studying 'maladjusted' girls in this period discovered incidents of incest, but like Professor Bridges, failed to make it an important factor in analysing the root causes of delinquency.[90] By the time the juvenile court was in operation, incest went the way of seduction: responsibility for this deviance was placed on the least powerful, the girl.[91] In a twist of irony, sexually victimized girls who rebelled against their situations and left the family home, searched out street life and modes of behaviour that landed them in institutions.[92]

Once the girl had acted out, separating herself from the abusive situation and taking up with other men seemingly of her own volition, court officials understood *her* to be the problem and not the abusive male. Incest was seen to be disrupting the social order, not because it was an expression of the power differential between daughters (who had little) and fathers (who were bestowed ultimate control in the family) but because it challenged the sanctity of the family as the fundamental social unit upon which society was built.

Conclusion

When adolescent girls appeared before the juvenile court, sexuality was placed at the centre of their cases. Doctors and probation officers probed their bodies and sexual histories, intensifying their construction as sex delinquents. In court, girls explained their 'debauched' states with a variety of rhetorical strategies. Some used seduction tales to emphasize their innocence; others demanded justice for rape and abuse; and many resisted dominant discourses about their sexual delinquency, rejecting the notion they were 'bad' and invoking a generational challenge to adolescent courtship, a trend that would spread especially in the 1940s.

Sources from the juvenile court suggest that girls in early-twentieth-century Montreal pursued sexual adventure but were also victims of rape and domestic sexual abuse. The juvenile court with its female caseworkers and medical professionals generated evidence of a gamut of sexual activities from adolescent romance to rape and incest. It upheld male sexual prerogative in families, however, choosing to downplay allegations of aggression and instead punishing errant female sexuality. Working-class families were often found complicit, not that the male aggressors were necessarily taken to court, but that their homes were condemned as unhygienic and immoral. Although domestic sexual abuse was increasingly addressed by early-twentieth-century psychologists and sociologists, it was not central to their explanations of delinquency and adolescent behaviour. In this court the experts collectively failed to use incest as an analytical category to explain delinquency leaving no room for girls to receive justice. Sexual delinquency, accompanied by a general rejection of obedience to parents made it difficult for girls to gain understanding or compassion in court; rather, this behaviour was used as evidence that the girls were the perpetrators of sexual deviance first at home and then on the streets.

Because of their gender, their age, and their class, adolescent girls might appear as naive, defenceless, and vulnerable in the juvenile court. They did, however, exhibit a certain capacity to assert themselves in the face of family members who abused them, court officials who condemned and did not believe them, and interrogations of their private lives. There were girls who maintained their stories in the face of damning evidence, but it was usually only the older girls, especially those brought to court in the 1940s, who were most effective in asserting their lives and claiming their sexuality.

chapter 7

Reform, Rehabilitation, and Riots: The Training School Experiment in Quebec

By the time she reached eighteen years of age Lorna H. knew well the Protestant system of 'care' in Montreal. Despite the Montreal Juvenile Delinquents' Court's (MJDC) preference for probation, Protestant institutions that kept girls off the streets, away from delinquent parents, and out of Catholic reformatories, proliferated in the early twentieth century. Lorna's relationship to the juvenile justice system began at age ten when the court declared her and her three siblings protection cases. Although baptized Roman Catholic, some confusion over her ethnic identity [1] initially resulted in her being funnelled through the Protestant network of care institutions. Responsibility for her fell to the Society for the Protection of Women and Children, which placed her with the venerable Ladies' Benevolent Society, a century-old Protestant institution designed for orphaned and abandoned children. She then was fostered out to private homes where she was 'taught the rudiments of a domestic occupation.' [2] Cheap domestic help had to be well behaved, though, and as she reached the age of fourteen her late nights and insubordination resulted in successive failed domestic placements and doomed attempts at reconciliation with extended family. Identified as a snatcher of silk stockings with attitudinal and behaviour problems, incarceration – or institutionalization – became an 'imperative.' By fifteen Lorna had traversed the narrow divide between sympathetic protection case and wilful delinquent girl. The juvenile court judge sent her to the Girls' Cottage Industrial School (GCIS) in 1928 for three years and made her a ward of the court until age nineteen. At the GCIS she did not settle easily into the rehabilitation regime designed for delinquent girls. During her years at the School, she successfully escaped and found her way to Montreal, where she was apprehended and brought back. At the conclusion of her sentence she was placed on parole in the city under the supervision of the school's field worker. Despite being given an allowance, clothing, and 'a good home,' her resistance to this placement led to a transfer to the supervised Young Women's Christian Association boarding house. At the next 'good home' she deserted and succeeded in eluding her parole officer for months, only to be found next in Chinatown. There she was arrested in the Oriental Hotel in the possession of cigarettes and the keys to a boarding house. Still a ward of the juvenile court, she again appeared before the judge. By this time the various Protestant organizations and institutions concerned with wayward girls had grown wary of her potential for rehabilitation. GCIS worker Dorothea H. Heney complained that this girl had been given reasonable opportunities and that her disorderly conduct did 'injustice to herself and undermine[d] the morale of the Industrial School.' Heney recommended Lorna's incarceration at one of the Soeurs du Bon Pasteur's facilities – the Women's Jail or the Maison de Lorette reform school. Thus her last act of defiance as an adolescent was met with a year-long sentence at the Catholic reform school run by the Soeurs du Bon Pasteur.

Lorna's story suggests the complexity of juvenile court dispositions and the role of religion in the treatment of pre-delinquent and delinquent girls. Lorna's journey through myriad Protestant agencies and ultimate condemnation to the Catholic reform school underscores the importance of cultural identities in the practice of juvenile justice. The two reform institutions for girls operating in Montreal in the first half of the twentieth century enjoyed distinct reputations based on their different understandings of discipline and treatment. Treating female delinquency through Catholic reform schools had been well entrenched in Quebec in the 1870s, a fact that alarmed Protestant child savers in Montreal and motivated them to action. On the eve of the juvenile court's opening, in an effort to save Protestant girls from the convent, the GCIS was founded.[3] Thus from the outset, the treatment and destiny of delinquent Protestant daughters were to be different from those provided to Catholic girls in the Soeurs du Bon Pasteur reform school. The most important distinction between the two institutions originated with the Protestant community's determination to open a training school, not a reform school. Just as magdalen houses for young prostitutes gave way to reform schools for girls in the latter part of the previous century, in the 1910s training schools challenged the outdated reform school. In Quebec, it was the Protestant, female, benevolent community that created this alternative to the nineteenth-century reform school.

The elite Protestant women who founded the GCIS built on a tradition of female benevolence that began in the early nineteenth-century with the Ladies' Benevolent Society and the Protestant Orphans Home. Originally concerned with orphans and abandoned children, in the twentieth century these organizations turned their efforts toward delinquent and pre-delinquent girls. While a de-institutionalization movement was well underway, reform schools persisted in the juvenile court era for delinquency and protection cases where adolescents' home lives were judged dangerous or inadequate. Protestant women eschewed the dated and what they considered monstrous convent reformatories in favour of modern training schools that offered the benefits of a proper home. These 'bright, cheery, home-like schools' modernized the youth incarceration experience, updating treatment in the name of 'care.'[4] From its rudimentary beginning, the GCIS embraced psychobiological models of adolescence and new methods to correct wayward female behaviour that promoted rehabilitation and normalization.[5] These facilities operated under the principle that a proper home atmosphere could empower delinquent girls and deliver them from a troubled adolescence to responsible young womanhood. This training school would be fashioned in stark contrast to the Soeurs du Bon Pasteur's reform school for girls: it was conceived of and promoted as a 'home, not a detention house for the wayward or underprivileged girl.'[6]

As we saw in chapter 2, from the mid-nineteenth century Canadians were determined that youthful offenders would be spared the incarceration experience of adults. In Montreal, Catholic religious communities constructed two reform schools in the latter half of the century, separating adolescents under sixteen from adults and housing them in sex-specific facilities. Early in the new century two more reform schools were built by the city's lay Protestant community such that by the time the MJDC opened in 1912 there were four operating in the city. The Soeurs du Bon Pasteur's reform school for girls, the Institut Saint-Antoine for Catholic boys, and the Boys' Farm and Training School for non-Catholic boys have received considerable attention but the smallest and perhaps the most innovative, the GCIS, has been overlooked.[7]

In 1911 the GCIS was found in time to receive the first non-Catholic girls processed by the MJDC. The two Montreal reform schools for girls represent distinct traditions of incarcerating females. While both had the intention of transforming delinquent girls into disciplined young women, they differed dramatically in architecture and programs, reflecting the class, religious, and ethnic orientation of their respective administrations. While nuns and Protestant philanthropists promised a gentler system of incarceration for girls and appeared distinct from 'total custodial institutions,'[8] they were not without contradictions.

In this chapter we find delinquent girls not on the street, at home, or in the court, but behind bars. Those associated with the GCIS would have objected to the reference to bars; indeed theirs was an experiment in surrogate family life, surely the antithesis of the prison experience. The purpose, design, and program of the training school were intended to reflect the most modern and progressive juvenile justice ideas on treatment of wayward girls. Discipline and punishment were not unknown at the school, revealing that its mission was at times compromised by the reality that it was, in fact, an incarceration facility. GCIS rhetoric and physical design suggest overwhelming empathy for the individual girl and a desire to inscribe in her qualities such as passive femininity demonstrable in her approach to housework, her married and maternal future, and willingness to forsake the sexual experience that likely landed her in the juvenile justice system. Years spent in the GCIS were intended to launch a girl from the difficulties of adolescence to mature young adulthood. Girls responded to their incarceration with a mixture of accommodation and resistance. Theirs was the last word at the GCIS in 1946 when escapes and escapades led to the end of an era in training school experimentation.

Incarceration as an Outcome of Girls' Cases

One of the aims of juvenile justice in the first half of the twentieth century was to avoid incarcerating youth, especially with adults. Probation was hailed as the latest innovation in delinquency treatment, yet it was not the only solution used. With new institutions designed specifically for children and adolescents, such as the detention home or the reform school, juvenile justice authorities persisted in locking girls away, either temporarily or for multiyear sentences. Table 7.1 shows that probation alone was used in only a minority of girls cases.

Similarly, in the 1930s and early 1940s, more than 30 per cent of juvenile court girls were incarcerated, at least briefly. In the 1930s, 24 per cent were given sentences in the city's reform schools and another 7.5 per cent were incarcerated for a temporary period then placed on probation. During the Second World War a third of girls appearing before the court for delinquent acts were incarcerated (see table 7.2). A growing proportion of juvenile court girls were sent home with a suspended

Table 7.1 Disposition of girls' cases, 1912, 1918, and 1924

Outcome	1912 no. (%)	1918 no. (%)	1924 no. (%)
Probation	16 (23)	53 (29.5)	19 (8.5
Incarceration	26 (37)	51 (28)	90 (40)
Temporary incarceration (<3 months); Probation	22 (31.5)	50 (28)	46 (20)
Sent home*	–	–	37 (16)
Other**	6 (8.5)	26 (14.5)	35 (15.5)
Total	70	180	227

*Sent home was not a category in 1912 and 1918.
**Other outcomes include: 1912: placed in an asylum (2); dismissed (1); not indicated (3). 1918: placed in an institution (2); dismissed (3); warrant not executed (11); placed in foster home (9); not indicated (1). 1924: placed in an institution (14); warrant not executed (2); discharged (5); suspended sentence (4); withdrawn (4); liberated (1); not found (1), not indicated (4).
Source: MJDC dossiers. (percentages rounded to nearest .5).

sentence provided they observe certain conditions. These conditions included obedience to parents, observation of curfew, and restricted, if not forbidden access, to particular friends. In conjunction with this conditional release, the court usually declared the girl a ward of the court until twenty-one years of age. This system meant that girls lived under a constant threat of a return to juvenile court and incarceration. This weapon was used by parents and probation officers to exact compliance from these girls. Therefore, in the experience but also the imagination of girls labelled delinquent, the reform school played a dramatic role in juvenile justice. As the number of admissions to reform schools indicates, over the course of the early-twentieth century, girls' presence behind bars did not diminish (see table 7.3). The facilities and incarceration experience, however, did vary over time, as we will see.

The Origins of Non-Catholic Reform Schools in Quebec

The MJDC incarcerated juvenile delinquents according to sex and religion. The two largest and oldest institutions served the Catholic population: the École de Réforme for boys was administered by the Frères de la Charité and the École de Réforme for girls was run by the Soeurs du Bon Pasteur. In the early-twentieth century, the Montreal Protestant elite founded private charities to administer reform and industrial schools for

Table 7.2 Outcome in girls' cases, Montreal Juvenile Delinquents' Court, 1930s and 1940s

Outcome	1930s no. (%)	1940s no. (%)
Probation	38 (16)	10 (5)
Incarceration	57 (24)	62 (31.6)
Temporary incarceration (<3 months) followed by probation	18 (7.5)	0
Placed*	26 (11)	20 (10)
Dismissed	16 (7)	8 (4)
Sent home	8 (3)	0
Sentence Suspended with conditions	72 (30)	88 (45)
Other**	4 (2)	7 (3.6)
Total	239 (100.5)	196 (99.2)

*Placed includes in an institution other than a reform school, or with a foster family.
**Other includes: warrant not executed; not indicated; or sent out of province.
Source: MJDC dossiers, based on a two-month sample from 1930, 1932, 1934, 1936, 1938, 1940, 1942, 1944.

non-Catholics. The first, the Boys' Farm and Training School at Shaw-bridge, Quebec, was established in 1908 by a group of Protestant businessmen who had previously been active in the Boys' Home of Montreal.[9] Its ties with the Protestant elite ensured its solvency, before the province became involved in running reform schools.[10] A cottage-style reformatory, the Boys' Farm was comprised a main two-storey building and six dormitories on a 250-acre farm. The boys worked on the farm, attended classes for three hours each day, were required to do military drill, say daily prayers, and participate in some form of recreation.[11]

The founding of the second Protestant institution was a response to the establishment of the MJDC. In 1911, in anticipation of the court opening the following year, the GCIS was founded by a group of female Protestant philanthropists. Although called an industrial school, which according to provincial statute was authorized to house children under fourteen as protection cases, this institution functioned also as a reformatory school, incarcerating delinquent girls sent by the juvenile court.[12] The GCIS began as a home in Outremont that supported a handful of girls and a matron.[13] Montreal philanthropists Beatrice and Mary Hickson opened the school in response to the need for facilities for non-Catholic delinquent girls. Within the first year, the school moved to a larger house on the south shore of Montreal. Two more moves were necessary before it

Table 7.3 Population of Montreal reform schools for girls
(on 31 December)

Year	Girls' Cottage Industrial School	École de Réforme
1911	(6)	29
1912	n/a	40
1913	n/a	51
1914	13	(60)
1915	17	99
1916	17	113
1917	16	138
1918	20	135
1919	no report	146
1920	13	118
1921	6	78
1922	12	53
1923	34	50
1924	31	66
1925	29	78
1926	39	90
1927	41	94
1928	34	92
1929	40	88
1930	39	108
1931	40	124
1932	32	109
1933	34	119
1934	33	140
1935	30	140
1936	39	138
1937	30	128
1938	39	175
1939	40	235
1940	n/a	n/a
1941	36	216
1942	31	206
1943	40	249
1944	32	215
1945	32	166

Sources: Quebec, Sessional Papers, Report of Inspectors of Asylums, Reform Schools and Industrial Schools for Province of Quebec, 1911–14; Quebec, Statistical Yearbook, 1914–46.

settled in the Eastern Townships, sixty miles from Montreal. There it stayed from 1922 to 1946. In the first years of operation this fledgling institution suffered financial uncertainty, using 'bazaars, raffles, concerts and every conceivable arduous form of collecting money' to keep it open.[14] Although the school had been incorporated under the Reformatory Schools Act, it did not receive sufficient funds from the government to cover its operating costs.[15] Only in 1921 did the school reach an agreement with the province that put them on the same financial footing as the Soeurs du Bon Pasteur.[16]

Thus by the time the juvenile court opened, four distinct reform schools built along religious lines and serving sex-specific populations were operating in Montreal. All four were privately run institutions, two by Catholic orders and the others by lay Protestant boards. The smallest, the GCIS, was perhaps the most ambitious in its attempt to be a true expression of progressive juvenile justice. Purposely designed as a critique of the older convent model of reform school and the only facility of its kind in the province, this institution became Quebec's best example of a training school.

'A good woman and a true home maker': The Purpose of the Training School for Girls

The aims and purpose of the GCIS were shaped in part by legal responsibility, and the class and ethnic biases of the board of directors and the superintendents, who through this school put into place 'modern' methods of social work. The federal Juvenile Delinquents' Act (JDA) (1908) and the provincial industrial and reform schools acts laid the framework for the functioning of the GCIS. The JDA defined juvenile delinquents as children in need of care, as opposed to criminals requiring incarceration. The directors of the school referred to the Act in explaining their purpose: 'That the care and custody and discipline of a Juvenile delinquent shall approximate, as nearly as may be, that which should be given by its parents, and that as far as practicable every Juvenile delinquent shall be treated not as a criminal, but as a misdirected, misguided child and one needing aid, encouragement, help and assistance.'[17]

The provincial legislation that legally founded the GCIS in 1912 declared the mandate of the school: 'to provide a home and facilities for the education, improvement and training of friendless, delinquent, incorrigible or destitute girls in the City of Montreal and elsewhere in the Province of Quebec and of organizing a training school.'[18] When the

MJDC opened in 1912, the GCIS began receiving non-Catholic girls between the ages of twelve and sixteen; parents were also entitled to commit their daughters, creating a category of 'voluntary' cases.

The nature of the retraining depended in large measure on the members of the Protestant elite who stood as directors of the school. The school was run by a female board of directors whose roster included prominent families like the Ogilvies and the McConnells. Many of the board volunteers were also eminent members of other organizations such as the Montreal Local Council of Women and the Committee of Sixteen. An all-male advisory board also represented the elite of Montreal, including Birks, Currie, Molson, and McConnell men. Their original motivation was to expand Protestant institutional care and divert girls from the Catholic reform school where English language and culture were not observed. Beyond this their aim was to implement a means of improving wayward Protestant girls' morals and potential. Their stated purpose for the school was to rehabilitate the delinquent girl into 'a good woman and a true home maker.'[19] The directors intended that the school would function as a social laboratory that took in delinquent girls and transformed them into women ready for lives of marriage and motherhood.

The purpose of this reform school was explicitly benevolent; what might be considered a prison for youths convicted by the juvenile court was reconceptualized as a 'training school.' The appellation 'training school' suggests education, not punishment, was the aim of the institution. The retraining of wayward girls started from the assumption that these girls were not criminals but misdirected children needing a home, discipline, and encouragement. In 1917, the superintendent wrote that the primary difficulty with the new charges was in convincing them that they were not being punished.[20]

When the industrial and reform schools opened in the latter half of the nineteenth century, their major function and intrinsic value had hinged on inducing a rupture with the inmates' past and providing them with an apprenticeship so they might be self-sufficient on release. By the early-twentieth century, imparting a good home experience was understood as the key to changing the behaviour and character of the inmates. The idea was that life at the GCIS would imitate a 'proper' home, one that many had been denied. The GCIS board believed that through 'faulty home training' the girls had failed to learn adequate standards of right and wrong and did not live up to the 'demands of community life.'[21] Because the girls tended 'to challenge the prevailing standards of human conduct ... [the officers of the school] must constantly hold before the girls the highest standards of living and cultivate within them an appreciation of the finer things in life.'[22] Compare this to the ethic the nuns attempted to instill in their charges: 'An honest and virtuous person, someone humble whatever their place in the social hierarchy has the right to hold her head high. They're taught to dress properly and nicely without finery ... [to] judge people not on dress, looks or words but according to their actions and behaviour.'[23]

From 1918 onwards the directors ushered in a new era, one in which a more sophisticated approach to incarcerating and training delinquents was taken. In that year, the directors appealed to experts to help them improve the GCIS. The advice led them to embrace a wider objective for the school. Maude E. Miner of the New York Probation and Protective Association encouraged them to see their mission and function as extending from protective work with girls in Montreal to retraining at the school in Sweetsburg to the reintegration of former delinquents.[24] Extending their mandate in this way required funds (which they did not have in 1918), and an expansion and professionalization of their staff. Quality of work at the school would be greatly enhanced, Miner advised, if a 'highly trained' social worker was employed as superintendent. This attack on the lack of serious credentials of the current superintendent, Miss E. Davies, was heeded and she was replaced.[25] Among Miner's other recommendations was a cottage system to separate the 'different types' of delinquents.

In the early 1920s an era of professionalization began: the directors moved the GCIS to a farm, developed a small-scale cottage system, and hired social workers as superintendents and follow-up personnel. The hiring of Nancy Stork in 1924 signalled an achievement of sorts for the school: well versed in social work methods, Stork had been assistant-superintendent at Toronto's Alexandria Industrial School for Girls. Although in its first decade GCIS operated as a small residential school for a handful of wayward girls sent by the court, once established at Sweetsburg under the direction of superintendent Stork, the institution matured into a 'social agency' committed to tackling 'predelinquency' and monitoring former inmates' reintegration into Montreal. The school became the crucial middle step between delinquency and a new life. In the 1920s Stork reiterated this idea when she insisted that the GCIS was 'not a place of punishment but of opportunity.'[26]

Stork's first report to the directors reflected in detail some of Miner's views about categorization of delinquent girls. Beginning with Nancy Stork and the follow-up program, delinquent girls received 'full treatment' that began upon being directed to the school and was unrelenting until the girls were 'safely and wisely readjusted in the community.'[27] She upheld the importance of the GCIS in the context of rescue work with sex delinquents. Considered far more effective than the 'occasional supervision' of club activities of the YWCA and other such organizations, she determined that institutionalization (and by extension the GCIS) was the only solution for sexually precocious girls.[28] In her work on Toronto, Carolyn Strange has also found moral reformation was the aim of incarceration in the late nineteenth century, but this was replaced in the 1910s with 'scientifically monitored rehabilitation projects' that were to facilitate a readjustment to society.[29]

In their annual reports in the late 1920s and 1930s it is evident that contemporary social work methods and terminology had been fully embraced, the thrust of which was individual assessment and treatment. In quoting American Margaret Reeves (author of *Training Schools for Delinquent Girls*, 1929), the administrators wrote that 'our work is not merely custodial but it is to carry out a programme of scientific study and treatment, adapted to the restoration of each emotionally disturbed and wayward girl.'[30] The officers at the school had long given up on the hereditary basis of delinquency and firmly believed in resocialization. This was the basis for designing treatment to suit individual needs: 'individualization is the keynote of all modern social progress.'[31] As one prominent GCIS worker, Dorothea Heney, commented: '[the GCIS girl] is labelled as incorrigible and delinquent – rather hackneyed terms which convey to the lay mind a picture of an individual more or less guilty of crime. If we accept Dr. Healy's interpretation of delinquency we recognize that it is merely a product of life experience, not predetermined by heredity but rather by the forces of that life experience and its various trends.'[32] With total abnegation of punishment at the school its function became to encourage 'health, both in body and mind, the development of self-control and self-direction towards useful ends or moral strength, vocational preparation and guidance for a career in which happiness and success can be achieved.'[33]

Through the 1930s and 1940s the stated purpose of the training school acknowledged the importance of feminine citizenship. In 1936 the GCIS's objects were 'to provide corrective training for the adolescent problem girl and to give her the opportunity to become a self-respecting, independent member of the community.'[34] This goal of transforming delinquent girls to lead socially 'useful' lives upon release speaks directly to the school's determination that girls would forget their pasts and become disciplined members of the larger Protestant community.

The GCIS's purpose, as articulated in law, involved providing shelter, clothing, and education for wayward girls. It also served its purpose in rescuing Protestant girls from the convent reform school. The Protestant community in Quebec formed a small minority but occupied an important place in Montreal's elite. This privileged position was critical for the raising of funds for the GCIS and in lobbying the provincial government. Although not financially vulnerable, the elite of this community was concerned that when daughters of working-class Protestants were sent to the Soeurs du Bon Pasteur, according to one report, they emerged 'scarcely able to speak their own language, and frequently desiring to join the Catholic Church.' Further, whereas the nuns offered no individual care or training, this alternative facility enabled the development of a true training facility for 'their' girls.[35] This conception began with constructing a homelike environment in a pastoral setting.

The Geography and Architecture of the Training School

The walls are bare and whitewashed; doors and floors are of natural wood; no paintings are to be seen; the consoling statues and angels are white ... the complete absence of colour produces a curious effect that is far from banal; it is pure and austere. The views do not suffer for it, since the windows offer marvellous panoramas and countryside of an ideal beauty..[36]

A cottage for twenty-five girls permits a wholesome home life to be lived. The girls would go out to other buildings for school and to the different industries, a few remaining at home to do the housework and cooking ... and would spend the evenings at home doing fancy work or reading; while, for bad weather, there could be a large, airy light playroom in the basement. This normal life could not fail to make a pleasant atmosphere and tend to normalize any girl.[37]

These quotations illustrate the striking difference in physical space between the two reform schools for girls and how the space reinforced the ideology behind each respective facility. The first, a description of the new industrial school at Laval-des-Rapides in 1915, is suggestive of the kind of atmosphere – pure and austere – created by the nuns in order to complete their 'difficult work' of retrieving lost souls.[38] Describing the proposals for an addition to the GCIS, the latter conjures up an image of a homey, familial existence, typical of late-nineteenth and early-twentieth-century women's institutions found in the United States and Britain.

During the 1910s the two girls' reform schools serving the Montreal area coincidentally both ended up being moved to the periphery of the city.[39] Both were separated from the city by water: the GCIS to the south on the St Lawrence, and the Maison de Lorette to the north on the Back River. In 1911 a one-and-a-half-storey old stone house was converted for the purposes of the GCIS; in 1915 juvenile delinquents were transferred from the provincial house on Sherbrooke Street to the old Moulin de Crochet at Laval-des-Rapides. The symbolism of physically removing the girls from Montreal should not be minimized: the Soeurs du Bon Pasteur and the GCIS board shared the belief that in order to effect positive change in inmates all ties with the city had to be severed and knowledge of it forgotten.

The pastoral setting for reform schools became a major feature in incarcerating youths beginning in the mid-nineteenth century. In part, this was a result of the belief in environmentalism but also with convictions about women and nature. In the 1850s the Lancaster Industrial School in Massachusetts set a standard for future institutions for girls. Believing that they could correct bad girl behaviour through 'tender incarceration,' those at the Lancaster School rejected the urban setting and traditional architecture of penal institutions and replaced them with a homey atmosphere in idyllic surroundings.[40] Located fifty miles from Boston in a picturesque landscape, the Lancaster School was the first in North America to implement ideas about socializing through 'pastoral simplicity.'[41] This idea became a trend with reform schools and women's reformatories constructed in the late nineteenth century. So powerful was the belief in reforming the individual in sanctuaries far from the madness of the city that new incarceration facilities such as the English inebriate reformatories were placed in the countryside.[42] Natural surroundings were also common for new women's residential institutions, such as college residences and boarding schools. The early-twentieth-century nurses' residence at Montreal's Royal Victoria Hospital, for example, was intentionally nestled into a woody site on Mount Royal, as Annmarie Adams has argued, 'because of its more natural, 'untouched' character.'[43]

Placing women in nature was an attempt to reinforce certain qualities and beliefs about women: that their delicate natures would be preserved or revitalized by healthy, outdoor living far from the perils of urban life. Nineteenth-century prescriptive notions about women's nature defined it as submissive, domestic, pious, and pure – traits that might also apply to rural life in contrast to its urban counterpart. Where better to correct a 'deviant' character that was produced in the city than the countryside? It also confirmed a notion of women as childlike or innocent.[44] The importance of the site of the reform school was not missed on the Soeurs du Bon Pasteur: 'The beautiful countryside is very favourable for the [girls'] state of health.'[45] Pure air and vistas of the beautiful river were key in setting the inmates on the right track.[46] In the interwar period the GCIS was moved to a farm in the picturesque Eastern Townships. Its rural location and 'wholesome atmosphere' was thought to have curative potential for the inmates' physical and moral health.[47]

A major difference between the two Montreal reformatories, in terms of physical space, was the convent style of one and the emulation of the middle-class cottage of the other. The homelike GCIS shared a common history with women's institutional architecture. The red-brick houses with white sash windows became a hallmark of nineteenth-century women's residential institutions – settlement houses, college residences, and reformatories. This Queen Anne–style was embraced as reform architecture for women's institutions because it 'embodied the cosy comforts of the English home.'[48] A well-known North American example of this is Hull House, the Chicago settlement house run by Jane Addams in the Progressive Era.[49] Feminist architectural historians suggest that the similarity of domestic and women's institutional architecture in the late-nineteenth century was no coincidence – it ensured that public institutions for women retained a private quality.[50] The major consistency among the women's residence, the boarding school, and the reform school was the attempt at a family-oriented home existence. But, it was a particular kind of family life, as Martha Vicinus reminds us: 'The surroundings [of women's residences], bespoke permanence, seriousness of purpose, and the same solidity that marked the middle-class families from which the bulk of the students came.'[51] Even though boarding houses and college residences were explicitly serving the purposes of the bourgeoisie by socializing its daughters into good wives and mothers in institutions that resembled middle-class homes, reform schools tended to adapt the same ethic that ultimately became a way of immersing working-class girls in middle-class values. Barbara M. Brenzel contends that the Lancaster Industrial School for Girls looked more like a New England academy than a house of detention.[52] The GCIS, in trying to emulate middle-class residential institutions also referred to the inmates as 'boarders.'[53]

A home at the water's edge in St Lambert, the first building (1911–15) was nicknamed the Marmalade Factory. It was nothing like a factory –

Figure 7.1 Girls' Cottage Industrial School, 1911–15 (GCIS, *Annual Report*, 1914)

nor a prison – in appearance but a single-family dwelling wrapped by a verandah and a wooden fence (see figure 7.1) Lacking the money to renovate, the directors had no choice but to suggest the six inmates and superintendent live in the house much as the previous tenants had, in all likelihood a middle-class family. A shed behind the house doubled as a school room, revealing the diminished importance of teaching the three *R*s over training in culinary arts, particularly the making of marmalade.

Within four years the population at the school doubled, necessitating a move to a larger home. When Lillias Molson offered to buy a larger house in St Lambert and rent it to the GCIS, the Directors eagerly accepted. This time, the building was a much more substantial house, a three-storey home with a high picket fence surrounding the generous property (see figure 7.2) The house could hold up to twenty girls and three residential staff persons. The superintendent noted its main advantage over the previous house was that it allowed for major training in the area of laundry work.[54]

Figure 7.2 Cottage Industrial School, 1915–22 (GCIS, *Annual Report*, 1918)

Two acts of fortune in the early 1920s enabled the GCIS directors to experiment with the mode of reform school they advocated. With the support of the Montreal Council of Social Agencies, the school signed a contract with the government resulting in a per capita annual grant of $120. Being placed on firm financial footing at the start of 1922 was complemented with the donation by J.W. McConnell of a forty-two-acre farm in Sweetsburg.[55] On this farm was a large home, a barn, and a schoolhouse. McConnell also provided funds to have the house remodelled to suit the purposes of the reform school. For the first time the directors were able to manipulate the interior physical space of the school to suit their purposes.

The directors chose to divide the interior of the big house into two parts in such a way that would not alter the external appearance of the residence. Each of the two sections contained a kitchen, living room, laundry, and sleeping quarters, and were staffed by two women. The first and larger of the sections comprised the original house where it was necessary to use dormitories for the girls' bedrooms. The extension or new wing provided cubicles for each girl to have a room of her own. Girls with venereal disease or who were considered highly immoral were kept in this part of the house.[56]

In the early 1920s the directors conceived of a three-cottage system to meet their needs concerning the segregation of the girls. The cottage system was developed for reforming children in the 1840s in Mettray, France, and came to North America in the 1850s.[57] From the time of its inception, the GCIS contained the name cottage in its title, although the design did not incorporate an elaborate cottage system until the 1950s when the institution was yet again relocated, this time to St Bruno. The GCIS began as model middle-class homes and by the end of its first decade was organized along the cottage plan. The first home would house 'diseased cases'; the second housed girls who had had 'definitely immoral experiences but [were] free from infection'; and the last would be for girls who were merely 'incorrigible.'[58] Not being in a financial position to build a third cottage, the directors decided to make do during 1923 and 1924 with a dormitory in the attic.[59]

Finally, in 1925, the gift of a 'generous friend' enabled the board to have an addition to the original house built. This separate building was joined to the main building by a covered passageway. The new building provided them with twenty-one separate bedrooms, two large bathrooms and toilets, a large sewing room, a recreation room, rooms for two staff members, and an attic for storage.[60]

The board of directors hailed this new building as a sign of substantial progress for the school because it meant a separate room for each girl – a nod to the belief in personalized, individual treatment. Separate bedrooms and segregation of inmates, according to the board of directors, made for 'a much more desirable arrangement.'[61] In several ways the individual bedroom system was a major modification to the dormitory-style of residence: it meant that each girl was allowed a certain amount of freedom to personalize her space; it reinforced bourgeois notions of privacy; and it enabled greater control over the social/sexual interaction of the inmates. In asserting the benefits of the individual bedroom Superintendent Nancy Stork wrote: 'Every girl should have at the end of a busy and full day her own little room, where she can be by herself, to meditate and think for a while, for we try to teach our girls to think seriously on many subjects. A girl cannot think, be she ever so inclined, with half a dozen girls jabbering around her. Then again she can be taught to take pride in the keeping of her own room in a neat and attractive manner, and she has more self-respect when she knows she has her own corner to keep her many little personal treasures from prying eyes, and from becoming public property.'[62]

As an example of how the school design ameliorated the condition of working-class girls, the superintendent quoted a letter that one recent arrival at the school wrote to her mother. 'Dear mother...for the first time in my life I have a room of my own; I can change it around the way I want to, they let us put up pictures, make curtains, dye our bedspreads, it's wonderful!'[63] But clearly the separation of the girls was not simply for the personal benefit of the individual girl.

The directors wrote: 'In an institution of this kind there is no greater hindrance to the training of the girls than the old dormitory system.'[64] Reformatories had long had a reputation for being dens of 'evil' and the directors of the GCIS articulated fears of certain worldly girls 'contaminating' others. The containment of adolescent sexuality went hand in hand with retraining delinquent girls as did preventing intimate relationships between inmates. Many of the inmates entered the school having had substantial sexual experience – indeed were viewed as having precocious knowledge of carnal desires. As Michelle Cale has argued for the case of the Victorian English reformatory system for girls, the authorities attempted to counter 'pernicious sexuality ... not from a horror of lesbianism in itself, since for many Victorians such a deviance had no actuality, but because they feared that an introduction to sexual feelings through the contact of girl with girl would inevitably lead to an awakening appetite for heterosexual activity which was both immoral and unfeminine.'[65] In 1942 the GCIS board of directors was informed by Dr Baruch Silverman, director of the Mental Hygiene Institute on the 'sex problem' in institutional care. The doctor dismissed the idea that girls had strong sex urges and asserted that lesbian activity was 'usually an expression of interest in or want of affection.'[66] The cottage system enabled the superintendent to physically separate the more 'innocent' girls from those with considerable experience; the separate bedrooms were necessary, then, to inhibit sexually experienced girls from seeking nocturnal pleasures that would 'inevitably' lead to the encouragement of inappropriate hetero- and homosexual behaviour.

The sheer number of juvenile delinquents at the Maison de Lorette made individual rooms out of the question. Also, the separate sleeping quarters were antithetical to convent architecture.[67] When the decrepit *moulin de crochet* was replaced in 1930, the new building maintained this tradition. The GCIS then became the first reformatory to experiment with 'modern' notions of retraining wayward girls through domestic architecture in a rural landscape that permitted girls a room of their own. Inmates coming from the working-class were likely never to have had their own living spaces. However folly it seems for the directors to promote a bourgeois notion of family life that would be far from the girls' reality, it was one of their means to effect rapid and thorough retraining.

None of the physical incarnations of the GCIS between 1911 and 1946 resembled the institutional space of penal facilities. At no time did the GCIS have the financing necessary to plan and construct a building for their purposes; however, their choices in renting and/or renovating houses represent some agency toward defining reformatory architecture. All former homes, the buildings reflected the directors' desire to recreate a middle-class experience for the inmates; yet, these 'homes' were also intended to be facilities where the latest methods of resocialization could be implemented. In the 1930s the GCIS commissioned plans for two additions that betray their commitment to modern social science. As physical outlet for adolescent girls became increasingly viewed as a key part of the training school's therapeutic environment, plans for a new gymnasium were requested. In the early 1930s the top floor of the unheated barn had been used as a makeshift gymnasium but it was clearly inadequate for modern recreation.[68] In 1933 the superintendent of the School also argued for another building that would serve the need to isolate certain girls. Literally called an isolation building, this new building was meant to fulfill three functions: it would be a receiving cottage for breaking in recent arrivals, a hospital for contagious or infectious inmates, and temporary residence for 'demoted' girls.[69] Although attempts to create a full cottage system were frustrated, the GCIS workers remained committed to a treatment facility that reflected a class bias and orientation toward contemporary beliefs about rehabilitating delinquent girls.

Boarders, Pupils, Inmates: Girls at the GCIS

When the GCIS opened its doors in 1911, the directors expected it would be a family-sized institution in which a handful of girls and young women would receive proper 'retraining.' The fledgling training school grew rapidly after a difficult first decade: once the school relocated to Sweetsburg in 1922, its population at December 31 rose to thirty and forty inmates, the maximum at any one time peaking at forty-six in 1927 (see table 7.3). The school's annual reports suggest that during the 1930s and 1940s between 50 and 60 girls were under care at the institution. The GCIS's Catholic counterpart also faced increases accelerated by the First World War, a slight decline in the early 1920s, and a steady rise in population through the 1930s and 1940s. The school was primarily established to receive girls between twelve and sixteen years of age but did accept voluntary cases up to age eighteen. The mean age therefore hovered around fifteen.[70]

In the 1910s, the inmates tended to be first-generation Canadians coming mainly from England, Ireland, and Scotland. This stands in sharp contrast to the inmates at the École de Réforme who were consistently and overwhelmingly Canadian-born. By the second decade of the school's history a noticeable shift had occurred: in the mid-1920s a survey of the inmates showed that more than 60 per cent were born in Canada.[71] The percentage of Canadian-born inmates continued to grow such that through the interwar period, only a tiny minority of new cases (sometimes only one girl) each year was born outside Canada. For example, of the twenty new cases in 1933, eighteen were born in Canada. Notwithstanding the fact that girls were largely Canadian, the GCIS continued to chart nationality by 'origin.' Thus Canadian-born girls were categorized according to the school's sense of their national heritage and ethnicity. Predominating among these countries of origin were England, Scotland, and Ireland; each year one or two girls also came from the United States, South Africa, Austria, Germany, the Soviet Union (Russia), France, and Romania. In the interwar period, girls whose families derived from China, Hungary, the Ukraine, and Syria were rare but could be found at the institution.[72] The vast majority of inmates were Canadians but many were daughters of immigrants.

Having been explicitly created for the incarceration of non-Catholics sentenced by the juvenile court, it follows that the majority of inmates were registered as Protestants. In the 1930s the annual reports indicate that the majority of these girls were Church of England, United Church or without church affiliation. Jewish and Greek Orthodox girls were also sent to the GCIS (see tables 7.4 and 7.5).

Between one-half and three-quarters of the inmates came from so-called broken families. Consistently less than half of the inmates could admit to having two living parents, and even then, the parents did not necessarily live together. Not many of the inmates were orphans but enough came from homes with only one parent to suggest to the directors a direct connection between delinquency and 'broken homes.'

Table 7.4 Birthplace and religion of Girls' Cottage Industrial School inmates

	Birthplace				Religion	
Year	Canada	U.S.	Other	Total	Protestant	Jewish
1915	5	–	12	17	17	–
1920	6	1	6	13	9	4
1925	29	1	15	45	40	5
1930	32	3	4	39	37	2
1935	27	1	2	30	27	3
1941	32	1	3	36	35	1

Source: Quebec, Statistical Yearbook, 1915–41.

A further profile of inmates at the GCIS is not possible from the statistical reports of the province nor the records of the GCIS. We can use Professor Bridge's 1926 study of the inmates that we saw in Chapter 3 to create a snapshot of the school's population. In 1926 there were 33 inmates when Professor Bridges visited. The inmates were mainly ethnic English, Irish, or Scottish. There were three Jewish inmates, and one who was labelled by the professor 'mulatto'. Eight had been born in Montreal, twelve in other parts of Canada, eight in Britain or Ireland, two in the United States, and three elsewhere.[73] This breakdown was similar to that of the Protestant boys at Shawbridge. Two-thirds of the young women were from the city and one-third from the countryside. The average age at the GCIS was seventeen, which was three years above the average age at Shawbridge.[74] Only five of the thirty-three had been attending school when they were committed to the reform school. Almost half (fourteen) were domestic servants most of whom were labelled sex delinquents. Parents tended to be from the skilled, semiskilled, or unskilled occupational categories. The family situations of most inmates illustrated to Professor Bridges the broken homes theory in action: only ten of the thirty-three had two parents at home. Three inmates were orphans, seven had lost their fathers, while four had lost their mothers. There were seven cases of separated parents, and two situations where the parents had never married.[75]

In addition to juvenile court–sentenced youths, the GCIS, like the other reform schools in Montreal, accepted, in fact relied upon, 'voluntary' cases. The latter were brought to the school by parents or guardians. The directors intended to receive only juvenile court cases but found in

Table 7.5 Girls' Cottage Industrial School, Religion and Nationality, Selected Years, 1925–1938*

1925	1928	1930	1935	1938
Total number 45	Total number 45	Total number 56	Total number 47	Total number 60
Religious affiliation	Religious affiliation	Religious affiliation	Religious affiliation	Religious affiliation
Protestants 40	Protestants 50	Protestants 54	Protestants 43	Protestants 57
Hebrews 5	Jewish 4	Jewish girls 2	Jewish girls 4	Jewish girls 3
Nationality by birth	Nationality by birth	Analysis of new cases (n = 15)	Analysis of new cases (n = 12)	Analysis of new cases (n = 22)
Canadian 29	Canadian 44	Nationality by birth	Religious affiliation	Religious affiliation
Scotch 3	English 5	Canadian born 14	Church of England 7	Church of England 6
English 9	Irish 2	American born 1	United Church 1	United Church 4
U.S.A. 1	United States 2	Nationality by origin	Welcome Hall Mission 1	Presbyterian 2
Foreign 3	Foreign 1	English 9	Christadelphian 1	Baptist 1
		Scotch 2	Protestant with no affiliation 1	Greek Orthodox 3
		Irish 1	Nationality by birth	No affiliation 5
		Austrian 1	Canadian born 11	Nationality by birth
		Belgian 1	British born 1	Canadian born 21
		German 1	Nationality by origin	British born 1
		Religious affiliation	English 8	Nationality by origin
		Church of England 6	Scotch 1	English 12
		United Church 4	Russian 2	Scotch 1
		Greek Orthodox 1	French 1	Russian 3
		Protestant with no affiliation 4		Chinese 1
				Roumanian 1
				South African 1
				Jewish 1

*Statistical information collected by the GCIS superintendents was not standardized. These tables retain the information as it was provided in the annual reports.
Source: 1925: GCIS, *Annual Report* (1925), 127; 1928: GCIS, *Annual Report* (1928), 12; 1930: GCIS, *Annual Report* (1930), 129; 1935: GCIS, *Annual Report* (1935), 51; 1938: GCIS, *Annual Report* (1938), 49.

the first years that these were not numerous enough to fill the school.[76] The Protestant boys' reform school at Shawbridge went through a similar crisis of undersubscription and actively recruited voluntary cases through an aggressive advertising campaign.[77]

In the 1910s various social agencies brought girls to the school. Those admitted by parents through a social agency were not covered by provincial funds and therefore parents were required to pay ten dollars per month. It seems, though, that no voluntary case was refused on the basis of inability to pay: the directors accepted as little as fifty cents per month. For this favour, however, parents would have to subject themselves to a means test by the school officials. The voluntary cases had to be under eighteen years of age and were not accepted for less than one year because 'the girls ha[d] much to unlearn before they beg[a]n to learn.'[78]

The directors preferred that the voluntary cases first be processed by the juvenile court and sentenced.[79] This prevented parents from breaking their one-year rule and interfering in the school's agenda. Parents' authority sometimes clashed with what the directors were hoping to achieve. The superintendent reported an incident involving a voluntary case who had been placed at the school in November 1917. At first the inmate wanted to escape and resisted her placement at the reform school, but within a short time 'had settled down for a proper training.'[80] The young woman's mother, however, felt the daughter ought to be earning money and withdrew her from the GCIS when a job was secured at a rubber factory. The superintendent provided this as evidence of how parents might sabotage the work and success of the school.[81] Also, in the 1920s the voluntary cases were deemed unsatisfactory because of parents 'who signed the agreement [and] wanted their children discharged before the time agreed upon expired, or before such times as the superintendent and Board of Directors considered it advisable.'[82] From the 1920s the numbers of voluntary cases dropped precipitously (see table 7.6).

After 1918 when the directors viewed their role as a social agency both to prevent and correct female delinquency, voluntary cases took on an important role at the school. The school staff felt they were more successful with 'predelinquent' girls of twelve or thirteen years; through preventive work at the school, younger, 'incorrigible' – but not delinquent – girls could be 'piloted into safety.'[83] This was a veiled protest against social agencies using them only as a last resort, and an admission that the efficacy of their work depended on the age of the inmate.

Beyond the young women who were impressionable and most manageable, the school also used the voluntary cases to get around the legally

Table 7.6 Court vs. Voluntary cases, 1913–41

Year	Court cases	Voluntary no. (%)	Total
1913	2	6 (75)	8
1914	4	10 (71)	14
1915	9	15 (62)	24
1916	6	23 (79)	29
1917	8	21 (72)	29
1918	7	26 (79)	33
1919	14	16 (53)	30
1924	22	9 (29)	31
1925	28	17 (38)	45
1926	31	20 (39)	51
1928	32	22 (41)	54
1929	32	21 (40)	53
1930	37	19 (34)	56
1931	38	18 (32)	56
1932	39	16 (29)	55
1933	38	17 (31)	55
1934	42	11 (21)	53
1935	41	6 (13)	47
1936	48	9 (16)	57
1937	51	4 (7)	55
1938	55	5 (8)	60
1939	56	4 (7)	60
1940	65	1 (1.5)	66
1941	59	0 (0)	59

Sources: For the 1910s, LAC, GCS, vol. 1, file 34, 'The GCS. Historical Report, Summary of Cases, 1919.' For the 1920s, 1930s, and 1940s, annual reports. The annual reports do not indicate voluntary admissions after 1941.

imposed age limit of sixteen for young offenders. The problem, as the directors saw it, was that there was no place to put 'older girls' (except the women's jail) because there was no provincial women's reformatory.[84] In the Recorder's court the first-time female offenders were given suspended sentences; that is, they were let off. The GCIS began receiving as voluntary cases these older girls between the ages of sixteen and eighteen and kept them up to age twenty-one; that is, the school argued that the age for juvenile delinquents ought to be raised to eighteen but before it was, in 1942, the voluntary category permitted the juvenile court and the

GCIS to incarcerate girls between sixteen and eighteen.[85] This had the effect of pushing up the average age at the school, which in the 1920s hovered around seventeen. The GCIS functioned as a reform school admitting non-Catholic girls and young women aged between twelve and sixteen from across the province of Quebec. Because they could be by order of the tribunal held until their twenty-first birthday, there was always a presence of older girls in the institution.

In the first decade, then, the majority – as much as 70 per cent – were voluntary cases. As the school expanded and juvenile delinquency was more actively policed and more girls were given sentences, court cases became more prominent, averaging about 64 per cent of the school's population in the 1920s. The annual reports indicate that the voluntary cases had to be limited because of the rise in court cases. Still, those that were committed tended to be older and less manageable. The reports of the school from the late 1930s and 1940s frequently mention the rising level of recalcitrance.[86]

On being sentenced or 'voluntarily' committed to the GCIS, the girls and young women were subjected to a thorough examination process. The testing revolved around measuring – in order to correct – physical, intellectual, moral, and spiritual shortcomings. The two most common forms of examination, mental testing and the physical exam, related to the alleged nature of delinquency itself: the most prominent reasons for being committed to a sojourn at the GCIS were sexual promiscuity (evidenced by venereal disease) and mental 'defectiveness' or feeblemindedness. From the beginning, mental testing and physical examinations had always been part of the initiation programming at the school.

In the 1920s the system was more formalized. Upon entering the school, the new arrival was isolated, given "complete" physical, mental, dental, and eye examinations and submitted to the appropriate treatment. Before being integrated into the school regime the new girl was escorted to the Montreal General Hospital or the Royal Victoria Hospital for a physical exam and a blood test to determine whether she had venereal disease. This system was replaced in the 1920s when the GCIS hired a female doctor who came out to the school to do these tests. As venereal disease had always been present in the population at the school, isolating the new inmate functioned to prevent 'cross infection.'[87] Testing positive for venereal disease led to treatment at the local Sweetsburg General Hospital. In the post–First World War period, the province got involved in the prevention of venereal disease, paying for the treatment through the Anti–Venereal Disease Campaign of the Board of Health.[88] Another function of the physical testing was to check for pregnancy. Pregnant inmates were not permitted to stay at the school but were hidden away at Bethany House until the child was born, after which time the inmate would be readmitted.

In the 1920s the mental testing of new inmates was carried out by members of the National Committee on Mental Hygiene in Montreal. Here the provincial board of health played less of a role. The directors routinely complained of a lack of facilities for the so-called feeble-minded: in Quebec there were no special classes in the public school system, much less institutions that could properly care for them, until the 1930s.[89] The directors were periodically concerned their reform school had become a dumping ground for the feebleminded. Still, the mental tests enabled the Directors to predict how bad the girl would be and how possible it was to retrain her.

Further to the physical and mental tests, the girls took eye examinations, had dental work and eventually chest x-rays for tuberculosis, and even foot repair.[90] Once all of this testing regime was completed, the field worker and/or the superintendent took family histories of the girls, and created a case report. The composite drawn from the interview and the tests enabled the superintendent to categorize the girls and place them in the appropriate living space and classes. The profile was also used by the field worker when the sentence expired to determine the inmates' future.

Whether through voluntary or court admissions, adolescent females were incarcerated for defying parents. Girls were most often charged with desertion, incorrigibility, and vagrancy. The sexual nature of their offences made incarceration popular with authorities and parents. Their sentences were lengthy – on average two years.

Program and Regime

Our school is a place where these mistakes are to be corrected ... a bright, home-like place, full of sunshine and cheerfulness and healthy activity.[91]

GCIS workers argued a causal link existed between substandard home lives and girls' descent into delinquency. In creating well-ordered surrogate homes for delinquent girls, superintendents provided their charges with what they perceived the girls' homes lacked. The training school program and regime promoted a respect for law, authority, and the family ideal and emphasized character building. The program focused on four areas of training: domestic, vocational, academic, and recreational. In the early years, retraining and education at the GCIS was circumscribed by the lack of funding: the girls spent most of their time doing chores, gardening and making preserves and other items that generated cash for the institution. Initially, formal education was limited and the only apprentice work available was in the area of domestic service. By the 1940s the GCIS's orientation reflected more the training-school ethic, prioritizing first academic then 'pre-vocational training coupled with a cultural and recreational programme.'[92] At the end of her incarceration at the institution, the girl was to leave the school with a fresh start on a new life, symbolized by the new set of clothing she donned for the occasion of her departure.

In the 1910s the domestic service training predominated at the institution. This orientation fit with the assumption that the feeblemindedness of inmates made them well suited for rudimentary 'feminine' work. An early aim of the administrators was to demonstrate the training school's efficacy in transforming delinquent girls into disciplined domestic servants. Through the interwar period the school boasted about their reputation for training in household sciences, which easily facilitated placing girls as domestic servants. In 1929, for example, the administrators boasted placing nine girls in 'responsible positions' as domestics, as well as several in businesses and factories.[93]

Consistent with girls' education in the early-twentieth century, the inmates at the GCIS learned the various aspects of domestic science: cooking (including bread making and preserving), laundry work, sewing and knitting, gardening, serving meals, and cleaning.[94] The inmates on kitchen duty began at 6:30 a.m. and continued until the dinner dishes were washed. During the 1910s this routine was interrupted only for meals, a walk, and an hour at the school.[95] The wash girls rose at 7 a.m. and began the day by cleaning the school. On Mondays they soaked the clothes and washed the superintendent's and assistant's clothes. Tuesdays they washed the house linen and on Wednesdays the inmates' clothes. Thursdays and Fridays were taken up with ironing, and Saturdays they cleaned the irons, wringers and buckets.[96]

In the 1920s a three- and four-month rotation system was developed so that girls spent a set period of time getting to know well each of the areas of housekeeping – the kitchen, laundry, and cleaning. All girls were taught to sew and they made their own dresses – to improve 'a girl's self-respect'[97] – a kind of school uniform. Teaching of 'every day usefulness,'[98] of course, served functions other than how to be domestic servants or homemakers: the regime disciplined the girls, taught them the value of industriousness, and cut the costs of the institution. All of the daily work of the institution was performed by the inmates under careful supervision.

The focus on domestic arts and sciences also served another purpose. In the 1920s those who administered the GCIS blamed unstructured home lives for delinquent behaviour. Following this reasoning, the program at the reform school centred on teaching girls 'the true way of making a home.'[99] 'Good, practical training is given in cooking, kitchen management, the general care of the home, laundry work, sewing and simple handicrafts,' was claimed in the annual report of 1934.The skills became increasingly geared to fitting the girl for a life as wife and mother and less as domestic servants. This required a shift in perception of the incarcerated girl and the capacity of the training school to erase her history and create possibilities for the future.

Eventually teaching the inmates how to run a well-ordered household evolved into an education in personal hygiene and decorum. The superintendents in the late 1930s began focusing on creating marriageable young women through manners and grooming lessons. In these classes the girls were taught the rudiments of makeup and generally how to appear poised and attractive to men. Contrast this with the Maison de Lorette rule that hair was to be kept short and held back with a barrett.[100] It was no secret that the majority of inmates at the GCIS were very familiar with men and sex; the aim, though, was to get them to attract husbands. Seeing that the girls had 'an unhealthy distorted view of sex', sex education was necessarily added to the curriculum.[101] Taught by a nurse, sex education was placed in the context of reproduction, both firmly viewed within marriage.[102] Mothercraft studies followed closely on the heels of the course on appropriate sexuality. Although the school banished to Bethany House (a home for the pregnant and unwed) any inmate discovered to be pregnant, the program included instruction on child development, feeding, bathing, and dressing a baby.[103] The orientation of these courses reflects the superintendents' beliefs about what delinquent girls had missed in their working-class homes.

The garden and poultry farm at the GCIS augmented the school's income and provided work considered wholesome and satisfying. Each girl was given a part of the garden in which to grow vegetables. Having the girls participate in the gardening, according to the superintendents, fostered a healthy sense of competition.[104] From the early years at the school the regime had included gardening but the most elaborate program was developed once they moved to Sweetsburg. In fact, the GCIS won first prize for the best garden in the townships at the annual Bedford Fair in 1927. That year, the garden took in $290 and provided the school with much of the needed produce for the year.[105] But Nancy Stork was quick to remind that the garden was not simply a money-making endeavour, that its value rested in its contribution to building character. Its virtues included occupying the girls during the summer months when the school was not in session.[106] The belief that the outdoors and farm work made a virtuous citizenry was also embraced by other reformatories like the Boys' Farm at Shawbridge.

A critical part of the training program for girls at the GCIS was instilling the value and virtues of volunteer work. During the First World War the girls were taught knitting and needlework so they might contribute to the Red Cross and Verdun Patriotic Society, redeeming themselves as valuable citizens.[107] In the late 1930s the girls joined the local chapter of the Junior Red Cross Society where they learned home nursing and first aid.[108] During the Second World War the girls again knitted for the Red Cross and increased the output of fruits and vegetables in their version of a victory garden.

The girls were also instructed in the value of producing items for personal gain. In many of the annual reports, the superintendents indicated that the girls sold bread, marmalade, eggs, produce, knitwear, embroidery, and clothing. In return they earned pocket money.[109] This work ethic orientation persisted after release from the school as girls were directed toward employment that would permit them 'some personal satisfaction.'[110]

Vocational training at the GCIS did not extend far beyond domestic training; however, there were other skills taught that would provide certain girls with opportunity for employment. In the 1930s the workers recognized that more extensive vocational training (beyond househod arts and handicrafts) was required if girls were to succeed in life after they were released.[111] In 1918 the staff began teaching typing, though by the 1940s they still ran a rather limited business preparation course. This does not compare favourably to boys' reform schools such as the Catholic Mont-St-Antoine where the inmates were taught a variety of trades.

Only slowly did the GCIS embrace academic training as an important method of reforming the girls' characters or improving their lives. The urgency of this form of training cannot be understated considering that illiteracy among the new arrivals was not uncommon. Within the first years of the GCIS, the administrators blamed the high rates of feeblemindedness among the girls on a lack of educational advantages and on Quebec's failure to implement compulsory education.[112] In the 1920s three hours of schooling per day was the norm at the school and this education ended at the seventh grade.[113] In part, the directors felt they could not afford a teacher more than part-time; only in the 1920s did the Protestant School Board of Montreal agree to finance one full-time teacher. Even with a teacher at the school all day, the inmates still would attend school for a half-day only.[114] The curriculum followed that of the local public school in Cowansville: reading, writing, arithmetic, geography, Canadian history, and hygiene.[115] Four hours of academics in the 1930s gave way in the early 1940s to the determination that each inmate would achieve Grade 10.[116] At the École de Réforme a modest emphasis on formal education was also evident: in the 1910s two hours per day were set aside for schooling, the rest of the day was taken up with sewing, cooking, and other household tasks.[117]

A Christian education was considered integral to resocialization at the turn of the century reform schools. This was perhaps most obvious at the institutions run by the Soeurs or the Frères: as their contemporaries saw it, religion was fundamental to any system of correction at the Écoles de Réforme.[118] The Soeurs du Bon Pasteur institutions featured, in order of importance, prayer, work, study, and recreation. The matrons who lived in the cottages at the GCIS with the girls were expected to be religious women,[119] although none of the staff were spiritual leaders. And, unlike at the Catholic reform school a chapel did not form part of the institutions themselves. This education therefore took place mostly outside the GCIS or by occasional visitors to the school. The superintendent did, however, establish morning and evening prayers and a Sunday evening prayer meeting.[120] On Sundays the girls were expected to attend the local Anglican Church. Putting the girls on the right path in preparation for their release included development of the habit of church-going. Once freed from the school, the authorities at the GCIS hoped church community groups would buffer the girls from their previous lives.[121] Jewish girls had limited religious education: only in preparation for Jewish holidays would a visitor, Mrs Rabinovitch of the Federation of Jewish Philanthropies of Montreal, address the girls' spiritual lives.[122]

Recreation and leisure played an important role in the resocialization process at the school and was central to character development. The significance of supervised play in correcting waywardness was prominent in the contemporary literature on juvenile delinquency. Field worker Dorothea Heney cited Margaret Reeves on this issue: 'Play is useful from a health point of view, but it has many additional values of equal or greater importance ... [it] is important because it contributes to the mental and moral development of a person quite as much as to physical health ... and a properly directed programme provides a greatly needed avenue for the expression of personality.'[123] Providing the girls with planned recreational activities was not always successful. Superintendent Bertie H. Frantz had attempted to get the girls to play outside but found the 'spirit of team work and fair play sadly lacking.'[124] Team work and play seemed to hold a key for resocializing the girls, however, and recreation retained its prominence in annual reports for decades. Each year, the superintendent wrote of attempts to get the girls to play baseball, which was often met with resistance.

Calming adolescent sexual urges was another important reason for well-managed play. Superintendent Nancy Stork quoted her former boss, Miss Lucy M. Brooking at the Alexandra School for Girls, on the reasons for physical activity: 'There must be a substitute given to the delinquent for the pleasure derived from the gratification of sensual cravings and unclean dissipation, and it is in the intoxication of a clean, hard-fought game that she will get the best substitute.'[125] In this way, recreation was preferred over work as a process to transform the girls' character.[126] The pressing need for better recreation facilities became all the more urgent when the superintendent admitted the girls were 'oversexed' and therefore needed more exercise![127]

By the end of the era the GCIS had fully embraced the training school ethic of preparing girls for life beyond the school. Premised upon the belief that girls came from 'unstable and poor home backgrounds' and faced personality problems, the school proposed four major components of the training:

1. Academic school to Grade X including stenography.
2. Practical training in home economics, mothercraft, gardening and poultry raising ...
3. Religious education, recreation, music, dancing and art.
4. Regular preventive and corrective health programme.[128]

A critical part of the institution's preventive and corrective health program involved a monthly clinic at the school run by the Mental Hygiene Institute in the late 1930s. At the time of the Second World War, the Marmalade Factory stood as the only thoroughly modern training school in Quebec.

The re-education of girls continued after their release from the training school through field or follow-up work. The follow-up program at the GCIS began in 1924 and was run by recent graduates of McGill's new School of Social Work. Ideally their task – commonly referred to as 'tracing up old girls' – was to help girls adjust to city life after a long period of training at the institution.[129] The workers met with girls at the school and parents in their homes to prepare for their reentry into society, found the girls jobs, and organized their leisure hours. Ideally, girls were kept at the training school until they were ready to embark on a responsible and independent life; in the words of Dorothea H. Heney, a long-standing field worker: 'It has always been our aim to protect and guide the under-privileged, misdirected girl until she loses the restlessness of adolescence and becomes a woman.'[130] By the 1930s the field department was responsible for ensuring that girls were prepared to earn a living on their own. The functions of the field department included:

1. To encourage the girls to put into practical use the training received at the School.
2. To inspire confidence in their own ability to succeed.
3. To guide them into work from which they are able to get personal satisfaction.
4. To maintain their interest in wholesome recreation.
5. To pave the way for a better understanding by the public, upon whose acceptance of the girls their successful adjustment to community life is contingent.[131]

Through the interwar period and into the Second World War field workers carried caseloads of more than 100 each year.[132]

Because the family ideal predominated in the rehabilitation of delinquent girls, it followed that the field workers would try to reintegrate them with their own families at the termination of their sentences or once paroled. Field workers often commented that the family was inadequate or needed rehabilitation too.[133] Dorothea H. Heney suggested many GCIS girls were orphaned or 'rendered homeless,' meaning that these girls could not return home.[134] Although there was 'no substitute for happy, normal family life,' too many girls' homes were deemed 'permanently broken' and did not inspire the field workers to let the girls reside with their families. Field workers attempted home rehabilitation but if unsuccessful rejected the family home as place for newly released GCIS girls. Family, in fact, was at times considered a 'great handicap' to the GCIS mission, offering the girl nothing but a return to a life of degradation.[135] Wartime exacerbated this trend: a majority of girls released from the training school during the Second World War were assessed as having inadequate parental supervision. 'Aftercare,' then, was increasingly located in surrogate homes including boarding and foster homes.[136]

That little store was put in the ability of the families of delinquent girls to reform factored into the field workers' determination to play midwife to a girl becoming an independent, responsible, female citizen ready for marriage. The kind of independence the worker hoped to inculcate in the girls was from her inadequate family and her delinquent past, including friends. The field workers therefore focused on making girls less dependent on their families and the institution through suitable employment. Domestic positions were the easiest to come by, but the field workers also noted that girls were securing positions in factories, hospitals (as ward maids and in diet kitchens), restaurants, and department stores (as clerks).[137]

Directing girls toward wholesome recreation on their release from the school was critical to build character and prevent the girls from falling back into old habits. The field workers used a network of anglophone agencies that catered to adolescent girls; girls were sent to the Young Women's Christian Association, Girl Guides, Canadian Girls in Training, settlement houses, and the Big Sisters Association. Directing girls to these 'wholesome' institutions was meant to counter the perennial attraction of the 'night club, the dance hall, and "John Barleycorn."'[138] During wartime the field workers also responded to the girls' demands to meet young men during leisure hours. Recognizing that girls 'look forward to marriage as their future security,' and because recruitment of young men into the armed forces made long courtships difficult and the temptation to rush into intimate relationships very likely, the GCIS workers became involved in supervising dating.[139] The field secretaries created ways for the girls to meet young men but also to discourage rash decisions to marry.

Discipline, Punishment, and Resistance

The GCIS and the Maison de Lorette reform schools were colloquially known as a cottage school and a convent, respectively. Yet these euphemistic names do not disguise the fact that girls were subject to constant supervision, disciplinary technologies known to prisons, and multiyear sentences. At the GCIS the superintendent and her assistant oversaw all activities and two supervising women lived in each cottage. A strict regime at the school meant every moment was planned, leaving the girls with little time to themselves. Gongs signalled the beginning of the day and mealtimes. When not doing housework or attending school, girls participated in organized recreation for a short period in the afternoons. Keeping the girls busy from morning until night strategically made sense in a reform school but exacted a toll on the staff, many of whom resigned because of ill health after several years at the GCIS. The reports of the superintendents suggest an intention to rule with warmth and acceptance of the delinquent; resistance, however, was met with discipline. The administrators were obviously attempting to conform to an ideology about juvenile penology that upheld treatment over punishment; in their reports even the word *punishment* was scratched out and replaced with 'treatment.'[140] The GCIS was not a home, it was an incarceration facility and the adolescent girls sent there were justifiably angry and difficult when their freedom was severely circumscribed for lengthy periods of time: girls averaged two-year sentences to ensure that 'proper' retraining took effect. Forcing inmates to unlearn their past lives involved a struggle and demanded a disciplinary code that inevitably contradicted some of their major principles of creating a family-oriented environment.

At the École de Réforme, the tradition of discipline had its roots in convent boarding schools. Rather than the homey environment of the women's reformatory, resocialization depended on a religious atmosphere that began with the architecture of the convent and permeated the programs and daily regimes. Micheline Dumont has written of the late-nineteenth-century girls' boarding schools 'The lives of boarders were characterized by silence in dormitories, the dining rooms, the parlours duly decorated with ferns, the chapel, the classrooms, and the recreation rooms. Here, the educational structure found a powerful means to reinforce religious, moral, and social values. Discipline guaranteed the submission expected of students. Submission was then described as women's most noble virtue.'[141] At the Maison de Lorette, girls demonstrated their submission by their 'piety, good conduct, and fondness of work.'[142]

Convincing a recent arrival at the GCIS that she was not there to be punished but 'retrained' in the context of a regimented and monotonous daily life would have been somewhat arduous, indeed. The superintendents exacted a standard of 'strict obedience, order and all possible perfection in [the inmates'] work' through constant supervision.[143]

Given that the inmates were incarcerated at the GCIS for transgressing behaviour fitting of a young woman, Superintendent Nancy Stork believed that obedience was at the heart of their retraining, and she insisted that her staff be unwavering disciplinarians.[144]

During Stork's regime in the 1920s each new arrival at the school faced a fortnight's quarantine. Contact with a nurse was all the young woman could expect.[145] This process of 'breaking in' new girls was done ostensibly for health reasons but the recent arrival surely experienced this as the creation of a dynamic in which she was to a large measure powerless and vulnerable. In order to begin the reinscription process toward a new feminine ideal, the girls' own clothing and personal effects were exchanged for clothing they made themselves at the institution, a symbolic move toward shedding their pasts.

The girls' days started early and never was one caught with 'fingers idle.'[146] Each inmate was to be out of bed by 6:00 a.m., 6:30 if they were on kitchen duty. Lights were out at 8:30 p.m. and talking afterwards was strictly forbidden. Inmates could not visit each other's bedrooms unless permission had been granted and borrowing from one another was prohibited. Hands were to be washed and hair brushed before each meal. Tidiness in the girls' bedrooms was mandatory, with marks lost for any sign of slovenliness. Communication with the outside world was carefully monitored: incoming and outgoing mail was read by the staff and inmates received letters only once a week. Visiting days were held on the first Saturday of the month for two hours in the afternoon, likely leaving some girls lonely and homesick.[147]

Embraced by early reform schools as an important method of discipline, corporal punishment was not endorsed at the GCIS in the early twentieth century. The underlying design of the school contradicted the use of it: a family environment and understanding of the individual precluded resorting to corporal punishment with even the most recalcitrant inmate. Brenzel also found at Lancaster that administrators considered physical violence as an unnecessary disciplinary measure, while similar institutions for boys in the same period did employ it.[148] In the reports of the superintendents to the board of directors at the GCIS, punishment was rarely discussed, though clearly certain young women were found to be unmanageable. The stated 'treatment' of the girls was to provide compassion rather than punishment, but it remains unclear if they resorted to corporal punishment up to the 1940s when their policies outlined their opposition to it.[149] In lieu of corporal punishment, inmates were placed in solitary confinement for breaking rules.[150] This usually consisted of sending the inmate to her room or to a special room reserved specifically for that purpose. In the 1940s the work manual for the staff made explicit that solitary confinement could not be used for indefinite periods, suggesting that it perhaps was in the past.

Withdrawal of privileges appears to have been the most common form of discipline. Also, the school increasingly used a rewards system to honour good behaviour: in the same way girls could be awarded privileges, they could be taken away. The biggest threat the superintendent held over the inmates was her right to haul them back into court and have their sentences extended.[151]

A shrewd mechanism for exacting a high level of discipline at the school involved placing inmates in charge of surveillance. Self-government, as the plan was called, came to the school in the late 1930s. Its primary purpose was to teach responsibility and leadership, but its divide-and-conquer method must have had appeal from a disciplinary standpoint. The two 'best girls' in each cottage were selected and called respectively president and secretary. The presidents were charged with reporting any misbehaviour and the secretaries with noting any shirking of duties. These two would meet each week with the staff of the GCIS, followed by a house meeting where the reports were made public. Girls could at that point ask questions and make comments. This routine to make inmates embarrass or alienate their peers was considered the latest in reform school techniques.[152] Designed to intrude upon inmates' informal hierarchy and allegiance system this scheme was meant to render young women and girls more manageable. Likely, though, girls grafted their own rules onto these schemes.

For all the attempts at creating a desirable, familial existence in a natural environment, the girls and young women committed to the GCIS were understandably angry and rebellious. They came to the school at the hands of parents who betrayed them and a justice system that showed its empathy through lengthy sentences. Programs at the training school were designed in their 'best interests' but required subscribing to a new subjectivity of passive femininity, industriousness, and renounced sexuality. Although no record of all incidents of resistance exists, the superintendents' reports shed some light on inmates' defiance at the GCIS. In the history of girls' reform schools there is evidence that female delinquents, though not typically considered violent, destroyed property, staged riots, and fought with workers at the school and each other. Girls' resistance could be overt and violent, verbal, and passive. The ultimate form of defiance at such institutions was, of course, the escape.

Girls, enraged over their sentences and the quarantine, exploded soon after arriving at the institution. In November 1928 the superintendent wrote of a recent arrival to the school who caused tremendous problems. A fifteen year old sent to the school for five years on a charge of vagrancy erupted in a violent tantrum that she eventually turned on herself. On her second night at the GCIS she tore up her bedding and her night clothes. The next morning she was found with a string tied around her neck. She defied the superintendent further by refusing to talk or to submit to mental examination. This final gesture frustrated Nancy Stork, who determined to have each new arrival assessed and categorized.[153]

This kind of rebelliousness at the school, the superintendents explained, was ordinarily confined to recent arrivals to the school. The inmates did not always act alone: two new girls who escaped for several hours were believed to have not yet 'settled.'[154] Those who attempted to escape often had just been committed.[155] Stork's mandatory quarantine, then, should be understood in this context, as an important period of isolation and psychological sedation. Stork wrote of the two girls. 'We feel justified in teaching them that discipline must be maintained, that the laws of the country must be obeyed, and that where there is not law there is no order or safety.'[156]

While some girls 'settled' and properly embraced the passive feminine ideal at the school, others ran from it. Lorna, the girl introduced at the beginning of this chapter, escaped from the school and managed to find her way back to the city. The determination of one group of girls from the GCIS was revealed by the physical risks they took: they nearly drowned in a river trying to make their way back to Montreal.[157] Escapes became common primarily because girls were young and miserable. Under the juvenile justice system in Quebec, it was not unusual for sentences to be two or three years in length and an inmate could not be released or paroled until she had served eighteen months of her sentence. This length of time must have felt like a lifetime for adolescent girls. Desperate to escape, one thirteen-year-old girl at the Maison de Lorette leapt from the third storey of the building. Badly hurt, she was incapable of carrying through with her plan. Incarcerated since she was ten, her repeated bad acts, verbal abuse and threats led to a five and a half year sentence at the Maison de Lorette.[158] Revenge came in 1940 when she became a gang leader and led a revolt that would become a model for rioters in 1945. Frustration and outrage likely led Stella L. to run away from the Maison de Lorette in 1931, shortly after being sen-

tenced to four years at the institution. In her case, a supervised walk
presented the right conditions for her and six others to scale the surrounding wall and flee through neighbouring woods. She was not found
for more than two and half years.[159]

Insolence and insubordination in inmates could be expected among a
group that were labelled incorrigible because they defied their parents.
Talking back extended from the home to the training school, especially
in the face of rules, regulations, and expectations. At Maison de Lorette,
the nuns reported that enraged girls took aim at the religious aspect of
their retraining. In Catholic institutions, both nuns and their piety were
models of the sexual repression, conformity and obedience demanded
of the girls. In the Maison de Lorette proper demeanour for adolescent
girls encompassed not only deference to the nuns' authority but also to
the Catholic faith and its symbols. A perennial 'problem' with one of the
girls, claimed a nun, was that she 'admits great contempt for all things
religious.'[160] The austere surroundings at the convent reform school
were intended to promote contemplation of religious vows; for example,
if the girls wanted to talk during work hours, they were permitted end-
less repetitions of the rosary. To protest the silence demanded of them,
the girls sang, screamed, and swore. French-Canadian swear words concern aspects of the Church and faith taken in vain; for example, 'Christ,'
'Chalice,' and 'tabernacle.'

Some acts were more benign than others: at the GCIS a girl stole wool
to make mittens, while another broke locks and doors and tried to set
fire to the institution.[161] Small indiscretions were met with ambivalence,
such as the case of the stolen wool; having turned it into a gift of mittens
for a relative, she managed to blur the line between appropriate productive feminine labour and delinquency.

After an initial acting-out period, some of the inmates turned to passive
resistance. Staff at the school contended daily with inmates' general dis-
interest in the programs, feeble attempts at academic courses, refusal to
perform duties properly, and a less than enthusiastic response to change.
Passive resistance as a strategy could backfire when it became the justification for an extension of sentence: one training school girl who showed
'no apparent progress' and who 'did nothing unless forced,' found her
original sentence of three years doubled.[162] Girls' indifference to disciplinary measures was also duly noted by reform school workers and used
against them. In a case from the Maison de Lorette, because 'reproaches
and punishment have left her indifferent' the nuns asked the juvenile
court judge to send her to the Women's Prison.[163]

Accommodation, feigned or real, characterizes the approach most girls took to their stay at the GCIS. Some girls may well have enjoyed the structured environment and regular meals and preferred life at the institution to their own homes. Freedom lost, however, could provoke girls into noisy accommodation. In the case of Jeanne who spent multiple years in the GCIS at the end of the 1930s was caught violating the rules of her parole in July 1940 and was placed in the Fullum Street Women's Jail in Montreal. There she wrote the juvenile court judge: 'I am fully aware of the penalty people have to pay for their foolishness and negligence, and what I thought was a good time was only tinsel and bright lights.'[164] This plea of acquiescence and accommodation got her three-month sentence reduced but once released to the field worker's care, she easily slipped out of sight and continued her pursuit of tinsel and bright lights.

Once liberated from training school, girls remained under the scrutiny of the field worker, who became yet another force to flee. Girls worked hard to elude the field worker, like Jane who ditched her worker three times, the last time when she deserted Bethany House, Montreal's home for pregnant, single, Protestant girls.[165] Another girl who had been paroled from the GCIS in the 1940s, and whose pregnancy was also discovered by a field worker eager to 'manage' her condition, took the ultimate escape route: marriage. The worker advised vigorously against the wedding but once the young woman had taken the step she crossed the threshold out of adolescence, and therefore out of the juvenile justice system's reach.[166]

Once paroled, GCIS girls sometimes stuck together on the outside. Jeanne, who had spent two and a half years at the GCIS when she was paroled in March 1940, preferred the company and advice of 'old girls' to that of her field worker. The field worker complained that she had contact with several former GCIS girls who were 'missing' from parole.[167]

Young women and girls at the GCIS were placed in quarantine on entering the institution, branded if they had venereal disease, then subjected to a routine with little free time. Further, they were forced to submit to a resocialization process and demonstrate that GCIS programs had transformed them. Considering that their 'crimes' were often sex delinquency or incorrigibility and that their sentences were somewhat harsh – five years for vagrancy – it should not be surprising that they rebelled in various ways. Discipline at the GCIS was carefully planned and maintained except for one brief period in the 1940s when it evaporated in the midst of high staff turnover.

The Rebellions of 1945–6 and the End of an Era

The Second World War produced and kindled a phenomenon known as the 'revolt of the adolescent.'[168] The city's two reform schools for girls erupted in chaos in autumn 1945 and the following spring, bringing these ignored penal institutions to public attention. When an investigation was called into the GCIS in June 1946 following the escape of a handful of inmates, it would be the second inquiry into the city's reform schools in six months. The closing of the GCIS that year signalled the end of an era in residential reform schools for girls in Quebec.

In a modern building not far from the Back River in Laval-des-Rapides, 250 female juvenile delinquents served their sentence terms under the surveillance of the Soeurs du Bon Pasteur (see figure 7.3)[169] One Sunday evening, 7 October 1945, a small group of inmates, following the lead of two gang members who had been placed in solitary confinement, staged a riot to protest unreasonable treatment at the institution. According to *La Presse*, the riot began in one of the dormitories and for one hour the girls blockaded themselves in and ravaged the room, throwing drinking glasses, religious statues, and furniture. The nuns, unable to regain control of the situation, called in the provincial police. Quelling the riot required ten officers. Eleven young women, aged sixteen to twenty, wearing nightshirts stained with blood were taken into police custody in straitjackets. The revolt made national headline news.[170] Girls who took part in the violent episodes in the 1940s claimed the nuns committed egregious acts against them. Punishment by ridicule included the forced wearing of paper tongues for having spoken when told not to, and the cutting of their hair on one side above one ear.[171] In the riot of October 1945, girls at the Maison de Lorette claimed they were protesting the use of solitary confinement, straitjackets, and general poor treatment. According to Rév. Mère Marie-Joseph du Christ, director of the Maison de Lorette, the girls had revolted to have their sentences reduced: 'They only sought to provoke a disturbance with the hope that we would put them back in the hands of the police who would detain them in the Fullum [women's] prison where – and this is important – they would go for only three or four months.'[172] In response to the girls' claim of inadequate clothing and poor food, the Reverend Mother stated that the girls wore the same clothing as the nuns and invited the members of the press to sample their meals.

The Montreal anglophone press claimed a revolt was not surprising: a lack of funds had allegedly led to inadequate food, clothing, and train-

Figure 7.3 Maison de Lorette, Laval-des-Rapides (Soeurs du Bon Pasteur, *Au Soir d'un Siècle* [Montreal: Le Bon Pasteur d'Angers, 1944], 64)

ing.[173] Called an 'accident' by cleric authorities and blamed on 'psycho-pathic girl delinquents' by juvenile court judge Gordon Nicholson, the riot brought to public attention the disturbing conditions under which girls were incarcerated.[174] 'L'affaire de Lorette,' as it was called in La Presse, prompted the Comité catholique de la Cour juvénile to investigate the conditions of the girls' reform school.[175]

The riot at Lorette sparked a public debate about which reform school (ultimately which community, Catholic or Protestant) treated incarcerated girls better. The Gazette pointed out the failure of the dormitory-style reform school: headlines raged 'Women of 21 and Children of Nine Detained in Same Home, Without Segregation, Director Reveals.'[176] This anglophone newspaper took the opportunity to itemize in dramatic fashion, the girls complaints: under 'concentration camp conditions' at the Maison de Lorette girls were given 'coarse, ugly clothing [and an] insufficient diet' and were subject to 'harsh treatment amounting to per-secution and lack of any real rehabilitation methods.'[177] Montreal's women's organizations called for a lay committee to assist the religious order 'to bring in new methods of training and care for girls committed to their charge.'[178] Mrs John O'Neill-Gallery, chair of the city's 1944 Delinquency Prevention Week, also deplored the conditions at the Mai-son de Lorette, especially the institution's refusal to pay girls for their work in the commercial laundry but also the lack of movies, radio, and newspapers. The Affaire Lorette laid bare the usage by the nuns of soli-tary confinement and straitjackets, which according to the Gazette, were found on the premises by the provincial police.[179]

Others came to the defence of the nuns. La Presse noted with some irony that on 8 October members of the GCIS softball team bolted from supervision, a fact that the anglophone press had ignored.[180] The news story emphasized that size mattered (37 inmates at GCIS compared to 250 at Maison de Lorette). With such a manageable number, the GCIS had become not a repressive regime but a school that required girls work only on a voluntary basis; where each girl had her own room; where they had reading groups, softball teams, and could sew their own skirts accord-ing to contemporary fashion. Yet the La Presse reporter noted that in court the rioters were in fact wearing short grey-blue dresses that were every bit as nice as those worn by GCIS girls.[181] The problem with the Mai-son de Lorette lay firmly with the girls: one article referred to the prob-lems of mental backwardness; in another they were 'les mutines,' little devils.[182] Some readers came to the defence of the nuns in the Gazette. Former convenor of the Catholic Big Sisters wrote that the nuns' regime was 'antiquated' but she 'constantly admired the extraordinary devotion and warm heartedness of the nun who directed the girls.' Arthur Saint-Pierre condemned the 'wild talk and senseless criticism hurled at the institution and the admirable women who therein sacrifice their lives to the welfare and redemption of wayward girls. There is more devotion to duty, more true charity toward the young inmates and more real competence in dealing with that class of children among the Sisters of the Good Shepherd, than among the whole lot of self appointed censors and busybodies, barring none, who have been assailing them these last several days.'[183]

A grandfather of one of the 'mutinous' hired a lawyer to file a writ of *habeas corpus* on behalf of his daughter who was being held in the women's jail. This was to protest that she had not been given the opportunity to register her plea and, though a minor, was held in the adult women's jail. The petition to the court outlined her defence: she was not subject to 'bad treatment' by the nuns but rather by older girls who were instructed at times by the nuns to oversee the younger girls. In this role, these girls 'practiced veritable sadism.'[184]

If long sentences or brutal treatment of inmates had led to the riot at the Maison de Lorette the opposite was the source of the troubles at the GCIS six months later. Also a private institution, the GCIS functioned under the tutelage of a superintendent, in recent years a trained social worker, who promoted an ethic of retrieving girls from their previous lives and retraining them into moral and disciplined young women.

One Friday evening in the spring of 1946, five youths from the GCIS escaped, went on a drinking bout, and 'acted promiscuously' with local young men who hid the escapees in 'barns, summer houses, sugar houses and sawmills.'[185] Having sneaked out of the GCIS, the youths indulged in cigarettes, rum, and 'wild orgies.' The provincial police apprehended them within days, collecting them from various locations including the sawdust pile of a mill near East Farnham. The statements of those captured not only indicted them for immorality but opened the institution to harsh criticism. Clearly this was not the first time the girls had escaped for a night of adventure – the girls' stories revealed that the school's alarm bells did not work, stealing the matron's keys was effortless, and poor night supervision of the inmates created the conditions for such behaviour.[186] This state of affairs at the thirty-five-year-old facility led to its closure.

Paradoxically, it had been the administrators' desire to teach proper socialization that led to this chain of events. A chaperoned dance held in February 1946 at the GCIS to which young men from the village had been invited had led to friendships. Connections made at this occasion were followed up on supervised bi-monthly visits to Sweetsburg. Dancing, caressing, and drinking were part of these Saturday visits. The girls took it from there to organize their own, unofficial visits to town, after 'lights out.'[187]

Staff difficulties experienced during the war – mainly that professional women were in high demand in the city and refused to live in Sweetsburg on mediocre salaries – had meant that discipline became a problem long before the outbreak. Judge Nicholson then visited the school and was appalled at its condition, and effectively closed it, citing it as a fire hazard: a 'menace to life and health.'[188] The buildings were sold and it would take five years and a guarantee of state funding from the new Department and Ministry of Social Welfare and Youth to reopen the facility.

Problems at the reform schools underscored the need for the province to make a larger commitment to regulating and supporting these institutions. In this sense, as Rains and Teram have shown, Quebec trailed far behind other North American jurisdictions in institutions for youth. Only in the post–Second World War period did reform schools fall under public control.[189] The causes of the two rebellions are manifold; however, it is perceivable that both institutions suffered because of inadequate funding. Also, the bold actions on the part of the female inmates suggest an unwillingness on their part to be passive in a system that saw fit to incarcerate them for minor transgressions.

Conclusion

In 1948 the Montreal Council of Social Agencies commissioned a report on the GCIS and its place in the treatment of girls in Montreal. Its author, Ethel Barger of the Park Ridge School for Girls in Illinois, took the opportunity to outline the differences between the training school and the Maison de Lorette. Even in the wake of the GCIS closure, the board was commended for their sense of responsibility to all categories of girls: 'feeble-minded, epileptic, psychopathic, psychotic, crippled, or normal.' Considering the lack of proper oversight by the state and chronic underfunding, Barger wrote, 'The wonder was not that there were blow-ups but that there were not more serious explosions.'[190] She concluded that the main challenge faced by the GCIS was the desire to implement an effective individual training program with such a varied population. While not entirely successful, Barger noted, it was a marked improvement on what had evolved at the Maison de Lorette. The latter institution was found to be clean and orderly but the program was judged 'meager.' Instead of individual training the Maison de Lorette girls spent much of their time working in the commercial laundry or at sewing. Days were spent in a silence broken only in the dining room. Mass care was not only worse than training experiment at GCIS, it was out of date.

In the early-twentieth century, 'bad girls' could be placed through a juvenile tribunal or parental recommendation in the École de Réforme or the GCIS. The experience of that placement was determined by religious and ethnic traditions expressed in the choice of location, architecture, and programs of each institution. In the École de Réforme, young women were given religious and moral retraining in a Catholic setting under the Soeurs du Bon Pasteur, and were taught to appreciate their station in life. The GCIS began as a pet project of a small group of Protestant Montreal women who believed that non-Catholic girls ought to be given a chance at rehabilitation through a 'proper' women's reformatory. It became, by the 1920s, a cottage-style training school with a professional staff well-educated in the modern techniques of social work. On the surface the GCIS experience was as far from the punitive style of the penitentiary or local jail as one might get: the philosophy and programs at the school reflected a desire to create a middle-class, 'homey' experience.

Adolescence was considered a time when women should learn to run a house and prepare to become wives and mothers. The GCIS did not believe in hereditary causes of juvenile delinquency, but it believed that through proper resocialization it could prepare the girls for their future domestic lives. They were taught to appreciate privacy and the 'finer' things in life. On leaving the GCIS the girls were given or made a new set of clothing to mark the beginning of their new life. The superintendents at the GCIS pioneered a new women's reformatory in the form of a girls' reform school where they implemented the latest ideas in social work. These women believed that what they were doing benefited not just the individual adolescent but also society in general. But to interpret a sojourn at the GCIS as a relief from working-class Montreal to a middle-class lifestyle in the Eastern Townships would be superficial.

The resocialization process involved breaking in the girls through isolation, a regimented daily routine, and schemes of surveillance. Girls responded with accommodation and resistance, melancholy and anger, conformity and violence. All eventually left the institution and were followed by field workers. This regulatory technique was intended to see girls delivered from adolescence and delinquence into maturity and young womanhood.

Conclusion

In recent years the long-forgotten dossiers generated by the first juvenile court in Quebec travelled from the dusty shelves of the Ministry of Justice's warehouse (also known as the Pré-archivage) to the basement of the Chambre de la Jeunesse to their final resting place in the hallowed Archives nationales du Québec à Montréal. This physical voyage from obscurity and neglect to prominence and accessibility finds a parallel in the place of juvenile justice and delinquency in Quebec history. Although dependent and delinquent children are ubiquitous throughout modern Quebec history, scholars until recently have scarcely included juvenile justice practice and politics in their writing of it. Yet Quebec's juvenile justice system participated in and reflected broad developments in the social, political, and cultural history of the province. Bringing to light records that until the 1990s lay dormant in poorly ventilated spaces, this study locates the child-centred movements, institutions, personnel, and 'clientele' that formed and informed the early juvenile justice system in Quebec.

Quebec's juvenile justice system was shaped by policies and people – from legislators and legal experts to citizens whose claim to expertise was limited to a concern for the well-being and control of youth – and thus was never static from its beginning in 1869 to the Second World War. In the latter part of the nineteenth century Quebec established reform schools for girls and boys, respectively. Although limited to the incarceration stage of criminal justice, the province gave birth to a juvenile justice system that embraced child saving and innovation. The system was subject to constant revision over the next century with the most dramatic change coming with the new juvenile court in Montreal in 1912. In juvenile court, surrogate parents were supposed to carefully investigate the adolescent's world and gently correct the delinquent's behaviour. Under the juvenile court system, probation was implemented to ensure family integrity and reduce the institutionalization of children, but also the observation of religious and cultural divisions within the city. During the Montreal Juvenile Delinquents' Court's (MJDC's) reign, delinquency and adolescence became research subjects and court personnel increasingly turned to expert knowledge to explain why youth might develop a recalcitrant personality and exhibit wayward tendencies.

The creation of a juvenile justice regime with its auxiliary institutions and variety of expert knowledges resulted in a dramatic potential for heightened regulation and punishment of the adolescent population. In the late-nineteenth century the creation of youth jails called reform schools led to a justification for locking up adolescents for years, often in the name of protection. Beyond juvenile prostitutes, reform schools were filled with daughters whose parents had complained about their behaviour to the City Recorder. The juvenile court depended upon working-class parents to identify their delinquent children and confess to their own failed disciplinary regimes. Physicians and mental health experts catalogued physical and psychological details regarding the adolescent. Probation officers filled in forms and wrote myriad versions of the adolescent's life and delinquencies.

Through both stages of development of Quebec's juvenile justice system gender and place figured prominently. Women prevailed in the justice system where girls were concerned, as proper 'care' providers and as experts on delinquent girls. While juvenile justice authorities across North America promoted the appropriateness of surrogate mothers and maternal governance when dealing with troublesome girls, in Quebec this was expressed in the context of Catholic social and political prominence. Montreal's delinquent girls were thus placed in a reform school run by a conservative religious order where they were dressed like nuns, observed silence and daily prayer, worked to keep the institution solvent, and learned domestic skills required of working-class women. Later this incarceration facility would be joined by a competing model of female reformatory, the training school. Largely funded and administered by the elite Protestant community, the Girls' Cottage Industrial School remained the only training school for girls in the province. In the city's juvenile court women also figured prominently where female probation officers exercised a maternal prerogative over adolescent girls. These emergent case workers followed the professional development of social service workers elsewhere but in MJDC, gender and professionalism coalesced with the predominant ethnic and religious contours of Montreal to produce confessional casework. One of the most significant results was that anglophone (Protestant and Jewish) girls were sent for psychological and intelligence testing decades prior to Catholic girls.

Negotiations emerged among adolescents and their parents, probation officers, and reform school administrators; probation officers and parents; and among juvenile justice personnel. These struggles were not simply about adolescent behaviour, they were about gender, ethnicity, religion and the state stepping, albeit slowly, into new territory. Often they were clashes centred on the contested definition of delinquency, on different cultural and religious orientations toward behaviour and treatment, and tensions over secular and religious solutions to delinquency.

When it came to female delinquents, most agreed that girls embodied delinquency. Girls' unrestrained sexuality, with its potential for unwed pregnancy, disease, and disgrace troubled French-Canadian and Irish Catholics, Jewish and Protestant Montrealers. Yet Montreal's girl problem resonated differently within each cultural community. Interwar French-Canadian nationalists worried about modern girl behaviour beyond sexuality; her refusal to attend mass or confession, and the rejection of a family and parish-centred lifestyle threatened the foundation of the 'race.' Members of the Federation of Jewish Philanthropies attended to the girl problem because the Main's delinquent girls held the power to damage the reputation of all Montreal Jews and therefore their bid for inclusion and citizenship. The Protestant community did not reject the modern girl's lifestyle but chose to influence it through modern methods of prevention and correction. These measures emphasized the rescue and retraining of working-class anglophone girls. Its *pièce de résistance* was the thoroughly modern training school that emphasized the bourgeois values of its benefactors. Thus female delinquents should not be collapsed into a sexualized identity; early-twentieth-century female adolescent experience involved complex relationships and levels of responsibility. Further, as contemporary critics of modern girlhood argued, it was their failure to follow in their mothers' footsteps, or conform to a model of bourgeois propriety that was the problem.

The impact of juvenile justice on individual girls was dramatic. Girls who were brought to the 'home of mercy,' also known as the Montreal Juvenile Delinquents' Court, experienced an intimidating process where their parents betrayed them, their bodies and stories were mined for the nature and extent of their delinquency, and they were made to promise to do better or they were sent to an incarceration facility. These Montreal juvenile court girls generally came from the poorer strata of urban society. In the first half of the twentieth century their adolescence took shape as they gathered more autonomy by going out to work, dating, and spending leisure hours in the company of friends far away from their homes and neighbourhoods. They contributed to the economy as workers and as consumers and to the family as wage-earners; in both cases their adolescence and subordinate positions accentuated their value. Adolescent girls became *les jeunes filles modernes* as they rewrote the scripts for daughters and young women and reconceptualized the city in their own terms. Juvenile justice for them meant the following could land them in court: a determination to keep their wages; refusal to work; failure to obey curfew; staying out all night; dating an 'inappropriate' boy; and talking back to parents.

Over the course of several months starting in the autumn of 1945 Montreal girls' contempt for the juvenile justice system unfolded in a violent riot at the Maison de Lorette reform school and a mass desertion from the Girls' Cottage School. What had happened to the child saving and maternal treatment intended for delinquent girls? What had happened to adolescent girls? In the nineteenth century child savers launched a persistent and successful campaign to liberate girls from local jails and rescue them from their street-centred lives. In 1945 the reform school girls schemed to graduate from the juvenile justice facility to the Women's Jail. Though tinged with some irony, this history speaks to the importance of examining both policies and practice inherent in a juvenile justice project.

The consequential events of 1945–6 were symptomatic of changes within the system and Quebec society more generally. The Second World War had put delinquency and youth back on the front pages across the country and in Quebec a series of policy changes circumscribed young people's freedoms. It was an era in which children and youth gained an unprecedented political presence, for better or worse. Several measures, such as the implementation in Montreal of a nighttime juvenile curfew in 1942 and compulsory schooling throughout the province in 1943, were aimed at children under fourteen and had the effect of extending childhood. It also solidified the beginning of adolescence at fourteen. With respect to delinquency, the dramatic change in age of the category, juvenile delinquent, in 1942 from under sixteen to under eighteen had significant ramifications for the juvenile court and for girls, especially those sixteen and seventeen. Thus adolescence and juvenile delinquency increasingly became focused on those aged fourteen to seventeen and this group generated extraordinary attention in Montreal, even before the eruptions of 1945 and 1946.

As the juvenile court expanded its jurisdiction over girls up to seventeen years of age, it was confronted with a cohort that was fully committed to its independence. Adolescent girls continued to be an important labour force and were sought out by wartime industries, the service sector, and other areas where labour shortages were felt. Unlike their older siblings who had limited options during the 1930s Depression, these girls enjoyed a widening of employment options accompanied by better pay. Montreal, a hub for recruited men, was also a centre of work, leisure, fashion, and entertainment. This combination meant Montreal's female adolescent population found jobs easily and were courted by the night-life that thrived during the war. Commentators worried about the high wages paid youth who could not exercise discretion over spending money and leisure time.

In the 1940s girls who formed gangs and rioted in the reform school were called psychopathic and 'too recalcitrant to be disciplined by nuns.' The wartime atmosphere generated concern that the rise in absentee parents had produced dislocated and delinquent youth. It is no mistake that in the early 1940s Montreal hosted a Delinquency Prevention Week and gave rise to the potential for a ministry of youth. As the war ended, Premier Maurice Duplessis justified the idea of a Minister of Youth: 'There is no possible survival for French-speaking Canada without assuring the future of our youth.'[1] The project to ensure the future of youth is related to the heightened regulation of adolescents in general, and gender specifically, in several ways. First, ensuring the future of youth is a euphemistic way of saying that the state would do its part to discipline and correct wayward youth. Second, part of the critique about wartime delinquency was directed at women, especially mothers, who had allegedly abandoned their sons and daughters. There was no shortage of mother blaming as the war drew to a close. Third, the fact that mothers had been proven to fall short of an effective regulatory force especially where controlling daughters was concerned meant a renewal of an old idea: the policewoman. In 1945 calls were again made for the reinstatement of policewomen to 'exercis[e] a restraining influence on young women and girls.'[2]

Concern over delinquency, at a height during the Second World War, ebbed and flowed over the course of the history of Quebec's juvenile justice system. The general panic over delinquency during the war was a national preoccupation, as was sexual delinquency during the 1910s.

Specific to the Montreal context were post–First World War anxieties over *les jeunes filles modernes* who eschewed the paths of their mothers and imperilled a nation. A *jeune fille moderne*, seventeen-year-old Jeannine is a good example. She hadn't been to confession since Easter when she was brought into juvenile court in the autumn of 1943. The complaint against her read like many launched against female delinquents since the opening of the court in 1912: failure to obey mother's wishes, refusal to work, immoral behaviour. Her mother had been married at seventeen and had eight children whom she raised in a 'good moral environment.' Jeannine, on the other hand, was out every night to movies, restaurants, and dance clubs and in the morning could not drag herself out of bed to go to work. Her modern lifestyle, based around dancing and smoking cigarettes, included a much more varied sexual life than her mother's likely did. Since sixteen, she admitted to having between twelve and fifteen lovers who in exchange for sex showed her 'un good time,' buying her meals and taking her on the town. She rejected the Catholic Church's strictures not only on sexuality (to be expressed only within heterosexual marriage) but also birth control, which she admitted diminished the fear of pregnancy. While she had had a job at a hat factory, she quit because she wanted more money. The problem here was that her mother had been widowed prior to the war and needed her income. Thus at seventeen she was declared a juvenile delinquent, made a ward of the court until twenty-one and sent home on certain conditions: that she dissociate from her girlfriends and boys with bad morals, that she stay away from night clubs, attend church, and stop being rude to her mother.[3] For six months her mother held these conditions over her. She broke by May 1944. Back in court, this girl was now in her nineteenth year and threatened with three years in the Soeurs du Bon Pasteur's reform school.

The turbulent war years were both liberating and constraining for modern girls like Jeannine. On the one hand jobs and better pay were widely accessible, a flourishing cultural scene provided nightly entertainment, and a hint of sexual liberation (or at least some relief from the threat of pregnancy) came with the growing availability of condoms. An important moment also came when Quebec women won the right to vote provincially in 1940. Yet for sixteen and seventeen-year-old girls other legislation seriously circumscribed their rights. Certainly as the age of the Quebec juvenile delinquent was raised to under eighteen girls were spared adult courtrooms and incarceration facilities; however, the offences that this older cohort could, after 1942, be brought to court for included being rude to parents, staying out late and refusing to go to confession – none of which have a parallel in the Criminal Code that pertained to those over eighteen. From the perspective of the state and most parents these girls now had the right to be rescued from their own bad behaviour. From the perspective of the girls, they now faced scrutiny from not only parents but also the state. While Jeannine's self-proclaimed identity was clearly beyond minor and dependent, the state did not define her that way, extending her surveillance to the age of twenty-one.

From the files of the Montreal Juvenile Delinquents' Court come the sounds of a thousand frustrated girls. Individually they appeared before the probation officer and the judge and awaited for adults to make decisions about them. Only rarely did girls act collectively against the system, as was the case in the Lorette riots. The juvenile justice system created the violence among adolescent girls verging on young womanhood. At the Maison de Lorette, the girls were taken with their bloodied bodies wrapped in straitjackets to the local jail. This episode, rather than draw attention to the girls' complaints, led to another round in the fight over 'race' and the superiority of Catholic versus Protestant institutions and models of rehabilitation. Montreal's particular ethnic configuration and politics resulted in a confessional arrangement for both probation and incarceration. The nuns' hold on the reform school lasted a century from its beginning in the late-nineteenth century. During the 1960s and 1970s citizens' groups came together to articulate what the girls already knew: reform schools were children's prisons by another name. Various investigations confirmed the problem of outdated youth facilities in the province. As the *Montreal Gazette* asked in 1975 on the eve of the Batshaw Report's release: 'What will it take to haul Quebec's juvenile system out of the Dark Ages?'[4]

The MJDC was the product of 'progressive' judicial reform and signalled the growth of the therapeutic state. Its architects made an exception for 'difference' in the world of criminal justice: based on chronological age those under sixteen (and later eighteen) would be treated not only separately but also differently from adults. In relation to its parent – the criminal justice system – juvenile justice was contrived as a better, 'progressive' system predicated not on punishment but on treatment. Gone was the adversarial system yet this progressive system pitted parents against their children. Rules of evidence were dismissed in favour of hearsay and gossip, and cases were based on the generating of material by new court employees who were not trained in law, but social work. Rarely were those brought into court and accused of delinquency represented by legal counsel. This experiment circumscribed the rights of juvenile delinquents in the name of protection of childhood and adolescence. The liberal interpretation of juvenile offences, the scarcity of defence counsel, and wide discretionary powers of judges would ultimately lead to a rejection of juvenile justice under the Juvenile Delinquents Act. As Lillian E. Mendolsohn and Sharon Ronald wrote in their history of the MJDC in 1969, by mid-century the system had become 'controversial,' 'outdated and unconstitutional.'[5] Such critiques have led to the formation of Montreal's Social Welfare and Youth Court in 1950, the Batshaw Report in 1975 (a scathing report of Quebec's youth facilities), the Young Offenders Act in 1984, and the Youth Criminal Justice Act of 2002.

The violence at the Maison de Lorette made headlines in 1945 and was mentioned again in 1995 in the '50 Years Ago Today' section of the *Globe and Mail.* This event appeared in the newspapers half a century ago and recently for very different reasons. In the former case it was news because the image of such violence and defiance by girls went against commonly held perceptions of what girls, even delinquent girls, were capable of. In the 1990s this episode was trotted out again because it confirmed what Canadians are increasingly thinking about young women – that they are 'just like boys' when it comes to aggression, violence, and delinquency.

In this so-called post-feminist age girls have been given the dubious status of being equal to boys in the realm of aggressive behaviour. Researchers and the media have focused in the last few years on the insidiousness of girls' behaviour especially when it comes to sexuality and aggression. Who can forget the oh-so-seductive cover of *Saturday Night* magazine in February 1996 where the headline around a scantily clad young woman warned 'Lock Up Your Sons!' Girls' sexuality had become aggressive and dangerous. In 1998 crime reporters told us of a 'reign of terror' of girl gangs at high schools across Canada. The experts were called in to comment; they claimed one of the barriers to addressing this problem is that we collectively still see girls in sugar and spice stereotypes – rather than as every bit as aggressive as boys.[6] Some researchers have offered a corrective to the 'girl violence is escalating out of control' theory: they suggest that it is 'girls' indirect aggression that is more widespread and considered something of a specialty among girls.'[7] Most infuriating is that it is seen as a visible sign that girls and women have achieved equality in our society. I wonder, though, if there is not another way of understanding today's young women and their aggression – as resistance/as frustration/

as a product of girls living in a society that does tell them that they are equals, but where their experience tells them something quite different.

Today the triumph of a conservative discourse that denies the familial and social power relations that shape girls' behaviour seems complete. What one seems loath to acknowledge is the general acceptance of violence against girls. Recently, headlines raged: 'Chaining Up Errant Daughter No Crime, Jury Rules.' In half a day a jury acquitted a mother who had forcibly confined her daughter to prevent her from leaving the house. The fifteen year old was an habitual juvenile offender in the mother's eyes: breaking rules about going out, dating a man far older than herself, and finally getting pregnant. The newspaper seemed to excuse the criminal actions of the mother because she was 'at her wits' end' dealing with her delinquent daughter. This story might have taken place a century ago but it in fact occurred while this book was being written. It suggests that the way adolescent daughters spark outrage and exasperation have changed little over the twentieth century. Defiance and insubordination are likely familiar to all parents of teenage daughters; adolescent girls for their part assume independence by rejecting parents, dating beyond their peer group and without parental approval, using drugs and alcohol, and engaging in early sexual activity. While some of us would likely agree with the Crown Attorney that the mother committed a criminal act with that chain, using 'excessive and cruel force' to control her daughter, clearly a jury of the mother's peers supported the need for a little vigilante action when it comes to bad girls. Our collective hair pulling over this behaviour has led to a malignant tolerance for violence against adolescent girls; perhaps a legacy of juvenile justice did violence to adolescent girls – a chain around their waists.

Notes

Introduction

1 *Les jeunes filles modernes* can be translated as 'young, modern girls.'
2 See Bettina Bradbury, *Working Families: Age, Gender, and Daily Survival in Industrializing Montreal* (Toronto: McClelland and Stewart, 1993).
3 Library and Archives of Canada (hereafter LAC), W.L. Scott Papers, MG 30, C27, vol. 6, file 20 A35.4, 'Genesis of the Juvenile Delinquents Act,' 50–1.
4 For example, see Jean Trépanier and Françoise Tulkens, *Délinquance et protection de la jeunesse aux sources des lois belges et canadiennes sur l'enfance* (Montreal and Ottawa: Les Presses de l'Université de Montréal et de l'Ottawa, 1995); Jean Trépanier, 'Origins of the Juvenile Delinquents Act of 1908: Controlling Delinquency Through Seeking its Causes and through Youth Protection,' in *Dimensions of Childhood*, ed. Russell Smandych, Gordon Dodds, and Alvin Esau (Winnipeg: Legal Research Institute, 1991) and 'Protéger pour prévenir la délinquance: l'émergence de la Loi sur les jeunes délinquants de 1908 et sa mise en application à Montréal,' in *Entre surveillance et compassion: l'évolution de la protection de l'enfance au Québec: des origines à nos jours*, ed. Renée Joyal (Sainte-Foy: Les Presses de l'Université du Québec, 2000), 49–95; Renée Joyal, 'L'act concernant les écoles d'industrie (1869): une mesure de prophylaxie sociale dans un Québec en voie d'urbanisation,' *Revue d'histoire de l'Amérique française* 50:2 (Fall 1996): 227–40 and 'L'évolution des modes de contrôle de l'autorité parentale,' *International Journal of Canadian Studies* (Winter 1993): 73–84.
5 In the aftermath of the Conquest, the colony that would become Quebec did not implement British common law, but held on to French civil law. For the implications and development of Quebec's Civil Code, see Brian Young, *The Politics of Codification* (Montreal: McGill-Queen's University Press, 1994). See also Bradbury, *Working Families*.

6 MJDC, 7 January 1944, #5622.
7 Steven L. Schlossman and Stephanie Wallach, 'The Crime of Precocious Sexuality: Female Juvenile Delinquency in the Progressive Era,' *Harvard Educational Review* 48:1 (1978): 65–94. See also Steven L. Schlossman, *Transforming Juvenile Justice: Reform Ideals and Institutional Realities, 1825–1920* (Dekalb: Northern Illinois University Press, 2005), introduction.
8 Mary E. Odem, *Delinquent Daughters: Protecting and Policing Adolescent Female Sexuality in the United States, 1885–1920* (Chapel Hill: University of North Carolina Press, 1995); Meda Chesney-Lind, *Girls, Delinquency and Juvenile Justice* (Belmont, CA: Brooks/Cole, 1992); Linda Mahood, *Policing Gender, Class and Family: Britain, 1850–1940* (London: UCL Press, 1995); Ruth Alexander, *The 'Girl Problem': Female Sexual Delinquency in New York, 1900–1930* (Ithaca, NY: Cornell University Press, 1995).
9 Alexander, '*Girl Problem,*' 2; Odem, *Delinquent Daughters,* 136.
10 Éric Pierre and David Niget, 'Filles et garçons devant le tribunal des enfants et adolescents d'Angers de 1914 et 1940: un traitement différencié,' in *Femmes et justice pénale, XIX–XX siècles,* ed. Christine Bard, Frédéric Chauvaud, Michelle Perrot, and Jacques-Guy Petit (Rennes: Presses Universitaires de Rennes, 2002), 327–38, at 330.
11 Denise Riley, '*Am I that Name?' Feminism and the Category of 'Woman' in History* (Minneapolis: University of Minnesota Press, 1988).
12 Anne Meis Knupfer, *Reform and Resistance: Gender, Delinquency, and America's First Juvenile Court* (New York: Oxford University Press, 2001), 4.
13 Girls' Cottage School, *Annual Report* (1932), 123.
14 Joanne Meyerowitz, *Women Adrift: Independent Wage Earners in Chicago, 1880–1930* (Chicago: University of Chicago Press, 1988); Carolyn Strange, *Toronto's Girl Problem: The Perils and Pleasures of the City, 1880–1930* (Toronto: University of Toronto Press, 1995).
15 The identities of girls and their friends and family have been disguised to respect the conditions of access.
16 In order to understand the way girls were processed by the new juvenile court, I began with an examination of every case for the years 1912 (n = 70), 1918 (n = 180), and 1924 (n = 227). I then conducted a two-month per year sample for each even-numbered year between 1912 and 1945 (n = 611). A comparison to boys' cases was conducted through a 10 per cent sample of 1918 (n = 100), as well as the 1929 study of the court by Herman H. Ross.
17 Linda Gordon, *Heroes of Their Own Lives: The Politics and History of Family Violence* (New York: Penguin Books, 1988); and Joan W. Scott's response in *Signs* 15:4 (Summer 1990); see also reaction to her work in *International Labour and Working Class History* 31 (Spring 1987); and Kathleen Canning, 'Feminist History after the Linguistic Turn: Historicizing Discourse and Experience,'

Signs 19 (Winter 1994): 368–404. Karen Tice, *Tales of Wayward Girls and Immoral Women: Case Records and the Professionalization of Social Work* (Urbana and Chicago: University of Illinois Press, 1998), introduction.

18 Annalee Golz, 'Uncovering and Reconstructing Family Violence: Ontario Criminal Case Files,' in *On the Case: Explorations in Social History,* ed. Franca Iacovetta and Wendy Mitchinson (Toronto: University of Toronto Press, 1999), 289–311.

19 Iacovetta and Mitchinson, *On the Case,* 9.

20 Karen Dubinsky, 'Afterword: Telling Stories About Dead People,' in Iacovetta and Mitchinson, *On the Case,* 364.

21 Jacques Donzelot, *The Policing of Families* (New York: Pantheon, 1979); Anthony M. Platt, *The Child Savers: The Invention of Delinquency* (Chicago: University of Chicago Press, 1969); Ellen Ryerson, *The Best-Laid Plans: America's Juvenile Court Experiment* (New York: Hill and Wang, 1978); Neil Sutherland, *Children in English-Canadian Society: Framing the Twentieth Century Consensus* (Toronto: University of Toronto Press, 1976).

22 See Mahood, *Policing Gender, Class and Family;* Alan Hunt, *Governing Morals: A Social History of Moral Regulation* (Cambridge: Cambridge University Press, 1999); John McLaren, Robert Menzies, and Dorothy E. Chunn, eds, *Regulating Lives: Historical Essays on the State, Society, the Individual, and the Law* (Vancouver: UBC Press, 2002); Carolyn Strange and Tina Loo, *Making Good: Law and Moral Regulation in Canada, 1867–1939* (Toronto: University of Toronto Press, 1997).

23 Mahood, *Policing Gender, Class and Family,* 12.

24 Ibid., 13. See also Gordon, *Heroes of Their Own Lives.*

25 See T. Myers, 'The Voluntary Delinquent: Parents, Daughters and the Montreal Juvenile Delinquents' Court in 1918,' *Canadian Historical Review* 80:2 (June 1999): 242–68.

26 Odem, *Delinquent Daughters,* 158.

27 Kelly Hannah-Moffat's work on Foucault's governmentality is instructive here. She argues that while expert knowledges emerged to identify, classify, monitor, and treat the deviant, an 'analysis of women's penal strategies shows how everyday systems of governance and nonexpert women's knowledges have been used to reform and regulate prisoners.' *Punishment in Disguise: Penal Governance and Federal Imprisonment of Women in Canada* (Toronto: University of Toronto Press, 2001), 14.

28 Tamara Myers and Joan Sangster, 'Retorts, Runaways and Riots: Patterns of Resistance in Canadian Reform Schools for Girls,' *Journal of Social History* 34:3 (Spring 2001): 669–97.

29 Karlene Faith, *Unruly Women: The Politics of Confinement and Resistance* (Vancouver: Press Gang, 1993); Estelle Freedman, *Their Sisters Keepers: Women's*

Prison Reform in America, 1830–1930 (Ann Arbor: University of Michigan Press, 1981); Carol Smart, *Women, Crime and Criminology* (London: Routledge and Kegan Paul, 1976); Lucia Zedner, *Women, Crime and Custody in Victorian England* (Oxford: Clarendon Press, 1991).

30 Meda Chesney-Lind and R.G. Shelden, *Girls, Delinquency, and Juvenile Justice* (Pacific Grove, CA: Brooks Cole, 1992); Meda Chesney-Lind, *The Female Offender: Girls, Women, and Crime* (Thousand Oaks, CA: Sage, 1997).

31 Odem, *Deliquent Daughters*; Alexander, 'Girl Problem'; Knupfer, *Reform and Resistance*; Joan Sangster, *Girl Trouble: Female Delinquency in English Canada* (Peterborough, ON: Broadview Press, 2002).

32 Pamela Cox, *Gender, Justice and Welfare: Bad Girls in Britain, 1900–1950* (Basingstoke: Palgrave, 2003), 15.

33 Joan Sangster, 'Creating Social and Moral Citizens: Defining and Treating Delinquent Boys and Girls in English Canada, 1920–65,' in *Contesting Canadian Citizenship: Historical Readings*, ed. Robert Adamoski, Dorothy E. Chunn, and Robert Menzies (Peterborough: Broadview Press, 2002), 354.

34 Andrée Lévesque, *Making and Breaking the Rules: Women in Quebec, 1919–1939* (Toronto: McClelland & Stewart, 1994); 'Mères celibataires et infanticides à Montréal, 1914–1930,' in Bard, Chauvaud, Perrot, and Petit, *Femmes et justice pénale*. Marie-Aimée Cliche's work weds family, legal, and social history in Quebec, with an emphasis on children and youth. See 'Un secret bien gardé: l'inceste dans la société Québécoise,' *Revue d'histoire de l'Amérique française* 50:2 (1996): 201–26; 'Les fille-mères devant les Tribunaux de Québec, 1850–1969,' *Recherches sociographiques* 32:1 (1991): 9–42; 'Est-ce une bonne méthode pour élever les enfants? Un debat sur punitions corporelles dans les courriers du coeur au Québec, 1925 à 1969,' *Canadian Historical Review* 82:4 (2001): 662–89.

35 Véronique Strimelle, 'La gestion de la déviance des filles et les institutions du Bon Pasteur à Montréal (1869–1912),' PhD diss., Université de Montréal, 1998; Jean-Marie Fecteau, *La liberté du pauvre: crime et pauvreté au XIXe siècle Québécois* (Montreal: vlb éditeur, 2004), ch. 5; Sylvie Ménard, *Des enfants sous surveillance: la rééducation des jeunes délinquants au Québec (1840–1950)* (Montreal: vlb éditeur, 2003).

36 Evidence for this case comes from MJDC, 8 June 1928, #1980.

37 Joan Sangster, *Regulating Girls and Women: Sexuality, Family, and the Law in Ontario, 1920–1960* (Toronto: Oxford University Press, 2001), 131.

38 *La Presse*, 7 June 1927, 3.

Chapter 1

1 Institutions for children – asylums, orphanages, industrial schools – were considered necessary but underwent serious revision, especially by Chil-

dren's Aid Societies that preferred to 'place' children in Homes. David J. Rothman, *The Discovery of the Asylum: Social Order and Disorder in the New Republic* (Boston: Little, Brown, 1971); P.T. Rooke and R.L. Schnell, *Discarding the Asylum: From Child Rescue to the Welfare State in English-Canada, 1800–1950* (Lanham, MD: University Press of America, 1983); Peter Holloran, *Boston's Wayward Children: Services for Homeless Children, 1830–1930* (Boston: Northeastern University Press, 1994); Steven L. Schlossman, *Transforming Juvenile Justice: Reform Ideals and Institutional Realities, 1825–1920* (Chicago and De Kalb: Northern Illinois Press, 2005).

2 Pamela Cox examines the discourses of protecting and punishing children in her book, *Gender, Justice and Welfare: Bad Girls in Britain, 1900–1950* (Aldershot: Ashgate, 2003).

3 Paul-André Linteau, *Histoire de Montréal depuis la confédération* (Montreal: Les Editions du Boréal, 2000), 40.

4 See Holloran, *Boston's Wayward Children*; Linda Mahood, *Policing Gender, Class and Family* (Edmonton: University of Alberta Press, 1995); Huguette Lapointe-Roy, *Charité bien ordonné: le premier réseau de lutte contre la pauvreté à Montréal au 19e siècle* (Montreal: Boréal, 1987); Jan Noel, '"Femmes Fortes" and the Montreal Poor in the Early Nineteenth Century,' in *Changing Roles of Women in the Christian Church*, ed. L. Muir and M. Whitely (Toronto: University of Toronto Press, 1995).

5 Mahood, *Policing Gender, Class and Family*, 42.

6 Susan E. Houston, 'The "Waifs and Strays" of a Late Victorian City: Juvenile Delinquents in Toronto,' in *Childhood and Family in Canadian History*, ed. Joy Parr (Toronto: McClelland Stewart Ltd, 1982), 131; Peter C. Baldwin, 'Nocturnal Habits and Dark Wisdom: The American Response to Children in the Streets at Night, 1880–1930,' *Journal of Social History* 35:3 (2002): 593–69; Timothy Gilfoyle, 'Street-Rats and Gutter-Snipes: Child Pickpockets and Street Culture in New York City, 1850–1900,' *Journal of Social History* 37:4 (Summer 2004): 853–70.

7 See Barbara Littlewood and Linda Mahood. 'Prostitutes, Magdalenes, and Wayward Girls: Dangerous Sexualities of Working-Class Women in Victorian Scotland,' *Gender and History* 3 (1991): 160–75; Christine Stansell, *City of Women: Sex and Class in New York, 1789–1860* (New York: Alfred A. Knopf, 1986).

8 Heather Shore, 'Cross Coves, Buzzers, and General Sorts of Prigs: Juvenile Crime and the Criminal "Underworld" in the Early Nineteenth Century,' *British Journal of Criminology* 39:1 (1999): 10–24.

9 See Neil Sutherland, *Children in English-Canadian Society: Framing the Twentieth-Century Consensus* (Toronto: University of Toronto Press, 1976), 98–9; Jean Trépanier, 'Protéger pour prévenir la délinquance: l'émergence de la

loi sur les jeunes délinquants de 1908 et sa mise en application à Montréal,' in *Entre surveillance et compassion: l'évolution de la protection de l'enfance au Québec: des origines à nos jours*, ed. Renée Joyal, (Sainte-Foy: Les Presses de l'Université du Québec, 2000), 49–95, at 51.

10 D. Owen Carrigan, *Juvenile Delinquency in Canada: A History* (Concord, ON: Irwin Publishing, 1998), ch. 1.

11 In her study of nineteenth-century British juvenile justice, Linda Mahood suggests that it 'represented the failure of the criminal justice system and society to provide minimal levels of justice and support,' ch. 5.

12 Cited in Jean-Marie Fecteau, Sylvie Ménard, Jean Trépanier, and Véroniquee Strimelle, 'Une politique de l'enfance délinquante et en danger: la mise en place des écoles de réforme et d'industrie au Québec (1840–1873),' *Crime, Histoire, Société* 1:2 (1998): 75–110, at 85.

13 Fecteau et al., 'Une politique,' 79–80; Sutherland, *Children in English-Canadian Society*, 98.

14 These resolutions are cited in the Report of the Inspectors of Prisons and Asylums for 1865, as cited in Sylvie Ménard, *Des enfants sous surveillance: la rééducation des jeunes délinquants au Québec (1840–1950)* (Montreal: vlb editeur, 2003), 44–5.

15 Act for the More Speedy Trial and Punishment of Juvenile Offenders, S. Prov. C. 1857 c. 29.

16 This provision was part of a larger Act whose aim was to improve public institutions such as asylums, prisons and hospitals. Acte pour établir des prisons pour les jeunes délinquants, pour la meilleure administration des asiles, hôpitaux et prisons publics, et pour mieux construire les prisons communes. 20 Vict. 1857, c. 28.

17 At the helm was Andrew Dickson, who had in the 1850s contributed to the debate over what to do with problem children through his reports.

18 Fecteau et al., 'Une politique,' 88–9. Anne Duret, 'L'enfermement comme forme de punition du garçon délinquant au Québec (1857–1930),' MA thesis, Université d'Ottawa, 1988.

19 Carrigan, *Juvenile Delinquency in Canada*, 45.

20 The 1869 acts referred to *écoles de réforme*; the official English translation was 'reformatory schools.' I will also use the term *reform schools*.

21 Québec, An Act respecting Industrial/Reform Schools, 32 Vict., c. 17 and c. 18, 1869.

22 Initially there was no minimum age set. In 1884 a minimum age was set at seven and then in 1890 at four. Two years later, in 1892, it was set at six. Similarly the maximum age fluctuated from less than 14 in 1869 to less than twelve in 1884 and back to less than fourteen in 1894. Joyal, 'L'act concernant les écoles d'industrie (1869): Une mesure de prophylaxie sociale dans

un Québec en voie d'urbanisation,' *Revue d'histoire de l'Amérique française* 50:2 (Fall 1996): 227–40, at 237.

23 See Joyal, 'L'act concernant,' 235.

24 Michael Ignatieff, *A Just Measure of Pain* (London: Penguin Books, 1978).

25 Kelly Hannah-Moffat, *Punishment in Disguise: Penal Governance and Federal Imprisonment of Women in Canada* (Toronto: University of Toronto Press, 2001), 32.

26 Renée Joyal, 'L'évolution des modes de contrôle de d'autorité parentale,' *International Journal of Canadian Studies*, Special Issue (Winter 1993): 75; and 'L'act concernant,' 232. Joyal notes specifically the appeals of Reverends Baile (of the Sulpiciens), Ramsay (of the Miséricorde), and Taschereau (future archbishop and cardinal).

27 Jean-Marie Fecteau, 'La construction d'un espace social: les rapports de l'église et de l'état et la question de l'assistance publique au Québec dans la seconde moitié du XIXe siècle,' in *L'histoire de la culture et de l'imprimé.* ed. Yvan Lamonde and G. Gallichan (Quebec: Presses de l'Université Laval, 1996), 61–90; Huguette Lapointe-Roy, *Charité bien ordonné: le premier réseau de lutte contre la pauvreté à Montreal au 19e siècle* (Montreal: Boréal, 1987); Philippe Sylvain and Nive Voisine, *Histoire du catholicisme québécoise: les XVIIIe et XIX siècles*, vol. 2 (Montreal: Boréal, 1991); Janice Harvey, 'Upper Class Reaction to Poverty in Mid-19th-Century Montreal: A Protestant Example,' MA thesis, McGill University, 1978.

28 Fernande Roy, *Histoire des idéologies au Québec aux XIXe et XXe siècles* (Montreal: Boréal, 1993), 35.

29 In 1867 a Ministry of Public Instruction had been established by the province. This was abolished in 1875 and replaced by a Department of Public Instruction that was comprised of two committees, a Catholic one and a Protestant one. Members of the former included clergymen.

30 Roy, *Histoire des idéologies*, 35–6.

31 The child as 'un être faible' was a popular belief. Protestants as well as Catholics debated the 'natural' state of the child. See Nancy Christie, *Engendering the State: Family, Work, and Welfare in Canada* (Toronto: University of Toronto Press, 2000), especially ch. 1.

32 On the 'multicultural upper crust,' legal elites in Quebec, and their pluralistic legal orientation, see Brian Young, *The Politics of Codification: The Lower Canadian Civil Code of 1866* (Montreal and Kingston: McGill-Queen's University Press, 1994).

33 Jean Trépanier, 'Protéger pour prévenir la délinquance'; D. Owen Carrigan, *Crime and Punishment in Canada: A History* (Toronto: McClelland and Stewart, 1991), 415.

34 Carrigan, *Crime and Punishment*, 416.

35 Sutherland, *Children in English-Canadian Society*, ch. 8; John Bullen, 'J.J. Kelso and the 'New' Child-Savers: The Genesis of the Children's Aid Movement in Ontario,' in *Dimensions of Childhood* ed., Russell Smandych, Gordon Dodds, and Alvin Esau (Winnipeg: Legal Research Institute, 1991), 135–58; Andrew Jones and Leonard Rutman, *In the Children's Aid: J.J. Kelso and Child Welfare in Ontario* (Toronto: University of Toronto Press, 1981); P.T. Rooke and R.L. Schnell, *Discarding the Asylum: From Child Rescue to the Welfare State in English Canada* (New York: University Press of America, 1983).

36 Library and Archives of Canada (hereafter LAC), W.L. Scott Papers, MG 30, C 27, Vol. 6, File 20, A.35.4, W.L. Scott, 'Genesis of the Juvenile Delinquents Act.'

37 Sutherland, *Children in English-Canadian Society*, chs. 8 and 9.

38 I made this point in my dissertation, 'Criminal Women and Bad Girls: Regulation and Punishment in Montreal, 1890–1930,' McGill University, 1996, 158–9; Pierre Dubois and Jean Trépanier, 'L'adoption de la loi sur les jeunes délinquants de 1908: études comparées des quotidiens montréalais et torontois,' *Revue d'histoire de l'Amérique française* 52:3 (Winter 1999): 345–81.

39 Dubois and Trépanier, 'L'adoption,' 364.

40 Scott, 'Genesis of the Juvenile Delinquents Act,' 80. See also letter concerning the petition from Katherine Weller (Montreal CAS) to W.L. Scott, 6 March 1908, LAC, MG 30, C27, vol. 7, 25A.35.4.

41 Scott, 'Genesis of the Juvenile Delinquents Act,' 58–59; *La Presse*, 7 February 1908, 4; Dubois and Trépanier, 'L'adoption,' 379.

42 Scott, 'Genesis of the Juvenile Deliquents Act,' 83.

43 See Sutherland, *Children in English-Canadian Society*, ch. 8.

44 Anthony M. Platt, *The Child Savers: The Invention of Delinquency* (Chicago: University of Chicago Press, 1969); Ellen Ryerson, *The Best-Laid Plans: America's Juvenile Court Experiment* (New York: Hill and Wang, 1978); Schlossman, *Transforming Juvenile Justice.*

45 Quebec, An Act respecting Juvenile Delinquents, 1910, 1 Geo. V, c. 26. Section VI of the act established the Juvenile Delinquents' Court in Montreal. It stipulated that the juvenile court judge be chosen from judges of the sessions, police magistrates, or magistrates performing their duties in the city of Montreal.

46 Quebec, An Act respecting Juvenile Delinquents, 1910, 1 Geo. V, 26.

47 Quebec, *Débats de l'Assemblée Législative*, 12th legislature, 2nd session, 6 May 1910, 493. Author's translation.

48 Quebec, *Débats*, 12th legislature, 2nd session, 493. There is no doubt that the Canadian juvenile court system borrowed from the first American juvenile tribunals in Chicago and Denver and, Montreal juvenile court judges fol-

lowed closely the model of juvenile justice practiced in the United States and in English Canada.

49 Unofficially the court began its work months earlier. The MJDC was situated at 209 Champs de Mars until the early 1930s when it was moved to St. Denis Street.

50 Lucien A. Beaulieu, 'A Comparison of Judicial Roles under the JDA and YOA,' in *The Young Offenders Act: A Revolution in Canadian Juvenile Justice*, ed. Alan W. Leschied, Peter G. Jaffe, and Wayne Willis (Toronto: University of Toronto Press, 1991), 131. Beaulieu writes that the trial 'was to be summary in nature, almost as if the alleged offence was trivial.' See also Schlossman, *Transforming Juvenile Justice*, 58–9.

51 E. Gouin, 'La Cour Juvénile de Montréal,' *La revue canadienne* (December 1913).

52 Paul-André Linteau, *Histoire de Montréal depuis la Confédération*, 2nd ed. (Montreal: Editions Boréal, 2000), 161–2.

53 Fecteau et al., 'Une politique,' 75–110; Jean-Marie Fecteau, 'La construction d'un espace social: les rapports de l'église et de l'état et la question de l'assistance publique au Québec dans la seconde moitié du XIXe siècle,' in *L'histoire de la culture et de l'imprimé*, ed. Yvan Lamonde and G. Gallichan, (Quebec: Presses de l'Université Laval, 1996), 61–90.

54 On French-English relations as 'race relations' see Vic Satzewich and Li Zong, 'Social Control and the Historical Construction of "Race,"' in Bernard Schissel and Linda Mahood, eds, *Social Control in Canada* (Toronto: Oxford University Press, 1996), 263–87, at 271–4.

55 See Judge Seth Leet on the issue. Archives nationales du Québec à Québec, Correspondance du Procureur-Général, E 17, Letter to Hon. Sir Lomer Gouin, from Seth Leet, 12 December 1910; and letter to the editor of the *Montreal Witness*, December 1910.

56 *Le Devoir*, 17 April 1915, 1.

57 Nancy Christie, *Engendering the State: Family, Work, and Welfare in Canada* (Toronto: University of Toronto Press, 2000), 39.

58 Those over fourteen charged with an indictable offence could be brought into the regular criminal justice system at the juvenile court judge's discretion.

59 Canada, An Act respecting Juvenile Delinquents, 7–8 Edward VII, c. 40.

60 Ibid.

61 Province of Quebec, *Revised Statutes of Quebec*, 1909, Article 4036.

62 Quebec, An act to amend the Revised Statutes of Quebec, 1909, respecting Juvenile Delinquents, 3 Geo. V, c. 39. Assented to December 1912.

63 Judge Choquet fully supported the widening of the description of delin-

quency in the JDA. Choquet to Lomer Gouin, 28 November 1912, Quebec, *Documents de la Session* (1912).

64 For a discussion of 'immoral' boys, see Tamara Myers, 'Embodying Delinquency: Boys' Bodies, Sexuality and Juvenile Justice in Early Twentieth-Century Quebec,' *Journal of the History of Sexuality* 14:4 (October 2005).

65 Bruno Théorêt, 'Régulation juridique pénale des mineur-es et discrimination à l'égard des filles: la clause de 1924 amendant la Loi sur les jeunes délinquants,' *Canadian Journal of Women and the Law* 4 (1990–1): 539–55, at 541. See also Revised Statutes of Canada, 1927.

66 MJDC, *Annual Report* (1918); 1915 and 1916.

67 LAC, Girls' Cottage School Papers, MG 28, I 404, vol. 1, file 20, Bridges, 'A Study of a Group of Delinquent Girls, 1926.'

Chapter 2

1 Jean-Marie Fecteau, Sylvie Ménard, Jean Trépanier, and Véronique Strimelle, 'Une politique de l'enfance délinquante et en danger: la mise en place des écoles de réforme et d'industrie au Québec (1840–1873),' *Crime, Histoire, Société* 1:2 (1998): 75–110; Sylvie Ménard, *Des enfants sous surveillance: la rééducation des jeunes délinquants au Québec (1840–1950)* (Montreal: vlb editeur, 2003); Véronique Strimelle, 'La gestion de la déviance des filles et les institutions du Bon Pasteur à Montréal (1869–1912),' PhD diss., Université de Montréal, 1998; Renée Joyal, 'L'évolution des modes de contrôle de l'autorité parentale,' *International Journal of Canadian Studies*, Special Issue (Winter 1993): 73–84, at 74–5; and her 'L'act concernant les écoles d'industrie (1869): une mesure de prophylaxie sociale dans un Québec en voie d'urbanisation,' *Revue d'histoire de l'Amérique française* 50:2 (Fall 1996): 227–40.

2 Joyal, 'L'évolution'; and her 'L'act concernant les Écoles d'Industrie.'

3 Jacques Donzelot, *Policing of Families* trans. Robert Hurley (New York: Pantheon Books, 1979); Anthony Platt, *The Child-Savers: The Invention of Delinquency* (Chicago: University of Chicago Press, 1969).

4 See, for example, the work of Strimelle, 'La gestion,' and Ménard, *Des enfants*; Anne Duret, 'L'enfermement comme forme de punition du garçon délinquant au Québec (1857–1930),' MA thesis, Université d'Ottawa, 1988; and Danielle Lacasse, 'Du délinquant à ouvrie qualifié: le Mont-Saint-Antoine, 1945–1964,' *Histoire sociale/Social History* 22:44 (November 1989): 287–316.

5 For a critique of this reform innovation, see Michael Ignatieff, *A Just Measure of Pain: The Penitentiary in the Industrial Revolution, 1750–1850* (London: Macmillan, 1978); David J. Rothman, *The Discovery of the Asylum: Social Order and*

Disorder in the New Republic (Boston: Little, Brown, 1971); Michel Foucault, *Discipline and Punish: The Birth of the Prison* (New York: Vintage Books, 1977).

6 For an overview, see D. Owen Carrigan, *Crime and Punishment in Canada: A History* (Toronto: McClelland and Stewart, 1991).

7 Karlene Faith, *Unruly Women: The Politics of Confinement and Resistance* (Vancouver: Press Gang Publishers, 1993) ch. 3; Estelle B. Freedman, *Their Sister's Keepers: Women's Prison Reform in America, 1830–1930* (Ann Arbor: University of Michigan Press, 1981).

8 Barbara M. Brenzel, *Daughters of the State: A Social Portrait of the First Reform School for Girls in North America, 1856–1905* (Cambridge, MA: MIT Press, 1983); Lucia Zedner, *Women, Crime, and Custody in Victorian England* (Oxford: Oxford University Press, 1991), c. 121; Freedman, *Their Sister's Keepers*; Nicole Hahn Rafter, *Partial Justice: Women, Prisons, and Social Control* (New Brunswick, NJ: Northeastern University Press, 1985).

9 Rafter, *Partial Justice*, 23.

10 Freedman, *Their Sister's Keepers*, 47; see also Rafter, *Partial Justice*, 45–6.

11 Lucia Zedner, *Women, Crime and Custody in Victorian England* (Oxford: Oxford University Press, 1991), 116–21; and Freedman, *Their Sisters' Keepers*, 22–4; Kelly Hannah-Moffat, *Punishment in Disguise: Penal Governance and Federal Inprisonment of Women* in Canada (Toronto: University of Toronto Press, 2001), ch. 1.

12 T. Ploszajska, 'Moral Landscapes and Manipulated Spaces: Gender, Class and Space in Victorian Reformatory Schools,' *Journal of Historical Geography* 20:4 (1994): 413–29.

13 Hannah-Moffat, *Punishment in Disguise*, 52.

14 Ibid., 56–70; and Carolyn Strange, 'The Criminal and Fallen of Their Sex: The Establishment of Canada's First Women's Prison, 1874–1904,' *Canadian Women and the Law* 1:1 (1986); and Carolyn Strange, 'The Velvet Glove: Maternalistic Reform at the Andrew Mercer Ontario Reformatory for Females, 1874–1927,' MA thesis, University of Ottawa, 1983.

15 Rafter, *Partial Justice*; Freedman, *Their Sisters' Keepers*; Zedner, *Women, Crime and Custody*.

16 Strange, 'The Criminal and Fallen of Their Sex' and 'The Velvet Glove.'

17 Rafter, *Partial Justice*.

18 J. Douglas Borthwick, *History of the Montreal Prison from A.S. 1784 to A.D. 1886* (Montreal: A. Periard, 1886), 225. See also Borthwick, *From Darkness to Light: History of the Eight Prisons Which Have Been, or Are Now, in Montreal from A.D. 1766 to A.D 1907 – Civil and Military* (Montreal: The Gazette Printing Co., 1907).

19 Strimelle, 'La gestion,' 89. See also Province of Quebec, *Sessional Papers*, Reports of the Inspectors of Prisons, especially 1867 and 1868.
20 Quebec, *Sessional Papers*, 'Report of the Inspectors of Prisons' (1875).
21 Freedman, *Their Sisters' Keepers*, 46. Note that private, religious-based institutions were also common in the United States, although they tended to be peripheral to the juvenile justice system.
22 Henri de Courcy, *Les servantes de Dieu en Canada: essai sur l'histoire des communautés réligieuses de femmes de la province* (Montreal: John Lovell, 1855), 102; Strimelle, 'La gestion,' 96.
23 Soeurs du Bon Pasteur, *Annales de la Maison Saint-Domitille* (Montreal: Imp. de l'Institution des Sourds-Muets, 1919), 15. See also Gaetan Beronville, *Saint Mary Euphrasia Pelletier: Foundress of the Good Shepherd Sisters* (Westminster, MD, 1959) and Sister Mary of St Marine Verger, *Practical Rules for the Use of the Religious of the Good Shepherd for the Direction of the Classes* (Angers, 1898).
24 Philippe Sylvain and Nive Voisine, *Histoire du catholicism québécois: le XVIIIe et XIXe siècles*, Vol. 2, *Réveil et consolidation (1840–98)* (Montreal: Boréal, 1991), 28. Bourget's travels to France in the 1840s had resulted in the successful recruitment of several female religious orders, including the Soeurs du Bon Pasteur. He also encouraged the establishment of Canadien orders: the Soeurs de la Providence in 1843, the Soeurs de la Miséricorde (1846), Soeurs du Saint-Nom de Jésus et Marie (1843), and the Soeurs de Sainte-Anne (1850). By the1870s Montreal accommodated a large number of religious orders operating a complex network of institutions. By the end of the century there were over thirty women's religious orders in Quebec, covering a wide spectrum of social service work with the poor, the orphaned, the infirm, the mentally ill, and the aged.
25 De Courcy, 'Les servantes de Dieu,' 102.
26 Soeurs du Bon Pasteur, *Au Soir*, 32.
27 Soeurs du Bon Pasteur, *Annales des Religieuses de Notre-Dame de Charité du Bon Pasteur d'Angers à Montréal, 1844–1896*, vols. 1–2.
28 Soeurs du Bon Pasteur, *Fêtes Jubilaires 1844–1894* (Montreal, 1894), 7.
29 *Au Soir*, 120–1. Peter Holloran, *Boston's Wayward Children: Services for Homeless Children, 1830–1930*, (Boston: Northeastern University Press, 1994), 127. In the United States, these institutions were private and not as fundamental to the juvenile justice system as were the Soeurs in Montreal. Anne Meis Knupfer has found that with the establishment of the juvenile court in the twentieth century approximately 15 per cent of Chicago's delinquent girls were sent to the House of the Good Shepherd. '"Rectifying ... the hampering causes of delinquency": The Chicago Home for Girls, 1900–1935,' *Journal of Illinois History* 2 (Spring 1999): 17–38, at 17. However, as she notes in her

monograph, *Reform and Resistance: Gender, Delinquency, and America's First Juvenile Court* (New York: Routledge, 2001), in the first decade of the twentieth century, the House of the Good Shepherd was consistently overcrowded with nearly five hundred girls at any one time.

30 De Courcy, 'Les servantes,' 104.

31 Lapointe-Roy, 214.*Charité bien ordonnée: le premier réseau de lutte contre la pauvreté à Montréal au 19e siècle* (Montreal: Boréal, 1987).

32 Soeurs du Bon Pasteur, *Fêtes Jubilaires,* 27.

33 Jacques Laplante, *Prison et ordre social au Québec* (Ottawa: Les Presses de l'Université d'Ottawa, 1989), 78.

34 See Tamara Myers, 'Criminal Women and Bad Girls: Regulation and Punishment in Montreal, 1890–1930,' PhD diss., McGill University, 1996, ch. 5, 'The Soeurs du Bon Pasteur and the "Brébis fugitives et rebelles": Incarcerating Women in Montreal, 1870–1930.'

35 Soeurs du Bon Pasteur, *Au Soir,* 120–1.

36 Andrée Lévesque, 'Deviant Anonymous: Single Mothers at the Hôpital de la Miséricorde in Montreal, 1929–1939,' Canadian Historical Association *Historical Papers* (1984): 168–86.

37 WCTU (Montreal), *Annual Report* (1887), 19.

38 Ibid., 20.

39 Here I am drawing a distinction between these nuns and women's organizations that were instrumental in confronting young women on the streets, at railway stations, and in a variety of commercial amusements locales. The Soeurs du Bon Pasteur certainly did use the press to recruit a clientele for their Sanatorium Sainte-Euphrasie, an asylum for 'nervous disorders' – primarily alcohol and drug addiction. See *La Revue Moderne*, November 1924, as cited in Lévesque, *Making and Breaking the Rules: Women in Quebec, 1919–1939* (Toronto: McClelland and Stewart, 1994), 39. The Soeurs du Bon Pasteur were not strictly a cloistered, contemplative order. I use the term to emphasize how they lived separate from society in convents but unlike nuns who were truly cloistered, these nuns embraced 'good works' which led to contact with the world beyond the convent. For a discussion on the differences see Elizabeth Smyth, 'Professionalization among the Professed: The Case of Roman Catholic Women Religious,' in E. Smyth et al., *Challenging Professions: Historical and Contemporary Prespectives on Women's Professional Work* (Toronto: University of Toronto Press, 1999), 237.

40 The Montreal Young Women's Christian Association was founded in 1874 and quickly embraced the challenge of finding solutions to problems facing the city's recent arrivals from rural Quebec and the British Isles. See Diana Pedersen, '"Keeping Our Good Girls Good": The YWCA and the "Girl Prob-

lem," 1870–1930,' *Canadian Woman Studies* 7:4 (Winter 1986); and 'Providing a Woman's Conscience: The YWCA, Female Evangelicalism, and the Girl in the City, 1870–1930,' in *Canadian Women: A Reader*, ed. Wendy Mitchinson et al. (Toronto: Harcourt, 1996), 194–210. Also focusing on preventive strategies was Montreal's Working Girls Association, an organization directing girls to inexpensive but morally safe lodgings, employment services, opened a reading room downtown in the mid-1870s. This Protestant organization also noted the desperate living conditions facing working 'girls.' In an exposé on the reading room the abominable crowded and amoral living spaces were revealed as the source of young women's unacceptable behaviour: 'Can We Blame Them That They Hurry Out from This to Seek Air and Amusement on the Streets? '*Montreal Witness*, 8 February 1875.

41 Andrée Lévesque, 'Éteindre le red light: les réformateurs et la prostitution à Montréal entre 1865 et 1925,' *Urban History Review* 17:3 (February 1989): 191–201.

42 Christine Stansell, *City of Women: Sex and Class in New York, 1789–1860* (Urbana and Chicago: University of Illinois Press, 1986), 180–2.

43 Linda Mahood, *The Magdalenes: Prostitution in the Nineteenth Century* (London: Routledge, 1990), 117.

44 Ibid., 118.

45 The nineteenth-century notion of fallen women included what one American historian has defined as 'a broad category including prostitution, tramps and nearly every adult woman who challenged middle-class assumptions about domesticity.' Jeffrey Adler, 'Streetwalkers, Degraded Outcasts, and Good-for-Nothing Huzzies: Women and the Dangerous Class in Antebellum St. Louis,' *Journal of Social History* 25:4 (1992): 737–55, at 740.

46 *Montreal Witness*, 5 January 1875.

47 City of Montreal, Recorder's Court Archives, 26 January 1903.

48 Ibid., 7 May 1907.

49 Ibid., 12 December 1908.

50 Quebec, *Sessional Papers* (1910), 'Report of the Lady Superior.'

51 See Pamela Cox, 'Rescue and Reform: Girls, Delinquency and Industrial Schools, 1908–1930,' PhD diss., University of Cambridge, 1996, 5. Cox suggests this has to do with low numbers and a desire to train girls to be urban domestic servants. As Barbara Brenzel illustrates, the first American reform school for girls, the Lancaster, was based on a cottage system. Brenzel, *Daughters of the State.*

52 Archives du Bon Pasteur, 'Diverse Categories de Personnes Recues Depuis le Début de Notre Oeuvre à Montréal,' 2.

53 Lacasse, 'Du délinquant,' 291.

54 Quebec, An Act respecting Reformatory Schools, 32 Vict., c. 18, 1869. According to Judge F.-X. Choquet, of the Cour des sessions de la paix (and later of the Juvenile Delinquents' Court) this was later changed to 'not less than 2 years.' Library and Archives of Canada, Montreal Local Council of Women, MG 28, I 164, vol. 7, file 7–4–B, Letter from F.-X. Choquet, 26 July 1910.

55 Strimelle, 'La gestion,' 210.

56 Ibid., xii.

57 Ibid., 193–4.

58 Ibid., 192. Between 1869 and 1912, 68 per cent of inmates at the reformatory school were between 13 and 16. (Strimelle, 'La gestion,' 186) Compare this to boys who were largely incarcerated for property offences and offences against the person. Sylvie Ménard has found that a large majority of boys sent to the Mont-Saint-Antoine reform school were petty thieves, whereas vagrants made up 18.9 per cent of the population between 1873 and 1909. Ménard, 'Des enfants,' 156.

59 Quebec, An act respecting industrial schools, 32 Vict., c. 17, 1869.

60 Montreal, Recorder's Court Archives, 27 May 1907.

61 Strimelle, 'La gestion,' 110.

62 Ibid., 179.

63 Michelle Cale, 'Girls and the Perception of Sexual Danger in the Victorian Reformatory System,' *History* 78:253 (June 1993): 201–17, at 209.

64 Hannah-Moffat, *Punishment in Disguise: Penal Governance and Federal Imprisonment of Women in Canada* (Toronto: University of Toronto Press, 2001), 19.

65 Soeurs du Bon Pasteur, *Au Soir,* 120–1.

66 Micheline Dumont and Nadia Fahmy-Eid, *Les couventines: l'éducation des filles au Québec dans les congrégations religieuses enseignantes, 1840–1960* (Montreal: Boréal, 1986). Marie-Paule Malouin, *Ma soeur, à quelle école allez-vous? Deux écoles de filles à la fin du XIXe siècle* (Montreal: Fides, 1985).

67 See Brian Young, 'Édouard-Charles Fabre,' *Dictionary of Canadian Biography,* vol. 12, *1891 to 1900* (1990): 300–5, at 302.

68 Strimelle, 'La gestion,' 229.

69 Soeurs du Bon Pasteur, *Annales de la Maison Ste-Domitille,* 34–5. Author's translation.

70 Strimelle, 'La gestion,' 104.

71 Soeurs du Bon Pasteur, *Au Soir d'un siècle,* 97. Author's translation.

72 Strimelle, 'La gestion,' 221.

73 Duret, 'L'enfêrmement,' 124–5; Ménard, 'Des enfants,' 233–4.

74 The commercial laundry was founded in 1888. Soeurs du Bon Pasteur, *Annales du Soeurs du Bon Pasteur,* vol. 1 (1895), 277.

75 Soeurs du Bon Pasteur, *Annales du Soeurs du Bon Pasteur,* vol. 1 (1895), 277.
76 Strimelle, 'La gestion,' 166.
77 Quebec, *Sessional Papers,* Report of Inspectors of Prisons, etc. [1908–1909], Report of the Superioress of the Montreal Reformatory for Girls, 29 December 1908.
78 Soeurs du Bon Pasteur, *Annales de la Maison Ste-Domitille* (Montreal: Imprimeur de l'Institut des Sourds-Muets, 1919), 244.
79 Ibid., 243–4.
80 Quebec, *Sessional Papers,* Report of the Inspectors of Prisons, etc., 'Report of the Lady Superior of the Montreal Reformatory School for Girls,' 13 January 1914.
81 Strimelle, 'La gestion,' 235.
82 Ibid., 225.
83 Foucault, *Discipline and Punish,* ch. 1.
84 Strimelle, 'La gestion,' 226.
85 Quebec, Sessional Papers, 'Reports of Inspectors of Prisons,' 1908–1909, Report of the Superioress of the Montreal Reformatory School for Girls, 29 December 1908.
86 Strimelle, 'La gestion,' 226.
87 Tamara Myers and Joan Sangster, 'Retorts, Runaways and Riots: Patterns of Resistance in Canadian Reform Schools for Girls,' *Journal of Social History* (U.S.) 34:3 (Spring 2001): 669–97.
88 Strimelle, 'La gestion,' 174.
89 Ibid., 240.
90 For an overview of late-nineteenth-century English-Canadian reformers' preference for 'a wholesome family environment' over institutionalization see Neil Sutherland, *Children in English-Canadian Society: Framing the Twentieth-Century Concensus* (Toronto: University of Toronto Press, 1976), 100. See also Patricia Rooke and R.L. Schnell, *Discarding the Asylum: From Child Rescue to the Welfare State in English Canada* (Lanham, MD: University Press of America, 1983).
91 Lévesque, *Making and Breaking,* 55.
92 The École de Réforme occupied a separate building on the grounds of the Sherbrooke Street monastery. It was situated at the corner of Cadieux and Norbert Streets.

Chapter 3

1 *Montreal Herald,* 9 August 1910, 1 and 6.
2 *Montreal Herald,* 12 August 1910.

3 Cynthia Comacchio, 'Dancing to Perdition: Adolescence and Leisure in Interwar English Canada,' *Journal of Canadian Studies* (Autumn 1997): 6.

4 As cited in Comacchio, 'Dancing to Perdition,' 7.

5 Mary E. Odem, *Delinquent Daughters: Protecting and Policing Adolescent Female Sexuality in the United States, 1885–1920* (Chapel Hill and London: University of North Carolina Press, 1995), 95; Regina G. Kunzel, *Fallen Women, Problem Girls: Unmarried Mothers and the Professionalization of Social Work, 1890–1945* (New Haven: Yale University Press, 1993), 62–3; Ruth M. Alexander, *The 'Girl Problem': Female Sexual Delinquency in New York, 1900–1950* (Ithaca: Cornell University Press, 1995), 37.

6 See Carolyn Strange, 'From Modern Babylon to a City Upon a Hill: The Toronto Social Survey Commission of 1915 and the Search for Sexual Order in the City,' in *Patterns of the Past: Interpreting Ontario's History*, ed. Roger Hall et al. (Toronto: Dundurn Press, 1988), 255–77; and *Toronto's Girl Problem* (Toronto: University of Toronto Press, 1995).

7 Andrée Lévesque, 'Éteindre le red light: les réformateurs et la prostitution à Montréal entre 1865 et 1925,' *Urban History Review* 17:3 (February 1989): 191–201.

8 *La Bonne Parole* (official journal of the FNSJB), 1:10 (December 1913): 3. Author's translation.

9 Major J.G. Fitzgerald, 'The Advisory Committee on Venereal Diseases for Military District No. 2,' *Public Health Journal* 9:2 (February 1918): 49. Also in 1918, Ontario established a royal commission on venereal disease and feeblemindedness. The repressive state reaction to the perceived crisis is the subject of Mary Louise Adams's 'In Sickness and in Health: State Formation, Moral Regulation, and Early VD Initiatives in Ontario,' *Journal of Canadian Studies* 28:4 (Winter 1993–4): 117–130.

10 Danielle Lacasse, *La Prostitution féminine à Montréal, 1945–1970* (Montreal: Boréal, 1994).

11 Committee of Sixteen, *Preliminary Report*, 9.

12 Ibid.

13 Among its twenty-six original members were: Anglican minister Rev. Herbert Symonds, Methodist Rev. Dr E.I. Hart, Rev Father Gauthier of St James Parish, Dr Alfred K. Haywood of the Montreal General Hospital, Dr W.W. Chipman of the Montreal Maternity Hospital, J. Howard T. Falk of McGill's Social Service Department, Miss L.E.F. Barry of the Catholic Social Service Guild, W.B. Colley of the Salvation Army, Mrs F. Wilson Fairman, President of the Sheltering Home, Eleonor Tatley of the Local Council of Women, Miss B. Glassman of the Federation of Jewish Philanthropies, Lady Hingston of the Catholic Social Service Guild, Dr Samuel C. Schwartz of Temple Emanu El,

Miss Mabel C. Jamieson of the Montreal YWCA, Miss Bessie Hall of the University Settlement, and Kathleen Moore of the Girls' Cottage Industrial School.

14 Committee of Sixteen, *Fourth Annual Report* (1923), 6.

15 Committee of Sixteen, *Preliminary Report*, 20–1.

16 Ibid., 23–5.

17 Ibid., 27–31.

18 *Montreal Gazette*, 12 November 1918, 7.

19 Committee of Sixteen, *Preliminary Report*, 33. These conclusions were also published in *Social Welfare*, 1 September 1919, 290.

20 Odem, *Delinquent Daughters*, 122–3.

21 Committee of Sixteen, *Preliminary Report*, 10.

22 Ibid., 10.

23 Rev. Dr H. Symonds, 'The Social Evil,' Council for Social Service, *Bulletin* 19 (December 1918), 6.

24 Montreal Juvenile Delinquents Court (hereafter MJDC), 3 October 1918, #5421.

25 Committee of Sixteen, *Preliminary Report*, 40.

26 'The Committee of Sixteen,' *Social Welfare*, 1 September 1919, 290.

27 Kathy Peiss, *Cheap Amusements: Working Women and Leisure in Turn-of-the-Century New York* (Philadelphia: Temple University Press, 1985); Strange, *Toronto's Girl Problem*.

28 Evanston Hart, *Wake Up! Montreal! Commercialized Vice and Its Contributories* (Montreal: Witness Press, 1919), 7.

29 Strange, *Toronto's Girl Problem*, ch. 5.

30 Ibid., 125.

31 Cynthia Comacchio, '"The Rising Generation": Laying Claim to the Health of Adolescents in English Canada, 1920–1970,' *Canadian Bulletin of Medical History* 19 (2002): 139–78, and 'Dancing to Perdition,' 5–35.

32 'Les Policières,' *La Bonne Parole* 7:2 (April, 1919): 2.

33 Andrée Lévesque, *Making and Breaking the Rules: Women in Quebec, 1919–1939* (Toronto: McClelland and Stewart, 1994), 55.

34 See Susan Mann Trofimenkoff, *The Dream of Nation: A Social and Intellectual History of Quebec* (Toronto: Gage Publishing, 1982), 223–4.

35 'Journal des Oeuvres,' *La Bonne Parole* 25:12 (December 1937): 11. Author's translation.

36 In *La Semaine Religieuse de Montréal*, the Montreal clergy frequently railed against female behaviour and fashion in the 1920s and 1930s.

37 'Le clergé chez Monseigneur,' *La Semaine Religieuse de Montréal* 77:2 (10 January 1921): 20–3.

38 'Mentalité de la jeune fille de la ville,' *La Bonne Parole* 18:4 (April 1930): 13. Author's translation.

39 'Causes de la déchéance morale des familles,' *La Bonne Parole* 20:6 (June 1932): 1–3; see also 'Mentalité de la jeune fille de la ville,' *La Bonne Parole* 18:4 (April 1930): 12–13.

40 'Emploi du salaire et des loisirs,' *La Bonne Parole* 10:1 (January 1922): 11.

41 Ibid., 11. Author's translation.

42 'La jeunesse aujourd'hui,' *La Bonne Parole* 12:11 (November 1924): 6.

43 'Obstacles au développement de l'esprit familial,' *La Bonne Parole* 18:4 (April 1930): 6. Author's translation.

44 'Monsieur, Madame, Le Cinéma et l'Enfant,' *La Bonne Parole* 11:11 (January 1915): 3; see also Lévesque, *Making and Breaking*, 70.

45 Herman R. Ross, 'Juvenile Delinquency in Montreal,' MA thesis, McGill University, 1932, 33. Montreal had no shortage of cinemas. In the winter of 1920 the following theatres were fined for permitting access to minors: Canada Moving Picture Hall, Napoleon Palace, Maisonneuve Hall, Midway Hall, Maple Leaf Palace Hall, Crystal Palace, the Regent, the Mont Royal, and the Globe Hall. City of Montreal, Recorders Court Archives, January–February, 1920.

46 'Les Cinémas et Théâtres,' *La Bonne Parole* 10:12 (December 1922): 12. See also Yvan Lamonde and Pierre-François Hébert, *Le cinéma au Québec: essai de statistique historique (1896 à nos jours)* (Quebec: Insitut québécois de recherche sur la culture, 1981).

47 'Emploi du salaire et des loisirs,' *La Bonne Parole* 10:1 (January 1922): 12.

48 'Les Cinémas et Théâtres,' *La Bonne Parole* 10:12 (December 1922): 12.

49 *La Presse*, 7 June 1927, 3. He also included dance and pool halls.

50 Lévesque, *Making and Breaking*, 71.

51 Ibid., 56–60.

52 'Emploi du salaire et des loisirs,' *La Bonne Parole* 10:1 (January 1922): 12.

53 Suzanne Marchand, *Rouge à lèvres et pantalon: des pratiques esthétiques féminines controversial au Québec, 1920–1939* (Montreal: Editions Hurtubise, 1997), 15.

54 R.P. Archambault, 'Une Entrevue du Président du Tribunal des jeunes délinquants de Montréal,' *Parents chrétiens sauvez vos enfants du cinéma meurtrier* (Montreal: L'oeuvre des tracts [No.91], 1927): 16. Author's translation.

55 Ethel MacLachlan, 'The Delinquent Girl,' *Social Welfare*, December 1921, 54.

56 Archambault, 'Une Entrevue,' 16.

57 *La Presse*, 7 June 1927, 3.

58 'Causes de la déchéance morale des familles,' *La Bonne Parole* 20:6 (June 1932): 2.

59 'Obstacles au développement de l'esprit familial,' *La Bonne Parole* 18:4 (April 1930): 6. Author's translation.

60 'Mentalité de la jeune fille de la ville,' *La Bonne Parole* 18:4 (April 1930): 13. Author's translation.

61 'Causes de la déchéance morale des familles,' *La Bonne Parole* (June 1932): 4.

62 'Obstacles au développement de l'esprit familial,' *La Bonne Parole* 18:4 (April 1930): 6. Author's translation.

63 Ibid.

64 Ibid., 7. Author's translation.

65 Ibid., 6–7.

66 Ibid., 6. Author's translation.

67 Louise Bienvenue, *Quand la jeunesse entre en scène: l'Action catholique avant la Révolution tranquille* (Montreal: Boréal, 2003), ch. 1.

68 ANQQ, E17, file 6371, 1937.

69 Marie Hamel, 'La Protection de la Jeune Fille,' *Canadian Welfare* 17:6 (November 1941): 22–4.

70 Jeffrey Keshen, 'Wartime Jitters over Juveniles: Canada's Delinquency Scare and Its Consequences, 1939–1945,' in *Age of Contention: Readings in Canadian Social History, 1900–1945*, ed. Jeffrey Keshen (Toronto: Harcourt Brace, 1997), 365.

71 *Montreal Gazette*, 22 January 1941; 15 June 1942; 1 March 1944.

72 Keshen, 'Wartime Jitters,' 365.

73 *La Presse*, 19 October 1945, 5. Author's translation.

74 *Montreal Gazette*, 11 March 1944, 6.

75 LAC, MG 28, I 10, vol. 87, file 1856, 1941–43 Delinquency (General), 'Juvenile Delinquency ... Part of the Price We Pay for Victory.'

76 Trofimenkoff, *The Dream of Nation*, 256–6.

77 R.P. Valère Massicotte, *La délinquence juvénile et la guerre* (Montreal: Oeuvre des Tracts, April 1944), 13.

78 *La Presse*, 11 March 1944, 29. Author's translation.

79 *Montreal Gazette*, 11 March 1944, 6.

80 Ibid., 9 March 1944, 3; 11 March 1944, 13.

81 Jeffrey A. Keshen, *Saints, Sinners, and Soldiers: Canada's Second World War* (Vancouver: UBC Press, 2004), 136.

82 Library and Archives of Canada, Canadian Council on Social Development, I 10, vol. 87, file 1856.

83 See Marie Hamel, 'Jeunes Délinquants,' *Canadian Welfare* 17:2 (May 1941): 32–3 and 'La Protection de la Jeune Fille,' ibid. 17:6 (November 1941): 22–4.

84 Comacchio, '"The Rising Generation."'

85 Bruno Théorêt, 'Psychiatry, Juvenile Justice, and Delinquent Identity: A Case Study at the Juvenile Court of Winnipeg, 1930–1959,' *Journal of Human Justice* 6:1 (Autumn 1994): 64–77.

86 Henry Herbert Goddard, *The Kallikak Family: A Study in the Heredity of Feeble-Mindedness* (New York: Macmillan, 1919).

87 Danielle Lacasse, 'Du délinquant à ouvrier qualifié: le Mont-Saint-Antoine, 1945–1964,' *Histoire sociale / Social History* 22:44 (November 1989): 287–316, at 298.

88 Soeurs du Bon Pasteur, *Au Soir* (Montreal: Le Bon Pasteur d'Angers, 1944), 107–8.

89 For an example of this process see Elizabeth Lunbeck, *The Psychiatric Persuasion: Knowledge, Gender, and Power in Modern America* (Princeton: Princeton University Press, 1994), introduction.

90 Ibid., 63.

91 Angus McLaren, *'Our Own Master Race': Eugenics in Canada, 1885–1945* (Toronto: McClelland and Stewart, 1990), 41.

92 Ibid., Theresa R. Richardson, *The Century of the Child: The Mental Hygiene Movement and Social Policy in the United States and Canada* (Albany: State University of New York Press, 1989), 64; see also James W. Trent, Jr, *Inventing the Feeble Mind: A History of Mental Retardation in the United States* (Berkeley: University of California Press, 1994).

93 McLaren, *'Our Own Master Race,'* 25.

94 LAC, MLCW, vol. 7, Committee on Mental Deficiencies, Carrie M. Derick, 'The Social Menace of Feeblemindedness,' 5.

95 Ibid.

96 LAC, MLCW, vol. 7, file: Committee on Mental Deficiencies, 'The Montreal Local Council of Women and Mental Defectives,' (n.d.), 1.

97 Lunbeck, *Psychiatric Persuasion*, 56.

98 Richardson, *Century of the Child*, 79.

99 Anne Meis Knupfer, *Reform and Resistance: Gender, Delinquency, and America's First Juvenile Court* (New York: Oxford University Press, 2001), 37.

100 Théoret, 'Psychiatry, Juvenile Justice, and Delinquent Identity,' 73.

101 Kunzel, *Fallen Women*, 53.

102 See her article in the *Public Health Journal*, 5 (1914): 212–18, cited in McLaren, *'Our Own Master Race,'* 41.

103 GCIS, *Annual Report* (1917), 14 and GCIS, *Annual Report* (1924), 123.

104 Dorothy Ross, *G. Stanley Hall: The Psychologist as Prophet* (Chicago: University of Chicago Press, 1972); Joseph Kett, *Rites of Passage: Adolescence in American* (New York: Basic Books, 1977).

105 G. Stanley Hall, *Adolescence: Its Psychology and its Relation to Physiology,*

Anthropology, Sociology, Sex, Crime, Religion and Education (New York: D. Appleton and Company, 1904).

106 Alexander, 'Girl Problem,' 38–9; Odem, *Delinquent Daughters*, 101.

107 Edith Abbott and Sophisba P. Breckinridge, *The Delinquent Child and the Home* (New York: Arno Press, 1970 [c. 1912]).

108 Odem, *Delinquent Daughters*, 103–6.

109 Ibid., 103.

110 Lucy Brooking, 'A Study of the Delinquent Girl,' *Social Welfare* (1 April 1921): 182.

111 Kathleen W. Jones, *Taming the Troublesome Child: American Families, Child Guidance, and the Limits of Psychiatric Authority* (Cambridge, MA: Harvard University Press, 1999), 44–5.

112 William Healey, *The Individual Delinquent: A Text-book of Diagnosis and Prognosis for All Concerned in Understanding Offenders* (Boston: Little Brown, 1915).

113 Jones, *Taming the Troublesome Child*, 46–7.

114 GCIS, *Annual Report* (1930), 127. See also Ross, 'Juvenile Delinquents,' 62.

115 Mona Gleason, *Normalizing the Ideal: Psychology, Schooling and the Family in Postwar Canada* (Toronto: University of Toronto Press, 1999), 24.

116 Rose Henderson, 'Child Labour, Delinquency, and the Standards of Living,' *Social Welfare* 2:1 (October 1919): 16.

117 Henderson, 'Child Labour,' 16.

118 *Canadian Nurse* 12:9 (September 1916) 492.

119 Brooking, 'A Study of the Delinquent Girl,' 181.

120 *Canadian Nurse* 12:9 (September 1916): 492.

121 *Montreal Herald*, 28 July 1922, 6; Ross, 'Juvenile Delinquency,' 35.

122 Cited in Alexander, '*Girl Problem,*' 39; *Young Working Girls: A Summary of Evidence from Two Thousand Social Workers* (Boston, New York: Houghton Mifflin, 1913).

123 Symonds, 'The Social Evil,' 6.

124 Archives du Bon Pasteur, 'Oeuvre des jeunes délinquants.'

125 Henderson, 'Child Labour,' 17.

126 Frank T. Sharpe, 'Stopping before Starting,' *Child and Family Welfare* 9:5 (January 1934): 42.

127 Canadian Jewish Congress National Archives, MB 1, Series B, Box 1, File: Juvenile Neighbourhood House, letter from Mrs E.M. Berliner, Juvenile Aid Department to the Executive Committee, Federation of Jewish Philanthropies, 28 May 1926, 2.

128 Odem, *Delinquent Daughters*, 105.

129 Jones, *Taming the Troublesome Child*, 8 and ch. 7.

130 Big Sister Association (hereafter BSA) (Montreal), *Annual Report* (1939), 54.

131 BSA, *Annual Report* (1943), 85.

132 *Montreal Standard*, 3 December 1938, 7.

133 See Gordon Mundie, 'The Problem of the Mentally Defective in the Province of Quebec,' *Canadian Journal of Mental Hygiene* (July 1919): 123–9.

134 ANQQ, E17, Correspondance du Procureur-Général, 2332–13, Letter from Dr Mundie to Dr L.J. Lemieux, 6 May 1913.

135 Other reform organizations similarly pursued mental hygiene experts. The Montreal Local Council of Women hired Isa Cole to do testing for them. A graduate of the Boston School for Social Work, Cole had extensive experience in progressive psychiatry at the Social Service Department and psycho-neurological clinic of the Massachusetts General Hospital. In 1916, she was asked to introduce social service work at Montreal's Maternity Hospital. Throughout 1918, Cole ran tests on juvenile delinquents, women arrested by the city's policewomen, and inmates at the Hervey Institute for Dependent Citizens. According to Carrie Derick, Cole used the Huey and Stanford revisions of the Binet and Simon tests to determine mental ages of those she examined. Derick, 'The Social Menace,' 5–6; McLaren, '*Our Own Master Race*,' 24.

136 GCIS, *Annual Report* (1914), 7.

137 This complaint was lodged in annual reports of the GCIS throughout the 1920s.

138 GCIS, *Annual Report* (1918), 8.

139 Ibid. (1925), 119; Rockefeller Archive Center (hereafter RAC), RFA, RG 1.2, box 4, file 29, 'Interview of Alan Gregg with Dr. W.T.B. Mitchell, October 3, 1936,' and R.G 1.1 Series 427 Canada, file 7, Folder Canadian National Committee for Mental Hygiene, Reports, 1926–38.

140 Mitchell was the head of the mental hygiene clinic and professor of mental hygiene; Bridges was a professor of abnormal psychology in the McGill faculty of medicine. RAC, Laura Spellman Rockefeller Memorial Foundation Fonds, Series 3, box 32, folder 345, McGill University, 1929–34, Letter from Sir Arthur Currie, 4 November 1931. See also RAC, Rockefeller Foundation Archives, RG 1.1, Series 427, box 1, folder 3, Canadian National Committee for Mental Hygiene, 1927–29, Memorandum Re: Mental Hygiene at McGill University, c. 1927; and folder 6, CNCMH 1938–1940, 'Canadian National Committee for Mental Hygiene – Summary, August 1939.'

141 Richardson, *Century of the Child*, 117; Gleason, *Normalizing the Ideal*, 24.

142 Montreal Health Survey Committee, *Survey, Public Health Activities, Montreal October 1928* (Montreal: Metropolitan Life Insurance Co., 1928), ch. 26, 'Mental Hygiene.'

143 J.W. Bridges, 'A Study of a Group of Delinquent Girls,' LAC, GCS, vol. 1, file 20, 21–2.

144 Ibid., 11.

145 Ross, 'Juvenile Delinquency in Montreal,' 62. See also GCIS, *Annual Report* (1930), 127.

146 Bridges, 'A Study' 13–15.

147 Ibid., 20.

148 Ibid., 5.

149 Knupfer, *Reform and Resistance*, 30.

150 Marjorie L. Moore, 'Treatment without Operating,' *Child and Family Welfare* (March 1934): 43.

151 'Jeunes Délinquants,' *Canadian Welfare Summary*, 15 May 1941, 32.

152 Yolande Tétreault, 'L'adolesence: exposé psychologique,' *La Bonne Parole* 36:5 and 6 (May and June 1946): 4. This issue includes several articles on various aspects of adolescence. Author's translation.

153 MJDC, 28 January 1942, #237.

Chapter 4

1 *Montreal Daily Star*, 29 February 1908, 9.

2 Amanda Glasbeek, 'Maternalism Meets the Criminal Law: The Case of the Toronto Women's Court,' *Canadian Journal of Women and the Law* 10 (1998): 480–502; Dorothy E. Chunn, *From Punishment to Doing Good: Family Courts and Socialized Justice in Ontario, 1880–1940* (Toronto: University of Toronto Press, 1992); Mary E. Odem, *Delinquent Daughters: Protecting and Policing Adolescent Female Sexuality in the United States, 1885–1920* (Chapel Hill: University of North Carolina Press, 1995).

3 Women were accepted to the Quebec bar in 1941. On legal professionalism and female judges see Dorothy E. Chunn, 'Maternal Feminism, Legal Professionalism and Political Pragmatism: The Rise and Fall of Magistrate Margaret Patterson, 1922–1934,' in *Canadian Perspectives on Law and Society: Issues in Legal History*, ed. W. Wesley Pue and Barry Wright, (Ottawa: Carleton University Press, 1988), 91–117.

4 Elizabeth J. Clapp, *Mothers of All Children: Women Reformers and the Rise of Juvenile Courts in Progressive Era America* (University Park, MD: Pennsylvania State University Press, 1998).

5 See Carol Baines, et al., eds, *Women Caring: Feminist Perspectives on Social Welfare* (Toronto: Oxford University Press, 1991); Kelly Hannah-Moffat, *Punishment in Disguise: Penal Governance and Federal Imprisonment of Women in Canada* (Toronto: University of Toronto Press, 2001), 22–3.

6 Child Welfare Exhibition, *Souvenir Pamphlet* (Montreal, 1912), 30.

7 Ignace-J. Deslauriers, j.c.s., ed., *Les tribunaux de Québec et leurs juges* (Cowansville, QC: Les Editions Yvon Blais, 1987), 176.

8 *Montreal 1535–1914. Biographical 3* (1914), 594; Jocelyn Saint-Pierre, 'Cléophas Beausoleil,' *Dictionary of Canadian Biography,* vol. 13, *(1901–10),* 55–6; Deslauriers, *Les tribunaux de Québec,* 176; *Montreal Gazette,* 1 January 1927, 4; and Tamara Myers, 'François-Xavier Choquet,' *Dictionary of Canadian Biography* (forthcoming).

9 *Montreal Gazette,* 24 October 1907, 4.

10 There exists fragmentary evidence of the history of the Children's Aid Society of Montreal. Mendolsohn and Ronald claim that the Children's Aid Society was created 11 November 1907. Lillian E. Mendelsohn and Sharon Ronald, 'History of the Montreal Juvenile Court,' MSW thesis, McGill University, 1969, 20. The Montreal press reported that the inauguration of the Montreal CAS occurred on 1 February 1908. *Le Canada,* 4 February 1908, 5.

11 *Montreal Herald,* 3 January 1912, 9; 8 June 1912, 15.

12 Ibid., 6 January 1912, 2. Author's emphasis.

13 Ibid., 13 June 1914, 35.

14 Ibid., 6 June 1912, 2.

15 *Le Devoir,* 23 March 1912, 9.

16 Clapp, *Mothers of All Children,* 130–1.

17 Rose Henderson, 'The Juvenile Court,' *Canadian Municipal Journal* (March 1916): 84.

18 Judge Choquet, 'The Juvenile Court,' *Canadian Municipal Journal* 10:6 (June 1914), 232–3. For an analysis of the early workings of the Montreal Juvenile Delinquents' Court see Tamara Myers, 'The Voluntary Delinquent: Parents, Daughters and the Montreal Juvenile Delinquents' Court, 1918,' 80:2 *Canadian Historical Review* (June 1999). Choquet retired in April 1922, although his replacement, J.-O. Lacroix claimed he worked for the court for thirteen years. *La Presse,* 4 January 1927, 7. See 'First Evidence of Retirement,' *Montreal Herald,* 11 April 1922, 1; and 'Resignation of Judges Accepted,' *Montreal Herald,* 20 April 1922, 3. According to the *Gazette* (1 January 1927, 4), he remained 'in charge' of the court until November 1923. Choquet died at seventy-five on 31 December 1926. The cortege included senators F.L. Beique and Donat Raymond and several ministers and judges.

19 'L'inauguration du tribunal des jeunes délinquants,' *Le Devoir,* 23 March 1912, 9.

20 Scott, 'Juvenile Delinquents Act,' 50–1.

21 Henderson, 'The Juvenile Court,' 84.

22 *Montreal Herald,* 8 June 1912, 15.

23 Ibid.

24 *Montreal Gazette,* 3 January 1912, 3.

25 Quebec, *Débats*, 6 May 1910, 493. Quebec politicians were determined that in their delinquents would be '*traités dans un esprit paternel.*'

26 Henderson would have been well aware of the tensions surrounding the sole juvenile court in the province. Just one year prior to her article professing Choquet's talent, *Le Devoir* took aim at the Protestant and 'American' character of the court, suggesting that he had been too influenced by Progressives from the United States.

27 *Montreal Herald*, 28 October 1909, 13.

28 Library and Archives Canada (hereafter LAC), Montreal Local Council of Women, MG 28, I 164, Vol. 7, 'Reformatory Committee Correspondence and Reports, 2 of 2 (1909–22, 1931),' letter from Judge Choquet to Mrs Warwick Chipman, 26 July 1910.

29 In Canada the use of probation as an alternative to incarceration began with the JDA. This method of disposition distinguished the juvenile courts from criminal courts. See D.W.F. Coughlan, 'The History and Function of Probation,' in *Lawful Authority: Readings on the History of Criminal Justice in Canada*, ed. R.C. Macleod (Toronto: Copp Clark Pitman, 1988).

30 Archives nationales du Québec à Québec, Correspondance du Procureur-Général, E17, file 2939/1915 and 4494/1916.

31 Scott, 'Juvenile Delinquents Act,' 62.

32 Jean Trépanier, 'Origins of the Juvenile Delinquents Act of 1908: Controlling Delinquency Through Seeking Its Causes and through Youth Protection,' in *Dimensions of Childhood*, 225; Jean Trépanier and Françoise Tulkens, *Délinquance et protection de la jeunesse aux sources des lois belges et canadiennes sur l'enfance* (Montreal and Ottawa: Les Presses de l'Université de Montréal et de l'Ottawa, 1995), 33.

33 Alison J. Hatch and Curt T. Griffiths, 'Child Saving Postponed: The Impact of the Juvenile Delinquents Act on the Processing of Young Offenders in Vancouver,' in *Dimensions of Childhood*, ed. Russell Smandych, Gordon Dodds, and Alvin Esau, 233–66.

34 Canadian Welfare Council, *Juvenile Court in Canada: Being a Brief Description of Juvenile Court Organization in the Provinces* (Ottawa: Publication No. 121, 1942), 16.

35 In 1912 the original committee members included religious and lay leaders of three communities as well as women involved in social reform. In the Catholic contingent were both francophones and anglophones: Rev Canon Gauthier, Lady Margaret Josephine Hingston, Caroline Béique, Marie Mignault, Madames Chevrier, Moreau, and Miss Murphy. The Protestant members included Rev Dr Symonds, Rev F.R. Griffin, William Maxwell, Owen Dawson, Mrs F.H. Waycott, Mrs H.W. Weller, and Mrs Stewart Taylor. The

Jewish community was represented by Lyon Cohen and Max Goldstein. *Montreal Gazette*, 3 January 1912, 3.

36 Mendelsohn and Ronald, 'History of the Montreal Juvenile Court,' 30.

37 Quebec, Sessional Papers, 'Report of the Administrator of the detention house for Young Delinquents of the City of Montreal,' 1914. In the first years of the court's operation, education at the Detention House consisted of twice weekly sessions conducted by a voluntary teacher. Due to the 'success' of the juvenile court, however, the facility was almost immediately inadequate: overcrowding led to the disposition of those awaiting trial to reform schools, especially of girls. Lillian E. Mendelsohn and Sharon Ronald, 'History of the Montreal Juvenile Court,' MSW thesis, McGill University, 1969, 25–6.

38 Quebec, *Sessional Papers* (1914).

39 A scandal erupted when the new building was constructed without a proper detention home. The new building was not used until such a facility was built, delaying the move for years.

40 This is according to a reporter who was permitted a rare invitation to visit the court by Judge Robillard. Basil C. Fitzgerald, 'Problem of Juvenile Delinquency Increases in Extent and Variety; Judge Robillard's Huge Task,' *Montreal Standard*, 3 December 1938, 7.

41 LAC, CCSD, MG 28, I 10, vol. 85, Juvenile Courts, Quebec-Maritimes, 1938–41 file, 'Juvenile Court of Montreal: Detention Home,' May 1938.

42 *Le Devoir*, 17 April 1915, 1; *Montreal Herald*, 8 June 1912, 15; *Canadian Municipal Journal*, March 1916, 84.

43 'Is Chosen Clerk of Juvenile Court,' *Montreal Herald*, 19 January 1912, 6.

44 On maternalism see Seth Koven and Sonya Michel, 'Womanly Duties: Maternalist Politics and the Origins of Welfare States in France, Germany, Great Britain, and the United States,' *American Historical Review* 95 (October 1995): 1076–108; Seth Koven and Sonya Michel, 'Introduction: "Mother Worlds,"' in *Mothers of a New World: Maternalist Politics and the Origins of Welfare States*, ed. Seth Koven and Sonya Michel (New York: Routledge, 1993), 1–42; Molly Ladd-Taylor, *Mother-Work: Women, Child Welfare, and the State, 1890–1930* (Urbana: University of Illinois Press, 1994); Molly Ladd-Taylor, 'Toward Defining Maternalism in U.S. History,' *Journal of Women's History* 6 (Fall 1993): 110–13.

45 Koven and Sonya Michel, *Mothers of a New World*, 4.

46 Clapp, *Mothers of All Children*.

47 Platt, *The Child Savers*, ch. 4.

48 Ladd-Taylor, *Mother-Work*, 75.

49 Nancy Christie, *Engendering the State: Family, Work, and Welfare in Canada* (Toronto: University of Toronto Press, 2000), 29 and 44–5.

50 W.L. Scott, 'The Juvenile Delinquents Act,' *Canada Law and Times Review,* as cited in Jeffrey S. Leon, 'The Development of Canadian Juvenile Justice: A Background for Reform,' *Osgoode Hall Law Journal* 15 (1977): 71–106, at 92–3.

51 Odem, *Delinquent Daughters,* 129 and 155.

52 Hannah-Moffat, *Punishment in Disguise,* 43.

53 Glasbeek, 'Maternalism,' 482.

54 Dorothy Chunn, '"Just Plain Everyday Housekeeping on a Grand Scale": Feminists, Family Courts, and the Welfare State in British Columbia, 1928–1945,' in *Law, Society, and the State: Essays in Modern Legal History,* ed. Louis Knafla and Susan Binnie (Toronto: University of Toronto Press, 1995), 384.

55 Ibid.

56 Clubwomen were middle- and upper-class philanthropists who volunteered to work for various reform organizations often through Protestant and Catholic churches.

57 This unification of women's groups in the MLCW obscures the fact that there was likely only loose agreement on the definition and importance of various social problems and very probably women disagreed over appropriate solutions. Both linguistic and religious groups included a range of conservative and progressive thinkers, allowing for coalitions and divisions. In terms of child welfare issues, as Nancy Christie argues for Ontario, theological debates 'raged' over the sinful or innocent state of childhood (*Engendering the State,* 25) which would influence the remedy (home or institution) sought for problem children.

58 Marie Lavigne, Yolande Pinard, and Jennifer Stoddart, 'The FNSJB and the Women's Movement in Quebec,' in *A Not Unreasonable Claim: Women and Reform in Canada, 1880s–1920s,* ed. Linda Kealey (Toronto: Women's Press, 1979), 71–88, at 76–7.

59 Karine Hébert, 'Une organisation maternaliste au Québec: la Fédération nationale St-Jean-Baptiste et la bataille pour le vote des femmes,' *Revue d'histoire de l'Amérique française* 52:3 (Winter 1999): 315–44; also her Master's thesis, 'Une organisation maternaliste au Québec, la Fédération nationale St-Jean-Baptiste 1900–1940,' Université de Montréal, 1997. On Christian feminism and maternalism see also Susan Pedersen, 'Catholicism, Feminism, and the Politics of the Family during the Late Third Republic,' in Koven and Michel, *Mothers of a New World,* 246–76.

60 Denyse Baillargeon, 'Fréquenter les gouttes de lait: l'expérience des mères montréalaises, 1910–1965,' *Revue d'histoire de l'Amérique française* 50:1 (1996), 29–68.

61 Lavigne, Pinard, and Stoddart, 'The FNSJB and the Women's Movement,' 73; Clio Collective, *Quebec Women: A History* (Toronto: Women Press, 1987), 251.

62 Cited in Lavigne, Pinard, and Stoddart, 'The FNSJB and the Women's Movement,' 73.

63 In early 1908 the press noted the inauguration of the Montreal CAS. See *La Patrie*, 3 February 1908, 12; *Le Canada*, 4 February 1908, 5, cited in Dubois and Trépanier, 'L'adoption de la loi sur les jeunes délinquants de 1908: études comparées des quotidiens montréalais et torontois,' *Revue d'Histoire de l'Amérique française* 52:3 (Winter 1999), 376.

64 LAC, MLCW, MG 28 I 164, vol. 7, Reformatory Committee Corr. (1 of 2). Report of Reformatory Committee, 16 March 1910, 2.

65 Mme F.-L. Béique, *Quatre-vingts ans de souvenirs: histoire d'une famille* (Montreal: Les Editions Canadienne-Française, 1939), 265.

66 For histories of the GCIS see '50 Years of Growing: Girls' Cottage School,' and Kathleen Moore, 'History of the Girls' Cottage School, 1911–1946,' (1950), in LAC, Girls Cottage School Collection, MG 28, I 404, vol. 2, file 21 and 22, respectively.

67 Tamara Myers, 'Women Policing Women: A Patrol Woman in Montreal in the 1910s,' *Journal of the Canadian Historical Association* (Ottawa 1993): 229–45.

68 *La Bonne Parole*, 6:4 (June 1918): 14. Author's translation.

69 Jean Turmel, *Le Service de Police de Montréal, 1796–1971*, vol. 2 (Montreal: Service de Police de la C.U.M., 1974), 61; LAC, MLCW, MG 28, I 164, vol. 7, Women's Patrols, K. Chipman, 'The Employment of Women Patrols.'

70 LAC, MLCW, K. Ward file, K. Chipman, 'The Employment of Police Women,' 1918.

71 Scholars have attempted to get around the equal rights/maternal feminist dichotomy that has been used to describe turn-of-the-century female reformers' political ideology. As Molly Ladd-Taylor and others have argued, a distinction must be made between 'maternalists' and feminists. Maternalists, according to Ladd-Taylor, believed in '(1) a uniquely feminine value system based on care and nurturance; (2) that mothers perform a service to the state by raising citizen-workers; (3) that women are united across class, race, and nation by their common capacity for motherhood and therefore share a responsibility for all the world's children; and (4) that ideally men should earn a family wage to support their 'dependent' wives and children at home' (p. 3). Feminists on the other hand did use motherhood rhetoric but were not maternalists per se because they advocated economic and political independence for women (p. 7). Linda Gordon uses a similar definition of maternalism that includes the assumption that women were 'uniquely able to lead certain kinds of reform campaigns' and that women exhibited a

parental role vis-à-vis the poor. She appropriately points out that while maternalism might appear to be paternalism in feminine garb, the distinction is that maternalism functioned under the assumption that women were subordinate to men. Linda Gordon, *Pitied but Not Entitled: Single Mothers and the History of Welfare* (Cambridge, MA: Harvard University Press, 1994), 55.

72 Clapp, *Mothers of All Children*, 14.

73 Virginia Woolf used this phrase when discussing the addition of women to history. Virginia Woolf, *A Room of One's Own* (London: Panther Books, 1977, 1929), 45.

74 Hatch and Griffiths, 'Child Saving Postponed,' 259. See Helen Gregory MacGill, *The Juvenile Court in Canada* (Ottawa: Canadian Council on Child Welfare, 1925); and 'The Relation of the Juvenile Court to the Community,' *Canadian Journal of Mental Hygiene* 1:3 (October 1919): 232–6.

75 In her assessment of Margaret Patterson's appointment to the Toronto Women's Court, Dorothy Chunn writes, 'Her elevation to the Bench did not constitute a feminist victory per se but, rather, the electoral triumph of "uplift" politics.' Dorothy E. Chunn, 'Maternal Feminism, Legal Professionalism and Political Pragmatism: The Rise and Fall of Magistrate Margaret Patterson, 1922–1934,' in *Canadian Perspectives on Law and Society: Issues in Legal History*, ed. W. Wesley Pue and Barry Wright (Ottawa: Carleton University Press, 1988), 93.

76 Denyse Baillargeon, 'L'assistance maternelle de Montréal (1912–1961): un exemple de marginalisation des bénévoles dans le domaine des soins aux accouchées,' *Dynamis* 19 (1999): 382. Author's translation.

77 On the marginalization of volunteer women see Baillargeon, 'L'assistance.'

78 Clio Collective, *Quebec Women*, 245.

79 Chunn, 'Maternal Feminism.'

80 Henderson, 'The Juvenile Court,' 84.

81 Clapp, *Mothers of All Children*, 181. Clapp observes the similarities but points out an important difference: that *parens patriae* philosophy was often promoted within legal language, not an explicitly gendered one.

82 *Montreal Daily Herald*, 27 January 1912, 27. Mrs Louise deKoven Bowen, chair of the Chicago Juvenile Court Committee claimed in 1904 that her work was 'formative rather than reformative.' Cited in Clapp, *Mothers of All Children*, 174–5.

83 Henderson, 'The Juvenile Court,' 84.

84 Margaret Hodge quoted in the *Montreal Daily Star*, 13 June 1914, 35.

85 ANQQ, E17, File 4541, 1910, Letter from CAS of Montreal to Sir Lomer Gouin, 27 September 1911. This letter outlines the intended membership of the Catholic and non-Catholic Juvenile Court Committees and indicates that

Miss M. Clément and Mrs R.W. Henderson have worked as probation officers for two years.

86 *Montreal Herald*, 27 January 1912, 27.

87 Marie Mignault was appointed 1 July 1915 and died 12 January 1936. ANQ,
E17, 1936, file 765.

88 LAC, WL Scott Collection, MG 30, C27 vol. 6, File 23A35.4, letter from W.L.
Scott to Mrs Weller, 21 December 1907.

89 Letter from Scott to Weller.

90 ANQQ, E 17, 1919, file 2412.

91 Henderson wrote 'Woman and War,' n.d. See Joan Sangster, *Dreams of Equal-
ity* (Toronto: McClelland and Stewart, 1989), 111. Obituary in *Globe and
Mail*, 1 February 1937 and *Daily Clarion*, 1 February 1937, 1; *Who's Who in
Canada*, 1936–37, 497.

92 Carol Lee Bacchi, *Liberation Deferred? The Ideas of the English-Canadian Suf-
fragists, 1877–1918* (Toronto: University of Toronto Press, 1983), 91.

93 Later she would seek admission to the Quaker's Society of Friends. See Will
C. van den Hoonaard, 'Rose Henderson: Biographical Zoning and the
Bahà'í Context of Her Social Activism,' paper presented to the Canadian
Historical Association, Toronto, 2002.

94 Rose Henderson, 'Save and Starve,' *Labor World / Le Monde Ouvrier* 25
November 1916; Rose Henderson, 'Victim of Poverty,' ibid., 6 January 1917.
I would like to thank Peter Campbell for sharing his research on Rose
Henderson with me.

95 Linda Kealey, *Enlisting Women for the Cause: Women, Labour, and the Left in
Canada, 1890–1920* (Toronto: University of Toronto Press, 1998), 234–5.

96 According to the *Daily Clarion* (1 February 1937, 1), her antiwar activity was
directly related to her 'release' from the court.

97 ANQQ, E17, 5007/19, 1919. Letter from the Hon. Sec. of the Imperial
Order of the Sons of the Empire to Sir Lomer Gouin, 3 October 1919.

98 Seized documents and discussion arising are in ANQQ, E17, 5007/19,
1919. See also Kealey, *Enlisting Women*, 218.

99 ANQQ, E17, 1919, file 5007, Letter to Monsieur Lanctot, 6 October 1919.

100 ANQQ, E17, 1919, file 5007, Letter from Rose Henderson to Attorney General, 13 December 1919; also see 1920, File 1593, Letter to Attorney General Taschereau, 31 March 1920. This letter notes that Henderson was
suspended for three months and then resigned her job. The letter from
Henderson's letter is requesting compensation for lack of pay pending the
government's decision on her case; $175 was authorized. The MJDC also
noted in their Annual Report (1919) that Henderson had been replaced by
Miss I.M. Mitchell in December 1919.

101 See Peter Campbell, 'Working-Class Hero: Rose Henderson and the Canadian Left, 1919–1920,' paper presented to the Canadian Historical Association, Toronto, 2002.
102 *Montreal Herald*, 27 January 1912, 27.
103 Ibid.
104 *Labor World / Le Monde Ouvrier*, 15 April 1916.
105 *Montreal Herald*, 27 January 1912, 27.
106 Clapp, *Mothers of All Children*, 177.
107 Karen W. Tice, *Tales of Wayward Girls and Immoral Women: Case Records and the Professionalization of Social Work* (Urbana and Chicago: University of Illinois Press, 1999), 20. The process of organizing a case around the delinquent had the effect of making her stand 'in relief ... all major items of information appear as predicates' of her (Dorothy E. Smith, *The Conceptual Practices of Power: A Feminist Sociology of Knowledge* [Toronto: University of Toronto Press, 1990], 90). The practice of case recording, Dorothy Smith reminds us (90–1), requires 'standardized methods of observation and investigation, categories, interpretive schemata and practices,' thus creating a hierarchy of knowledge in which the author becomes the powerful and the object (in this case the delinquent girl) has limited opportunity to shape the narrative of her life and is deprived of access to the completed file.
108 Quebec, An Act respecting Reform Schools, 55–56 Vict, 1892, c. 27. Reaffirmed in 1909, Revised Statutes of Quebec article 3680.
109 LAC, Canadian Council of Social Development, MG 28, I 10, vol. 31, 'Juvenile Delinquency Court Conference, 1929.'
110 Smith, *Conceptual Practices*, 4.
111 Tice, *Tales of Wayward Girls*, 9.
112 On bureaucratic knowledge and the form see Mary Louise Adams, 'In Sickness and in Health: State Formation, Moral Regulation, and Early VD Initiatives in Ontario,' *Journal of Canadian Studies* 28:4 (Winter 1993–94): 117–30, at 127.
113 Quebec Civil Code, 1866; for the origins of paternal power in French law see Pierre Petot, *Histoire du droit privé français: la famille* (Paris: Editions Loysel, 1992), 365–83. On mothers' rights within the family see Clio Collective, *Quebec Women*, 255.
114 Margaret Little, *'No Car, No Radio, No Liquor Permit': The Moral Regulation of Single Mothers in Ontario, 1920–1997* (Toronto: Oxford University Press, 1998), 19. Also critical of her stand on mothers' pensions, see Bacchi, *Liberation Deferred?* 123.
115 LAC, W.L. Scott, MG 30, C 27, vol. 7, file 26 A35.4, letter introducing Henderson to W.T. White, Minister of Finance, 26 February 1913.

116 Rose Henderson, 'The Juvenile Court by One Who Knows,' *Woman's Century*, March 1916, 28.
117 *Montreal Herald*, 27 January 1912, 27.
118 Henderson, 'The Juvenile Court,' [*Canadian Municipal Journal*] 84.
119 *Montreal Herald*, 27 January 1912, 27.
120 Henderson, 'The Juvenile Court, By One Who Knows,' [*Women's Century*] 28.
121 Molly Ladd-Taylor, *Mother-Work*, 75.
122 MJDC, 13 June 1916, #3244.
123 MJDC, 29 August 1912, #492a. Author's translation.
124 MJDC, 5 June 1912, #259.
125 *Montreal Herald*, 8 June 1912, 15.
126 MJDC, 13 January 1914, #1539.
127 MJDC, 23 October 1912, #622.
128 MJDC, 10 October 1912, #593.
129 MJDC, 14 June 1912, #285.
130 Henderson, 'The Juvenile Court,' *Woman's Century*, September 1915, 17.
131 On surveillance of the working-class family see Andrew J. Polsky, 'The Odyssey of the Juvenile Court: Policy Failure and Institutional Persistence,' *Studies in American Political Development* 3 (1989): 166–72; Jacques Donzelot, *The Policing of Families* (New York: Pantheon, 1979), 103–4. On the deinstitutionalizing of children see Neil Trépanier, 'Origins of the 'Juvenile Delinquents Act,' 216; Sutherland, *Children in English-Canadian Society: Framing the Twentieth-Century Consensus* (Toronto: University of Toronto Press, 1976), 100; Andrew Jones, 'Closing Penetanguishene Reformatory: An Attempt to Deinstitutionalize Treatment of Juvenile Offenders in Early Twentieth-Century Ontario,' *Ontario History* 70 (1978): 227.
132 Choquet, 'The Juvenile Court,' 232.
133 My numbers are based on reading each of the seventy files for 1912. See Jean Trépanier, 'Protéger pour prévenir la délinquance,' in *L'évolution de la protection de l'enfance au Québec: des origines à nos jours*, ed. Renée Joyal (Montreal: Presses de l'Université du Québec, 2000), 82–3.
134 MJDC, 1912, #44, 124, 147, 367, 609.
135 MJDC, 1912, #565.
136 On this issue see Regina Kunzel, *Fallen Women, Problem Girls* (New Haven: Yale University Press 1994); Carolyn Strange, *Toronto's Girl Problem* (Toronto: University of Toronto Press, 1995); and Tamara Myers, '*Qui t'a débauchée?* Female Adolescent Sexuality and the Juvenile Delinquents' Court in Early Twentieth-Century Montreal,' in *Family Matters: Papers in Post-Confederation Canadian Family History*, ed. Lori Chambers and Ed Montigny (Toronto: Canadian Scholars Press, 1998), 377–94.

137 Little, 'No Car,' 9; and Marianna Valverde, *The Age of Soap, Light and Water: Moral Reform in English Canada* (Toronto: McClelland and Stewart, 1991).

138 J.O. Lacroix was educated in law at the Montreal branch of Université Laval and was called to the Quebec bar in 1898. He worked as a Recorder for Ville St Pierre and judge of the sessions. Appointed in 1923, Judge Lacroix served eight years at the MJDC, until he fell ill in late 1931. He died in January 1937. He was also involved in Liberal politics. 'Judge J.O. Lacroix had Noted Career,' *Montreal Herald*, 12 January 1937, 3.

139 J.O. Lacroix, MJDC *Annual Report* (1924), 8–9.

140 Herman R. Ross, 'Juvenile Delinquency in Montreal,' MA thesis, McGill University, 1932, 45–6.

141 'Need of Domestic Court Stressed by Judge Lacroix,' *Montreal Herald*, 2 June 1932, 3.

142 ANQQ, E17, file 1563/1932.

143 'Solomon Presides in Juvenile Court,' *Montreal Standard*, 10 March 1934; 'Le tribunal pour enfants à Montréal, '*La Jeunesse Ouvrière*, December–January 1935, 10; 'Standard Sees Juvenile Delinquents Treated with a Wise Eye to Future,' *Montreal Standard*, 15 October 1932 and 'Problem of Juvenile Delinquency Increases in Extent and Variety; Judge Robillard's Huge Task,' 3 December 1938.

144 Federation of Jewish Philanthropies, Juvenile Aid Department, *Annual Reports* (1932 to 1937).

145 *Canadian Child Welfare News*, January–April 1924; May–July 1924, 40–1.

146 For example, MJDC, 17 January 1938, #86, Bertheline P.; 15 January 1940, #56 Georgette L.

147 *Le Devoir*, 26 June 1939, 9.

148 *Montreal Daily Star*, 27 June 1941, 1.

149 MJDC, 24 January 1944, #5744.

150 Province of Quebec, An Act to Constitute a Child Aid Clinic, 9 George VI, c. 25. June 1945.

151 Invited to speak before the Young Men's Hebrew Association in February 1914, Henderson urged the Jewish community to get involved in tackling Jewish delinquency from the vantage point of the voluntary committee. *Canadian Jewish Times*, 13 February 1914. On Henderson's view of Jewish juvenile delinquency see Rose Henderson, 'The Needs of Our Children,' *Canadian Jewish Chronicle*, 8 November 1918, 3.

152 Born in 1868 in Poland, Lyon Cohen grew up in a small town in Ontario and eventually moved to Montreal. A successful industrialist and philanthropist who joined other wealthy English Montrealers in Westmount,

Cohen founded the *Jewish Times* in 1897 and worked at both promoting Jewish rights in Quebec and Jewish welfare. He served as president of the Federation of Jewish Philanthropies in 1923–24. Maxwell Goldstein was a Quebec-born lawyer who worked for Jewish civil rights in the province. He was the founding president of the Federation of Jewish Philanthropies of Montreal in 1917. Gerald Tulchinsky, *Taking Root: The Origins of the Canadian Jewish Community* (Toronto: Lester Publishing, 1992), 208 and 150–1.

153 Paul-André Linteau, *Histoire de Montréal depuis la Confédération*, 2nd ed. (Montreal: Boréal, 2000), 325; Tulchinsky, *Taking Root*, 158. See also Jacques Langlais and David Rome, *Jews and French Quebecers: Two Hundred Years of Shared History* (Waterloo, ON: Wilfrid Laurier University Press, 1991); Ira Robinson and Mervin Butovsky, eds, *Renewing Our Days: Montreal Jews in the Twentieth Century* (Montreal: Véhicule Press, 1995); Joe King, *From the Ghetto to the Main: The Story of the Jews of Montreal* (Montreal: Montreal Jewish Publication Society, 2001).

154 See Tamara Myers, 'On Probation: The Rise and Fall of Jewish Women's Antidelinquency Work in Interwar Montreal,' in *Negotiating Identities in 19th- and 20th-Century Montreal*, ed. Bettina Bradbury and Tamara Myers (Vancouver: UBC Press, 2005), 175–201. See also Daniel J. Walkowitz, *Working with Class: Social Workers and the Politics of Middle-Class Identity* (Chapel Hill: University of North Carolina Press, 1999), 66–72.

155 Ida Seigler, 'Juvenile Crime in Its Relation to the Jewish Child,' *Canadian Jewish Chronicle*, 25 October 1918.

156 Choquet, 'The Juvenile Court,' 232. Beyond Jewish he may have referred to children belonging to the Greek Orthodox church.

157 Ibid.

158 Cited in King, *From the Ghetto*, 94.

159 *Canadian Jewish Chronicle*, 29 October 1915.

160 MJDC, *Annual Report* (1921); Linteau, *Histoire de Montréal*, 318.

161 Ross, 'Juvenile Delinquency in Montreal,' 27.

162 Federation of Jewish Philanthropies, *Annual Report* (1921), 75.

163 Ibid. (1918), 24.

164 Ibid. (1923), 61.

165 Ibid.

166 Ibid. (1925), 60.

167 Ibid. (1921), 73–5.

168 CJCNA, Federation of Jewish Philanthropies, MB 1, Series B, Box 1, File 21, Juvenile Aid, 'Proposed By-Laws of the Juvenile Aid Society,' c. 1924.

169 Federation of Jewish Philanthropies, *Annual Report* (1923), 60.

170 CJCNA, MB1, Series B, Box 1, File 21, Letter from Millie W. Berliner to Executive Committee, Federation of Jewish Philanthropies, 28 May 1926.

171 Federation of Jewish Philanthropies, *Annual Report* (1936), 60.

172 Ibid. (1930), 72.

173 CJCNA, MB1, Series B, Box 1, File 21, 'Juvenile Neighbourhood House,' Letter from Millie Berliner (Chair of the JDA) to the Executive Committee, Federation of Jewish Philanthropies, 28 May 1926, 1.

174 Walkowitz, *Working with Class*, 68.

175 ANQQ, E17, 656/21, 1921. See also Dorothy Feigleson, 'Why Have We Juvenile Delinquency?' *Canadian Jewish Chronicle*, 2 September 1921, 6.

176 This was a modest sum. A complaint in 1924 resulted in Sigler's salary being raised to $1200. ANQQ, E17, 6072/24.

177 Federation of Jewish Philanthropies, *Annual Reports* (1929, 70; 1930, 67; 1934, 55; 1936, 57; 1937, 60).

178 Walkowitz, *Working with Class*, ch. 2.

179 Tice, *Tales of Wayward Girls*, 56.

180 Quoted in ibid.

181 MJDC, 11 June 1924, #476.

182 MJDC, 13 December 1924, #1072.

183 Federation of Jewish Philanthropies, *Annual Report* (1930 and 1932).

184 CJCNA, MB 1, Series B, File 21. Letter to Joel B. Saxe, Chairman of the Juvenile Aid Department from Chairman of the Executive Committee, 23 December 1930.

185 See, for example, MJDC, 25 January 1930, #77.

186 Pierre Anctil, 'Interlude of Hostility: Judeo-Christian Relations in Quebec in the Interwar Period, 1919–1939,' in *Quebec Since 1800: Selected Readings*, ed. Michael D. Behiels (Toronto: Irwin Publishing, 2002), 399.

187 Ibid., 401–2.

188 Ibid., 407, 405.

189 Federation of Jewish Philanthropies, *Annual Report* (1938), 25.

190 ANQQ, E17, Département du Procureur-Général, 8859–1938, Note to M. Georges Léveillé, from L'Assistant-procureur général, 10 June 1938. Author's translation.

191 Note to Léveille; Paul Monty was interested in clearing out the old guard in juvenile court. ANQQ, E17, 4589–1937. Author's translation.

192 ANQQ, E17, 1938, File 8859, Letter from L'Assistant-procureur général to M. Georges Léveillé, 10 June 1938.

193 ANQQ, E17, 1938, File 8859, Letter to Edouard Asselin from W.R. Bulloch, 4 July 1938.

194 Letter to Asselin from Bulloch; Letter to Frank W. Horner, 5 July 1938.

195 Walkowitz, *Working with Class*, 67–8.

196 For example, in her annual and monthly reports from the early 1930s Levitt at times saw as many non-court cases as court cases. Further the non-court 'offences' do not appear to be out of the purview of the court's mandate: theft, unmarried mothers, incorrigibility, desertion and immorality, truancy, neglect, etc. (*Annual Report* 1931). CJCNA, Federation of Jewish Philanthropies, MB 1, Series B, box 1, 1921–39, Juvenile Aid Department, files 19 and 20.

197 ANQQ, E17, File 8859, Letter from Frank W. Horner to Edouard Asselin, 12 July 1938.

198 LAC, MG 28, V88, Jewish Family Services of the Baron de Hirsch Institute, vol. 12, file November 21, 1937 to 27 November 1941, Minutes of Meeting of Child Welfare Committee, 16 May 1939.

199 CJC NA, MBI, FJP, Series B, box 10 1944–1946, file 35, Jewish Child Welfare Bureau 1945, Letter from Esther G. Levitt to Mr S. Hershon, 8 January 1945.

Chapter 5

1 Archives nationales du Québec à Montréal, Fonds Cour des jeunes délinquants de la cité de Montréal (hereafter MJDC), TL 483, 14 January 1924, #34. Author's translation.

2 This information is derived from Annual Reports of the MJDC. Only an incomplete set of reports exists, therefore I have augmented them with my exhaustive study of girls before the court in 1912, 1918, and 1924, as well as Herman Ross's 1929 study of the court. I also conducted a two-month sample of the following years: 1914, 1916, 1920, 1922, 1926, 1928, 1930, 1932, 1934, 1936, 1938, 1940, 1942, 1944. Of the reports that do exist, nationality and religion were not always specified and often statistics were not broken down by sex.

3 Based on annual reports from 1919, 1920, 1921, 1924, 1927, and 1937.

4 Archives municipales de Montréal, Département de Police, *Annual Reports*, 'Statistiques des Crimes et Délits,' 1920s. The arrests of girls for desertion reached an annual high of 102 in 1924. From the late 1920s to 1945 the number of girls arrested explicitly for desertion ranged from 10 to 39.

5 Département de Police, *Annual Report* (1924), 33–5 and 39.

6 MJDC, 11 April 1912, #124; 19 April, 1912, #147; 27 February 1912, #44; 22 April 1912, #148; 1 April 1912 #109. Also 'living as a common prostitute,' 15 October 1912, #609; and 25 April 1924, #333.

7 MJDC, 17 September 1924, #782.

8 MJDC, 27 April 1918, #4846; 13 May 1918, #4891; and 11 June 1924, #476.

9 MJDC, 6 October 1924, #852.

10 MJDC, *Annual Report* (1915).

11 MJDC, *Annual Reports* (1910s).

12 See David Wolcott, 'Juvenile Justice before Juvenile Courts: Cops, Courts, and Kids in Turn-of-the-Century Detroit,' *Social Science History* 27:6 (2003): 109–36; and '"The Cop Will Get You": The Police and Discretionary Juvenile Justice, 1890–1940,' *Journal of Social History* 35:2 (2001): 349–71.

13 Archives municipales de Montréal, Département de Police, *Annual Reports* (1930–9).

14 Ibid. (1945–9).

15 Tamara Myers, 'The Voluntary Delinquent: Parents, Daughters, and the Montreal Juvenile Delinquents' Court in 1918,' *Canadian Historical Review* 80:2 (June 1999): 242–68.

16 Every tenth case concerning boys was examined in 1918, n = 100.

17 The largest number, 81 (36 per cent), were brought forward by mothers, followed by fathers at 47 (21 per cent).

18 From a sample of 239 cases from 1930, 1932, 1934, 1936, and 1938. I examined all female cases that came to court over the course of a two-month period in each of these years. In their 10 per cent sample of cases from the MJDC, the Centre d'histoire de la regulation social at UQAM found that 25 per cent of complaints were made by family members and overall about 27 per cent of cases involving girls. See David Niget, 'Jeunesses populaires sous le regard de la justice: naissance du tribunal pour enfants à Angers et Montréal (1912–1940),' PhD diss., Université d'Angers, 2005, ch. 6.

19 From a sample of 196 cases from 1940, 1942, and 1944. Two months were examined for each of these years.

20 MJDC, 16 June 1938, #998. Author's translation.

21 MJDC, 30 June 1926, #2855.

22 Dorothy M. Chunn, 'Boys Will Be Men, Girls Will Be Mothers: The Legal Regulation of Childhood in Toronto and Vancouver,' *Sociological Studies in Child Development* 3 (1990): 87–110, at 97.

23 Compulsory schooling was implemented in Quebec in 1943. In the early-twentieth century, the Montreal school system was run by two separate commissions, the Catholic and the Protestant. Protestant girls had access to schooling up to Grade 11, whereas only private schools run by female religious orders offered Grades 9 to 11 for Catholic girls.

24 MJDC, 25 January 1930, #77.

25 MJDC, 18 June 1932, #473.

26 MJDC, 17 January 1940, #67.

27 Denyse Baillargeon, *Making Do: Women, Family and Home in Montreal during the Great Depression* (Waterloo, ON: Wilfrid Laurier University Press, 1999), 34–41 and ch. 3.

28 Bettina Bradbury, 'Gender at Work at Home: Family Decisions, the Labour Market, and Girls' Contributions to the Family Economy,' in *Canadian Family History,* ed. Bettina Bradbury (Toronto: Copp Clark Pitman, 1993), 178.

29 Ibid., 185.

30 MJDC, 8 February 1924, #93. The court intervened, sending her back to the reform school. Author's translation.

31 *Labour Gazette,* August 1914, 185.

32 Canada, *Census,* 1911, vol. 6, Occupations of the People, 250–62. Approximately 6000 of 40,000 workers were in domestic service. See also Marie Lavigne and Jennifer Stoddart, 'Ouvrières et travailleuses montréalaises, 1900–1940,' in *Les femmes dans la société québécoises,* ed. Marie Lavigne and Yolande Pinard (Montreal: Boréal Express, 1977), 127.

33 MJDC, 16 August 1912, #450; 6 November 1912, #655; 7 November 1912, #656; 5 April 1918, #4775; 17 April 1918, #4816; 1 August 1918, #5179.

34 MJDC, 18 June 1932, #473; see also 11 January 1932, #24, where a thirteen year old similarly earned two dollars in a home with no children.

35 MJDC, 1 August 1918, #5186.

36 *Labour Gazette,* February 1915, 921. The Montreal reporter for the *Labour Gazette* also gave the impression that during the summer months domestic servants from the countryside return home to work (June 1915), 1407. In *La Bonne Parole,* the FNSJB announced it would open an employment bureau to funnel requests for girls and women for factory, store, or office work (December 1913).

37 *Labour Gazette,* June 1916, 1273.

38 Report of the Royal Commission on Industrial Training and Technical Education, Part IV, (1913), 1978.

39 *Labour Gazette,* August 1913, 148. Report of the Royal Commission on Industrial Training and Technical Education, Part IV, (1913), 1974.

40 *Labour Gazette,* September 1914, 368, and November 1914, 570.

41 *Labour Gazette,* July 1915, 55.

42 *Labour Gazette,* November 1914, 571.

43 *Labour Gazette,* December 1914, 676.

44 Report of the Royal Commission on Industrial Training and Technical Education, Part IV, (1913), 1978.

45 MJDC, 5 April 1918, # 4775.

46 MJDC, 11 September 1918, #5336.

47 Big Sister Association (hereafter BSA), Incorporated (Montreal), *Annual Report* (1939), found in the journal *Welfare Work in Montreal*, 54.

48 BSA, *Annual Report* (1939), 55.

49 Jennifer Stephen, 'The "Incorrigible," the "Bad," and the "Immoral": Toronto's "Factory Girls" and the Work of the Toronto Psychiatric Clinic,' in *Law, Society, and the State: Essays in Modern Legal History*, ed. Louis A. Knafla and Susan W.S. Binnie (Toronto: University of Toronto Press, 1995), 414.

50 MJDC, 28 January 1944, #5779.

51 MJDC, 18 June 1942, #1483.

52 MJDC, 19 June 1936, #730; 11 January 1938, #51.

53 MJDC, 18 June 1932, #473.

54 Linda Gordon, *Heroes of Their Own Lives: The Politics and History of Family Violence* (New York: Penguin, 1988), 188–9. See also Bettina Bradbury, *Working Families: Age, Gender and Daily Survival in Industrializing Montreal* (Toronto: McClelland and Stewart, 1993), ch. 4, and Joan Sangster, *Earning Respect: The Lives of Working Women in Small-Town Ontario, 1920–1960* (Toronto: University of Toronto Press, 1995), ch. 2.

55 MJDC, 31 May 1918, #4975.

56 Ibid., report of Probation officer Rose Henderson, 10 June 1918.

57 MJDC, 4 July 1924, #459.

58 MJDC, 4 January 1924, #1. This case illustrates how the juvenile court's mandates – to police and protect youth – overlapped. The father, for his part, stated that he agreed to Dorothy's confinement not because of his menacing behaviour but rather because she '*a deserté mon toit sans permission et de plus est incorrigible et incontrolable.*'

59 Herman R. Ross, 'Juvenile Delinquency in Montreal,' MA thesis, McGill University, 1932, 62.

60 Suzanne Marchand, *Rouge à lèvres et pantalon: des pratiques esthétiques féminines controversées au Québec, 1920–1939* (Montreal: Editions Hurtubise, 1997), 65.

61 MJDC, 29 June 1942, #1558. My translation.

62 MJDC, *Annual Report* (1917).

63 MJDC, 14 January 1924, #34.

64 MJDC, 24 September 1918, #5396.

65 MJDC, 1 April 1912, #109.

66 MJDC, 25 February 1918, #4673.

67 MJDC, 3 September 1918, #5308.

68 MJDC, 27 January 1930, #83.

69 MJDC, 14 March 1924, #208.

70 Anne Meis Knupfer, *Reform and Resistance: Gender, Delinquency, and America's First Juvenile Court* (New York: Oxford University Press, 2001), 72.

71 MJDC, 28 March 1924, #261; 14 March 1924, #208.
72 MJDC, 13 January 1928, #1508; 11 January 1930 #12.
73 MJDC, 24 September 1918, #5396.
74 MJDC, 18 June 1942, #1483. Author's translation.
75 MJDC, 10 October 1918, #5454; 13 August 1924, #680.
76 MJDC, 4 March 1918, #4706.
77 MJDC, 18 December 1924, #1089.
78 MJDC, 10 January 1944 #5640; 7 January 1944, #5622.
79 MJDC, 17 January 1944, #5697.
80 MJDC, 29 January 1944, #5797.
81 Marchand, *Rouge à Lèvres*, 15.
82 *Montreal Herald*, 19 June 1918, 2.
83 MJDC, 12 January 1944, #5653.
84 Mary E. Odem, *Delinquent Daughters: Protecting and Policing Adolescent Female Sexuality in the United States, 1885–1920* (Chapel Hill: University of North Carolina Press, 1995), 104; Knupfer, *Reform and Resistance*, 68.
85 MJDC, 11 January 1932, #24; 27 June 1934, #829; 25 January 1930, #77; 8 January 1932, #16; 15 January 1926, #2382.
86 Montreal *Daily Star*, 14 August 1926.
87 This is clear from the dating histories taken by the court. See also Denise Lemieux and Lucie Mercier, *Les femmes au tourant du siècle, 1880–1940: ages de la vie, maternité et quotidien* (Quebec: Institut québécois de recherche sur la culture, 1989), ch. 4. Dating rituals are also featured in fiction: see, for example, Gabrielle Roy's *The Tin Flute*.
88 Baillargeon, *Making Do*, 48.
89 MJDC, 3 April 1924, #284.
90 MJDC,13 August 1924, #671.
91 MJDC, 13 January 1928, #1508.
92 MJDC, 12 September 1918, #5339.
93 Denyse Baillargeon has shown that while families and the Catholic Church remained resolute that premarital sex was a mortal sin and immoral, young women who were pregnant on their wedding day did not necessarily suffer criticism and condemnation; Baillargeon, *Making Do*, 51.
94 MJDC, 12 September 1918, #5339.
95 MJDC, 3 April 1924, #284.
96 MJDC, 2 April 1924, #235.
97 Steven Maynard, 'Through a Hole in the Lavatory Wall: Homosexual Subcultures, Police Surveillance and the Dialectics of Discovery,' *Journal of the History of Sexuality* 5 (1994): 207–41.
98 Carolyn Strange, *Toronto's Girl Problem* (Toronto: University of Toronto Press, 1995), 136.

99 '"Thrill Seekers" Are Fewer as Juvenile Delinquency Here Shows Improvement,' *Montreal Standard*, 26 October 1935.
100 Joan Sangster, *Regulating Girls and Women: Sexuality, Family, and the Law in Ontario, 1920–1960* (Toronto: Oxford University Press, 2001), ch. 5.
101 Elizabeth Pleck, *Domestic Tyranny: The Making of American Social Policy Against Family Violence* (New York: Oxford University Press, 1987). On family violence in Quebec see Marie-Aimée Cliche, 'Un secret bien gardé: l'inceste dans la société traditionelle Québécoise, 1858–1938,' *Revue d'histoire de l'Amérique française* 50:2 (Fall 1996); Kathryn Harvey, 'To Love, Honour and Obey: Wife-Battering in Working Class Montreal, 1869–79,' *Urban History Review* 2 (October 1990): 128–40; Peter Gossage, 'La marâtre: Marie-Anne Houde and the Myth of the Wicked Stepmother in Quebec,' *Canadian Historical Review* 76:4 (December 1995): 563–97.
102 Gordon, *Heroes of Their Own Lives*, 179.
103 MJDC, 19 August 1918, #5254.
104 MJDC, 14 April 1924, #303.
105 MJDC, 8 June 1928, #1982.
106 MJDC, 30 June 1928, #1978.
107 This case was discharged.
108 MJDC, 27 June 1928, #2060.
109 Kate Boyer, 'Place and the Politics of Virtue: Clerical Work, Corporate Anxiety, and Changing Meanings of Public Womanhood in Early Twentieth-Century Montreal,' *Gender, Place and Culture* 5:3 (1998), 261–76, at 268. See also Sarah Deutsch, *Women and the City: Gender, Space and Power in Boston, 1870–1940* (New York: Oxford University Press, 2000), 78–9.
110 This literature begins in the 1960s but really explodes in the 1970s when runaways become an international concern. For a recent study on the experiences of youths on the streets in Canadian cities, see J. Hagan and B. McCarthy, *Mean Streets: Youth Crime and Homelessness* (Cambridge: Cambridge University Press, 1997).
111 MJDC, 25 February 1918, #4673.
112 MJDC, 5 February 1918, #4650.
113 MJDC, 27 January 1930, #83.
114 MJDC, 2 April 1924, #235.
115 MJDC, 1 February 1924, #78.
116 Increasingly, wage-earning women sought out accommodations, resulting in a rash of boarding-house openings. Religious orders and women's organizations attempted to meet the demand and direct women into respectable lodgings, but demand far outstripped availability. During the First World War, the Montreal Local Council of Women protested the uncon-

trolled spread of boarding houses and mounted a campaign to have these establishments licensed. LAC, MLCW, MG 28, I 164, vol. 6, Projects, 'Plan to License and Supervise all Boarding and Rooming Houses.'

117 YWCA (Montreal) *Annual Report* (1916–17).

118 LAC, MLCW, MG 28, I 164 vol. 6, Projects, 'Plan to License.'

119 Ibid., K. Chipman to Mrs Plumptre, 30 April 1918.

120 Boarding houses were inspected by Elizabeth Wand, one of the city's first policewomen, who in 1918 investigated the way independent women lived in the city. LAC, MLCW, MG 28, I 164, vol. 7, K. Ward [*sic*] Protection Officer, Correspondence and Reports, 1918–19, 'Resume of Work for Local Council of Women,' July 1918; and YWCA, *Annual Reports*.

121 Royal Commission on Industrial Training and Technical Education, Part IV (1913), 1978.

122 Ruth Rosen and Sue Davidson, eds, *The Maimie Papers* (Indianapolis: Feminist Press, 1977), 183.

123 MJDC, 24 March 1924, #246. Rose Anna M., a fifteen year old, made seven dollars a week and rented a room with her boyfriend at 146 Ste Elizabeth Street for four dollars.

124 MJDC, 24 January 1944, #5743.

125 MJDC, 1 February 1924, #78.

126 MJDC, 24 September 1918, #5396.

127 MJDC, 3 April 1924, #235.

128 MJDC, 23 March 1918 #4749; 3 January 1918, #4580.

129 MJDC, 22 April, 1924, #301.

130 MJDC, 31 May 1918, #4975.

131 MJDC, 22 March 1924, #231.

132 MJDC, 2 May 1924, #347.

133 MJDC, 2 May 1924, #236. The province refused to honour indeterminate sentences and changed it to two years at GCIS. Archives Nationales du Québec à Québec (hereafter ANQQ), E17, 1924, File 3158, Letter from the Honorable Secretaire de la Province, 7 July 1924.

134 MJDC, 25 April 1924, #295.

135 Gordon, *Heroes of Their Own Lives*, 188.

136 MJDC, 17 April 1918, #4816.

137 R.L. Simons and L.B. Whitebeck, 'Sexual Abuse as a Precursor to Prostitution and Victimization Among Adolescent and Adult Homeless Women,' *Journal of Family Issues* 12:3 (September 1991): 361–79; Meda Chesney-Lind and Randall S. Shelden, *Girls, Delinquency, and Juvenile Justice* (Pacific Grove, CA: Brooks/Cole, 1992), 35.

138 MJDC, 18 February 1924, #130.

139 Christine Stansell, *City of Women: Sex and Class in New York, 1789–1860* (New York: Alfred A. Knopf, 1986), 179.
140 MJDC, 7 January 1932, #11. Simonne was sent to the Maison de Lorette for an indeterminate sentence.
141 Odem, *Delinquent Daughters,* 56.
142 Chesney-Lind and Sheldon, *Girls, Delinquency,* 35.
143 Anny V. MJDC, 26 January 1934, #95; Annie B. 4 June 1936, #655. Anny's mother ran a boarding house and had been arrested for selling liquor without a licence; she had never attempted to find her daughter or report her. Probation officer Fales-Jones felt that the girl 'had no chance in her home to make good' and had her sent to the Girls' Cottage School for two years. Annie was given four years at the same institution.

Chapter 6

1 Andrée Lévesque, *Making and Breaking the Rules: Women in Quebec, 1919–1939* (Toronto: McClelland and Stewart, 1994).
2 Christine Stansell, *City of Women: Sex and Class in New York, 1789–1860* (Urbana and Chicago: University of Illinois Press, 1986), 127.
3 This term is Steven Schlossman and Stephanie Wallach's. See 'The Crime of Precocious Sexuality: Female Juvenile Delinquency in the Progressive Era,' *Harvard Educational Review* 48:1 (February 1978): 65–95.
4 On 'rhetorical sameness' in case files and the 'repetitive rhetorical strategies' used by the interrogated see Annalee Golz, 'Uncovering and Reconstructing Family Violence: Ontario Criminal Case Files,' in *On the Case: Explorations in Social History,* ed. Franca Iacovetta and Wendy Mitchinson (Toronto: University of Toronto Press, 1999), 290; Steven Maynard, 'Horrible Temptations: Sex, Men, and Working-Class Male Youth in Urban Ontario, 1890–1935,' *Canadian Historical Review* 78:2 (June 1997): 201.
5 Kathleen Jones, *Taming the Troublesome Child: American Families, Child Guidance, and the Limits of Psychiatric Authority* (Cambridge, MA: Harvard University Press, 1999), 33. See, for example, the 1907 Illinois amendment.
6 Bruno Théorêt, 'Régulation juridique pénale des mineur-es et discrimination à l'égard des filles: la clause de 1924 amendant la Loi sur les jeunes délinquants,' *Canadian Journal of Women and the Law* 4 (1990–1): 539–55, at 541. See also Revised Statutes of Canada, 1927.
7 Théorêt, 'Régulation juridique,' 548; Ruth Alexander, Mary Odem, and Steven Schlossman found that sexual activity defined female juvenile delinquency in the Progressive Era. The Los Angeles Juvenile Court's interest in sexual activity of young women served 'to instill fear among single, working-

class females about the public or private expression of sexual interest or desire.' Mary E. Odem and Steven Schlossman, 'Guardians of Virtue: The Juvenile Court and Female Delinquency in Early 20th-Century Los Angeles,' *Crime and Delinquency* 37:2 (April 1991): 186–203, at 197 and 200. Ruth Alexander, *The 'Girl Problem': Female Sexual Delinquency in New York, 1900–1930* (Ithaca, NY: Cornell University Press, 1995).

8 Cited in Théorêt, 'Régulation juridique,' 547. Regina Juvenile Court Judge Ethel MacLachlan also agreed with finding a way to control young women's sexual behaviour. LAC, W.L. Scott Papers, MG 30, C27, vol. 8, file 30 A.35.4, Letter from Ethel MacLachlan to Judge Mott, 20 February 1924, 1.

9 This location was changed to the detention house in subsequent years.

10 MJDC, 15 January 1938, #63.

11 MJDC, 25 January, 1934 #120.

12 MJDC, 19 June 1932, #481.

13 Regina Kunzel, *Fallen Women, Problem Girls: Unmarried Mothers and the Professionalization of Social Work, 1890–1945* (New Haven: Yale University Press, 1993), 103–4.

14 MJDC, 19 June 1928, #2023.

15 MJDC, 20 January 1938, #95.

16 MJDC, 2 June 1942, #1323; 17 January 1944, #5693.

17 MJDC, 16 December 1924, #1078.

18 MJDC, 17 June 1936, #697. Author's translation.

19 MJDC, 28 January 1944, #5779. Author's translation.

20 See for example, MJDC, 29 January 1944, #5797.

21 MJDC, 30 September 1943, #5029.

22 See Kunzel, *Fallen Women,* 109–11.

23 MJDC, 22 September 1924, #760.

24 MJDC, 25 October 1924, #917.

25 MJDC, 13 January 1944, #5670.

26 MJDC, 15 January 1930, #31.

27 On narratives of sexual danger see Judith Walkowitz, *City of Dreadful Delight* (Chicago: University of Chicago Press, 1992).

28 Karen Dubinsky, *Improper Advances: Rape and Heterosexual Conflict in Ontario, 1880–1929* (Chicago: University of Chicago Press, 1993); Constance Backhouse, *Petticoats and Prejudice* (Toronto: Osgoode Society, 1991); Mary Odem, *Delinquent Daughters: Protecting and Policing Adolescent Female Sexuality in the United States, 1885–1920* (Chapel Hill: University of North Carolina Press, 1995), 50.

29 Graham Parker, 'The Legal Regulation of Sexual Activity and the Protection of Females,' *Osgoode Hall Law Journal* 21 (1983): 187–224.

30 Dubinsky, *Improper Advances*, 85.

31 See Joan Sangster, 'Incarcerating "Bad Girls": The Regulation of Sexuality through the Female Refuges Act in Ontario, Canada, 1920–45,' *Journal of the History of Sexuality* 7:2 (1996): 239–75; Franca Iacovetta, 'Delinquent Girls, Working-Class Parents, and the Family Courts,' in *On the Case: Explorations in Social History*, ed. Franca Iacovetta and Wendy Mitchinson (Toronto: University of Toronto Press, 1999); Lori Chambers, 'Courtship, Condoms, and Getting Caught: Working-Class Sexual Behaviour in Ontario 1921–61,' paper delivered to the Canadian Historical Association, August 1995.

32 On tales of seduction, see the Committee of Sixteen, *Preliminary Report on Vice in Montreal*, 1918. See also Dubinsky, *Improper Advances*; Carolyn Strange, *Toronto's 'Girl Problem': The Perils and Pleasures of the City* (Toronto: University of Toronto Press, 1995).

33 Woman's Christian Temperance Union, Montreal *Annual Report* (1887), 20.

34 *Montreal Witness*, 27 September 1912. CJCNA, A. Blumenthal Scrapbook, Bobine ZE140.

35 Lévesque, *Making and Breaking the Rules*. 62.

36 MJDC, 25 April 1924, #295.

37 Beth L. Bailey, *From Front Porch to Back Seat: Courtship in Twentieth-Century America* (Baltimore: Johns Hopkins University Press, 1988), 19. Bailey argues that the automobile was generally the favourite of early-to-mid-twentieth-century dating couples (p. 86). In Denyse Baillargeon's sample she found that the working-class women had access to automobile rides if they dated taxi drivers or widows who had used modest insurance sums to buy cars. Baillargeon, *Making Do: Women, Family and Home in Montreal during the Great Depression* (Waterloo, ON: Wilfrid Laurier University Press, 1999), 48.

38 As cited in Virginia Scharff, *Taking the Wheel: Women and the Coming of the Motor Age* (New York: The Free Press, 1991), 204.

39 MJDC, *Annual Report* (1917), cited *Montreal Herald*, 20 February 1918, 6.

40 Scharff, *Taking the Wheel*, 140.

41 MJDC, 28 January 1930, #79. Author's translation.

42 MJDC, 28 January 1938, #150.

43 MJDC, 11 June 1920, #7426.

44 MJDC, 31 May 1924, #434.

45 Karen Dubinsky and Adam Givertz, 'It Was Only a Matter of Passion: Masculinity and Sexual Danger,' in *Gendered Pasts: Historical Essays in Femininity and Masculinity in Canada*, ed. Kathryn McPherson, Cecilia Morgan, and Nancy M. Forestell (Toronto: Oxford University Press, 1999), 69.

46 See MJDC, 12 January 1934, #49.

47 MJDC, 12 September 1918, #5339.

48 MJDC, 4 November 1918, #5491.
49 MJCD, 19 June 1942, #1495.
50 Campaigns directed at regulating young women's behaviour during wartime
    spread out across North America. Maude Miner, Director of the Committee
    on Protective Work for Girls in the United States, spearheaded a national
    campaign to prevent the moral downfall of teenage girls in the area of mili-
    tary training camps. In 1918 she was invited to Montreal to give advice on
    controlling wayward girls. Committee of Sixteen, *Preliminary Report*, 10.
51 MJDC, 2 June 1924, #441. Another girl told the probation officer that she
    had been seduced by a boarder when she was very young. MJDC, 13 October
    1924, #878.
52 MJDC, 13 June 1944, #6713.
53 MJDC, 5 September 1924, #739. The judge asked: 'Est-ce qu'il a sorti son
    affaire et l'a-t-il mis sur la tienne? As-tu crié? As-tu saigné? Tu n'as pas été
    avec d'autres?'
54 MJDC, 11 January 1938, #46.
55 MJDC, 10 January 1936, #25.
56 MJDC, 19 June 1936, #730.
57 MJDC, 14 June 1944, #6724.
58 In 1918 I found 9 (of 181) cases that explicitly dealt with revelations of
    domestic sexual abuse. In 1924 the cases numbered 19 of almost 300 cases.
    This is likely a low incidence. Odem has found that 14 per cent of her sam-
    ple of girls in the Los Angeles Juvenile Court were the victims of physical or
    sexual assault in their homes.
59 Linda Gordon, *Heroes of Their Own Lives: The Politics and History of Family Vio-
    lence* (New York: Penguin, 1988), 227.
60 This is not to suggest that women were believed or treated better in rape trials
    where assailants were prosecuted. In fact, 'promiscuity' and general social
    behaviour of rape victims featured prominently in defendants' cases. See Kate
    Boyer, 'What's a Girl Like You Doing in a Place Like This? A Geography of Sex-
    ual Violence in Early 20th-Century Vancouver,' *Urban Geography* 17 (1996):
    286–93. Carolyn Strange's work on rape reveals the reasons why some men
    were prosecuted for rape, pointing to the conjunction of sexism, classism, and
    racism in the judicial system. See 'Patriarchy Modified: The Criminal Prose-
    cution of Rape in York County, Ontario, 1880–1930,' in *Crime and Criminal Jus-
    tice: Essays in the History of Canadian Law*, ed. Jim Phillips, Tina Loo, and Susan
    Lewthwaite (Toronto: The Osgoode Society, 1994), 207–51.
61 Marie-Aimée Cliche, 'Un secret bien gardé: l'inceste dans la société tradi-
    tionnale Québécoise, 1858–1938,' *Revue d'Histoire de l'amérique Française* 50:2
    (Fall 1996).

62 Ibid.

63 Joan Sangster, 'Masking and Unmasking the Sexual Abuse of Children: Perceptions of Violence against Children in the "Badlands" of Ontario, 1916–1930,' *Journal of Family History* 25: 4 (October 2000), 504–26.

64 Susan Brownmiller, *Against Our Will: Men, Women, and Rape* (New York: Bantam, 1975). This perspective as a political strategy is evident in Canadian, law which recognizes rape as assault.

65 Catherine MacKinnon, *Toward a Feminist Theory of the State* (Cambridge, MA: Harvard University Press, 1989). Vikki Bell wades through the history of these debates in *Interrogating Incest: Feminism, Foucault and the Law* (London: Routledge, 1993), especially ch. 6, 'Making Monsters, Locating Sex: Foucault and Feminism Debate.'

66 Dubinsky, *Improper Advances*, 34.

67 As Joan Sangster has noted, even Children's Aid Societies and turn-of-the-century feminists tended to obscure incest through a preference for campaigns against physical abuse and parental neglect. Sangster, 'Masking.'

68 Elizabeth Pleck, *Domestic Tyranny: The Making of Social Policy against Family Violence from Colonial Times to the Present* (New York: Oxford University Press, 1987), 7.

69 Sangster, 'Masking,' 11.

70 Pleck, *Domestic Tyranny*, 127–8. Pleck specifically points to the work of Jacques Donzelot and Christopher Lasch.

71 MJDC, 29 June 1938, #1053.

72 MJDC, 12 September 1924, #763. ANQQ, E17, 1924, file 3085.

73 MJDC, 19 June 1928, # 2023. Violet M. Report of Fales Jones, 16 July 1928; Letter to Judge Lacroix from George Corbett [Society for the Protection of Women and Children], 4 April 1929; Letter from Miss Heney to Judge J.A. Robillard, 14 June 1932.

74 MJDC, 27 February 1924, #171.

75 Gordon found in her study of Boston protection cases that fathers would attempt to undermine incest claims by charging their daughters were delinquent; *Heroes of Their Own Lives*, 191.

76 Not uncommon in abuse cases was the defence that it was the father's responsibility to teach their daughters sexual education. See Cliche, 'Un secret bien gardé,' 214. '[Quelques pères] prennent comme prétexte que c'est leur devoir de faire l'éducation sexuelle de leur enfant.'

77 Gordon, *Heroes of Their Own Lives*, 229.

78 MJDC, 9 October 1924, #867. In this file are two letters from the father to Germaine in the winter of 1924–25 imploring her to write to him. The address was not indicated but he describes her cubicle of a room (*ta petite*

chambrette) and *la crèche*, suggesting she was in a maternity hospital like the L'hôpital de la Miséricorde. In these letters he pleads with her to contact him and threatens her with his 'unhappiness.' He warned her not to show his letters to her aunt and to keep the communication between them, attempting to maintain his former relationship with her.

79 MJDC, 9 October 1924, #867.

80 Bell, *Interrogating Incest*, 68–9.

81 In recent sociological literature on homeless youths (runaways) it has been determined that `youths are unlikely to run away and stay away from home when the decision means loss of valued rewards from family relationships'; L.B. Whitbeck and R.L. Simons, 'Life on the Streets: The Victimization of Runaway and Homeless Adolescents,' *Youth and Society* 22:1 (September 1990): 109.

82 MJDC, 9 December 1918, #5590.

83 MJDC, 5 April 1918, #4775; 11 June 1918, #5007.

84 This reflects the court's lack of interest in this matter rather than the low incidence of sibling incest: without sexual histories taken of the boys, it is impossible to know how many had had incestuous sex.

85 MJDC, 17 July 1916.

86 MJDC, 28 August 1924, #717.

87 MJDC, 12 September 1924, #756.

88 LAC, GCS, vol. 1, file 20, 'A Study of a Group of Delinquent Girls,' 5.

89 NA, GCS, vol. 1, file 26, 'Case Histories.'

90 Gordon, *Heroes of Their Own Lives*, 219.

91 Ibid., 221.

92 In the last twenty years, American criminologist Meda Chesney-Lind has argued that the juvenile justice system in the United States has criminalized girls' survival by punishing behaviour that was the result of physical and sexual abuse at home. Feminists have suggested we interpret their acts of 'delinquency' as self-assertion. E.Ward, *Father-Daughter Rape* (London: Women's Press, 1984), 154. See also Gordon and the process of girls regaining autonomy through running away, *Heroes of Their Own Lives*, 242.

Chapter 7

1 Once her father died in 1920, her mother decided to raise her as a Protestant.

2 MJDC, 8 June 1928, #1980. Report of George H. Corbett, Executive Secretary for the Society for the Protection of Women and Children.

3 The GCIS dropped 'industrial' from its name in the early 1930s becoming the Girls' Cottage School.

4   Emily Jaquays [President, Girls' Cottage Industrial School], 'What Is Our Mental Attitude to the Delinquent Girl?' *Social Welfare* (March 1927): 378.

5   On normalization, see Mary Louise Adams, *The Trouble With Normal: Postwar Youth and the Making of Heterosexuality* (Toronto: University of Toronto Press, 1997); Mona Gleason, *Normalizing the Ideal: Psychology, Schooling, and the Family in Postwar Canada* (Toronto: University of Toronto Press, 1999).

6   GCIS, *Annual Report* (1932), 121. Found in the journal *Welfare Work in Montreal, 1922–1930.*

7   On the boys' reform schools in Montreal, see Sylvie Ménard, *Des enfants sous surveillance: La rééducation des jeunes délinquants au Québec (1840–1950)* (Montreal: vlb editeur, 2003); Anne Duret, 'L'enfermement comme forme de punition du garçon délinquant au Québec (1857–1930),' MA thesis, University of Ottawa, 1988; Danielle Lacasse, 'Du délinquant à l'ouvrier qualifié: le Mont-Saint-Antoine, 1945–1964,' *Histoire sociale / Social History* 22:44 (November 1989): 287–316; and her 'Le Mont-Saint-Antoine: la répression de la délinquance juvénile à Montréal, 1873–1964,' MA thesis, University of Ottawa, 1986; and Prue Rains and Eli Teram, *Normal Bad Boys: Public Policies, Institutions, and the Politics of Client Recruitment* (Montreal and Kingston: McGill-Queen's University Press, 1992). On the Montreal reform school for girls, see Véronique Strimelle, 'La gestion de la déviance des filles et les institutions du Bon Pasteur à Montréal (1869–1912),' PhD diss., Université de Montréal, 1998. On the history of Canadian reform schools, see Paul W. Bennett, 'Taming "Bad Boys" of the "Dangerous Class": Child Rescue and Restraint at the Victoria Industrial School, 1887–1935,' *Histoire sociale / Social History* 21:41 (May 1988): 71–96; Indiana Matters, 'The Boys Industrial School: Education for Juvenile Offenders,' in *Schooling and Society in Twentieth-Century British Columbia*, ed. Donald Wilson and David C. Jones (Calgary: Detselig, 1980), 53–70; Neil Sutherland, *Children in English-Canadian Society: Framing the Twentieth Century Consensus* (Toronto: University of Toronto Press, 1976), esp. ch. 7; Joan Sangster, *Girl Trouble: Female Delinquency in English Canada* (Peterborough, ON: Between the Lines, 2002), ch. 5.

8   Bennett, 'Taming "Bad Boys,"' 71; Barbara M. Brenzel does not use the term *total institution* but does argue that at the Lancaster State Industrial School for Girls 'a period of reformist vision and loving care (gave way) to one of harsh judgment, rudimentary job training, and punitive custody.' Barbara M. Brenzel, *Daughters of the State: A Social Portrait of the First Reform School for Girls in North America, 1856–1905* (Cambridge, MA: MIT Press, c. 1983), 160.

9   The Boys' Home of Montreal took in working-class boys fourteen years of age and older to train them for employment. It often operated as a placement centre for the boys. The files of the Boys' Home are in the Library and

Archives Canada (LAC). LAC, Boys' Home/Weredale, MG 28, I 405, vol. 7, file 8, 'Testimony to the Royal Commission on Price Spreads,' 21 November 1934.

10 Rains and Teram, *Normal Bad Boys*, 8.

11 Ibid., 16–17.

12 This issue was officially resolved in 1922. An understanding with the Quebec Attorney-General's office allowed them to be both a reformatory school and an industrial school as long as the voluntary cases and court cases were kept separate. Archives nationales du Québec à Québec (hereafter ANQQ), Fonds Correspondance du Procureur-Général, E17, File 4047, Correspondence August–October 1922.

13 For histories of the GCIS see Anonymous, *50 Years of Growing: Girls' Cottage School*, (c. 1962) and Kathleen Moore, *History of the Girls' Cottage School, 1911–1946* (1950) in LAC, Girls' Cottage School (hereafter GCS), MG 28, I 404, vol. 2, files 21 and 22, respectively.

14 GCIS, *Annual Report* (1926), 114.

15 In fact, in the first ten years, the GCIS received only $400 from the provincial government. The original agreement suggested the school would be awarded $200 per year to run the school. In 1920 the province awarded the school $2,280 in back payments. GCIS, *Annual Report* (1922).

16 This meant $120 per capita per annum.

17 GCIS, *Annual Report* (1926), 117–18.

18 LAC, GCS, vol. 3, file 3, 'Annual Statement of the Girls' Cottage Industrial School ... to the Treasurer of the Province of Quebec for the Year Ending 31 December, 1915,' 7.

19 GCIS, *Annual Report* (1926), 124.

20 Ibid. (1917), 13.

21 LAC, GCS, vol. 2, file 15, 'Superintendent's Monthly Reports,' January 1935.

22 Ibid.

23 Soeurs du Bon Pasteur, *Annales de la Maison Saint-Domitille* (Montreal: Imp. de l'Institution des Sourds-Muets, 1919), 244. Author's translation.

24 GCIS, *Annual Report* (1918), 11.

25 Davies left soon after Miner's report but a replacement with the appropriate qualifications took a number of years to find.

26 GCIS, *Annual Report* (1926), 120.

27 Ibid. (1929), 126.

28 Ibid. (1925), 131.

29 Carolyn Strange, 'The Velvet Glove: Maternalistic Reform at the Andrew Mercer Ontario Reformatory for Females, 1874–1927,' MA thesis, University of Ottawa, 1983, 73.

30 GCIS, *Annual Report* (1930), 127.

31 Ibid.

32 Ibid.

33 Ibid.

34 Ibid. (1936), 49.

35 McGill University Archives, Montreal Council of Social Agencies Fonds, MG 2076, C30, File 50, 'Girls' Cottage School – Barger Report,' 1948.

36 *Annales de la Maison Ste-Domitille*, 1915, 315.

37 GCIS, *Annual Report* (1923), 189.

38 Archives du Bon Pasteur, 'Maison de Lorette – Laval-des-Rapides de 1915 à 1944: Oeuvre des Jeunes Delinquantes,' n.d., 1.

39 That same decade the Frères de la Charité de St-Vincent-de-Paul began talk of moving the Catholic boys reform school out of the city. The Juvenile Court judge wrote in 1914: 'Il est admis, et tous les auteurs qui traitent spécialement de la question du relèvement de la jeunesse, sont unanimes à le reconnaître, que l'influence de la campagne est sous tous les rapports de beaucoup préférable à celle de la ville pour en arriver aux fins que vous poursuivez.' Cited in Duret, 'L'enfermement,' 159.

40 Brenzel, *Daughters of the State*, 69.

41 Ibid.

42 Lucia Zedner, *Women, Crime, and Custody in Victorian England* (Oxford: Oxford University Press, 1991), 238–9.

43 Annmarie Adams, 'Rooms of Their Own: The Nurses' Residences at Montreal's Royal Victoria Hospital,' *Material History Review* 40 (Fall 1994): 29–41, at 32.

44 Reform and industrial schools for dependent and delinquent boys were also built outside city limits. See Bennett, 'Taming "Bad Boys,"' 76.

45 Archives du Bon Pasteur, 'Maison de Lorette – Laval-des-Rapides de 1915 à 1944: Oeuvre des Jeunes Delinquant,' 1. Author's translation.

46 Soeurs du Bon Pasteur, *Annales des religieuses de Notre-Dome de Charité du Bon-Pasteur d'Angers à Montréal*, vol. 2, *Monastère du Bon-Pasteur, 1895*, 310–11, and *Annales de la Maison Ste-Domitille*, 43.

47 GCIS, *Annual Report* (1932), 121.

48 Deborah E.B. Weiner, *Architecture and Social Reform in Late-Victorian London* (Manchester and New York: Manchester University Press, 1994), 74. See also Gwendolyn Wright, *Moralism and the Model Home: Domestic Architecture and Cultural Conflict in Chicago, 1873–1913* (Chicago: University of Chicago Press, c. 1980).

49 Helen Lefkowitz Horowitz, 'Hull-House as Women's Space,' *Chicago History* 12 (1983): 40–55.

50 See, for example, Adams, 'Rooms of Their Own,' 37.

51 Quoted in ibid., 33; and Martha Vicinus, *Independent Women: Work and Community for Single Women, 1850–1920* (Chicago: University of Chicago Press, 1985), 129.

52 Brenzel, *Daughters of the State*, 69.

53 LAC, GCS, vol. 2, file 1, 'At the Girls' Cottage School,' 30 December 1945.

54 GCIS, *Annual Report* (1915), 9.

55 Ibid. (1922), 44.

56 Ibid. (1923), 184, 187.

57 The Victoria Industrial School for Boys near Toronto was organized along the cottage system. See Bennett, 'Taming "Bad Boys,"' 75.

58 GCIS, *Annual Report* (1922), 45.

59 Ibid. (1923), 184. The architectural changes to the GCIS are documented in the National Archives GCIS Map Collection.

60 GCIS, *Annual Report* (1925), 131.

61 Ibid. (1922), 45.

62 Ibid. (1924), 123.

63 LAC, GCS, vol. 2, file 15, 'Superintendent's Monthly Reports,' 1945, 2.

64 GCIS, *Annual Report* (1925), 124.

65 Michelle Cale, 'Girls and the Perception of Sexual Danger in the Victorian Reformatory System,' *History* 78:253 (June 1993): 201–17, at 216.

66 LAC, GCS, vol. 3, file 15, 1 April 1942.

67 On convent architecture and material culture see Elizabeth W. McGahan, 'Inside the Hallowed Walls: Convent Life through Material History,' *Material History Bulletin* 25 (Spring 1987): 1–10, at 5. Orders that educated girls of the elite, however, often did offer separate rooms. See also Tania Marie Martin, 'Housing the Grey Nuns: Power, Religion and Women in fin-de-siècle Montréal,' MA thesis, McGill University, 1995.

68 GCIS, *Annual Report* (1933), 118.

69 Ibid.

70 According the annual reports of the 1940s the average age was 14.5 or 15.

71 For 1926 birthplace of inmates: 32 Canada, 2 Scotland, 1 Ireland, 11 England, 1 Newfoundland, 3 United States, 1 Foreign. (Total 51). Compare this to a decade earlier: in 1916 7 born in Canada out of 17 total. Quebec, *Statistical Yearbook*, 1916, 1926.

72 GCIS, *Annual Report* (1915–45). The annual reports from the 1940s do not indicate nationality.

73 LAC, GCS, vol. 1, file 20, J.W. Bridges, 'A Study of a Group of Delinquent Girls. The Girls Cottage School, 1926,' 2.

74 Ibid., 3.

75 Ibid., 4.

76 GCIS, *Annual Report* (1917), 8.

77 Rains and Teram, *Normal Bad Boys*, 21–4.
78 GCIS, *Annual Report* (1917), 9.
79 Ibid., 8.
80 Ibid., 14.
81 Ibid.
82 Ibid. (1924), 126.
83 Ibid. (1926), 114.
84 Ibid. (1923), 184.
85 Ibid. (1924), 126.
86 LAC, GCS, vol. 1, file 17, 'Report of the Superintendents,' 1936, 1940.
87 GCIS, *Annual Report* (1922), 45.
88 Ibid.
89 Ibid. There were asylums, such as the St-Jean-de-Dieu in Montreal for those considered mentally insane.
90 LAC, GCS, vol. 1, file 16, 'Report of the Medical Officer, 1940.'
91 GCIS, *Annual Report* (1926), 117.
92 Ibid. (1941), 76.
93 *Montreal Herald*, 15 January 1930, 3.
94 GCIS, *Annual Report* (1917), 9.
95 Quebec, *Sessional Papers* 1913, 'Report on Asylums, Reform Schools'
96 Ibid.
97 GCIS, *Annual Report* (1924), 120.
98 LAC, GCS, vol. 2, file 15, 'Superintendent's Monthly Reports, 1927.'
99 GCIS, *Annual Report* (1924), 120.
100 *La Presse*, 9 October 1945, 3. The girls at Lorette complained of a 'coiffure ridicule.'
101 LAC, GCS, vol. 1, file 32, 'General Policy,' 9.
102 LAC, vol. 1, file 17, 'Superintendent's Reports,' 1944, 3.
103 Ibid., 1942.
104 GCIS, *Annual Report* (1918), 15–16.
105 Harvest for 1927 in bushels: 300 potatoes, 50 winter turnips, 20 summer turnips, 40 carrots, 40 beets, 20 parsnips, 45 mangels (beets), 20 corn, 70 tomatoes, 5 cucumbers, and 3 salsify. This also included 1000 heads of cabbage, 60 pumpkins, 60 squash, 25 citrons, 700 quarts of strawberries, and 40 quarts raspberries. GCIS, *Annual Report* (1927), 127.
106 Ibid. (1932), 121.
107 Ibid. (1914).
108 Ibid. (1938), 48.
109 Ibid. (1927), 126.
110 Ibid. (1938), 48.

111 Ibid. (1933), 120.

112 Ibid. (1918), 8.

113 Ibid. (1924), 121.

114 By the 1940s the full day of school was implemented. LAC, GCS, vol. 2, file 1 'Newspaper Clippings,' 30 December 1945.

115 GCIS, *Annual Report* (1923), 187.

116 Ibid. (1943), 76.

117 LAC, MLCW, MG 28, I 164, vol. 7, file: Reformatory Comm. Corr. and Reports – 2 of 2 (1909–22, 1931), 'Brief Sketch of the Reformatory Work Done at the Good Shepherd,' 1913, 2.

118 LAC, MLCW, vol. 7, file: Reformatory Comm. 'Brief Sketch,' 1.

119 GCIS, *Annual Report* (1924), 121.

120 Ibid. (1923), 188.

121 LAC, GCS, vol. 1, file 12, 'Report of the Follow-up Worker, 1926–28,' 1926, 3.

122 GCIS, *Annual Report* (1927), 127; LAC, GCS, vol. 1, file 17, 'Superintendent's Reports,' 1928.

123 *Annual Report* (1929), 127.

124 Ibid. (1923), 188.

125 Ibid. (1924), 121.

126 Ibid. (1932), 2.

127 LAC, GCS, vol. 1, file 17, 'Superintendent's Report,' 1941, 2.

128 See annual reports for the 1940s.

129 LAC, GCS, vol. 1, file 19, 'Visitor's Report, 1924–25.'

130 GCIS, *Annual Report* (1932), 124.

131 Ibid. (1939), 23.

132 Ibid. (1924–1945).

133 Ibid. (1944), 77.

134 Ibid. (1933), 120.

135 Ibid. (1928), 131.

136 Ibid. (1931), 127.

137 Ibid. (1938), 48.

138 Field Secretary Mrs M.K. Baker quoted in the *Montreal Daily Star*, 25 January 1939.

139 LAC, GSC, vol. 1, file 32, 'General Policy, n.d., 1942–1945,' 7 October 1942.

140 Ibid., 5.

141 Micheline Dumont, *Girls' Schooling in Quebec, 1639–1960*, Historical Booklet No. 49 (Ottawa: Canadian Historical Association, 1990), 15.

142 Quebec, *Sessional Papers* (1910), 'Report of the Superioress of the Montreal Reformatory School for Girls,' 25.

143 GCIS, *Annual Report* (1914), 9.
144 Ibid. (1928), 121.
145 Ibid, (1926), 121.
146 Ibid. (1914), 10.
147 Quebec, *Sessional Papers*, 'Report of Inspectors of Asylum, Reform Schools' 1913, 68–9.
148 Brenzel, *Daughters of the State*, 74; Bennett, 'Taming "Bad Boys,"' 90.
149 LAC, GCS, vol. 1, file 32, 'General Policy.'
150 For a history of disciplinary regimes in reform schools see Tamara Myers and Joan Sangster, 'Retorts, Runaways and Riots: Patterns of Resistance in Canadian Reform Schools for Girls,' *Journal of Social History* (USA) 34:3 (Spring 2001), 669–97; Peter Quinn, '"We ask for bread and are given stone': The Girls Industrial School, Parramatta, 1941–1961,' *Journal of the Royal Australian Historical Society* 75:2 (1989), 158–72, at 163.
151 LAC, GCS, vol. 1, file 32, 'General Policy,' 6.
152 LAC, GSS, vol. 2, file 6, 'Radio Talk,' 6.
153 LAC, GCS, vol. 2, file 15, 'Superintendent's Monthly Reports,' November 1928.
154 GCIS, *Annual Report* (1928), 129.
155 Ibid. (1917), 14.
156 LAC, GCS, vol. 1, file 17, 'Superintendent's Reports,' 1928, 2.
157 MJDC, 3 January 1944, #5601, Report to the Juvenile Court from GCS..
158 MJDC, 9 November 1936, #1481.
159 ANQQ, E17, File 2557, 1931.
160 MJDC, 27 January 1938, #142. Depositions from nuns at the Maison Ste-Domitille (industrial school), Asile Ste-Darie (Women's Prison) and Maison de Lorette (18 April 1940).
161 LAC, GCS, vol. 2, file 15 'Superintendent's Monthly Reports,' January 1936 and October 1935, respectively.
162 LAC, GCS, MG 28, I 404, vol. 1, file 26, Case files, 1941–42; MJDC, 27 June 1940, #1196.
163 MJDC, 27 January 1938, #142. Author's translation.
164 MJDC, 5 June 1940, #1098.
165 MJDC, 5 June 1940, #1098.
166 MJDC, 3 January 1944, #480.
167 MJDC, 5 June 1940, #1098.
168 The *Montreal Gazette* quoted a 'world authority on forensic psychiatry,' Dr Winfred Overholser, who laid responsibility for the recent crime waves on the rise of juvenile delinquency; *Montreal Gazette*, 24 January 1946.

169 A new building was constructed for juvenile delinquents in 1930.

170 'Révolte de détenues à la maison Lorette,' *La Presse*, 8 October 1945, 3; and 'Pour être plus tôt en liberté,' 9 October 1945, 3; *Globe and Mail*, 9 October 1945, 1.

171 The accusations were denied by the Soeurs. See 'Précisions sur Lorette,' *La Presse*, 11 October 1945, 21.

172 *La Presse*, 9 October, 1945, 3. Author's translation.

173 *Montreal Gazette*, 7 December 1945 and 8 December 1945.

174 *Montreal Herald*, 19 December, 1946. Judge Nicholson referred to the situation at Laval-des-Rapides when closing the Girls' Cottage School.

175 *La Presse*, 11 October 1945, 3.

176 *Montreal Gazette*, 10 October 1945, 11.

177 'Lay Body Proposed at Lorette House,' *Montreal Gazette*, 10 October 1945, 11.

178 Ibid.

179 Ibid.

180 La Première province dans le domaine social: Ce sera Québec d'ici trois ans, dit M. Dalton – En marge de la mutinerie de Lorette et de l'escapade de Sweetsburg,' *La Presse*, 20 October 1945, 27.

181 These dresses were shortened (cut up, really) by the girls themselves once inside the Women's Jail. They therefore appeared in court with bare knees. *La Presse*, 20 October 1945, 27.

182 See 'La Première province' and 'Les mutines de Lorette,' both in *La Presse*, 20 October 1945, 27.

183 *Montreal Gazette*, 18 October 1945, 8.

184 Ibid.

185 *Montreal Gazette*, 6 June 1946.

186 Ibid.

187 Ibid.

188 LAC, GCS, vol. 1, file 10, 'Report of the Board of Directors, 1946.'

189 Rains and Teram, *Normal Bad Boys*, 8. Both girls' reform schools suffered from their dependence on provincial funding; not until the 1950s did things change rapidly for the schools with the financial and administrative commitment coming from the newly created ministry of youth.

190 McGill University Archives, Montreal Council of Social Agencies, MG 2076, Barger Report, 4.

Conclusion

1 'Ministry of Youth Plan Is Announced,' *Montreal Gazette*, 27 August 1945, 20.

2 *Montreal Gazette*, 8 October 1945, 13.

3 MJDC, 30 September 1943, #5029.
4 *Montreal Gazette*, 22 December 1975, 3. See the Prevost Commission on Juvenile Justice (1970); the Committee for the Advancement of Justice for Children (1973); Batshaw Commission (1975).
5 Lillian Mendolsohn and Sharon Ronald, 'History of the Montreal Juvenile Court,' MSW thesis, McGill University, 1969, 1.
6 'Police Arrest Members of Girl Gang,' *Globe and Mail*, 22 January 1998, A12.
7 'Experts Report Girls as Aggressive as Boys but in Verbal Ways: First North American Conference on Subject Hears of Harm Done by False Rumours, Gossip,' *Globe and Mail*, 23 October 1999, A3.

Bibliography

Primary Sources

Archival Collections

Archives des Soeurs du Bon Pasteur d'Angers, Pierrefonds, QC
    École de réforme – Maison de Lorette
Archives municipales de la ville de Montréal
    Département/Service de Police de Montréal
    Recorder's Court, Annual Reports
    Press Clippings
Archives nationales du Québec, Montreal
    Fonds de la Cour des jeunes délinquants de la cité de Montréal
Archives nationales du Québec, Quebec
    Correspondance du Procureur-Général
Canadian Jewish Congress National Archives, Montreal
    Federation of Jewish Philanthropies
Cour municipale de Montréal
    Recorder's Court Dossiers
McGill University Archives
    Montreal Council of Social Agencies
Library and Archives of Canada
    Canadian Council of Social Development
    Girls' Cottage Industrial School
    Jewish Family Services of the Baron de Hirsch Institute
    Montreal Local Council of Women
    National Council of Women
    Society for the Protection of Women and Children [Montreal]

Summerhill Homes
W.L. Scott Papers
Rockefeller Archive Center
Laura Spellman Rockefeller Memorial Foundation Fonds
Rockefeller Foundation Archives

Books

Big Sister Association (Montreal). *Annual Reports.*
Borthwick, J. Douglas. *From Darkness to Light: History of the Eight Prisons Which Have Been, or Are Now, in Montreal from AD 1766 to AD 1907 – Civil and Military.* Montreal: Gazette Printing, 1907.
– *History of the Montreal Prison from A.D. 1784 to A.D. 1886.* Montreal: A. Periard, 1886.
Child Welfare Exhibition. *Souvenir Pamphlet.* Montreal: 1912.
Committee of Sixteen. *Preliminary Report of an Unofficial Organization upon the Vice Conditions in Montreal.* Montreal: Author, 1918.
– *Fourth Annual Report.* Montreal: 1922.
– *Some Facts Regarding Toleration, Regulation, Segregation and Repression of Commercialized Vice. Second Annual Report.* Montreal: 1919.
Courcy, Henri de. *Les servantes de Dieu en Canada: essai sur l'histoire des communautés réligieuses de femmes de la province.* Montreal: John Lovell, 1855.
Federation of Jewish Philanthropies [Montreal]. *Annual Reports.*
Girls' Cottage Industrial School. *Annual Reports.*
Goüin, Ed. P.S.S. *La Cour Juvénile de Montréal: son fonctionnement, ses résultats, ses ambitions.*
Montreal: Secrétariat de l'école sociale populaire, 1913.
Hart, Evanston. *Wake Up! Montreal! Commercialized Vice and its Contributories.* Montreal: The Witness Press, 1919.
Henderson, Rose. *Women and War.* Vancouver, 1920.
MacGill, Helen Gregory. *The Juvenile Court in Canada.* Ottawa: Canadian Council on Child Welfare, 1925.
Massicotte, R.P. Valère. *La Délinquence juvénile et la guerre.* Montreal: Oeuvre des Tracts, April 1944.
Montreal by Gaslight. 1889.
Montreal Council of Social Agencies. *Report of the Delinquency Committee.* Montreal: June 1945.
Montreal Health Survey Committee. *Survey, Public Health Activities, Montreal October 1928.* Montreal: Metropolitan Life Insurance, 1928.
Montreal: Historic, Romantic ... 1932.

Montreal Local Council of Women. *Annual Reports.*
Montreal Police Juvenile Guide. Montreal: L'imprimerie populaire limitée, 1950.
Moore, Kathleen. *History of the Girls' Cottage School, 1911–1946.* 1950.
National Council of Women of Canada. *Yearbooks.*
Saint-Pierre, Arthur, *L'oeuvre des congrégations religieuses de charité dans la province de Québec (en 1930)* Montreal: Editions de la Bibliothèque Canadienne, c. 1930.
School for Social Workers, McGill University, *Annual Reports.*
Sights and Shrines: An Illustrated Guide to Montreal. Montreal: A.T. Chapman, 1920.
Sister Mary of St Marine Verger, *Practical Rules for the Use of the Religious of the Good Shepherd for the Direction of the Classes* (Angers, 1898).
Soeurs du Bon Pasteur. *Annales de la Maison Saint-Domitille* Montreal: Imp. de l'Institution des Sourds-Muets, 1919.
– *Annales des religieuses de Notre-Dame de Charité du Bon-Pasteur d'Angers à Montréal,* vols. 1 and 2. Montreal: Monastère du Bon-Pasteur, 1895.
– *Au Soir d'un Siècle.* Montreal: Le Bon-Pasteur d'Angers, 1944.
– *Fêtes Jubilaires, 1844–1894.* Montreal, 1894.
Taschereau, Henri. 'Report on the Police Investigation and Its Results,' 18 February 1905.
Topping, C.W. *Canadian Penal Institutions.* Toronto: Ryerson Press, 1929.
Woman's Christian Temperance Union (Montreal). *Annual Reports.*
Wyles, Lilian. *A Woman at Scotland Yard: Reflections on the Struggles and Achievements of Thirty Years in the Metropolitan Police.* London: Faber and Faber, 1953.
Young Women's Christian Association (Montreal). *Annual Reports.*

Articles

Archambault, R.P. 'Une entrevue du président du tribunal des jeunes délinquants de Montréal.' *Parents chrétiens sauvez vos enfants du cinéma meurtrier.* Montreal: L'oeuvre des tracts [No. 91], 1927.
Brooking, Lucy. 'A Study of the Delinquent Girl,' *Social Welfare* (1 April, 1921): 182.
Choquet, Judge [François-Xavier]. 'The Juvenile Court,' *Canadian Municipal Journal* (June 1914): 232–3.
Fitzgerald, Major J.G. 'The Advisory Committee on Venereal Diseases for Military District No. 2.' *Public Health Journal* 9:2 (February 1918).
Haywood, Dr A.K. 'Vice and Drugs in Montreal.' *Public Health Journal* (January 1923): 1–18.
Henderson, Rose. 'Child Labour, Delinquency, and the Standards of Living,' *Social Welfare* 2:1 (October 1919): 16.

– 'The Juvenile Court.' *Canadian Municipal Journal* (March 1916): 84.
– 'The Juvenile Court by One Who Knows.' *Woman's Century* (March 1916): 28.
Jaquays, Emily. 'What Is Our Mental Attitude to the Delinquent Girl?' *Social Welfare* (March 1927): 378.
MacGill, Helen Gregory. 'The Relation of the Juvenile Court to the Community.' *Canadian Journal of Mental Hygiene* 1:3 (October 1919): 232–6.
Mundie, Gordon. 'The Problem of the Mentally Defective in the Province of Quebec.' *Canadian Journal of Mental Hygiene* (July 1919): 123–9.
Symonds, Dr H. 'The Social Evil.' Council for Social Service *Bulletin* 19. (December 1918).

Government Publications

Canada. *Report of the Royal Commission on Industrial Training and Education.* Ottawa, 1913.
Canada. *Report of the Royal Commission to Investigate the Penal System of Canada.* Ottawa, 1938.
Canadian Welfare Council. *Juvenile Courts in Canada being a Brief Description of Juvenile Court Organization in the Provinces.* Ottawa: Publication No. 121, 1942.

Secondary Sources

Books

Alexander, Ruth M. *The 'Girl Problem': Female Sexual Delinquency in New York, 1900–1950.* Ithaca, NY: Cornell University Press, 1995.
Atherton, William H. *Montreal, 1535–1914: Biographical.* Montreal: S.J. Clarke Publishing, 1914.
Bailey, Beth L. *From Front Porch to Back Seat: Courtship in Twentieth-Century America.* Baltimore: Johns Hopkins University Press, 1988.
Baillargeon, Denyse. *Making Do: Women, Family and Home in Montreal during the Great Depression.* Waterloo, ON: Wilfrid Laurier University Press, 1999.
Baines, Carol et al., eds. *Women's Caring: Feminist Perspectives on Social Welfare.* Toronto: McClelland and Stewart, 1991.
Béique, Mme F.-L. *Quatre-vingts ans de souvenirs: histoire d'une famille.* Montreal: Les Editions Canadienne-Française, 1939.
Beronville, Gaetan. *Saint Mary Euphrasia Pelletier: Foundress of the Good Shepherd Sisters.* Westminster, MD: 1959.

Bell, Vikki. *Interrogating Incest: Feminism, Foucault and the Law.* London: Routledge, 1993.

Bienvenue, Louise. *Quand la jeunesse entre en scène: L'Action catholique avant la Révolution tranquille.* Montreal: Boréal, 2003.

Bradbury, Bettina. *Working Families: Age, Gender, and Daily Survival in Industrializing Montreal.* Toronto: McClelland and Stewart, 1993.

Brenzel, Barbara. *Daughters of the State: A Social Portrait of the First Reform School for Girls in North America, 1856–1905.* Cambridge, MA: MIT Press, 1983.

Brodeur, J-P. *La délinquance de l'ordre. recherche sur les commissions d'enquête.* Montreal: Hurtubise, 1984.

Carrigan, D. Owen. *Crime and Punishment in Canada: A History.* Toronto: McClelland and Stewart, 1991.

– *Juvenile Delinquency in Canada: A History.* Concord, ON: Irwin Publishing, 1998.

Carrington, Kerry. *Offending Girls: Sex, Youth and Justice.* Sydney: Allen and Unwin Australia, 1993.

Chesney-Lind, Meda, and Randall G. Shelden. *Girls, Delinquency, and Juvenile Justice.* Pacific Grove, CA: Brooks/Cole, 1992.

Christie, Nancy. *Engendering the State: Family, Work, and Welfare in Canada.* Toronto: University of Toronto Press, 2000.

Chunn, Dorothy E. *From Punishment to Doing Good: Family Courts and Socialized Justice in Ontario, 1880–1940.* Toronto: University of Toronto Press, 1992.

Clapp, Elizabeth J. *Mothers of All Children: Women Reformers and the Rise of Juvenile Courts in Progressive Era America.* University Park: Pennsylvania State University Press, 1998.

Cox, Pamela. *Gender, Justice and Welfare: Bad Girls in Britain, 1900–1950.* Basingstoke: Palgrave, 2003.

Danylewycz, Marta. *Taking the Veil: An Alternative to Marriage, Motherhood, and Spinsterhood in Quebec, 1840–1920.* Toronto: McClelland and Stewart, 1987.

D'Emilio, John, and Estelle Freedman. *Intimate Matters: A History of Sexuality in America.* New York: Harper and Row, 1988.

Deslauriers, Ignace-J., ed. *Les tribunaux de Québec et leurs juges.* Cowansville, QC: Les Editions Yvon Blais Inc, 1987.

Deutsch, Sarah. *Women and the City: Gender, Space and Power in Boston, 1870–1940.* New York: Oxford University Press, 2000.

Donzelot, Jacques. *The Policing of Families,* trans. Robert Hurley. New York: Pantheon Books, 1979.

Dubinsky, Karen. *Improper Advances: Rape and Heterosexual Conflict in Ontario, 1880–1929.* Chicago: University of Chicago Press, 1993.

Dumont, Micheline. *Girls' Schooling in Quebec, 1639–1960.* Historical Booklet No. 49. Ottawa: Canadian Historical Association, 1990.

Dumont, Micheline, and Nadia Fahmy-Eid. *Les couventines. l'éducation des fille au Québec dans les congrégations religieuses enseignantes, 1840–1960.* Montreal: Boréal, 1986.

Faith, Karlene. *Unruly Women: The Politics of Confinement and Resistance.* Vancouver: Press Gang Publishers, 1993.

Fecteau, Jean-Marie. *La liberté du pauvre: crime et pauvreté au XIXe siècle québécois.* Montreal: vlb éditeur, 2004.

Foucault, Michel. *Discipline and Punish: The Birth of the Prison.* New York: Vintage Books, 1979.

– *The History of Sexuality.* Vol. 1. New York: Vintage Books, 1978.

Freedman, Estelle B. *Maternal Justice: Miriam Van Waters and the Female Reform Tradition.* Chicago: University of Chicago Press, 1996.

– *Their Sisters' Keepers: Women's Prison Reform in America.* Ann Arbor: University of Michigan Press, 1981.

Getis, Victoria. *The Juvenile Court and the Progressives.* Chicago: University of Chicago Press, 2000.

Gleason, Mona. *Normalizing the Ideal: Psychology, Schooling and the Family in Postwar Canada.* Toronto: University of Toronto Press, 1999.

Gordon, Linda. *Heroes of Their Own Lives: The Politics and History of Family Violence.* New York: Penguin Books, 1988.

– *Pitied but Not Entitled: Single Mothers and the History of Welfare.* Cambridge, MA: Harvard University Press, 1994.

Hagan, J., and B. McCarthy. *Mean Streets: Youth Crime and Homelessness.* Cambridge: Cambridge University Press, 1997.

Hannah-Moffat, Kelly. *Punishment in Disguise: Penal Governance and Federal Imprisonment of Women in Canada.* Toronto: University of Toronto Press, 2001.

Holloran, Peter. *Boston's Wayward Children: Services for Homeless Children, 1830–1930.* Boston: Northeastern University Press, 1994.

Hunt, Allan. *Governing Morals: A Society History of Moral Regulation.* Cambridge: Cambridge University Press, 1999.

Iacovetta, Franca, and Wendy Mitchinson, eds. *On the Case: Explorations in Social History.* Toronto: University of Toronto Press, 1999.

Ignatieff, Michael. *A Just Measure of Pain: The Penitentiary in the Industrial Revolution, 1750–1850.* London: Macmillan, 1978.

Jones, Kathleen W. *Taming the Troublesome Child: American Families, Child Guidance, and the Limits of Psychiatric Authority* Cambridge, MA: Harvard University Press, 1999.

Joyal, Renée, ed. *Entre surveillance et compassion: l'évolution de la protection de l'enfance au Québec: des origines à nos jours.* Sainte-Foy: Les Presses de l'Université du Québec, 2000.

Keshen, Jeffrey A. *Saints, Sinners, and Soldiers: Canada's Second World War.* Vancouver: UBC Press, 2004.

King, Joe. *From the Ghetto to the Main: The Story of the Jews of Montreal.* Montreal: Montreal Jewish Publication Society, 2001.

Knupfer, Anne Meis. *Reform and Resistance: Gender, Delinquency, and America's First Juvenile Court.* New York: Routledge, 2001.

Koven, Seth, and Sonya Michel, eds. *Mothers of a New World: Maternalist Politics and the Origins of Welfare States.* New York: Routledge, 1993.

Kunzel, Regina G. *Fallen Women, Problem Girls: Unmarried Mothers and the Professionalization of Social Work, 1890–1945.* New Haven, CT: Yale University Press, 1993.

Lacasse, Danielle. *La prostitution féminine à Montréal, 1945–1970.* Montreal: Boréal, 1994.

Lacelle, Claudette. *Urban Domestic Servants in 19th-Century Canada.* Ottaw: National Historic Parks and Sites, Environment Canada-Parks, 1987.

Ladd-Taylor, Molly. *Mother-Work: Women, Child Welfare, and the State, 1890–1930.* Urbana: University of Illinois Press, 1994.

Lamonde, Yvan, and Raymond Montpetit. *Le Parc Sohmer de Montreal, 1889–1919: un lieu populaire de culture urbaine.* Quebec: Institut Québécois de Recherche sur la Culture, 1986.

Langlais, Jacques, and David Rome. *Jews and French Quebecers: Two Hundred Years of Shared History.* Waterloo, ON: Wilfrid Laurier University Press, 1991.

Laplante, Jacques. *Prison et ordre social au Québec.* Ottawa: Les Presses de l'Université d'Ottawa, 1989.

Lapointe-Roy, Huguette. *Charité bien ordonnée: le premier réseau de lutte contre la pauvreté à Montréal au 19e siècle.* Montreal: Boréal, 1987.

Lemieux, Denise, et Lucie Mercier. *Les femmes au tournant du siècle 1880–1940.* Saint-Laurent, QC: Institut québécois de recherche sur la culture, 1989.

Lévesque, Andrée. *Making and Breaking the Rules: Women in Quebec, 1919–1939.* Toronto: McClelland and Stewart, 1994.

Linteau, Paul-André. *Histoire de Montréal depuis la Confédération.* 2nd ed. Montreal: Editions Boréal, 2000.

Little, Margaret. *'No Car, No Radio, No Liquor Permit': The Moral Regulation of Single Mothers in Ontario, 1920–1997.* Toronto: Oxford University Press, 1998.

Lunbeck, Elizabeth. *The Psychiatric Persuasion: Knowledge, Gender, and Power in Modern America* Princeton, NJ: Princeton University Press, 1994.

Mahood, Linda. *Policing Gender, Class and Family.* Edmonton: University of Alberta Press, 1995.

Malouin, Marie-Paule. *L'univers des enfants en difficulté au Québec entre 1940 et 1960.* Montreal: Bellarmin, 1996.

– *Ma soeur, à quelle école allez-vous? Deux écoles de filles à la fin du XIXe siècle.* Montreal: Fides, 1985.

Marchand, Suzanne. *Rouge à lèvres et pantalon: des pratiques esthétiques féminines controversées au Québec, 1920–1939.* Montreal: Editions Hurtubise, 1997.

Marquis, Greg. *Policing Canada's Century: A History of the Canadian Association of Chiefs of Police.* Toronto: University of Toronto Press, 1994.

McLaren, Angus. *'Our Own Master Race': Eugenics in Canada, 1885–1945.* Toronto: McClelland and Stewart, 1990.

McLaren, John, Robert Menzies, and Dorothy E. Chunn, eds. *Regulating Lives: Historical Essays on the State, Society, the Individual, and the Law.* Vancouver: UBC Press, 2002.

Ménard, Sylvie. *Des enfants sous surveillance: la rééducation des jeunes délinquants au Québec (1840–1950).* Montreal: vlb éditeur, 2003.

Meyerowitz, Joanne. *Women Adrift: Independent Wage Earners in Chicago, 1880–1930.* Chicago: University of Chicago Press, 1988.

Odem, Mary E. *Delinquent Daughters: Protecting and Policing Adolescent Female Sexuality in the United States, 1885–1920.* Chapel Hill: University of North Carolina Press, 1995.

Peiss, Kathy. *Cheap Amusements: Working Women and Leisure in Turn-of-the-Century New York.* Philadelphia: Temple University Press, 1985.

Petot, Pierre. *Histoire du droit privé français: La famille.* Paris: Editions Loysel, 1992.

Platt, Anthony. *The Child-Savers: The Invention of Delinquency.* Chicago: University of Chicago Press, 1969.

Pleck, Elizabeth. *Domestic Tyranny: The Making of American Social Policy Against Family Violence.* New York, Oxford University Press, 1987.

Pue, W. Wesley, and Barry Wright, eds. *Canadian Perspectives on Law and Society: Issues in Legal History.* Ottawa: Carleton University Press, 1988.

Rafter, Nicole Hahn *Partial Justice: Women in State Prisons 1800–1935.* Boston: Northeastern University Press, 1985.

Rafter, Nicole Hahn, and E. Stanko, eds. *Judge, Lawyer, Victim, Thief: Women, Gender Roles, and Criminal Justice.* Boston: Northeastern University Press, 1982.

Rains, Prue and Eli Teram. *Normal Bad Boys: Public Policies, Institutions, and the Politics of Client Recruitment.* Montreal and Kingston: McGill-Queen's, University Press, 1992.

Richardson, Theresa R. *The Century of the Child: The Mental Hygiene Movement and Social Policy in the United States and Canada.* Albany: State University of New York Press, 1989.

Riley, Denise. *'Am I That Name?': Feminism and the Category of 'Woman' in History.* Minneapolis: University of Minnesota Press, 1988.

Robinson, Ira and Mervin Butovsky, eds. *Renewing Our Days: Montreal Jews in the Twentieth Century*. Montreal: Véhicule Press, 1995.

Rooke, Patricia, and R.L. Schnell, *Discarding the Asylum: From Child Rescue to the Welfare State in English Canada*. Lanham, MD: University Press of America, 1983.

Rosen, Ruth and Sue Davidson, eds. *The Maimie Papers*. Indianapolis: Feminist Press, 1977.

Ross, Dorothy. *G. Stanley Hall: The Psychologist as Prophet*. Chicago: University of Chicago Press, 1972.

Rothman, David J. *The Discovery of the Asylum: Social Order and Disorder in the New Republic* Boston: Little, Brown 1971.

Roy, Fernande. *Histoire des idéologies au Québec aux XIXe et XXe siècles*. Montreal: Les Éditions du Boréal, 1993.

Ryan, Mary. *Women in Public: Between Banners and the Ballots, 1825–1880*. Baltimore: Johns Hopkins University Press, 1990.

Sangster, Joan. *Girl Trouble: Female Delinquency in English Canada*. Peterborough, ON: Broadview Press, 2002.

– *Regulating Girls and Women: Sexuality, Family, and the Law in Ontario, 1920–1960*. Toronto: Oxford University Press, 2001.

Scharff, Virginia. *Taking the Wheel: Women and the Coming of the Motor Age*. New York: Free Press, 1991.

Schissel, Bernard. *Blaming Children: Youth Crime, Moral Panics and the Politics of Hate*. Halifax: Fernwood Publishing, 1997.

Schissel, Bernard, and Linda Mahood, eds. *Social Control in Canada*. Toronto: Oxford University Press, 1996.

Schlossman, Steven. *Love and the American Delinquent: The Theory and Practice of 'Progressive' Juvenile Justice, 1825–1920*. Chicago: University of Chicago Press, 1977 (reprinted as Transforming Juvenile Justice: Reform Ideals and Institutional Realities, 1825–1920 [(Chicago and De Kalb, Northern Illinois Press, 2005)]).

Schneider, Eric. *In the Web of Class: Delinquents and Reformers in Boston, 1810s–1930s*. New York: New York University Press, 1992.

Smith, Dorothy E. *The Conceptual Practices of Power: A Feminist Sociology of Knowledge*. Toronto: University of Toronto Press, 1990.

Stansell, Christine. *City of Women: Sex and Class in New York, 1789–1860*. New York: Alfred A. Knopf, 1986.

Strange, Carolyn. *Toronto's Girl Problem: The Perils and Pleasures of the City, 1880–1930*. Toronto: University of Toronto Press, 1995.

Strange, Carolyn, and Tina Loo. *Making Good: Law and Moral Regulation in Canada, 1867–1939*. Toronto: University of Toronto Press, 1997.

Sumner, Colin. *The Sociology of Deviance: An Obituary.* London: Continuum, 1994.

Sutherland, Neil. *Children in English-Canadian Society: Framing the Twentieth-Century Consensus.* Toronto: University of Toronto Press, 1976.

Sylvain, Philippe, and Nive Voisine. *Histoire du catholicisme québécois: les XVIIIe et XIXe siècles.* Vol. 2. *Réveil et consolidation 1840–1898.* Montreal: Boréal, 1991.

Tice, Karen W. *Tales of Wayward Girls and Immoral Women: Case Records and the Professionalization of Social Work.* Urbana: University of Illinois Press, 1999.

Trépanier, Jean, and Françoise Tulkens. *Délinquance et protection de la jeunesse aux sources des lois belges et canadiennes sur l'enfance.* Montreal and Ottawa: Les Presses de l'Université de Montréal et de l'Ottawa, 1995.

Trofimenkoff, Susan Mann. *The Dream of Nation: A Social and Intellectual History of Quebec* Toronto: Gage Publishing, 1982.

Tulchinsky, Gerald. *Taking Root: The Origins of the Canadian Jewish Community.* Toronto: Lester Publishing Limited, 1992.

Turmel, Jean. *Police de Montréal, historique du service: premières structures et evolution de la police de Montreal: 1796–1971.* Vols. 1 and 2. Montreal: Service de la police de la CUM, 1971–4.

Valverde, Mariana. *The Age of Soap, Light and Water: Moral Reform in English Canada, 1885–1925.* Toronto: McClelland and Stewart, 1991.

Vicinus, Martha. *Independent Women: Work and Community for Single Women, 1850–1920.* Chicago: University of Chicago Press, 1985.

Walkowitz, Daniel J. *Working with Class: Social Workers and the Politics of Middle-Class Identity* Chapel Hill: University of North Carolina Press, 1999.

Walkowitz, Judith. *City of Dreadful Delight: Narratives of Sexual Danger in Late-Victorian London.* Chicago: University of Chicago Press, 1992.

Weiner, Deborah E.B. *Architecture and Social Reform in Late-Victorian London.* Manchester and New York: Manchester University Press, 1994.

Wright, Gwendolyn. *Moralism and the Model Home: Domestic Architecture and Cultural Conflict in Chicago, 1873–1913.* Chicago: University of Chicago Press, 1980.

Zedner, Lucia. *Women, Crime, and Custody in Victorian England.* Oxford: University of Oxford Press, 1991.

Articles

Adams, Annmarie. 'Rooms of Their Own: The Nurses' Residences at Montreal's Royal Victoria Hospital.' *Material History Review* 40 (Fall 1994): 29–41.

Adams, Mary Louise. 'Almost Anything Can Happen: A Search for Sexual Discourse in the Urban Spaces of 1940s Toronto.' *Canadian Journal of Sociology* 19:2 (1994): 217–33.

– 'In Sickness and in Health: State Formation, Moral Regulation, and Early VD Initiatives in Ontario.' *Journal of Canadian Studies* 28:4 (Winter 1993–4): 117–30.

Adler, Jeffrey S. 'Streetwalkers, Degraded Outcasts, and Good-for-Nothing Huzzies: Women and the Dangerous Class in Antebellum St. Louis.' *Journal of Social History* 25:4 (1992): 737–55.

– 'Vagging the Demons and Scoundrels: Vagrancy and the Growth of St. Louis, 1830–1861.' *Journal of Urban History* 13 (November 1986): 3–30.

Alaimo, Kathleen. 'Shaping Adolescence in the Popular Milieu: Social Policy, Reformers, and French Youth, 1870–1920.' *Journal of Family History* 17:4 (1992): 419–38.

Anctil, Pierre. 'Interlude of Hostility: Judeo-Christian Relations in Quebec in the Interwar Period, 1919–1939.' In *Quebec since 1800: Selected Readings*, ed. Michael D. Behiels, 396–423. Toronto: Irwin Publishing, 2002.

Baillargeon, Denyse. 'L'Assistance maternelle de Montréal (1912–1961): un exemple de marginalisation des bénévoles dans le domaine des soins aux accouchées.' *Dynamis* 19 (1999): 379–400.

– 'Fréquenter les Gouttes de lait: l'expérience des mères montréalaises, 1910–1965.' *Revue d'histoire de l'Amérique française* 50, 1 (1996): 29–68.

Baldwin, Peter C. 'Nocturnal Habits and Dark Wisdom: The American Response to Children in the Streets at Night, 1880–1930.' *Journal of Social History* 35:3 (2002): 593–611.

Beaulieu, Judge Lucien. 'A Comparison of Judicial Roles under the JDA and YOA.' In *The Young Offenders Act: A Revolution in Canadian Juvenile Justice*, ed. Alan W. Leschied, Peter G. Jaffe, and Wayne Willis, 128–45. Toronto: University of Toronto Press, 1991.

Bennett, Paul W. 'Taming 'Bad Boys' of the 'Dangerous Class': Child Rescue and Restraint at the Victoria Industrial School, 1887–1935.' *Histoire sociale / Social History* 21:41 (May 1988): 71–96.

Boris, Eileen. 'Restructuring the "Family": Women, Progressive Reform, and the Problem of Social Control.' In *Gender, Class, Race, and Reform in the Progressive Era* ed. Noralee Frankel and Nancy S. Dye, 110–126. Lexington: University of Kentucky Press, 1991.

Boyer, Kate. 'Place and the Politics of Virtue: Clerical Work, Corporate Anxiety, and Changing Meanings of Public Womanhood in Early Twentieth-Century Montreal.' *Gender, Place and Culture* 5:3 (1998): 261–76.

– 'What's a Girl Like You Doing in a Place Like This? A Geography of Sexual Violence in Early 20th-Century Vancouver.' *Urban Geography* 17 (1996): 286–93.

Bradbury, Bettina. 'Gender at Work at Home: Family Decisions, the Labour Market, and Girls' Contributions to the Family Economy.' In *Canadian Family History*, ed. Bettina Bradbury, 177–98. Toronto: Copp Clark Pitman, 1993.

– 'Pigs, Cows and Boarders: Non-wage Forms of Survival among Montreal Families, 1861–91.' *Labour / Le Travail* 14 (Fall 1984): 4–46.

Bullen, John. 'J.J. Kelso and the "New" Child-Savers: The Genesis of the Children's Aid Movement in Ontario.' In *Dimensions of Childhood*, ed. Russell Smandych, Gordon Dodds, and Alvin Esau, 135–58. Winnipeg: Winnipeg: Legal Research Institute, 1991.

Cahn, Susan. 'Spirited Youth or Fiends Incarnate: The Samarcand Arson Case and Female Adolescence in the American South.' *Journal of Women's History* 9:4 (Winter 1998): 152–80.

Cale, Michelle. 'Girls and the Perception of Sexual Danger in the Victorian Reformatory System.' *History* 78:253 (June, 1993): 201–17.

Canning, Kathleen. 'Feminist History after the Linguistic Turn: Historicizing Discourse and Experience.' *Signs* 19:2 (Winter 1994): 368–404.

Carlisle, Marcia. 'Disorderly City, Disorderly Women: Prostitution in Ante-Bellum Philadelphia.' *Pennsylvania Magazine of History and Biography* 110:4 (1986): 549–68.

Chesney-Lind, Meda. 'Girls' Crime and Woman's Place: Toward a Feminist Model of Female Delinquency.' *Crime and Delinquency* 35:1 (January 1989): 5–29.

– 'Women and Crime: The Female Offender.' *Signs* 12:1 (Autumn 1986): 78–96.

Chunn, Dorothy E. 'Boys Will Be Men, Girls Will Be Mothers: The Legal Regulation of Childhood in Toronto and Vancouver.' *Sociological Studies in Child Development* 3 (1990): 87–110.

– '"Just Plain Everyday Housekeeping on a Grand Scale": Feminists, Family Courts, and the Welfare State in British Columbia, 1928–1945.' In *Law, Society, and the State: Essays in Modern Legal History*, ed. Louis Knafla and Susan Binnie. Toronto: University of Toronto Press, 1995.

– 'Maternal Feminism, Legal Professionalism and Political Pragmatism: The Rise and Fall of Magistrate Margaret Patterson, 1922–1934.' In *Canadian Perspectives on Law and Society: Issues in Legal History*, ed. W. Wesley Pue and Barry Wright, 91–117. Ottawa: Carleton University Press, 1988.

Clapp, Elizabeth J. 'Welfare and the Role of Women: The Juvenile Court Movement.' *Journal of American Studies* 28 (1994): 359–83.

Cliche, Marie-Aimée. 'Est-ce une bonne méthode pour élever les enfants? Un debat sur punitions corporelles dans les courriers du coeur au Québec, 1925 à 1969.' *Canadian Historical Review* 82:4 (2001): 662–89.

– 'Les filles-mères devant les tribunaux de Québec, 1850–1969.' *Recherches sociographiques* 32:1 (1991): 9–42.

– '"Un secret bien gardé": L'inceste dans la société traditionelle québécoise, 1858–1938.' *Revue d'histoire de l'Amérique française* 50:2 (Autumn 1996): 201–26.

– 'Survivre à l'inceste dans les maison du Bon-Pasteur de Québec, 1930–1973.' *Nouvelles pratiques sociales* 14:2 (December 2001): 122–43.

Comacchio, Cynthia. 'Dancing to Perdition: Adolescence and Leisure in Interwar English Canada.' *Journal of Canadian Studies* (Autumn 1997): 5–35.

– '"The Rising Generation": Laying Claim to the Health of Adolescents in English Canada, 1920–1970.' *Canadian Bulletin of Medical History* 19 (2002): 139–78.

Coughlan, D.W.F. 'The History and Function of Probation.' In *Lawful Authority: Readings on the History of Criminal Justice in Canada*, ed. R.C. Macleod, 265–76. Toronto: Copp Clark Pitman, 1988.

Davies, Andrew. '"These Viragoes are no less cruel than the lads": Young Women, Gangs and Violence in Late Victorian Manchester and Salford.' *British Journal of Criminology* 39:1 (1999): 72–89.

Dubinsky, Karen and Adam Givertz. 'It Was Only a Matter of Passion: Masculinity and Sexual Danger.' In *Gendered Pasts: Historical Essays in Femininity and Masculinity in Canada*, ed. Kathryn McPherson, Cecilia Morgan, and Nancy M. Forrestell, 65–79. Toronto: Oxford University Press, 1999.

Dubois, Pierre, and Jean Trépanier. 'L'adoption de la loi sur les jeunes délinquants de 1908: études comparées des quotidiens montréalais et torontois,' *Revue d'histoire de l'Amérique française* 52:3 (Winter 1999): 345–81.

Fecteau, Jean-Marie. 'La construction d'un espace social: les rapports de l'église et de l'état et la question de l'assistance publique au Québec dans la seconde moitié du XIXe siècle.' In *L'histoire de la culture et de l'imprimé*, ed. Yvan Lamonde and G. Gallichan, 61–90. Quebec: Presses de l'Université Laval, 1996.

Fecteau, Jean-Marie, Sylvie Ménard, Jean Trépanier, and Véronique Strimelle. 'Une politique de l'enfance délinquante et en danger: la mise en place des écoles de réforme et d'industrie au Québec (1840–1873). *Crime, Histoire, Société* 1:2 (1998): 75–110.

Ferdinand, Theodore N. 'History Overtakes the Juvenile Justice System.' *Crime and Delinquency* 37:2 (April 1991): 204–24.

Gilfoyle, Timothy. 'Street-Rats and Gutter-Snipes: Child Pickpockets and Street Culture in New York City, 1850–1900.' *Journal of Social History* 37:4 (Summer 2004): 853–70.

Glasbeek, Amanda. 'Maternalism Meets the Criminal Law: The Case of the Toronto Women's Court.' *Canadian Journal of Women and the Law* 10 (1998): 480–502.

Golz, Annalee. 'Uncovering and Reconstructing Family Violence: Ontario Criminal Case Files.' In *On the Case: Explorations in Social History*, ed. Franca Iacovetta and Wendy Mitchinson, 289–311. Toronto: University of Toronto Press, 1999.

Gordon, Linda. 'Family Violence, Feminism and Social Control.' In *Unequal Sisters: A Multicultural Reader in U.S. Women's History*, ed. Ellen Carol Dubois and Vicki L. Ruiz, 141–156. New York: Routledge, 1990. .

– 'Feminism and Social Control: The Case of Child Abuse and Neglect.' In *What Is Feminism? A Reexamination*, ed. Juliet Mitchell and Ann Oakley, 63–84. New York: Pantheon Books, 1986.

Gossage, Peter. 'La marâtre: Marie-Anne Houde and the Myth of the Wicked Stepmother in Quebec.' *Canadian Historical Review* 76:4 (December 1995): 563–97.

Haine, W. Scott. 'The Development of Leisure and the Transformation of Working-Class Adolescence, Paris, 1830–1940.' *Journal of Family History* 17:4 (1992): 451–76.

Harvey, Kathryn. 'To Love, Honour and Obey: Wife-Battering in Working Class Montreal, 1869–79.' *Urban History Review* 2 (October 1990): 128–40.

Hatch, Alison J., and Curt T. Griffiths. 'Child Saving Postponed: The Impact of the Juvenile Delinquents Act on the Processing of Young Offenders in Vancouver.' In *Dimensions of Childhood*, ed. Russell Smandych, Gordon Dodds, and Alvin Esau, 233–66. Winnepeg: Legal Research Institute, 1991.

Hébert, Karine. 'Une organisation maternaliste au Québec: la Fédération nationale St-Jean-Baptiste et la bataille pour le vote des femmes.' *Revue d'histoire de l'Amérique française* 52:3 (Winter 1999): 315–44.

Horowitz, Helen Lefkowitz. 'Hull-House as Women's Space.' *Chicago History* 12 (1983): 40–55.

Houston, Susan. 'The 'Waifs and Strays' of a Late Victorian City: Juvenile Delinquents in Toronto.' In *Childhood and Family in Canadian History*, ed. Joy Parr, 129–42. Toronto: McClelland and Stewart, 1982.

Hubbard, Phil. 'Sexuality, Immorality and the City: Red-Light Districts and the Marginalisation of Female Street Prostitutes.' *Gender, Place and Culture* 5:1 (1998): 55–72.

Hurl, Lorna F., and David J. Tucker. 'The Michigan County Agents and the Development of Juvenile Probation, 1873–1900.' *Journal of Social History* 30:4 (Summer 1997): 905–35.

Iacovetta, Franca. 'Delinquent Girls, Working-Class Parents, and the Family Courts.' In *On the Case: Explorations in Social History*, Franca Iacovetta and Wendy Mitchinson, 312–37. Toronto: University of Toronto Press, 1999.

– *'Gossip, Contest and Power in the Making of Suburban Bad Girls: Toronto, 1945–60.' Canadian Historical Review* 80 (1999): 585–623.

Joyal, Renée. 'L'act concernant les écoles d'industrie (1869): une mesure de prophylaxie sociale dans un Québec en voie d'urbanisation.' *Revue d'histoire de l'Amérique française* 50:2 (Fall 1996): 227–40.

– 'L'évolution des modes de contrôle de l'autorité parentale.' *International Journal of Canadian Studies* (Winter 1993): 73–84.

Keshen, Jeffrey. 'Wartime Jitters over Juveniles: Canada's Delinquency Scare and Its Consequences, 1939–1945.' In *Age of Contention: Readings in Canadian Social History, 1900–45*, ed. Jeffrey Keshen, 364–86. Toronto: Harcourt Brace, 1997.

Koven, Seth, and Sonya Michel. 'Womanly Duties: Maternalist Politics and the Origins of Welfare States in France, Germany, Great Britain, and the United States.' *American Historical Review* 95 (October 1995): 1076–108.

Knupfer, Anne Meis. '"Rectifying ... the hampering causes of delinquency": The Chicago Home for Girls, 1900–1935.' *Journal of Illinois History* 2 (Spring 1999): 17–38.

Lacasse, Danielle. 'Du délinquant à ouvrier qualifié: Le Mont-Saint-Antoine, 1945–1964.' *Histoire sociale / Social History* 22:44 (November 1989): 287–316.

Lavigne, Marie, Yolande Pinard, and Jennifer Stoddart. 'La Fédération Nationale Saint-Jean-Baptiste et les revendications féministe au début du 20 siècle.' In *Travailleuses et féministes: les femmes dans la société québécoise*, ed. Marie Lavigne and Yolande Pinard, 199–16. Montreal: Boréal, 1977.

Lavigne, Marie, and Jennifer Stoddart. 'Ouvrières et travailleuses montréalaises, 1900–1940.' In *Travailleuses et feministes. les Femmes dans la société québécoise*, ed. Marie Lavigne and Yolande Pinard, 125–43. Montreal: Boréal Express, 1983.

Leon, Jeffrey S. 'The Development of Canadian Juvenile Justice: A Background for Reform.' *Osgoode Hall Law Journal* 15 (1977): 71–106.

Leschied, Alan W., and Peter G. Jaffe. 'Dispositions as Indicators of Conflicting Social Purposes Under the JDA and YOA.' In *The Young Offenders Act: A Revolution in Canadian Juvenile Justice*, ed. Alan W. Leschied, Peter G. Jaffe, and Wayne Willis, 158–690. Toronto: University of Toronto Press, 1991.

Lévesque, Andrée. 'Eteindre le red light: les réformateurs et la prostitution à Montréal entre 1865 et 1925.' *Urban History Review* 17:3 (February 1989): 191–201.

– 'Mères celibataires et infanticides à Montréal, 1914–1930.' In *Femmes et justice pénale, XIX–XX siècles*, ed. Christine Bard, Frédéric Chauvaud, Michelle Perrot, et Jacques-Guy Petit. Rennes: Presses Universitaires de Rennes, 2002.

Littlewood, Barbara, and Linda Mahood. 'Prostitutes, Magdalenes, and Wayward Girls: Dangerous Sexualities of Working-Class Women in Victorian Scotland.' *Gender and History* 3 (1991): 160–75.

Matters, Indiana. 'The Boys Industrial School: Education for Juvenile Offenders.' In *Schooling and Society in Twentieth Century British Columbia*, eds. Donald Wilson and David C. Jones, 53–70. Calgary: Detselig, 1980.

– 'Sinners or Sinned Against? Historical Aspects of Female Juvenile Delinquency in British Columbia.' In *Not Just Pin Money: Selected Essays on the History of Women's Work in British Columbia*, ed. Barbara Latham and Roberta Pazdro. Victoria: Camosun College, 1984.

Maynard, Steven. 'Horrible Temptations: Sex, Men, and Working-Class Male Youth in Urban Ontario, 1890–1935.' *Canadian Historical Review* 78:2 (June 1997).

– 'Through a Hole in the Lavatory Wall: Homosexual Subcultures, Police Surveillance and the Dialectics of Discovery.' *Journal of the History of Sexuality* 5 (1994): 207–41.

McGahan, Elizabeth W. 'Inside the Hallowed Walls: Convent Life through Material History.' *Material History Bulletin* 25 (Spring 1987): 1–10.

Myers, Tamara. 'On Probation: The Rise and Fall of Jewish Women's Antidelinquency Work in Interwar Montreal.' In *Negotiating Identities in 19th- and 20th-Century Montreal*, ed. Bettina Bradbury and Tamara Myers, 175–201. Vancouver: UBC Press, 2005.

– 'Qui t'a débauchée? Female Adolescent Sexuality and the Juvenile Delinquents' Court in Early Twentieth-Century Montreal.' In *Family Matters: Papers in Post-Confederation Canadian Family History*, ed. Lori Chambers and Ed Montigny, 377–94. Toronto: Canadian Scholars Press, 1998).

– 'The Voluntary Delinquent: Parents, Daughters and the Montreal Juvenile Delinquents' Court, 1918.' *Canadian Historical Review* 80:2 (June 1999): 242–68.

– 'Women Policing Women: A Patrol Woman in Montreal in the 1910s.' *Journal of the Canadian Historical Association* (1993): 229–45.

Myers, Tamara, and Joan Sangster. 'Retorts, Runaways and Riots: Patterns of Resistance in Canadian Reform Schools for Girls.' *Journal of Social History* (USA) 34:3 (Spring 2001): 669–97.

Noel, Jan. 'Women and Social Welfare in the Montreal Region, 1800–1833.' In *Changing Roles of Women in the Christian Church in Canada*, ed. L. Muir and M. Whitely, 284–98. Toronto: University of Toronto Press, 1995.

Odem, Mary E. 'Fallen Women and Thieving Ladies: Historical Approaches to Women and Crime in the United States.' *Law and Social Inquiry: Journal of the American Bar Foundation* 17:2 (1992): 351–62.

– 'Single Mothers, Delinquent Daughters, and the Juvenile Court in Early 20th-Century Los Angeles.' *Journal of Social History* 25 (Fall 1991): 27–43.

Oliver, Peter. 'To Govern by Kindness: The First Two Decades of the Mercer Reformatory for Women.' In *Essays in the History of Canadian Law*, vol. v. *Crime and Criminal Justice History*. ed. Jim Phillips, Tina Loo, and Susan Lewthwaite, 516–71. Toronto: Osgoode Society, 1994.

Parker, Graham. 'The Legal Regulation of Sexual Activity and the Protection of Females.' *Osgoode Hall Law Journal* 21 (1983): 187–224.

Pedersen, Diana. '"Building for the Womanhood of Tomorrow": Businessmen, Boosters and the YWCA, 1890–1930.' *Urban History Review* 15:3 (February 1987): 225–42.

Pedersen, Susan. 'Catholicism, Feminism, and the Politics of the Family during the Late Third Republic.' In *Mothers of a New World: Maternalistic Politics and the Origins of Welfare States*, ed. S. Koven and S. Michel, 246–76. New York: Routledge, 1993.

Pierre, Éric, and David Niget. 'Filles et garçons devant le tribunal des enfants et adolescents d'Angers de 1914 et 1940: un traitement différencié.' In *Femmes et justice pénale, XIX–XX siècles*, ed. Christine Bard, Frédéric Chauvaud, Michelle Perrot, and Jacques-Guy Petit, 327–38. Rennes: Presses Universitaires de Rennes, 2002.

Ploszajska, T. 'Moral Landscapes and Manipulated Spaces: Gender, Class and Space in Victorian Reformatory Schools.' *Journal of Historical Geography* 20:4 (1994): 413–29.

Quinn, Peter. '"We ask for bread and are given stone": The Girls Industrial School, Parramatta, 1941–1961.' *Journal of the Royal Australian Historical Society* 75:2 (1989): 158–72.

Reitsma-Street, Marge. 'Girls Learn to Care; Girls Policed to Care.' In *Women's Caring: Feminist Perspectives on Social Welfare*, ed. Carol Baines, Patricia Evans, and Sheila Neysmith, 106–37. Toronto: McClelland and Stewart, 1991.

Sangster, Joan. 'Creating Social and Moral Citizens: Defining and Treating Delinquent Boys and Girls in English Canada, 1920–65.' In *Contesting Canadian Citizenship: Historical Readings*, ed. Robert Adamoski, Dorothy E. Chunn, and Robert Menzies. Peterborough, ON: Broadview Press, 2002.

– 'Incarcerating "Bad Girls": The Regulation of Sexuality through the Female Refuges Act in Ontario, Canada, 1920–45.' *Journal of the History of Sexuality* 7:2 (1996): 239–75.

– 'Masking and Unmasking the Sexual Abuse of Children: Perceptions of Violence against Children in the "Badlands" of Ontario, 1916–1930.' *Journal of Family History* 25: 4 (October 2000): 504–26.

– '"Pardon Tales" from Magistrate's Court: Women, Crime, and the Court in Peterborough County, 1920–50.' *Canadian Historical Review* 74:2 (June 1993): 161–97.

Satzewich, Vic, and Li Zong. 'Social Control and the Historical Construction of "Race."' In *Social Control in Canada*, ed. Bernard Schissel and Linda Mahood, 263–87. Toronto: Oxford University Press, 1996.

Schlossman, Steven, and Mary Odem. 'Guardians of Virtue: The Juvenile Court and Female Delinquency in Early 20th-Century Los Angeles.' *Crime and Delinquency* 37:2 (April 1991): 186–203.

Schlossman, Steven, and Stephanie Wallach. 'The Crime of Precocious Sexuality: Female Juvenile Delinquency in the Progressive Era.' *Harvard Educational Review* 48:1 (February 1978): 65–95.

Shore, Heather. 'Cross Coves, Buzzers, and General Sorts of Prigs: Juvenile Crime and the Criminal "Underworld" in the Early Nineteenth Century.' *British Journal of Criminology* 39:1 (1999): 10–24.

Simons, R.L., and L. B. Whitebeck, 'Sexual Abuse as a Precursor to Prostitution and Victimization among Adolescent and Adult Homeless Women.' *Journal of Family Issues* 12:3 (September 1991): 361–79.

Smart, Carol. 'Disruptive Bodies and Unruly Sex: The Regulation of Reproduction and Sexuality in the Nineteenth Century.' In *Regulating Womanhood: Historical Essays on Marriage, Motherhood, and Sexuality*, ed. Carol Smart, 7–32. London: Routledge, 1992.

Smith, David. 'Juvenile Delinquency in Britain in the First World War.' *Criminal Justice History* 11 (1990): 116–45.

Smyth, Elizabeth. 'Professionalization among the Professed: The Case of Roman Catholic Women Religious.' In *Challenging Professions: Historical and Contemporary Perspectives on Women's Professional Work*, ed. E. Smyth et al., 234–54. Toronto: University of Toronto Press, 1999.

Stephen, Jennifer.'The "Incorrigible," the "Bad," and the "Immoral": Toronto's "Factory Girls" and the Work of the Toronto Psychiatric Clinic.' In *Law, Society, and the State: Essays in Modern Legal History*, ed. Louis A. Knafla and Susan W.S. Binnie, 405–39. Toronto: University of Toronto Press, 1995.

Strange, Carolyn. '"The Criminal and Fallen of Their Sex": The Establishment of Canada's First Women's Prison, 1874–1901.' *Canadian Journal of Women and the Law* 1:1 (1985): 79–92.

– 'From Modern Babylon to a City upon a Hill: The Toronto Social Survey Commission of 1915 and the Search for Sexual Order in the City.' In *Patterns of the Past*, ed. Roger Hall, William Westfall, and Laurel Sefton MacDowell, 255–77. Toronto: Dundurn Press, 1988.

– 'Patriarchy Modified: The Criminal Prosecution of Rape in York County, Ontario, 1880–1930.' In *Crime and Criminal Justice: Essays in the History of Canadian Law*, ed. Jim Phillips, Tina Loo, and Susan Lewthwaite, 207–51. Toronto: The Osgoode Society, 1994.

Taylor, C.J. 'The Kingston, Ontario Penitentiary and Moral Architecture.' *Histoire sociale / Social History* 12:24 (November 1979): 385–408.

Théorêt, Bruno. 'Psychiatry, Juvenile Justice, and Delinquent Identity: A Case Study at the Juvenile Court of Winnipeg, 1930–1959.' *Journal of Human Justice* 6:1 (Autumn 1994): 64–77.

– 'Régulation juridique pénale des mineur-es et discrimination à l'égard des filles: la clause de 1924 amendant la loi sur les jeunes délinquants.' *Canadian Journal of Women and the Law* 4 (1990–91): 539–555.

Tremblay, Pierre. 'L'évolution de l'emprisonnement pénitentiare, de son intensité, de sa fermeté et de sa portée: le cas de Montréal de 1845 à 1913.' *Canadian Journal of Criminology* 28:1 (1986): 47–68.

Tremblay, P., and G. Therriault. 'La punition commune du crime: la prison et l'amende à Montréal de 1845 à 1913.' *Criminologie* 18:1 (1985).

Trépanier, Jean. 'Origins of the Juvenile Delinquents Act of 1908: Controlling Delinquency through Seeking Its Causes and through Youth Protection.' In *Dimensions of Childhood*, ed. Russell Smandych, Gordon Dodds, and Alvin Esau, 205–31. Winnipeg: Legal Research Institute, 1991.

– 'Protéger pour prévenir la délinquance: l'émergence de la Loi sur les jeunes délinquants de 1908 et sa mise en application à Montréal.' In *Entre surveillance et compassion: l'évolution de la protection de l'enfance au Québec: des origines à nos jours*, ed. Renée Joyal, 49–95. Sainte-Foy: Les Presses de l'Université du Québec, 2000.

Trépanier, Jean, and Lucie Quevillon. 'Garçons et filles: la définition des problèmes posés par les mineurs traduits à la cour des jeunes délinquants de Montréal (1912–1950).' In *Femmes et justice pénale, XIX–XX siècles*, ed. Christine Bard, Frédéric Chauvaud, Michelle Perrot, and Jacques-Guy Petit, 339–52. Rennes: Presses Universitaires de Rennes, 2002.

Whitbeck, L.B., and R.L. Simons, 'Life on the Streets: The Victimization of Runaway and Homeless Adolescents.' *Youth and Society* 22:1 (September 1990): 108–25.

Wimhurst, Kerry. 'Control and Resistance: Reformatory Girls in Late Nineteenth Century South Australia.' *Journal of Social History* 18 (Winter 1984): 273–87.

Wolcott, David. 'Juvenile Justice before Juvenile Courts: Cops, Courts, and Kids in Turn-of-the-Century Detroit.' *Social Science History* 27:6 (2003): 109–36.

– 'The Cop Will Get You': The Police and Discretionary Juvenile Justice, 1890–1940.' *Journal of Social History* 35:2 (2001): 349–71.

Young, Brian. 'Édouard-Charles Fabre.' *Dictionary of Canadian Biography.* Vol. 12, *1891 to 1900* (1990): 300–5.

Unpublished Theses and Papers

Campbell, Peter. 'Working-Class Hero: Rose Henderson and the Canadian Left, 1919–1920.' Paper Presented to the Canadian Historical Association, Toronto, 2002.

Cox, Pamela. 'Rescue and Reform: Girls, Delinquency and Industrial Schools, 1908–1933.' PhD diss., University of Cambridge, 1996.

Douglas, Muriel H. 'History of the Society for the Protection of Women and Children from 1882 to 1966.' MSW Thesis, McGill University, 1967.

Duret, Anne. 'L'enfermement comme forme de punition du garçon délinquant au Québec (1857–1930).' MA thesis, Université d'Ottawa, 1988.

Harvey, Janice. 'Upper Class Reaction to Poverty in Mid-Nineteenth Century Montreal: A Protestant Example.' MA thesis, McGill University, 1978.

Hébert, Karine. 'Une organisation maternaliste au Québec, la Fédération nationale St-Jean-Baptiste 1900–1940.' MA thesis, Université de Montréal, 1997.

Lacasse, Danielle. 'Le Mont-Saint-Antoine: la répression de la délinquance juvénile à Montréal, 1873–1964.' MA thesis, Université d'Ottawa, 1986.

Martin, Tania Marie. 'Housing the Grey Nuns: Power, Religion and Women in fin-de-siècle Montréal.' MA thesis, McGill University, 1995.

Mayotte, A.S. 'Uses Made of a Mental Hygiene Clinic by a Boys' Training School.' MSW thesis, McGill University, 1949.

Ménard, Sylvie. 'L'Institut Saint-Antoine et la problématique de réforme des garçons délinquants au Québec (1873–1909),' PhD diss., Université du Québec à Montréal, 1998.

Mendelsohn, Lillian E., and Sharon Ronald. 'History of the Montreal Juvenile Court.' MSW thesis, McGill University, 1969.

Morton, Irving. 'Program Development at the University Settlement of Montreal.' MSW thesis, McGill University, 1953.

Myers, Tamara. 'Criminal Women and Bad Girls: Regulation and Punishment in Montreal, 1890–1930,' PhD diss., McGill University, 1996.

Niget, David. 'Jeunesses populaires sous le regard de la justice: naissance du tribunal pour enfants à Angers et Montréal (1912–1940).' PhD diss. Université d'Angers, 2005.

Ross, Herman R. 'Juvenile Delinquency in Montreal.' MA thesis, McGill University, 1932.

Strange, Carolyn. 'The Velvet Glove: Materialistic Reform and the Andrew Mercer Ontario Reformatory for Females, 1874–1927.' MA thesis, University of Ottawa, 1983.

Strimelle, Véronique. 'La gestion de la déviance des filles et les institutions du Bon Pasteur à Montréal (1869–1912).' PhD thesis, Université de Montréal, 1998.

van den Hoonaard, Will C. 'Rose Henderson: Biographical Zoning and the Bahà'í Context of Her Social Activism.' Paper presented to the Canadian Historical Association, Toronto, 2002.

Index

STUDIES IN GENDER AND HISTORY

General editors: Franca Iacovetta and Karen Dubinsky